The Making of a Sage

For Arnie,

Fourteen years ago I was in
your office, talking about
Rambam's 13 principles and
Scholem's "Revelation and Tradition".
Now I teach those texts in my
own Introduction to Judaism
course. It has been quite
a journey, and thank you for
all that you've done to help
me along the way.

Jon

This book was published with the support of the Mosse/Weinstein Center for Jewish Studies of the University of Wisconsin–Madison.

The Making of a Sage

A Study in Rabbinic Ethics

Jonathan Wyn Schofer

THE UNIVERSITY OF WISCONSIN PRESS

The University of Wisconsin Press
1930 Monroe Street
Madison, Wisconsin 53711

www.wisc.edu/wisconsinpress/

3 Henrietta Street
London WC2E 8LU, England

5   4   3   2   1

Printed in the United States of America

Library of Congress Cataloging-in-Publication Data
Schofer, Jonathan Wyn.
The making of a sage : a study in rabbinic ethics / Jonathan Wyn Schofer.
        p.   cm.
        Includes bibliographical references and index.
        ISBN 0-299-20460-X (hardcover: alk. paper)
        ISBN 0-299-20464-2 (pbk.: alk. paper)
        1. Talmud. Minor tractates. Avot de-Rabbi Nathan—Criticism, interpretation, etc.
2. Rabbinical literature—History and criticism.   3. Ethics in rabbinical literature.
4. Ethics, Jewish.   I. Title.
BM506.4.A943S36   2005
296.1´237—dc22   2004012862

Contents

Contents

Preface

The Making of a Sage offers the first theoretically framed examination of rabbinic ethics in several decades, asking questions such as: How did late ancient rabbis name and discuss their emotions, desires, and impulses? What ideals did they establish for character and action? How did they strive to transform themselves and attain those ideals? This study centers on a large and influential anthology entitled *The Fathers According to Rabbi Nathan* and situates that text within a broader spectrum of rabbinic thought relevant to character ethics. My analysis is based upon close examination of primary sources, with a developed theoretical account at the opening and briefer discussions framing the chapters.

Built on a foundation in scholarship concerning rabbinic literature and thought, this book is also intended for readers interested in the self, ethics, late antiquity, and the history of religions. Given my attention to a broad audience, I strive to explain every term and concept. Most technical discussions, whether about rabbis or about contemporary theory, are in the extensive notes. The introduction sets out the basic issues, followed by my account of ethical theory. Part 1 examines the corpus of *Rabbi Nathan*, identifying and responding to many challenges in reading an entire rabbinic text as a source for studying rabbinic thought. Parts 2 and 3 carry out the main thematic analyses centered on the ethical significance of the Torah and on conceptions of divine justice. The conclusion reflects upon the work as a whole and points to more advanced problems and issues.

This is a programmatic book, aiming to reinvigorate the study of late ancient or classical rabbinic ethics, provide new methodological foundations for research in rabbinic thought, and show how examination of rabbinic sources can inspire developments in the fields of ethics and history of religions. Perhaps the most distinctive aspect of the project is my particular way of combining philological and literary analysis with contemporary theory. Any such approach risks importing today's conceptual baggage into the late ancient world, and when people speak of the self and ethics in a cross-cultural context without discussion of the terms involved, then we should be suspicious that unexamined assumptions are present. At the same time, the study of rabbinic thought (including but not only ethics) requires us to enter this dangerous territory and to examine what we carry in.

We cannot do a purely inductive analysis of rabbinic ethics, for late ancient rabbis did not have a category that corresponds to "ethics" in scholarly and popular usage today. Early rabbis had a large vocabulary through which they set out norms for action and character: ideals that the sages *(ḥakhamim)* prescribe for students *(talmidim),* the ways that the tradition *(torah)* is to interact with basic impulses *(yetzer),* and the motivations and emotions that a person should maintain in relation to God, particularly love *('ahabah)* and fear or reverence *(yir'ah).* However, they did not employ a concept that draws these elements together. One response to this observation is to say that there is no such thing as rabbinic ethics and all we can do is track their own terms as they appear and are linked in the sources. I disagree, and I show over the course of this book that rabbis address a set of themes that are interrelated in ways that they do not explicitly identify. I name and analyze these themes employing contemporary terms such as ethics, self, and subjectivity and, in doing so, provide insights into overarching concerns and implicit meanings embedded in the texts.

My approach is to employ such categories by reflecting upon what they mean in contemporary scholarship and adapting them, in light of the sources, to build flexible descriptive tools rather than fixed concepts. More discussion of a term, though, does not mean more theory. Often my presentation involves paring down the specificity of my terms. To extend a common spatial metaphor: if a category is a container that may contain baggage, I try to clear out as much as possible in order to make room for rabbinic content. By the end of my introductory presentation, the self is defined in relation to imperatives and pronouns in the text, the subject is a standpoint of that self, and internalization is a metaphor. I have been especially attentive to this emptying of categories given that my initial definition of ethics draws from contemporary theory with roots in the writings of Aristotle, yet I do not accept interpretations that project medieval Jewish incorporations of Aristotelian philosophy backward in time to the early rabbis.

This is not the whole story, though, for I could go about the study of ethics with less conceptual apparatus than I offer. Another purpose of my theoretical work is linked with my goal of presenting rabbinic thought as simultaneously different and compelling. I strive to maintain a sense of the vast historical and cultural distance between rabbis' worldviews and our own, aiming to make the sources understandable but not necessarily palatable, and I do not highlight the aspects of their thought that would be most appealing today. This focus on difference is one of the ways that my analysis differs from modern Jewish ethics. At the same time, I work to make vivid both subtleties in the issues at stake and rabbis' creative ways of dealing with them. Expositing such compelling aspects of the sources demands a process of translation that is not only linguistic but also conceptual, explaining rabbinic modes of expression through a vocabulary that is recognized in today's academy and beyond.

A challenge in this conceptual translation is that rabbinic literature does many sophisticated things regarding ethics, but it does not present a theoretical account of the problems addressed. The language is highly concrete and allusive, including tropes, narratives, parables, and exegesis. In addition, the sources are not only descriptive but also prescriptive, with features that reveal a purpose of impacting the recipient in a direct manner. In order to exposit both the conceptual and the pedagogical features of this material, I both present tools for understanding metaphors and other tropes and set out an account of the relations between discourse, the self, and subjectivity. I see this aspect of my work as uncovering background or underlying understandings of the self and pedagogy, which are never named but still are crucial to the sources. My use of such categories aims to facilitate our scholarly imagination concerning *Rabbi Nathan* and its impact upon those who were shaped by its discursive world, not by ignoring or filtering out the literary, hermeneutical, and homiletic elements but by examining them carefully to see how form and content are intertwined.

I also see my work as contributing to the comparative and constructive study of ethics. I aim to give ethicists without a background in rabbinics access to this complex literature and to offer Jewish ethicists new perspectives on classical materials. In addition, I strive for a mutual illumination of theory and the analysis of texts: not only does the theory strengthen my interpretation but also the textual study leads to developments in the theory. Consideration of rabbinic literature provides an opportunity for today's readers to expand our thinking about ethics as well as the role of discourse in constituting what people are, the nature of the self, the formation of character, and the relation between choice and authority. This approach differs significantly from any attempt to "apply" a theory to a text. In the course of study, my text analysis and my conceptual work have continually developed together. I have employed something like an analogical imagination that juxtaposes rabbinic and contemporary discourse, refining my categories in the course of the analysis. The categories I started with are very different than those I have now. While my theoretical account is not meant to be universal, and it first and foremost constitutes a frame for the study of *Rabbi Nathan,* aspects of it can be drawn upon to address other cases.

There is a limit to what can be said in a preamble, and the real value in, and challenges for, my theoretical approaches and methodology will appear in the study itself—how effectively I formulate the categories, carry out the interpretation, and show the relation between the two. I would like to conclude this preface, though, with an invitation for the reader to enter this debate. In the years that I have worked on this project, I have considered many options: incorporating feminist and postcolonial approaches more extensively, drawing upon psychoanalytic or structuralist models, speaking in greater detail to contemporary concerns, or cutting back the entire discussion of theory. In addition, as I discuss at length below, there are many rabbinic sources to examine and ways to handle them. Now that this initial project has been completed, I would like to direct these possibilities outward, to inspire future projects as we move forward in the study of ethics during the next decades.

Acknowledgments

I have worked on this project for a long time, and many people have supported me in the process. I would first like to thank Robert Mandel and the staff at the University of Wisconsin Press for their great work in transforming a manuscript into a book, as well as Mary Magray for her careful copyediting. Many of the later revisions were done during a fellowship year while at the Stanford Humanities Center, and before that I spent much of two summers writing while receiving support from the University of Wisconsin Graduate School.

My two graduate advisers have contributed in significant ways to my scholarship after my doctorate while also encouraging new directions in my research: Frank Reynolds read numerous versions of the introduction and conclusion and has been a regular source of counsel, and Michael Fishbane read the full manuscript in close to the present form, giving extremely valuable support and observations. At the University of Wisconsin, I have benefited from my colleagues in the Department of Hebrew and Semitic Studies, the Mosse/Weinstein Center for Jewish Studies, and the Religious Studies Program. Michael Lyons read through the entire manuscript twice, offering extensive comments concerning both content and style, and he compiled the indices. I also was able to teach this material to fantastic groups of undergraduate students in two different semesters.

In working closely on one text, I felt a sense of connection with others who have covered the same terrain, and I have been able to meet or correspond with some of them. My study draws extensively upon the important recent scholarship by Menahem Kister, and I could not do my work if he had not first done his. Marc Bregman offered me his time and thoughts at early stages in the project. Jacob Neusner offered thoughts and assistance soon after the dissertation was completed. Anthony Saldarini passed on his mantle, in a sense, giving me his manuscripts and some very thoughtful advice in what I learned later would be our only meeting.

Many others have helped through comments on specific chapters or general discussion of the book as a whole, including but not only Elizabeth Shanks Alexander, Mark Berkson, Daniel Block, Daniel Boyarin, Mark Csikszentmihalyi, Jerome Copulsky, Marilynn Desmond, Wendy Doniger, Natalie Dohrmann, John Dunne, Arnold Eisen, Amy Feinstein, James Fernandez, Robert Cass Fisher, Charlotte Fonrobert, Anna Gade, Deborah Green, Ze'ev Gries, Greg Grieve, Charles Hallisey, Kelly Hayes, Joshua Holo, Philip J. Ivanhoe, Valentina Izmirlieva, Martin Jaffee, Leonard Kaplan, Paul Kollman, Thomas A. Lewis, Jonathan Malamy, Charles Mathewes, Sara McClintock, Louis Newman, Peter Ochs, Shubha Pathak, Eli Reich, Richard Rosengarten, Ishay Rosen-Zvi, Michael Satlow, Aaron Stalnaker, Despina Stratigakos, D. Andrew Teeter, David Tracy, Richard Weiss, Azzan Yadin, and Lee Yearley. I was editing the page proofs for this book when I met Amram Tropper and learned of his recent study, *Wisdom, Politics, and Historiography: Tractate Avot in the Context of the Graeco-Roman Near East* (Oxford: Oxford University Press, 2004). I believe that an engagement between our two lines of research would be very productive, but here I have not been able to carry that out.

Some portions have appeared in journal articles, and I thank the editors for permission to reprint material here: "The Redaction of Desire: Structure and Editing of Rabbinic Teachings Concerning *Yeṣer* ('Inclination')," *Journal of Jewish Thought and Philosophy* 12, no. 1 (2003): 19–53, see http://www.tandf.co.uk; "Spiritual Exercises and Rabbinic Culture," *Association for Jewish Studies Review* 27, no. 2 (2003): 203–26; and "Self, Subject, and Chosen Subjection: Rabbinic Ethics and Comparative Possibilities," *Journal of Religious Ethics* 33 (2005).

Throughout these past years I have learned, shared, and grown increasingly closer with my immediate family, and this book is dedicated to them: Syra Shariff, Nina Shariff, Evan Schofer and Ann Hironaka, Don Cherco, and most of all my mother, Susan Cherco.

Conventions

Abbreviations of the Central Texts

Fathers	The Mishnaic tractate *'Abot,* or "The Fathers"
Rabbi Nathan	*'Abot de Rabbi Natan*
Rabbi Nathan A	*'Abot de Rabbi Natan,* version A
Rabbi Nathan B	*'Abot de Rabbi Natan,* version B

The edition that I cite most often is Solomon Schechter and Menahem Kister, *Avoth de-Rabbi Nathan: Solomon Schechter Edition* (New York: Jewish Theological Seminary, 1997). I cite this edition of *Rabbi Nathan* by "version and chapter, page." A1,2 means version A, chapter 1, page 2; A6–7,27–35 means version A, chapters 6–7, pages 27–35. Readers of the printed edition or a translation can look up citations by chapter. If I cite Schechter's introduction or appendices, I do so by noting, "Schechter, *Rabbi Nathan,* page."

Transliteration

All translations of Hebrew and Aramaic texts are my own. In order to make the material accessible to nonspecialists, I have used the following transliteration system.

Hebrew/Aramaic: ' b g d h v z ḥ ṭ y k/kh l m n s ' p/ph tz q r ś/sh t

a: ḥataph-pataḥ, pataḥ, qamatz
e: sheva', ḥataph-segol, segol, tzeyreh
i: ḥiriq, ḥiriq-yod
o: ḥataph-qamatz, ḥolem, ḥolem-vav
u: qubbutz, shuruq
ey: tzeyreh-yod

Conventions

Greek: a b g d e z ē th i k l m n x o p r s t u ph ch ps ō

For proper names, I omit diacritics and substitute *k* for *q*. When quoting other scholars who transliterate, I follow their usage.

The Making of a Sage

Introduction

In what ways did rabbis of late antiquity examine human emotions, desires, and ways to transform them? Did they create sophisticated works of literature in which they discussed these issues? Do we have tools for expositing them? These questions do not yield simple answers, for rabbinic sages appear to have been primarily concerned with matters such as the development of the law or *halakhah,* the nature of "Torah," or tradition, God's involvement in the world, and the status of "Israel" or the Jews. Their interests in what we might call the self and its cultivation, then, were channeled through questions concerning how one should comport oneself while carrying out ideals prescribed in the law, how immersion in tradition impacts one's emotions and desires, how God responds to various actions and states, and so on. With this qualification, though, in this book I examine and emphasize the importance of rabbinic thought concerning the shaping of desire and emotion. I focus upon a large and influential text with rich material on these topics, and I set out methodological tools for analyzing its concepts and imagery.

The classical rabbinic sages were known as *hakhamim*—men distinct for their *hokhmah,* or wisdom. They and their followers constituted a movement of Jewish religious elites in late ancient Palestine and Babylonia that emerged after the destruction of the Jerusalem Temple by the Romans in 70 CE. The movement or network probably coalesced in the second century, and our earliest textual sources are a bit later.[1] Rabbis claimed they inherited a tradition that went back to Moses at Sinai, and their creative work to develop that tradition resulted in a tremendous volume of texts known as the Mishnah, Midrash, and Talmuds. Their influence among Jews, who were a colonized people in the Roman and Persian empires, may not have been significant during the second through sixth centuries when many of these texts were compiled. Considered in the context of late antiquity, rabbinic literature gives us a window into the struggle to construct ideals that would, in later time periods, come to be normative for the great majority of Jews, including those of the present day.

In considering classical rabbinic thought, a key issue concerns our scholarly unit of analysis. Should we center upon a rabbinic term, a corpus, a given rabbi and the teachings attributed to him, rabbinic literature as a whole, a modern conceptual formulation, or some combination of these?[2] I do not believe that we need to have one answer to this question—each approach has its own possibilities and dangers. This project centers on a text, or more specifically a family of texts, known as *The Fathers According to Rabbi Nathan.*[3] *Rabbi Nathan* is arguably the most significant example we have of rabbinic ethical literature—collections that show a distinct concern with ethical instruction, often as conveyed through short sayings. While several of these texts can be characterized as handbooks or manuals,[4] *Rabbi Nathan* is structured primarily as a commentary that cites and then reflects upon such maxims. Examples include:

> The Men of the Great Assembly . . . said three things: Be patient in judgment, raise up many disciples, and make a fence for the Torah. (A1,2; also B1,2; *Fathers* 1:1)

> [Yose ben Yoezer says]: Let your house be a meeting place for the sages, sit in the very dust of their feet, and drink with thirst their words. (A6,27; B11,27; *Fathers* 1:4)

> Rabbi Yehoshua says: The malicious eye, the bad impulse, and hatred of creatures cast a man out from the world. (A16,62; B30,62; *Fathers* 2:11)

Rabbi Nathan comments upon maxims such as these through a variety of genres. For example, the instruction of the Men of the Great Assembly to "raise up many disciples" is developed through an account of a dispute between two groups, the followers of Hillel and of Shammai. The issue at stake is what kind of students should be accepted or "raised up" for rabbinic teaching.

The House of Shammai upholds an elitist position, wanting only students who are already wise, humble, and rich. The House of Hillel, whose opinion is usually followed by later rabbis, takes a more egalitarian stance:

> ["Raise up many disciples."][5] For the House of Shammai says: A man should only teach one who is wise, humble, of noble birth, and rich. The House of Hillel says: One should teach all people, for there were many rebellious ones in Israel, yet they were drawn[6] to the study of Torah, and from them emerged righteous, pious, and upright men. (A3,14)

For the House of Hillel, the imperative of the Men of the Great Assembly becomes a call to "raise up" through the study of Torah "many" righteous, pious, and upright "disciples." Underlying the ideal of teaching all people is the claim that Torah, or rabbinic tradition, transforms the rebellious into righteous, pious, and upright persons. The study of Torah is not only intellectual but rather affects the student in a holistic manner, changing character to accord with rabbinic values. Solomon Schechter, who compiled the first critical edition of *Rabbi Nathan,* has made this point in elegant terms: "The occupation with the Torah was, according to the Rabbis, less calculated to produce schoolmen and jurists than saints and devout spirits."[7]

The argument I develop herein is similar, though perhaps adjusted to say that these rabbis, through study of Torah and service of God, aimed to become and produce "schoolmen and jurists" who were, at the same time, "saints and devout spirits." This process is a crucial element of rabbinic ethics. I elaborate upon my definition of ethics below, but for now a key formulation is that *Rabbi Nathan* presents complex accounts of what people are at origin or by nature (the rebellious), what ideal people are and do (the righteous, pious, and upright), and processes of transformation between the given and the ideal (the study of Torah).

How does the study of Torah transform an aspiring sage? Consider a narrative about the early career of perhaps the most prominent sage in *Rabbi Nathan,* Rabbi Akiba. The story appears in the commentary to the maxim of Yose ben Yoezer, "Let your house be a meeting place of the sages, sit at the dust of their feet, and drink with thirst their words." While several accounts of Rabbi Akiba's life appear in rabbinic literature, each with a distinct rhetorical focus,[8] in *Rabbi Nathan* he is a model for an adult immersing himself in the tradition. He begins to study at a late age, goes to the great sages of the day, learns under adverse circumstances, shows great talent and ability, and ultimately succeeds and becomes wealthy. Rabbi Akiba appears as a figure who can be upheld in response to anyone who wishes to avoid studying Torah based on age, adversity, or desire for worldly prosperity.[9]

The narrative opens by emphasizing the transformative impact of Torah upon the heart. When the story begins, the hero is an uneducated man who understands neither the workings of nature nor the text of the Torah. He sees a rock that has been worn away by water. Others explain this phenomenon through the first part of a verse from the Book of Job, "water carves away rocks" (Job 14:19). Rabbi Akiba draws from these words a teaching that offers hope for shaping his heart through Torah:

> What was the start of Rabbi Akiba? They said: He was forty years old and had not studied anything. One time [Akiba] was standing at the mouth of

a well. He asked, "Who chiseled out [*ḥiqeq*] that rock?" They said, "The water, which continuously falls upon it, every day." They said, "Akiba, do not you read in Scripture, 'Water carves away [*shaḥaqu*] rocks. . . .'" (Job 14:19).[10] Rabbi Akiba reasoned on his own from the minor to the major case: just as the soft wears away the hard, how much the more so that the words of Torah, which are hard as iron, will hollow out my heart, which is flesh and blood. (A6,28–29)

The focus on water may be inspired by the third part of Yose ben Yoezer's maxim—"drink with thirst their words"—which implies the metaphor that sagely teachings are a liquid that quenches and nourishes. More generally, the motifs of water, rock, and a well have deep resonance in the Bible and in traditions of late antiquity that draw upon it. A well or spring may represent wisdom, Torah, God, or the sage himself who flows with knowledge. A stone can be a metaphor for resistant or rebellious tendencies.[11] Rabbi Akiba's reasoning places the figures of water and stone on a continuum of soft-hard, stating that "the soft [water] wears away the hard [stone]." If this metaphor were applied in a direct analogy to the Torah and the heart, it would imply that the process of transformation is a slow wearing away of the hard and unformed heart. However, he does not draw a direct analogy but an *a fortiori* argument. Reversing the two figures' positions on the continuum, he asserts that the heart is not hard stone, but soft and receptive flesh and blood. Torah is not soft water, but hard iron. If soft water can wear away the stone, then iron-hard Torah has more than enough power to "hollow out my heart." According to these new metaphors, Torah is a highly powerful agent, the heart is extremely receptive, and the process of transformation is rapid.[12]

Along with analysis of these metaphors, it is important to note that the hermeneutical move that generates the teaching—the interpretation of Job 14:19—actually reverses the simple or contextual meaning of the verse. The full verse says, "Water carves away rocks, its torrents wash away earth, so You destroy human hope," yet Rabbi Akiba interprets the verse in a way that brings him hope for hollowing out his heart. The complexity of Torah for late ancient rabbis is evident here. Many of them saw their Scripture as divinely given, and at the same time their modes of interpretation reveal tremendous amounts of innovation in their encounter with its discourse.

In its exegetical context, then, the story is part of a multilayered teaching. The reader or listener is instructed to sit at the dust of his teachers' feet and drink with thirst their words. In doing so, he will learn words of Torah that wear away and reform his emotions and desires. A crucial point is the role of subordination in this process. A student is to be "low" in relation to the sage's mouth as "high," "dirty" in relation to an implied "clean" teacher, and "soft" and receptive in relation to the words of Torah as "hard" and transformative. This subordination is linked with internalization: drinking the words of the sages and having Torah hollow out the heart (and perhaps fill it as well). These tropes are only part of the story, however. An equally crucial point is that this process is not coerced. A student is not threatened with force along with the instruction to sit at a teacher's feet. Rabbi Akiba elects to engage in the study of Torah for his own goals of transformation, and we also see in the very process of midrash that the study of Torah is an active and inventive process.

This picture of ethical transformation is exemplary of a dynamic that I trace through the sources. The central thesis of this book is that significant portions of *Rabbi Nathan* instruct a student to become a sage through chosen and cultivated relations of subordination to the sage and community, the tradition of Torah, and God, along with internalization of discourse connected with these three authorities.[13] A central challenge, then, will be to understand the complex interplays between this subordination and internalization, on one hand, and choice and creativity on the other.

The Project and Intended Audiences

My project is a theoretically informed descriptive analysis of late ancient rabbinic ethics centered on *The Fathers According to Rabbi Nathan.*[14] *Rabbi Nathan* is often characterized as a commentary upon the influential tractate of the Mishnah entitled *The Fathers,* which has become the most commented upon text in all of rabbinic literature, in part because of its incorporation into Jewish liturgy.[15] As many have observed, *Rabbi Nathan* is our best source for understanding how these sayings were employed in late antiquity. This is not to say, though, that *Rabbi Nathan* presents the original meanings of the sayings. As we will see, we often find in *Rabbi Nathan* explicit adaptation or reinterpretation of the material it comments upon, especially when it preserves material from before the rabbinic period. Strictly speaking, *Rabbi Nathan* is a commentary to a shorter and earlier version of *The Fathers* than the one that appears in the Mishnah. The relation between the texts is quite complex, and *Rabbi Nathan* may have developed in competition with the extant version of *The Fathers.*[16] However we sort out these issues, *Rabbi Nathan* is itself one of the largest anthologies of rabbinic ethical material that we have, representing many centuries of editorial work. It now appears as an extracanonical tractate to the Babylonian Talmud with commentaries of its own.

I attend both to the ways that the text represents ethical matters and to the role of its pedagogical discourse in the process of transformation itself.[17] My analysis centers upon close literary examination of individual passages in their distinctiveness, building inductively to make broader claims about the work as a whole and framing the study of native terminology with contemporary categories of analysis. This work aims to further three realms of scholarship, centering on rabbinic literature, Roman late antiquity, and comparative ethics. For rabbinicists, I reopen an area of inquiry—ethics— that has been latent since the important work of Max Kadushin in the midtwentieth century.[18] Since then, methods for handling rabbinic texts have changed significantly, and setting out an approach to *Rabbi Nathan* as a source for rabbinic ethics is a central concern of this book. There is currently a strong foundation for my study in detailed examinations of the manuscripts and printed editions, of literary structure and broad themes, and of certain passages and terms. I draw this work into a project that strives to read the text as a whole, understanding it as an important part of rabbinic thought and culture.[19] My work also provides extensive treatments of major concepts in rabbinic thought, particularly Torah and divine justice, surveying their full range of uses in this important text and setting out methodological approaches for studying them in other sources as well.

For scholars of Roman late antiquity, I contribute to current research on self-formation among philosophical and religious elites in the Empire.[20] The most influential and controversial framing of the issues has been articulated by Michel Foucault, who has argued that elites of late antiquity had a distinct and intense focus on "the care of the self." Foucault's historical claims have undergone much criticism, but his basic point both draws upon and has been developed by many specialists in the field, including Pierre Hadot's work on spiritual exercises and Peter Brown's on sexual renunciation. My project brings a new dimension to this research, which has focused on philosophical schools and Christianity but has had little to say about rabbinic Judaism, and specifically I examine Hadot's category of "exercise" in detail. At the same time, it is extremely difficult to contextualize *Rabbi Nathan* in history and geography with precision. In chapter 1a I discuss the relations between text and context as well as the kinds of historical claims that this study makes possible.[21]

For scholars of comparative ethics and history of religions, the central problem of my work is conceptualizing the role of external authority or power in the self-formation of religious elites. In many cultural and religious contexts, people attain virtues and forms of freedom through entering into subordinate relations with particular authorities. This important dynamic is, I believe, still undertheorized, despite much work that comes close to the mark. Integrating scholarship on virtue ethics with that on discourse and ritual, I frame this feature of rabbinic ethics as chosen, elected, or willed "subjection." My analysis also leads to refinements in other categories used in ethics, including tradition, theology, and metaphor.

Though the project has these three dimensions, it is fundamentally unified and holistic. Since there is no classical rabbinic term that corresponds with ethics in the full scope that the word has today, any account of rabbinic ethics requires an encounter between ancient texts and contemporary theory. I make that encounter explicit. At the same time, in the descriptive endeavor I employ the methods and address the concerns of specialists in rabbinics and the late ancient world. A fundamental contention of this book, then, is that while individual readers may situate themselves in one or two of these groups of scholars, all of these approaches are necessary to understand the rabbinic ethics of *Rabbi Nathan.*

Rabbinic Ethics

In the rest of this introduction, I present a theoretical frame in character ethics appropriate for the sources I examine. My account draws upon many thinkers, but in overall approach I am particularly inspired by the work of Paul Ricoeur. Like Ricoeur, I aim to bring together (but not collapse) scholars and approaches that are often separated: the study of thought and the study of culture, character ethics and deontological ethics, and virtue ethics and subject formation. Also like Ricoeur's ethical theory in *Oneself as Another,* I do not present a systematic account but one that works from layer to layer. His studies of identifying reference, the speaking subject, action, agency, narrative identity, ethics, and then ontology build upon each other from more elemental to more complex features, but each section takes on distinct problems and addresses a distinct body of scholarly literature.[22] I present my theoretical work in four sections: a general presentation of character ethics, an examination of the role of discourse in ethics, a treatment of the self and subject as addressed by pedagogical discourse, and then a more developed account of ethics centered on the formation of the subject.

I begin by mapping the field of ethics as including procedural- and character-based approaches.[23] The first addresses procedures of reasoning leading to a given action, responding to the question, "What should I do?" Procedural ethics itself has variants, such as those focusing on rules or laws (deontological ethics) and those focusing on results (consequentialist or more specifically utilitarian ethics). Ethicists may engage in casuistry that poses a conflict between the two priorities, such as a situation when one must break a law ("do not kill") in order to achieve some important purpose ("to save many lives"). Character ethicists, in contrast, situate a given action or decision in the context of character and a life plan. They study virtue and notions of a good life, centering on questions such as, "How ought I to live? What kind of person should I be?"[24]

There are significant conceptual differences between character and procedural ethics. The two approaches represent differing understandings concerning the role of reason in determining action. The choice to focus on the self and character implies that examining rational processes and the immediate moment of decision making yields only a partial account of how people act. Character ethicists examine reason as linked with, not separate from, emotions and habits, and they situate individual decisions in the context of a person's dispositions, narratives, and ideals for a good life. While the two approaches can be articulated as competing and mutually exclusive, I believe (for both theoretical and descriptive projects) that we need to address their interrelations along with their conflicts. The formation of character often involves, in some form or another, rules or laws that guide action, and from the other direction, a set of laws or commands often implies some understanding of what humans are and should be.[25]

Rabbinic ethics has both procedural and character elements, and my study examines a large text in which themes of character and its formation are highly prominent. *Rabbi Nathan* is a collection of non-legal material *('aggadah)* that reflects upon rabbinic law *(halakhah)* through concepts such as Torah and divine justice, setting out ideals for the comportment that one should maintain while engaging in legally prescribed action and beyond. In this text and others, ethics is not in competition with law but a way of orienting to it, and concerns with character generally encompass and frame procedural matters.[26] My conceptual starting point is encompassed in the question: How does a person or group understand (a) what people are at origin or by nature (b) what ideal people are and do, and (c) processes of transformation from the given to the ideal? This starting point in many ways has its roots in Aristotelian thought, but I believe it is flexible enough to open up inquiries far beyond the tradition of ethics that sees him as a key figure. In contemporary terms, it can encompass both the insights of virtue ethicists (particularly Alasdair MacIntyre) and scholars of the subject and its formation (particularly Michel Foucault).[27]

The first element—what people are at origin or by nature—concerns the starting point of ethical transformation. How do religions construct, or at least provide the context for, notions of what is instinctive or spontaneous in a person? What emotions, desires, and motivations are defined as unformed or uncultured? We do not find a comprehensive treatment of these topics in *Rabbi Nathan.* A crucial category is the *yetzer,* or "inclination, impulse," which often denotes a site of innate tendencies toward transgression. In many cases, however, innate tendencies are treated on an occasional basis, or they are implied in other concepts. For example, the pervasive theological imagery of God's justice tends to presume, on the part of humans, self-interested desire and fear.

The second element—what ideal people are and do—concerns the ultimate state or *telos.* What notions of virtue, flourishing, perfection, or liberation define the goals of ethical transformation? In *Rabbi Nathan,* these ideals are most often portrayed in the literary figures of the sages, such as Rabbi Akiba. In some cases, the ideal sage is a person whose desires are fully shaped by the discourse of Torah and the practices it upholds. In others, the ideal person is one who has transcended self-interested desire and fear to attain a state of divine-centered love and awe. Rabbinic ideals for character are not separated from worldly and spiritual benefits. If all is right in the world, the sage should receive both wealth and mystical reward (such as death by a kiss from God) in response to righteous action.

The third element of my formulation—the processes of cultivation, formation, or transformation[28]—sets out the path that one must take to attain ethical ideals. What enables a person to reach a given *telos* from her or his original state? Processes of transformation may center upon both practice (including ritual and exercises) and discourse or "language in use." *Rabbi Nathan* is an instance of pedagogical discourse, presuming and reflecting upon the practices set out by rabbinic law.[29] In doing so, the text presents three key points of religious authority—the sage, Torah, and God. I attend closely to ways that the text portrays these authorities and the ways that the aspiring sage should orient toward them.[30]

Ethics and Discourse

My theoretical framing, as it stands to this point, sets up an account of how *Rabbi Nathan* depicts the process of ethical transformation, but not how it functions in that very process. *Rabbi Nathan* is an instance of discourse that upholds discourse (the teachings of the sages, the words of Torah, and concepts and tropes describing God) as central to one's transformation. Since the text presents itself as an element of both the sages' teachings and the Torah, it should impact the listener or reader in a direct manner. In addition, as I discuss below, the genres of the text reveal a strong concern with not only description but also instruction and persuasion. A theoretical frame for studying this pedagogical material requires an account of the relations between discourse, the self, ethics, and the broader society and culture that rabbis inhabit.

I first turn to Alasdair MacIntyre's account of narrative and ethics. He writes that the human is "essentially a story-telling animal." Narrative provides a bridge between intention, social context, and history that enables one to find intelligibility in actions and unity in life. Each person's telling of stories, however, is intricately linked with stories told by others. He writes, "I can only answer the question 'What am I to do?' if I can answer the prior question 'Of what story or stories do I find myself a part?'" Narrative selfhood has a dual sense of creativity and conditioning, with two key elements: being the subject of a history that is "my own and no one else's" and being part of an interlocking set of others' narratives, in which one is both accountable to others and can ask them for an account.[31] MacIntyre's formulation is extremely insightful but leads to a number of problems, the first being a need for attention to ways that social processes condition narratives and, more broadly, discourse in general. His own theorizing situates narratives in relation to practices and tradition, but while he defines tradition as being "socially embodied," he gives few tools for thinking about this sociality.[32] David Harvey, however, sets out a dialectical framework for the study of social processes that provides a valuable base for considering narrative or discursive selfhood.

Harvey, like MacIntyre, emphasizes that humans are conditioned by discourse but not in a passive manner. Summarizing in the first person, he states that people receive and respond to discourse in ways that are often very creative: "I take in ideas and thoughts through listening and reading. I gain a sense of selfhood thereby but in the process reformulate and transform words and in projecting them back in society change the social world."[33] Harvey situates discourse in a broader "map" of social processes that includes six "moments"—discourse, power, beliefs/values/desires, institutions, material practices (he locates the body here),[34] and social relations. He specifies, "Each moment is constituted as an *internal relation* of the others within the flow of social and material life. Discourses internalize in some sense everything that occurs at the other moments. . . . Discourses express human thought, fantasy, and desire. They are also institutionally based, materially constrained, experientially grounded manifestations of social and power relations. By the same token, discursive effects suffuse and saturate all other moments within the social processes."[35] I am less persuaded by the way Harvey characterizes the specific "moments" than by his overall picture, which presents discourse as deeply intertwined with other elements in social processes including the embodied self: the other elements appear internal to discourse, yet at the same time discourses "suffuse and saturate" them (I will discuss the concept of "internalization" further below).

This map provides an important corrective to MacIntyre, situating discourse in a broader context of social processes and reminding us that, even if we choose to focus on discourse, it is only a portion of the social world. Harvey cautions that, "to privilege discourse above other moments is insufficient, misleading, and even dangerous." Examination of any single moment does not give understanding into the totality of social processes. There is a significant difference between studying discourse and the social processes internalized in it and insisting, "the whole world is nothing other than a text."[36] The latter point is particularly important for the case of *Rabbi Nathan*. If we want to avoid overly simple historicizing, we have to keep in mind the gaps between social processes as represented in the text and social processes as enacted by living human beings. At the same time, we need remember that this literature was created, taught, and studied by actual people, even if we have little knowledge about them.

MacIntyre, then, offers tools for thinking about discourse as central to the self, and Harvey presents a valuable corrective concerning the place of discourse in relation to material practices and social relations. Another problem in drawing upon MacIntyre's formulation of narrative is that *Rabbi Nathan* does not preserve the raw narratives of individuals trying to find intelligibility in their own lives. Rather, it is a highly edited discourse of instruction. Ricoeur offers a corrective that is crucial here. Like MacIntyre, he approaches the self by way of narrative, arguing at length that narrative mediates temporal and spatial aspects of existence, the links between action and agent, and processes of self-interpretation.[37] He also asks, how do the "stories told in the thick of everyday life" that MacIntyre focuses upon interrelate with composed and stylized instances of discourse, such as religious texts? Ricoeur responds that literature is "an immense laboratory for thought experiments" that contributes to self-examination in real life. Humans may "appropriate" these narratives when they characterize agency and organize the experiences and events that make up their lives. He concludes with a reminder that "narrative is part of life before being exiled from life in writing; it returns to life along multiple paths of appropriation" but "at the price of unavoidable tensions" that he discusses at length.[38]

Study of *Rabbi Nathan* leads me to qualify and develop these general points in two ways. First, while *Rabbi Nathan* is a plural and multivocal work, it is still a prescriptive text: it presents itself as being part of a tradition with divine origin, and its voices instruct in correct comportment and action. Ricoeur's framing in terms of "thought experiments," then, does not capture the authority asserted within the text for its own instruction (and I believe that this issue would arise in considering other sources that are central to religious traditions).[39]

Second, while MacIntyre and Ricoeur single out narrative as a key form of mediation, in *Rabbi Nathan* the central genre of the text is the short maxim of instruction. The compilers of the text build upon these maxims through commentary that includes narratives along with lists and midrash. All of this material is available to the recipient for characterizing intention and agency, for organizing the experiences of life to give them meaning and intelligibility, and more generally for reflection concerning norms and ideals. This observation raises an important question: if narrative is not the primary genre in this text and in rabbinic literature generally, then can we still assume that, for those who engage with the text, narrative has greater status than other discursive forms? In other words, does cross-cultural study push us to give up the centrality of narrative as the preeminent genre through which humans describe and construct their lives? Or should we argue that lists, exegetical passages, aphorisms, and so on all provide material for self-description that is narrative at heart? I would at least consider the former possibility.

More generally, I would like to take a moment to highlight the potential of a discursive approach—such as the one I have set out drawing upon MacIntyre, Harvey, and Ricoeur—for cross-cultural study. Part of the point, I believe, is that the terms we and others have for talking about what people are (including ego/id/superego, the will, the heart/mind, emotions, lists of virtues, a good and bad *yetzer,* and so on) are part of specific socially and culturally conditioned discourses. They do not denote hypostatic entities that can be the bases for our analysis. Rather, all can be examined as ways that discourse enables humans to describe and constitute who we are.

This scholarly approach takes as its starting point a broad and dialectical map of social processes, which itself can be debated but probably should include the body with all its inchoate processes, discourses that both describe and constitute it, and other dimensions of the social and natural world that discursive bodies interact with.

Self and Subject

Given this account of discourse and ethics, what is the self? A study of character ethics requires some general term to denote what humans are, such as self, person, or *anthropos*. I set out the self as my most general category, knowing that any scholarly appeal to the self in a comparative context has dangers, and these dangers are particularly salient given that rabbinic literature has no corresponding term. More generally, the English word "self" carries significant conceptual baggage and tends to be associated with (often oversimplified) Enlightenment formulations that present selfhood as bounded, individual, and autonomous. A comparative study of the self, however, strives not to impose such a view upon other cultures but to show the contingent and constructed nature of all selves and to examine the range of possibilities for understanding the self and its vicissitudes.[40]

Within the maxims and their commentary, personal pronouns (such as I, you, he, she, and they) can have a special role in being locations where the discourse indexes or opens to the reader or listener. As indicators whose referent can shift depending on the speaker, recipient, and context of the utterance, they are the points in the text where someone can enter and apply concepts, tropes, narratives, and so on to him- or herself. Rabbinic selves, then, are indexed by such pronouns. I believe that some version of this linguistic turn (and Ricoeur seems to embark on something like this himself), in the context of a project whose sources lead us to focus upon discourse as central to describing and constituting human beings, is the most productive way to recast the self for comparative purposes.[41] The fact that the word "self" is itself a pronoun (of an odd sort) is a nice complement to this point, though I am not sure how much we should make of it.[42]

Three qualifications are in order. First, focusing on self as indexed by pronouns is not saying that the self is entirely linguistic—there may be significant parts of the self and its formation that are not conditioned by language. Second, not all pronouns in the text have broad referents, and the scholar has to identify those that potentially indicate human beings, or in an androcentric discourse, at least men in some generalized sense. Third, pronouns are not the only ways that the text describes and addresses selves: other examples include terms for a person or human being *('adam)* and general phrases such as "anyone who . . ." *(kol ha . . .)*.[43]

From this account of the self, I move to the subject. Ricoeur draws upon the work of Emile Benveniste to argue that "I" and "you" are distinctive among pronouns in indicating the "subjects of utterance"—the speaker/writer and recipient of a given instance of discourse.[44] In *Rabbi Nathan* generally, this subject is most often invoked not through an "I" but rather through the implied "you" of imperatives that appear in maxims of instruction. If the text says, "[You] make a fence for your words," then the implied pronoun is the discursive space in which the subject can appropriate the predication as, "I should make a fence for my words." If the text says, "[You] appoint for yourself a teacher," then the ideal subject would respond, "I should appoint for myself a teacher." The subject, then, is a specific form that the self can take—the self may be indicated in a variety of ways (impersonally as "he" or "they," for example), but the subject is specifically the stance of an "I." While I believe that the axis "I" and "you" is crucial for subjectivity in discourse, such appropriation can occur in relation to third-person instructions as well. The text may instruct, "He should say, 'Woe is me, perhaps retribution will come upon me today.'" Here, the third-person pronoun "he" is the place where one can shift the utterance to, "I should say to myself, 'Woe is me . . .'"

The subject delineates a rich and messy terrain, characterizing the self as it speaks, experiences, knows, chooses, and acts. There are a number of ambiguities in the contemporary use of the category. Several variations of the term itself appear in scholarship—subject, subjective, subjectivity, subjection, subjectivation—and there is no agreement concerning their relation or differences. Also, theorists disagree as to the specific features of the subject, as there are interrelations but no clear identity between speaking, consciousness, knowledge, choice, and agency.[45] My discussion herein is not meant to be a full treatment of the concept but a formulation that helps to further descriptive and comparative study. I focus upon three terms and treat them as intertwined: the "subject" as one standpoint of the self, "subjectivity" as the abstract state of being a subject, and "subjection" as the process of developing or intensifying that standpoint.

When I say that the subject is a standpoint and not a part of the self, I mean that I am not positing a substance or entity within the human being. Rabbis may employ hypostatic images in describing themselves, but my analytical tools are not.[46] Rather, the subject is a position in two respects. The first is the sense of the speaking subject that says "I" to a "you," as I discussed above. The second is a characterization of agency through an analogy to language: just as within a sentence the subject is a particular position in which a pronoun may be located, so the subject is a position or a standpoint that the self may take for itself or in which it may find itself through its relations with others. The relation between a subject and predicate in a sentence is then a key starting point for reflecting upon the relation between agent and action.

This grammatical analogy is particularly provocative given that my descriptive work concerns texts, so the material I have to work with are subjects and predicates in language. Given that I employ the category as a heuristic tool for descriptive study, further specification of subjectivity requires engagement with our sources. As I have stated above, my study shows that the instruction preserved in *Rabbi Nathan* prescribes that the self form itself as a subject through chosen and cultivated relations of subordination to external authorities along with the internalization of certain discourses. My theoretical account of ethics, then, has to address four more elements: the self forming itself as a subject, subordination, internalization, and the authoritative other.

Ethics and Subject Formation

How do we understand the connection between the subject, as addressed and instructed by *Rabbi Nathan,* and ethics? Here I draw from the work of Michel Foucault, who has studied the subject in and through specific historical discourses, practices, and institutions. All of these condition, and are conditioned by, "power," which should be understood as a matter of "ability"—such as the ability to create, produce, distribute, coerce, punish, destroy, define, categorize, or control.[47] Over the course of his career, Foucault has set out three approaches or "axes" for the study of the subject: how it knows and is known (studied in *The Order of Things*), how it is formed through relations with others (studied in *Discipline and Punish*), and how it forms itself through relations with itself (studied in parts 2 and 3 of *The History of Sexuality*). He characterizes the third axis as ethics, yet ethics does not occur in isolation from the other two. We should never underestimate the complexity of the relations between these three axes, and all are relevant for the understanding of any given subject.[48]

I believe that this latter point is extremely important for ethicists to consider, since the field tends to acknowledge but not analyze the social forces that condition dispositions and habits. In Western philosophy, this tendency goes back to Aristotle, though there have been notable exceptions such as G. W. F. Hegel. For my study of rabbis, I have found Foucault particularly useful, and my key point here is that we should not read his work on "the care of the self" in isolation from his studies of knowledge and power (a similar impulse underlies my situating MacIntyre's and Ricoeur's accounts of discourse in Harvey's map of social processes).[49]

Returning to the rabbis by way of Foucault's three axes—first, rabbinic subject formation existed within a particular knowledge system, one centered upon the exegesis of the Bible and of earlier sages' teachings. For several hundred years, the procedures of expression and justification known as midrash, mishnah, and gemara were the dominant bases of rabbinic knowledge production. There were significant variations within these approaches, and they were not the only forms available. Nonetheless, they provided a certain constancy that marks classical rabbinic or talmudic thought as distinct from the forms of knowledge that mark earlier and later periods. The ethical instruction of *Rabbi Nathan* is firmly situated within this epistemological universe.[50]

As for their relations with others, *Rabbi Nathan* describes and addresses males once they have entered a rabbinic community and says little about child rearing or the forces that impact a person at very young ages.[51] That community consisted of men with expertise in a particular way of speaking and writing who gradually attained religious and judicial leadership of Jewish communities. Rabbis cannot be classified in any simple sense through terms such as "dominant" or "subordinate." Rather, they existed in a diffuse network of power relations, most notably those based on nation,[52] gender, and elite status. In relation to the Romans they were colonized. In relation to women they benefited from and reinforced a patriarchal society. In relation to other Jews, they strove both to attain distinct and privileged positions in society and to interact with and influence others. I elaborate upon each of these points in part 1.

The third dimension of subject formation is the ethical. Foucault defines ethics in terms of an internal relationship—the self constituting itself as an ethical subject.[53] *Rabbi Nathan,* though, does not present an ideal of a pure, unmediated relation of the self with itself but rather a self that forms itself through relations with particular others, specifically chosen and cultivated relations of subordination to external authorities. Certain ethical theories address this aspect of character formation. For example,

Foucault himself sets out the category "mode of subjection," but his descriptive work on Greco-Roman philosophy says little about subordination. Ricoeur briefly discusses submission and enduring, and MacIntyre considers philosophy to be a craft and emphasizes the importance of obedient trust in a teacher—but neither develops these points fully.[54] In order to theorize subordination as part of ethics, I draw upon another element in the scholarship on the subject, a pun between (a) the subject/predicate analogy discussed above, and (b) the sense of being "subjected to" some greater authority or power, such as being the subject of a king. This pun highlights an intertwining of self-identification and agency with subordination to powerful others.[55]

This intertwining is highly complex and varies from case to case. In rabbinic ethics, on one hand, character formation is undertaken by aspiring elites who willingly enter a community and take on certain relationships. Within that context, they encounter specific discourses and likely appropriate them in creative ways (remember the great innovation in rabbinic exegesis, as evident in Rabbi Akiba's reworking of a biblical verse from Job). On the other hand, any man joining the community would already have developed prejudices and dispositions through social formation, which would have influenced his decision to enter, and the community itself centers on authoritative figures that would affect his preferences. *Rabbi Nathan* calls upon rabbis to elect, intensify, and to a degree control certain subordinations in order to intensify their own agencies. Through this orientation to greater powers, the rabbinic self extends itself beyond its original capacities, attaining fundamental expansions of itself. I believe that the tensions implicit in a notion of chosen or willed subjection captures, as well as a contemporary category can, the tensions between choice and creativity and subordination to authority present in such an ethic.

The particularity of the authority is crucial. Rabbis affirm subjection to Torah and to God, but this in many ways counters or evades subjection to the colonial power of Rome. They also reject rival religious and philosophical groups of their times. Through their tradition and deity, rabbis seek freedom from such oppressive or competing authorities.[56] In addition, it is crucial not to collapse all forms of subordination. While the theoretical roots of the pun between subjectivity and subordination center upon the figures of a lord/master and a bondsman/servant/slave,[57] we should not impose these images upon all cases. There are multiple ways that *Rabbi Nathan* envisions chosen subordination to Torah and to God, and an important part of this study will be to gather and analyze the range of possibilities.

I emphasize that, while I am developing these theoretical tools in relation to the case of *Rabbi Nathan,* subordination is central to self-formation in many religious contexts. My formulation should not be interpreted as reinforcing the widespread and highly problematic image that Judaism is a religion centered upon a harsh and authoritative God, while other religions do not call for subordination. More fundamentally, we should move beyond any assumptions that ethical outlooks centering upon subordination are somehow not as good as those that do not. This task is more difficult than it might seem, largely because of deep biases in Western cultures that have their roots in early modernity and, before that, certain aspects of Christianity that include anti-Jewish polemic. While I do not present a fully comparative analysis, part of my goal in setting out a theoretical framework for examining ethics and chosen subjection is to open up the possibilities for cross-cultural examination of such dynamics.

I certainly do not claim that subjection is a universal feature of ethics, but I hold that self-cultivation through subjection is both widespread and very important, and that comparative study could be extremely productive. Recent studies of medieval Christian monasticism, modern Christian theology, contemporary Muslim women, and ancient Manichean ritual present phenomena that could be explained in these terms, and I believe that the categories can also illuminate important aspects of many Chinese, Hindu, and Buddhist ethical outlooks.[58] Such calls for subordination tend to be linked with an extremely hopeful sense that the self can expand in fundamental ways through engagement with powers external to it, along with the sober observation that this process is not easy and may not be pleasant. Whether or not this hope and this observation are correct is a matter of constructive inquiry. For descriptive and comparative projects, the key point is that these assertions underlie many ethical stances.

In the ethical instruction of *Rabbi Nathan,* subordination to external authorities is linked with various ways of internalizing discourse.[59] The concept of internalization appears often in contemporary theory. As I discussed above, Harvey claims that each element in his map of social processes internalizes the others. For example, discourses internalize power, beliefs and values, institutions, material practices, and social relations. Humans are porous, absorbing elements of their ecosystem as well as language and other aspects of their surrounding society.[60] Ricoeur also appeals to internalization at several points in his treatment of character formation. He argues that dispositions are formed through identification with, or internalization of, values, norms, ideals, models and heroes. In addition, while most practices are fundamentally interactive and learned from others, people can internalize such interaction and come to "play alone, garden alone, do research alone in a laboratory, in the library, or in one's office."[61]

This focus upon internalization at important points by two very different thinkers can probably be explained in terms of trends in contemporary theory, and we have to be careful not to import such theoretical freight into late antiquity. More generally, a crucial question is, what does it mean to "internalize" something? What does Harvey mean when he writes that discourse internalizes other social processes or that bodies internalize practices? Surely these are not the same (one involving representation, the other habituation and memorization), and neither is identical with the physical internalization of food, drink, or oxygen by the body.[62] The category of internalization is best understood as a metaphor, framing the self in terms of the opposition inside/outside and asserting that movement occurs from without to within. The specific features of any given case of internalization are points for analysis, not decisions to be made at the theoretical level. In *Rabbi Nathan* internalization (like subordination) is portrayed through figurative imagery, and I examine in detail the numerous rabbinic tropes that depict selves forming themselves through internalization of that which is outside.

This dynamic of subordination and internalization is to occur, according to *Rabbi Nathan,* in relation to external authorities. At a very basic level, this study begins with, and focuses on, that which is other to the self—the ethical discourse of *Rabbi Nathan.* We encounter rabbinic selves only as the voices in the text call out to and describe them. Here an observation by Louis Althusser is salient. He writes that authoritative others—whether individuals, communities, institutions, traditions, or deities—actively hail, recruit, or beckon their subjects. They entice or compel potential initiates as well as devotees. In turning to this voice, the recipient becomes a subject.[63] This point is especially relevant to *Rabbi Nathan,* for it is a text that calls out: through its maxims, the sages speak to "you," the audience, upholding their movement, tradition, and deity.

Such authorities can be seen in the broader theoretical context of relations between self and other—all selves exist in relation to others, and the relation between self and other is crucial for ethics.[64] There exists a tremendous scholarly literature on the category of the other, and I note just a few key points. First, there are many different others, some powerful or authoritative, some vulnerable and needing aid, and some equal to, or peer with, the self. In *Rabbi Nathan,* subject formation centers primarily upon authoritative others, though peers are crucial to the process, and a caring response to the vulnerable is certainly a key feature of a cultivated sage's character. Second, relations between self and other can vary tremendously. Even in the specific case of an authoritative other that is embraced in the context of ethics, religious elites may prescribe vastly differing ideals for comportment, such as love, awe, care, duty, filial piety, and freedom. In *Rabbi Nathan* ideals concerning these relations are set out through tropes and through prescriptions for specific emotional responses. Third, as scholars we can never be sure of the ontological status of others. Given critical scholarship beginning with Ludwig Feuerbach, all claims concerning the ultimate nature of otherness have to be regarded with at least initial suspicion as having their origins in forces different than those claimed to be. To take the grandest and most obvious example, God and the traditions that emerge from revelation may be nothing more than manifestations of society, or unconscious drives, or economic relations, or a whole host of possible profane processes.[65]

My descriptive project, though, is not in any simple sense one of either suspicion or retrieval but one in which both impulses are present and mutually intensify each other like juxtaposed complementary colors in a painting. This dual commitment is particularly important since aspects of *Rabbi Nathan* that differ with modern and postmodern sensibilities are often crucial to its complex accounts of what selves are and could be. For example, rabbis' elitism and sexism are entangled with their persuasive visions of community and fellowship. Their intense traditionalism is at the same time radically innovative, and innovations are often expressed through forms of interpretation whose dynamics contrast greatly with modern rationality. Their accounts of a calculating deity that rewards and punishes are central to a complex theory of action and a sophisticated pedagogical rhetoric. I strive for an analysis of this material that highlights its compelling features, its foreign and perhaps disturbing elements, and the ways that the compelling and disturbing are often deeply connected.

The Text and Its Sages

The creators of rabbinic texts were editors who received, adapted, expanded, and arranged earlier materials. Contemporary scholars debate the methods we should employ for thematic studies drawing upon such sources, and I am largely a pluralist in these matters. There are many ways one could frame a treatment of a given topic, and each has its possibilities and dangers. Taking a single text as my primary unit of analysis allows me to examine editorial work at various levels, including that of the entire compilation, though a constant risk is overemphasizing the hands of the editors or attributing a false unity to the process of compilation. When I consider the ethics of *Rabbi Nathan* in relation to rabbinic thought broadly construed, two dangers are overparticularizing (claiming that this text represents the viewpoint of only one school or set of compilers) or overgeneralizing (claiming that this text represents rabbinic thought as such).[1]

Rabbi Nathan is a large and significant anthology of ethical material that represents an important strand of rabbinic ethical thinking and debate. The text includes a diverse range of teachings, and that diversity allows me to examine themes that have wide resonances in rabbinic literature. At the same time, like all rabbinic texts, *Rabbi Nathan* preserves many features that are specific to its stream of compilation. Despite its size, *Rabbi Nathan* surely does not represent all of rabbinic thought: its creators were selective and at times contentious. While I treat *Rabbi Nathan* as a key example for investigating rabbinic ethics broadly construed, I also identify the distinct features of the text in contrast with others produced by the movement. Part of my work will be to discuss the many groups of people that are excluded from its ethics, and one way that I signal that *Rabbi Nathan* represents a strand and not the totality of rabbinic views is to avoid the use of the definite article before the word "rabbis." *Rabbi Nathan* reveals what (certain) rabbis state, but not what (all of) "the rabbis" believed.[2]

How, though, do we read a rabbinic text as a whole? What is the relation between this text and the classical rabbinic sages of Roman late antiquity, many of whom are portrayed in the text itself? *Rabbi Nathan* has an extremely complicated history of composition and editing, and we only understand small parts of it. Within the textual family, we find multiple recensions and a diversity of views and opinions, and beyond *Rabbi Nathan* there are challenges of contextualization in relation to other rabbinic material as well as to history. This section responds to such problems, first addressing the issues in delineating the text of *Rabbi Nathan,* situating it in contexts, and identifying the overall picture of a rabbinic community portrayed in the material. Then I examine the genres and literary structure of the text as a whole, including its maxims, their arrangement, the commentary upon them, and narratives within the commentary. My focus is on pedagogical features—how the text instructs its audience. Finally, I consider methodological questions in understanding the thought presented by the text, particularly its concepts and tropes. Everything that I discuss here is crucial for understanding *Rabbi Nathan,* but the generality of these points in relation to other rabbinic sources varies. My accounts of midrash and narrative probably can be applied to many other rabbinic sources, as can the procedures I set out for studying concepts and tropes. Much of my discussion of text and context, and my analysis of maxims, would be applicable to *The Fathers* as well as *Rabbi Nathan,* though the arrangement of maxims, their commentary, and aspects of the communal ideals are particular to *Rabbi Nathan.*

1a   *Rabbi Nathan* and Its Contexts

What constitutes the text? *The Fathers According to Rabbi Nathan* really designates a group of texts, as there are a number of writings, often with significant differences, which have that title. Today's academic readers of rabbinic Hebrew likely encounter *Rabbi Nathan* in one of two sources: the printed edition of the Babylonian Talmud (as part of the extracanonical tractates), and Solomon Schechter's edition of 1887. Most scholars make use of Schechter's compilation, which is the first critical edition ever done of a rabbinic text and an incredible work. He arranged two different versions side by side: one based on printed editions labeled "A," and the other labeled "B." Drawing upon manuscripts, medieval quotations, and other sources, he made some corrections within the main text (at times making this explicit, at other times not), presented comments at the bottom of each page, and included several appendices with further notes and a full manuscript. Schechter's book has many flaws, and it is difficult to navigate, but it is a tremendous achievement and still the standard reference.[1] This marks not the end but the beginning of the challenges. In the years since Schechter, critical studies of manuscripts and *geniza* fragments have been done by Louis Finkelstein, Marc Bregman, and, most recently and extensively, Menahem Kister.[2] One of the manuscripts that Schechter used for *Rabbi Nathan A* was lost in the Holocaust, and Finkelstein was able to make use of a manuscript that Schechter did not have. Both Kister and Bregman have given us reason to see complexities in recension beyond the dichotomy of A and B.[3]

My method concerning this diversity of writings is threefold. First, I aim to support all of my fundamental arguments through *Rabbi Nathan A,* and specifically the printed edition. Why the printed edition? The textual history of *Rabbi Nathan* is so complex that no one manuscript can be designated as best for identifying some original text. The printed edition surely is flawed, but given that no manuscript is unequivocally superior, I use the writings that came to be disseminated most widely and that the reader can consult most easily. I strive not to base any key interpretation on a passage for which the printed edition is clearly faulty. In cases of textual problems, sometimes I still quote from that edition but do not draw upon the problematic elements in my analysis. Other times, I follow corrections suggested by Schechter or later scholars, and I indicate when I do so.[4] Unless otherwise specified, when I write *"Rabbi Nathan,"* this is shorthand for "the printed edition of *Rabbi Nathan A.*"

Second, when there are interesting points or supplements to my basic arguments, I quote and analyze manuscripts of *Rabbi Nathan A* and *Rabbi Nathan B*. Otherwise, much valuable material for understanding rabbinic ethics would be ignored. I specify when I am not drawing from the base text. Third, through footnotes, I aim to cite and reference all relevant materials, so that the reader can have access to the full range of possibilities present in the textual family that is denoted by *Rabbi Nathan* as well as in other rabbinic texts. My major claims, moreover, are on a level of generalization that should have application beyond *Rabbi Nathan,* but the form and degree of this application is largely a matter for further research.

Date and Duration

Setting out the context of *Rabbi Nathan* is no simple matter. The relation between text and context is problematic for any work of literature, and recent scholarship on intellectual and literary history has reflected upon the complexities involved. Dominick LaCapra, for example, sets out six "overlapping areas of investigation," considering the relations of a text to the author's intentions, the author's life, society, culture, the corpus of a writer, and structures or forms of discourse.[5] This consideration of context as multifaceted is an important starting point for studying rabbinic materials, for we cannot presume a uniform standard or method for contextualizing texts across the cultures of Roman late antiquity. *Rabbi Nathan* can be quite productively contexualized in relation to forms of discourse (such as maxims of instruction, midrash and other forms of commentary, and narrative) and with significant qualifications, in relation to society and culture. However, on the creator's intentions, life, and corpus, the texts I examine differ significantly from much Roman and Christian material of the time, which can be situated in relation to particular authors and speakers, dates, and events. These authors and speakers, moreover, reflected upon themselves, and some were honored publicly through statues. By contrast, the rabbinic movement developed literature through anonymous compilers who avoided reference to history beyond a few key events.[6]

Rabbi Nathan, like other rabbinic sources, was not written by an author. Even if we allow the theoretical point that the author is alive as a function of scholarly discourse, we cannot carry out that function with *Rabbi Nathan.* Specifically, we should not presume that the text was written at a particular time and place, that it has stylistic unity and conceptual coherence, and that it can be situated in relation to a distinct historical event or situation.[7] We do not even know when or why the text came to be attributed to "Rabbi Nathan," though a figure named Rabbi Nathan appears on the first page, which may have inspired the title.[8] The text was created over centuries by editors who preserved and transmitted teachings from their past, but not in a manner that allows us to treat the material as historically reliable in any simple sense. At the same time, they did not impose their own views strongly enough that we can consider the accounts to be authored compositions.

Some rabbinic sources are more amenable to historical contextualization than others. In certain cases, discrete units can be situated through comparison with Roman or early Christian material. As for entire texts, Saul Lieberman emphasized the importance of the Palestinian Talmud for historical study of second- and third-century Palestine.[9] The Babylonian Talmud brings all sorts of challenges, but at least the editors followed certain conventions for distinguishing earlier from later materials. The Mishnah can be identified as a distinct text from the gemara, or talmudic commentary. The gemara in turn distinguishes tannaitic teachings (first to second centuries CE) from amoraic (third to fifth centuries CE) and later ones. Even if scholars are suspicious concerning the accuracy of the early material, at least there is something with which to work. Also, researchers have often had great success in identifying likely source material in earlier texts such as the Tosephta, Palestinian Talmud, and midrashic collections, comparing them with the Babylonian gemara to identify the work of redaction.[10] *Rabbi Nathan,* by contrast, appears to be a tannaitic work of Roman Palestine. The text is almost entirely in Hebrew, and most all the sages named in the text are from Palestine during the first and second centuries CE or earlier. However, scholars have long been aware that the final version of the text is much later, and Menahem Kister's recent analysis makes clear that we cannot read *Rabbi Nathan* in any transparent way as a source for early rabbinic material. At the same time, contextualizing *Rabbi Nathan* in later periods also presents difficulties. As Kister and others have shown, both internal evidence and comparison between versions indicate a fluid set of texts that went through many stages of editing, not a single compiler at a single time.[11]

While many still take *Rabbi Nathan* to be the equivalent of a talmudic tractate to the mishnaic text of *The Fathers,* this analogy fails in ways that are methodologically significant. Since the base text of *Rabbi Nathan* is a shorter and arguably earlier collection of maxims than *The Fathers,* the texts probably developed in parallel for a long period of time—perhaps sometimes in competing rabbinic circles and sometimes not. The particular wording and arrangement of the maxims in *Rabbi Nathan* often differs from that of *The Fathers* in important ways. *The Fathers* cannot be treated as the text upon which *Rabbi Nathan* comments, but as another branch in a textual family whose trunk does not exist except in the scholarly imagination. If there is a "Tosephta" to *The Fathers,* it is also material found within *Rabbi Nathan.* The important distinctions between Mishnah and commentary, and between sources and redaction, are then much more difficult to delineate than they are for talmudic sources.[12] As others who have worked on these materials, I treat the maxims that form the base of *Rabbi Nathan* as being part of that text, not, as Talmudists treat the Mishnah, a different text (though, as I discuss below, *Rabbi Nathan* has an internal hierarchy of meaning, with the commentary often distinguished from the base text). Comparisons with parallel sources also tend to yield ambiguities. While sometimes we find relatively clear cases of older material reworked in *Rabbi Nathan,* for many of the passages that I focus upon, the parallels offer differently redacted materials rather than the sources of *Rabbi Nathan.*

How, then, do we situate *Rabbi Nathan* in time and space, history and geography? The printed edition and extant manuscripts of *Rabbi Nathan* all date from the medieval period, starting in the fourteenth century. The earliest *genizah* fragment may be from the ninth century or earlier.[13] However, there is little in the text that reveals explicit concern with the world of the later Geonic or medieval periods, such as existence in a Mediterranean Islamic or European Christian society.[14] The final editors of the text seem to have been shapers rather than creators of the material we find.

How early is that material? This is a difficult and hotly disputed question. The sages named in the text lived from the second century BCE to the third century CE. Scholars have attempted, with some success, to reconstruct formulations and meanings from that time,[15] but generally *Rabbi Nathan* is not a reliable source for historical information about rabbis in the first centuries. There are significant disjunctive points in the text, where we can see later commentators preserving, yet struggling with or transforming, earlier viewpoints. I give great attention to these, because they reveal in stark terms the interests of the commentators, but they do not correlate across the text such that we can identify datable strata. Each case has to be treated individually. The text probably was still being compiled during the Christianization of the Roman Empire in the fourth century CE, and it may have undergone changes after the shift to an Islamic context in the seventh century, though we find little if any explicit representation of those contexts. Figures and events of the first two centuries, then, provided the material through which later rabbis reflected upon their own communities as well as imperial culture and power.

Delineating the date of *Rabbi Nathan,* then, does not lead us to a static point of crystallization or origin. The text primarily indicates a Palestinian setting (though many have noted signs of Babylonian editing, particularly for *Rabbi Nathan A*). It began to be compiled in the second century CE or earlier, grew by accretion, and attained its full form sometime between the sixth and ninth centuries, perhaps even going through further changes afterwards. *Rabbi Nathan* can be situated in multiple temporal contexts, depending on whether one is trying to recover early material, identify editorial shaping, or trace the reception of the text through later commentary and transmission. Anthony Saldarini has argued that the overall ethos of the text is probably amoraic, but Kister's emphasis on later features always has to be considered.[16] The most significant source we have for studying classical rabbinic ethics is, in notable respects, postclassical.

What are the methodological implications of these observations? I suggest four points. First, as scholars drawing upon *Rabbi Nathan* have done for a long time, we have to begin by treating each passage individually in its local literary context, comparing it with parallels elsewhere, and from that work building an account of the entire text (if this latter stage is possible, and I believe it is). Second, we need to address the possibility that meanings may have changed over the time that the text was compiled. Generally, since I focus on the contours of the text as an edited whole, I situate it in relation to sources from the later part of the late ancient rabbinic period.

Third, I strive to read the text with a dual interpretative commitment. On one hand, I work to identify particularity by looking for disjunctions within the text that reveal differences between its versions or conflicts between the compilers of one stage and those of another. On the other, I determine the nature and degree of regularities, such as common terminology that underlies different stances and limits in the diversity of opinion within *Rabbi Nathan*. Fourth, to the extent that the text does reveal regularities, it is important not to force them into a history of events. Fernand Braudel's well-known insights are crucial here. He calls upon scholars to address multiple temporalities in history, from the short-term event, to intermediate cycles such as economic fluctuations over a half-century (conjuncture), to much longer durations: "History exists at different levels, I would even go so far as to say three levels but that would be only in a manner of speaking, and simplifying things too much. There are ten, a hundred levels to be examined, ten, a hundred different time spans."[17] Though much of my book centers on particulars, the overall argument is one of regularities in late ancient rabbinic thought. The major disjunctions within the text occur between the commentary and maxims attributed to sages who would have lived before 70 CE. Moreover, the differences within *Rabbi Nathan,* and even between it and other rabbinic sources, are far smaller than the differences between *Rabbi Nathan* and either Second Temple or Geonic ethical materials. To use a well-known spatial metaphor, I spend most of the time examining specific trees, but the ultimate goal will be to map a major forest of classical rabbinic ethics.[18]

Scholastic Rabbinism

All of this caution and skepticism concerning the relation between text and context is in tension with a long line of scholarship on *Rabbi Nathan* that situates the material in relation to tannaitic and amoraic rabbis and that compares them to Greco-Roman philosophical schools. This scholarship tends to see a fairly close relation (though not identity) between the world presented by the text and the world of the compilers. From the standpoint of today's scholarship on both the text and the rabbinic movement, such claims represent overly strong historicizing and have to be taken with much caution. At the same time, while some scholars have compared small passages in *Rabbi Nathan* with Christian sources, and while Babylonian influences are well known, historians have not provided an alternative framework for contextualization.[19]

Given these points, I build upon observations made by Anthony Saldarini and his predecessors. I present them primarily as typologies or heuristic tools, but my skepticism concerning their historical significance is not absolute. My stance concerning the relation between the text of *Rabbi Nathan* and the early rabbis is that, as we now have the text, the sages are first and foremost literary figures. They may have lived, and most probably did, but we encounter them as bearers of sayings and characters in stories, all of which are highly stylized. My primary approach to them is not as historical persons whom I try to reconstruct but as literary figures that are central to pedagogical discourse.[20]

At the same time, we should allow for the possibility that some form of *Rabbi Nathan* probably existed in late ancient rabbinic circles, disseminated in and through living teachers and students through memorization and recitation. We do not know exactly how much of the text existed at what point, nor when it was written down.[21] It is conceivable that some of the sages who appear in the text may have, as historical persons, been involved in early stages of compiling the material. Perhaps a living Rabbi Akiba actually edited a collection of sayings that become the basis of this commentary, and maybe, despite all our scholarly doubt, there was a Rabbi Nathan involved in the process—even if they had a small part in creating the text as we now have it. At still another level, the later editors who compiled the text were likely shaped by it, with their own education centered on the collective memory of earlier sages as preserved in maxims and narratives.

Saldarini has characterized *Rabbi Nathan* as distinctly "scholastic," meaning that it presents and presumes the social context of a school or disciple circle that is comparable to Greco-Roman philosophical schools. This school or disciple circle includes a founder who is valued for his teachings as well as behavior; groups of disciples emphasizing fellowship, study, and teaching; communal meals; and some degree of distance from the rest of society.[22] His comparisons are part of a larger scholarly picture that presents rabbinic sages not as an essential and isolated community, but as playing on the broader discursive field of spiritual elites in the eastern Roman Empire. Like other rabbinic texts, *Rabbi Nathan* indicates a multilingual environment, having Aramaic sections and many Greek loan words interspersed in its Hebrew. More specifically, genres that are prominent in *Rabbi Nathan*—maxims, genealogical lists, and narratives—have been the center of comparison with Greco-Roman thought.[23]

While sages participated in the broader social context of late antiquity, a significant aspect of this participation was evasion of, or suspicion toward, Roman culture and imperial power. In addition, as Seth Schwartz argues, "[T]he rabbis were emphatically *not* normal elites or subelites of the eastern part of the Roman Empire." One distinctive aspect of the movement was the claim of expertise in multiple realms of activity. Rabbis strove to excel not in one area but in rhetoric, conceptual thought, legal thought and practice, miracle working, and more. All of this activity was channeled through, and legitimated by, their tradition of Torah and especially their exegesis of the Hebrew Scriptures. Consideration of rabbis in relation to other elites of late antiquity, then, is best understood not as a matter of arguing for similarities or differences, but of opening up more complex analogical comparisons.[24]

The sages who appear in the text teach a small circle of disciples, making up an urban or semiurban community centered on study. In many respects, these comments hold for all rabbinic texts. *Rabbi Nathan* is distinct among rabbinic sources in having a particular concern with the dynamics of this setting—the comportment that teachers have toward students, students toward teachers, and students with other students. As Saldarini writes, the text "does not give a complete description of the Rabbis nor does it recount how they lived, but rather how they ought to live as members of a school."[25] The disciple circle sets the context for the cultivation of virtue, particularly forms of self-restraint. The sages of *Rabbi Nathan* praise humility, patience, and the control of speech, and they condemn in strong terms those who are arrogant or who engage in gossip and slander. Study is both an intellectual activity and a way of life that distinguishes the participants from the broader society.[26]

In a scholastic setting the relations between teachers and students are a central concern. In *Rabbi Nathan,* sages instruct teachers to "raise up many students" and to "be careful" with their words in their teaching of Torah.[27] As was noted above, students are instructed by the Second Temple period sage Yose ben Yoezer, "Let your house be a meeting place for the sages, sit in the very dust of their feet, and drink with thirst their words" (A6,27; B11,27; *Fathers* 1:4). One passage in the exegesis of this maxim specifies the student's subordination to the sage, "For every word that emerges from your mouth, let him receive it upon himself in awe, fear, trembling, and shaking" (A6,27). This fourfold emotional response appears earlier in *Rabbi Nathan* to describe Moses's state when receiving the Torah at Sinai (A1,1). The student, then, is to take on the same relation toward his teacher as Moses took before God during revelation. In other rabbinic sources, these emotions describe people's state when reading edicts of emperors.[28] The affirmed subjection of student in relation to teacher, then, is characterized through the terminology of imposed subjection to Roman imperial power.

The teachings regarding students often address the day-to-day concerns. For example, many numerical lists categorize students according to their propensities. One of these compares students to four objects— a sponge, a sifter, a funnel, and a strainer. The sifter is the best of the instruments because it gathers the good and casts out the bad. The implied metaphor is that knowledge is a substance that may be retained or lost, so the ideal students are those who retain good rabbinic teachings and reject others. Other lists set out typologies of students according to their aspirations, where they sit in class, how they ask and answer questions, and their economic background.[29]

Students are instructed to eat together, worship together, read together, and, if they were unmarried, sleep together. Yehoshua ben Parahiah, a sage of the Second Temple period, is portrayed as saying, "Appoint for yourself a teacher, acquire for yourself a fellow [*haber*], and judge every man with the scales weighted in his favor" (A8,35; B19,39; *Fathers* 1:6).[30] The word "fellow" (*haber*) is a crucial technical term that in pharisaic and tannaitic times denotes a member of an elite association whose members maintain stringent standards of purity, particularly concerning diet.[31] In later literature, the word has a range of meanings centering on sharing and friendship, including the sense of a "fellow" in maintaining piety, righteousness, purity, or Torah study.[32] One commentary upon "acquire for yourself a fellow" states:

> How so? This teaches that a man should acquire a fellow for himself, that he will eat with him, drink with him, study Scripture with him, study Oral Torah with him, sleep with him, and reveal to him all his secrets— secrets of Torah and secrets of *derekh 'eretz*. (A8,36; B18,40)

We can see here a prescription for an interpersonal homosocial spirituality, in which men work together to transform themselves and follow divine precepts. The fellowship of peers extends through much of the student's life, day and night. The community also appears to have its version of peer counseling. While rabbinic literature does not have the focus on confession that emerges in Christian literature, this passage calls upon the students to have intimate communication with each other, sharing their personal and perhaps mystical "secrets."[33]

Distinctions

The scholastic ethos of *Rabbi Nathan* is defined not only by internal relations but also through contrast with those outside the disciple circle. Key features that define the ideal sage are nation, gender, and status—the sages contrast themselves with Romans, with women, and with various other Jews in their surroundings.[34] To a large degree, these separations are present throughout rabbinic culture, for the movement consisted of men from a colonized group in the Roman Empire who regarded themselves as elites in purity and sanctity. However, for each case, *Rabbi Nathan* has certain positions that can be contrasted with other rabbinic sources.

The teachings of *Rabbi Nathan* are generally consistent in portraying Romans as brutal colonizers. The text has long and much-embellished accounts of the destruction of the Jerusalem Temple in 70 CE, the ensuing poverty and oppression, and persecutions following the Bar Kokhba rebellion in the second century.[35] The narratives portray a highly ambivalent response to this situation. While sages show a deep suspicion of the governing powers, they also embrace political moderation and willingness to work with the dominant regime. Pragmatic concerns appear to be primary. This position can be seen in a well-known narrative about Rabban Yohanan ben Zakkai during the events of 70 CE in Jerusalem. The highly fictionalized story appears in several sources, including both versions of *Rabbi Nathan,* the Babylonian Talmud, and a Palestinian midrashic compilation. All versions present Rabban Yohanan ben Zakkai taking a conciliatory stance, criticizing radical Jews who want to fight the Romans, and making a deal with the Roman leadership in order to establish a rabbinic academy at Yavneh such that rabbinic tradition could continue despite the end of Temple worship. These materials have been extensively studied, and I highlight key features of the unit in *Rabbi Nathan.*[36]

In *Rabbi Nathan* we find less attention than in other sources to Rabban Yohanan ben Zakkai's encounters with Jewish rebels in the city and the long period of the siege. Rather, *Rabbi Nathan* emphasizes Rabban Yohanan ben Zakkai as a decisive and strong exemplary figure, and it gives relative weight to the postdestruction possibilities for a new scholastic community. The literary context in *Rabbi Nathan* is an extended commentary on the maxim of Simeon the Righteous, "The world rests upon three things: upon the Torah, upon the [Temple] service, and upon good deeds." The exegesis of this maxim centers on rabbinic life after the destruction of the Temple, both affirming the importance of the Temple and asserting that rabbinic study and practice can substitute for it.[37] In *Rabbi Nathan A,* the story appears as part of the commentary to "good deeds," while the compilers of *Rabbi Nathan B* place it under the topic of Temple service.

In both cases, surrounding the escape scene is an extensive elaboration of violence done by Romans, who conquer the city and catapult a pig's head onto the altar.[38] In the end, priests of the Temple throw their keys to the heavens while shouting to God that they are not worthy to hold them, and the patriarchs of Genesis, wherever they may be, cry as well. Within this context, certain details in narration and phrasing draw attention to the partnership between Rabban Yohanan ben Zakkai and the soon-to-be emperor Vespasian. The rabbi's success is his "good deed" that allows the continuity of rabbinic practice when there is no Temple. A key feature that I emphasize is the way that the compilers of *Rabbi Nathan* juxtapose the sage's alliance with the Roman leader and Roman violence against Jews.[39]

The themes of desire and responsibility run through the story. The narrative framing states clearly where the editor places blame, for the opening line is, "When Vespasian came to destroy Jerusalem . . ." Vespasian, however, sends a message to the city that attempts to shift agency to the Jews:

> You idiots, why do you want [*mebaqqeshim*] to destroy this city and want [*mebaqqeshim*] to burn the Temple? For what do I request [*mebaqqesh*] from you but that you send me one bow or one arrow and I will go from you? (A4,22)

Vespasian asserts the legitimacy of imperial rule. If the Jews resist, knowing that the Romans will respond by destroying the city, then they must "want" to destroy their own city. He frames his desire for a symbol of surrender (a bow or arrow) with the same terminology *(mebaqqesh,* from the root *b.q.sh.),* intensifying the rhetoric: the Jews "want" to destroy the city, and he only "wants" a small admission of defeat.

The Roman's words come right after the opening statement that Vespasian came to destroy the city, so it is clear that the narrative voice opposes such a framing of the issues. Given this opposition, it is particularly striking that the rabbinic hero, Rabban Yohanan ben Zakkai, affirms Vespasian's stance:

> My children, why do you destroy this city and want [*mebaqqeshim*] to burn the temple, for what does he request [*mebaqqesh*] from you but one bow or one arrow, and he will go from you? (A4,22)

The sage aligns himself with the Roman, configuring the scene in the same language of request—the Romans merely want *(mebaqqesh)* a bow or arrow, and in not giving in, the people show that they want *(mebaqqeshim)* to destroy the city. After this scene, word reaches Vespasian that Rabban Yohanan ben Zakkai is one of "those who love the Caesar."

The concern with wanting or requesting appears later in the story, when the rabbi and Vespasian meet. The Roman offers to his ally, "What can I give to you?" Rabban Yohanan ben Zakkai responds,

I request [*mebaqqesh*] from you only Yavneh, so that I can go and teach students, fix prayer, and fulfill all commandments there. (A4,23)[40]

According to the legend, this final request brings the survival, or perhaps even birth, of the rabbinic movement in the wake of the Temple's destruction. God may not be present in tangible ways at that moment, but a human alliance between a sage and a Roman leader establishes a new locale for a religious movement focused not on a sacred center but on teaching, prayer, and observance of commandments.[41] After making this deal, Rabban Yohanan ben Zakkai mourns the destruction, from a distance.

How should we interpret these features of the narrative? The opening line and later details concerning the destruction convey a strong picture of Roman responsibility and viciousness. However, the rabbinic hero speaks in the words of the colonizers (not only to the colonizers, when he might have to, but to other Jews), and his actions make possible the continuation of the movement. I think that the narrative does not seek a resolution of this conflict but rather presents it in striking terms.[42] Given that situation, *Rabbi Nathan* portrays Rabban Yohanan ben Zakkai as the only figure in the story who does not "want" to destroy Jerusalem; both the Romans and the radical Jews do.[43]

In addition to political moderation, rabbis counsel and model reliance upon their relationship with God to improve their status in the world. In some cases, rebellion is channeled into theology, with sages asserting that God will ultimately vanquish the oppressor. Or they turn their attention from the political forces at work to inquire concerning God's justice or their own sin. This move has a subversive dimension, as it implies that the true agent in history is God and not the Romans.[44] Generally, the rabbinic affirmation that their God is "a king" implies that the worldly government is not the ultimate power working on earth. So, in part 3, when I examine rabbinic chosen subjection to their God, we should see this as an alternative or counter to Roman subjection.

A second axis of contrast through which the scholastic community of *Rabbi Nathan* defines itself is gender. The text, like all rabbinic sources, is written by men and for men, so the ethical instruction presented through the sages is androcentric, meaning that it centers upon a perspective that is distinctively male. Rabbinic ethics, then, is intertwined with a vision of masculinity.[45] The discourse of *Rabbi Nathan* tends to criticize, blame, and exclude women, yet along with these negative stances, there are voices and tendencies that show a more sympathetic viewpoint.

Criticism centers on the rabbinic values of observing commandments, controlling speech, and restraining sexual desire: women are portrayed as failing in observance, engaging in improper speech, and inciting male sexual desire. Such views may be expressed through biblical characters. Extended discussions of the Garden of Eden portray Eve as failing to observe God's commandment not to eat from the Tree of Knowledge, and they blame her for human mortality and even for killing Adam. One passage concerning the Israelites' time in the desert accuses Miriam of malicious speech toward Moses and considers this act to be the cause of her own leprosy. Beyond biblical figures, ethical instruction in *Rabbi Nathan* presents women as distracting students from the study of Torah, as causing disruption in the community through generating gossip, or as sources of improper sexual temptation (I will examine cases of the latter below in part 2).[46] This literary construction of women reinforces the disciple circle as a male setting, and *Rabbi Nathan* does not represent women as teachers, students, or otherwise engaging in traditional discourse.[47]

Given this general picture, it is important to note several subtleties. First, there are other rabbinic sources that elaborate in great detail both norms and ideals concerning women. *Rabbi Nathan,* by contrast, centers on men. The text may presume or justify, for example, laws concerning menstruation or marriage, but there is little debate concerning specific practices.[48] Second, there are some rabbinic sources that reveal openness to the idea that women may study Torah, so while the exclusion in *Rabbi Nathan* is not unique, it also does not represent all of rabbinic literature.[49] Third, within the textual family of *Rabbi Nathan,* there are significant differences between versions A and B. *Rabbi Nathan B* has longer discussions of Adam and Eve in Eden, with more negative portrayals of Eve. Also, the most explicit disparaging statements about women appear in *Rabbi Nathan B* and not in *Rabbi Nathan A.*[50] While much of this material has parallels in other rabbinic sources, *Rabbi Nathan B* has a misogynistic bent that is notable.[51]

Neither version of *Rabbi Nathan,* however, presents a unified and monolithic account of gender relations. While the text configures the disciple circle as excluding women, it also implies that rabbis must depend on their spouses if they want to attain ideals of a good life. Like other rabbinic sources, *Rabbi Nathan* does not call for men to separate completely from women, but rather for a life of study that exists along with marriage and bearing children, thus fulfilling the biblical commandment to "be fertile and increase." Men rely on women for hospitality to their fellows and perhaps for money to support a life of study. An ideal woman, in this account, displays her virtue through upholding her husband's scholastic activity.[52]

Certain passages counter the general critical stance toward women. I have noted discussions of Eden that blame Eve for human mortality, but these passages arise in the text through association with an initial discussion that shows Adam to be faulty in his relation with God. Other passages, concerning the aftermath of conflict with Rome in 70 CE, single out the suffering of young women as exemplifying the suffering of the broader community.[53] We find even in *Rabbi Nathan B* strong voices that differ with misogynist views. One teaching criticizes fathers who marry off their daughters when they are minors. Another important voice appears in response to a list enumerating "four characteristics of women but not of men," which are gluttony, jealousy, laziness, and eavesdropping. The next passage, attributed to Rabbi Yose, says, "Just as there are four characteristics of women, so too, there are four of men"—the very same qualities.[54]

Rabbi Nathan, then, presents ideals for a community of men who separate themselves from women for the sake of study, though this separation presumes a larger context in which men marry and in many ways are dependent upon women. The specific features of this text's sexism are conditioned by its concern for men (rather than the regulation of women) and its ideals of controlling both speech and sexual desire (presenting women as problematic in relation to both). While the most prevalent orientation toward women is criticism and blame, there are notable differences between the two versions of the text, and within each version we find multiple voices, a number of which soften or resist such disparagement.

The third line of distinction that is crucial for the sages of *Rabbi Nathan,* along with nation and gender, is their status as religious elites with unique piety and connection to God. This status is primarily symbolic rather than material. *Rabbi Nathan* portrays sages as associating with the wealthy but not necessarily having great means themselves.[55] They differentiate themselves from, and sometimes criticize, the larger population of Jews, whom they call "the people of the land" *('am ha-'aretz).* Such separation can be seen in a list of standards for the "fellows" of the community:

> Anyone who takes upon himself [*meqabbel 'alav*] four things will be accepted [*meqabbelin 'oto*] as a fellow [*ḥaber*]: he does not go to the graveyard, he does not raise thin cattle, he does not give a raised offering or tithe to a priest of the common people [*'am ha-'aretz*], and he does not fix pure food with a common person [*'am ha-'aretz*] or eat impure foods in purity. (A41,132)

This passage employs standard rabbinic terminology for the admission of a candidate into the group *(q.b.l.)* and prescribes certain requirements. He must uphold a communal ethic of not raising thin cattle, perhaps because they disrupt neighbors in searching for food. In his personal practice, he has to maintain scrupulous purity with regard to location (not entering a graveyard), diet, and people around him. Most important for the present discussion, he must maintain a separation from the "people of the land," or *'am ha-'aretz,* emphasizing the rabbinic desire for distinction through purity, particularly regarding food matters. Along with this separation, however, other passages reveal that rabbis desired public support, including invitations into people's homes to teach, and they aspired to be leaders of communities beyond their circle.[56]

The rabbinic sages were not the only religious group seeking influence among Jews in late antiquity. In *Rabbi Nathan,* competitors are often indicated by the term *minim*—those who, from the perspective of rabbis, were "sectarians."[57] *Rabbi Nathan* also reveals a distinct tension with independent Jewish figures, who appear as the "Early Pious Ones" or *ḥasidim ri'shonim.* The *ḥasidim* appear in rabbinic literature as pious and often ascetic individuals who were close to, but not part of, the rabbinic movement and its precedents.[58] The compilers of *Rabbi Nathan* have an extremely ambivalent response to such figures. In some cases *ḥasidim* appear as moral exemplars, displaying the highest degrees of self-control and fellowship, but other passages are critical of their practices and purity standards.[59] For example, a hyperbolic maxim of the sage Hillel asserts, "One who does not attend the sages is guilty of death." The commentary in *Rabbi Nathan* includes a story describing a priest who independently follows the practices of the *ḥasidim (middat ḥasidut).* Rabban Yohanan ben Zakkai sends a student to examine his activities, and the solitary pious man is found to be faulty in his diet, failing to maintain appropriate levels of purity.[60]

At the level of literary compilation, Shmuel Safrai has noted that certain anthologies of rabbinic ethical literature—most notably *Derekh Eretz Zuṭa* and *Seder Eliyahu*—preserve ideals and concepts that were central to the *ḥasidim.*[61] While I believe that his argument and its implications need further refinement, it is notable that there are identifiable points of difference or perhaps disagreement between *Rabbi Nathan* and these other compilations (I discuss one case below in chapter 3b). Such contrasts may indicate tensions between the scholastic and theologically moderate communities that generated *Rabbi Nathan* and other groups that embraced more independent, ascetic, and miracle-oriented forms of Judaism.

In addition to differentiation from the "people of the land" and from other Jewish elites, *Rabbi Nathan* reveals distinct interests within the rabbinic movement. The language and the rabbis named in the text indicate that *Rabbi Nathan* arose, at least initially, out of Palestinian communities rather than Babylonian. Within Palestinian rabbinism, perhaps the most important point of contrast is between the compilers of *Rabbi Nathan* and those who aspired to Jewish political leadership in the position of patriarch, as is evident in a comparison between *The Fathers* and *Rabbi Nathan*. *The Fathers* includes a prominently placed genealogy that culminates in Rabbi Yehudah the Patriarch and his descendants, and this text is now found in the Mishnah, whose compilation is attributed to the same Rabbi Yehudah. In *Rabbi Nathan,* this genealogy is either absent (in *Rabbi Nathan A*) or placed in a peripheral location (in *Rabbi Nathan B*). Some have also linked the name "Rabbi Nathan" with a Babylonian rabbi who was a contemporary of Rabbi Yehudah the Patriarch, seeing the text of *Rabbi Nathan* as emerging from this other rabbi's circle.[62] As Jewish elites, then, the compilers of *Rabbi Nathan* appear to have been Palestinian, moderate (not only politically but theologically), and separate from, though not overtly challenging, the authority of the patriarchate.

A Place to Sit

The distinct ethos of *Rabbi Nathan,* then, can be identified through the text's affirmations and exclusions. Sages prescribe intense relationships among those inside the community: both horizontal relations among peers and vertical relations between students and their teachers. These relationships occur within a community that separates itself from a variety of others. This combination of internal fellowship and external exclusion conditions the distinct piety and ethics articulated in *Rabbi Nathan* for a particular movement of male religious elites among a nation colonized by a larger empire.

In this scholastic community, the would-be sage is not a solitary individual agent, but a man who cultivates himself through a network of relationships. While there are rabbinic sources that present universalist values, at least in some form,[63] the ethics of *Rabbi Nathan* presumes a locative religiosity in which one must place oneself in a distinct hierarchical community that provides social and cosmic order, rather than an open or utopian vision that calls for transcending one's cultural particularity. Such self-locating is portrayed in very concrete terms through narratives of Rabbi

Eliezer ben Hyrcanus (first century CE) and Rabbi Akiba (early second century CE). According to legends in *Rabbi Nathan,* these sages start their study late, after realizing the value of Torah in adulthood. Their careers begin when they go to the major rabbinic teachers of their day. We read of the twenty-two-year-old Eliezer that he "sat himself before Rabban Yohanan ben Zakkai in Jerusalem" (A6,30). When the forty-year-old Akiba began to study, he first sat with his son in grade school and then, after reading the entire Torah, "sat before Rabbi Eliezer and Rabbi Yehoshua" (A6,29). A crucial and early step in ethical transformation is, literally and figuratively, sitting in the right place.[64]

1b The Text Instructs

Authoritative individuals, communities, traditions, and deities actively call out to their subjects, and the discourse of *Rabbi Nathan* in particular has features that do so. The distinctive and most fundamental literary genre is a short maxim or epigram, attributed to a named sage, which often appears in the second person. Through this form, the sages speak to "you," the audience. Moreover, this call is elaborated and developed through the editors' arranging of these maxims, their commentary upon them, and the concepts and tropes that pervade this material. In the following sections I examine these elements of the text and highlight their importance for ethical instruction.

The Sages' Maxims

As a literary figure, the sage's primary function in *Rabbi Nathan* is to instruct the listeners or readers through short, compact statements that I refer to as sayings, maxims, or epigrams. The maxims of *Rabbi Nathan* reveal specific stylistic and rhetorical conventions.[1] The first saying in *Rabbi Nathan* is attributed to the Men of the Great Assembly, a group that supposedly existed after the biblical prophets:

> The Men of the Great Assembly received [the Torah] from Haggai, Zechariah, and Malachi, and they said three things: Be patient in judgment, raise up many disciples, and make a fence for the Torah. (A1,2; also B1,2; *Fathers* 1:1)

This maxim has two features that, as Yonah Fränkel has observed, appear frequently in *The Fathers* and *Rabbi Nathan,* particularly among statements attributed to sages who would have lived prior to the destruction of the Second Temple.[2] First, the utterance is an imperative—"Be patient . . . raise up . . . make a fence . . ." In this case the Hebrew is plural, but in others the imperative can be framed in the second person singular or in the third person. In contrast with the commands of the Pentateuch — which present divine law spoken through Moses to all of Israel — the imperatives of *Rabbi Nathan* are human teachings spoken by sages to their followers, and they do not have the status of *halakhah,* or rabbinic law.

Second, the maxim is a cluster of three ideas. In the instruction of the Great Assembly, the numerical dimension is highlighted explicitly — "said three things" — and three distinct imperatives are present. The tripartite dimension can appear in other forms, such as a list of three nouns. For example, the next maxim, in the name of Simeon the Righteous, declares, "The world rests upon three things: upon the Torah, upon the [Temple] service, and upon deeds of loving kindness" (A4,18; B5,18; *Fathers* 1:2). In still other cases, we see a list of three items without a heading. Such groups may have originally expressed a single idea, but the exegesis of *Rabbi Nathan* tends to atomize them and sometimes highlights a particular element.[3] The compact nature of the statements, along with the pattern of threes, implies that they were likely memorized, perhaps in the context of popular education for children.

Fränkel has also pointed out that the sayings of Hillel, who lived around the time of Herod, differ significantly from the above pattern. These maxims are in Aramaic rather than Hebrew, and they are not second-person imperatives but indicatives in the first or third person. For example, one cluster of sayings is:

> A name raised up is a name destroyed.
> He who does not increase [*mosiph*], ceases [*yaseph*].[4]
> He who does not learn is guilty of death.
> He who makes use of the crown perishes.
> (A12,48; A12,56; B27,56–57;
> *Fathers* 1:13)

This sequence of four Aramaic sayings has several types of parallelism, including repetition ("name" in the first line), puns (*mosiph* and *yaseph* in the second), and number of words — the unit as a whole has a pattern of 4 words / 3 words / 4 words / 3 words.[5]

Many epigrams found in *Rabbi Nathan* fit neither the pattern of the tripartite imperative nor that of Hillel. Perhaps the most common form of these other statements asserts a relation of cause and effect through the expression "Anyone who [*kol ha-*] . . . will . . ."[6] For example,

> Rabbi Hanina ben Dosa says: Anyone whose [*kol ha-*] fear of sin is prior to his wisdom, his wisdom is established. (A22,74; B32,69)

> Rabbi Akiba says: Anyone who [*kol ha-*] takes a *peruṭah* [a small coin] from the community fund, when he is not in need, will not pass from the world before he is in need [of charity] from his fellow. (A3,15)

Such maxims instruct through specifying the consequences of a given action, whether positive or negative, spiritual or material. Still other rabbinic epigrams begin with a question. For example, Rabban Yohanan ben Zakkai asks his students, "Go out and see, what is [*'eyzehu*] the good way [*derekh ṭobah*] to which a man should cling in order that he enter through it to the world to come?" The question is followed by a series of answers by students—a good eye, a good fellow (*ḥaber*), and so on. This format of question and answer, some argue, is similar to rhetorical styles in Hellenistic philosophical schools and may give us a glimpse into the dynamics of classroom pedagogy in late antiquity.[7]

In addition to these various forms of epigram—imperatives, first- and third-person statements, and questions—we find in *Rabbi Nathan* numerical lists. These lists, along with their exegeses, make up about a third of the text. Many center on the Torah: they may compile the contents of the Written Torah (such as the generations from Adam to Noah and Noah to Abraham, or the names of the Holy Spirit), the formal features of the Written Torah (unusual marks in the vocalization of the text), or contents of the rabbinic Oral Torah (miracles in Jerusalem). Such lists may not appear to be ethical instruction, but the ensuing exegesis often interprets the items or the entire list with pedagogical interest. This concern can be quite explicit, as when commentary begins, "What need do inhabitants of the world have of this? It is to teach you that . . ." There are also many cases in which the list itself conveys ethical values through techniques such as contrasting qualities of the sage and the fool, listing the qualities of good students, and articulating the dynamics of divine reward and punishment.[8]

Rabbinic wisdom sayings, then, are short, compact units of discourse with distinct stylistic features that convey ethical and theological teachings as part of instruction and guidance.[9] Such maxims are the most fundamental way that *Rabbi Nathan* hails or beckons its subjects, and as prescriptive utterances that point to ideals for which the reader or listener should strive, they constitute the most basic way that *Rabbi Nathan* sets out processes of change, formation, or transformation from one's present state to a sagely one.

Arrangement of Maxims

Throughout the classical rabbinic period and beyond, maxims were center points for ethical reflection, and they were gathered in collections of rabbinic ethical literature.[10] Generally, in both *Rabbi Nathan* and *The Fathers,* the arrangement is not according to topical or formal features, but rather based on the sages to whom the sayings are attributed.[11] Many maxims honor specific sages, introduced by a phrase such as "Rabbi X would say." We cannot assume that a given sage, as a historical person, actually said the maxims that appear in his name, but such attributions are crucial to the creation of sages as literary figures.[12]

In *Rabbi Nathan* and *The Fathers* we find five groups of sayings, arranged according to the following attributions or numerical features:

1. A genealogy presenting a transmission of Torah from Moses to the prophets, elders, and Men of the Great Assembly, and then to Hillel and Shammai (A1–13; B1–27);
2. Rabban Yohanan ben Zakkai and his students in the first and early second centuries CE (A14–18; B28–31);
3. Sages of the House of Shammai who lived during the first century BCE and the first century CE (A19–22; B32 and 34);
4. The "Four Who Entered the Garden" of the early second century CE (A23–26; B33 and 35);
5. Numerical statements, grouped largely by ten, seven, and four (A31–41; B36–48).[13]

Given this arrangement, *Rabbi Nathan* can be analyzed as an anthology of several lists, each of which has rhetorical force. The first is a genealogy of teaching and learning. It conveys, despite historical gaps, an unbroken chain of Torah transmission from Moses to Hillel and Shammai. Such a genealogy is characteristic of Hellenistic schools in late antiquity, linking the founders of the tradition to present or recent teachers.[14] The list of *Rabbi Nathan* legitimates the rabbis' tradition as linked with divine revelation, reinterprets the prophets and elders of the Bible as proto-sages, and excludes for the most part priests and kings.[15]

The second list extends the genealogy to encompass the first and second generations of tannaitic rabbis, centering on the legendary founder of the study house at Yavneh, Rabban Yohanan ben Zakkai. In the mishnaic *The Fathers* we find a genealogy of patriarchs preceding Rabban Yohanan ben Zakkai and his students, but these figures are absent or placed in more peripheral locations in *Rabbi Nathan* (as noted in chapter 1a, *The*

Fathers thus legitimates the patriarchate in a way that *Rabbi Nathan* does not).[16] In both *The Fathers* and *Rabbi Nathan,* the chronological sequence breaks down at the third group, moving back to earlier sages.[17] The fourth list, most prominent in *Rabbi Nathan A,* presents rabbis known for their philosophical or mystical speculations in the *pardes* (garden). It is not clear, though, what significance we should give to this grouping or how we should read it in relation to narrative accounts of this garden.[18]

Finally, we come to the list of lists, the compilation of numerical catalogues. Within this section, the collection of lists of ten has a crucial role. It begins with creation, presenting ten utterances with which God created the world. It moves to listing of generations from Adam to Noah, then Noah to Abraham, then trials of Abraham, then discussions of the time that Israel was in Egypt and the desert, then various other materials, and finally comes to an extended list and discussion centering on Jerusalem (A31–35,90–106; B36–39,90–108; *Fathers* 5:1–5). This literary unit, then, presents a genealogy linking creation to Jerusalem—the city of the Temple. The emphasis on creation and Jerusalem complements the opening genealogy that excludes priests and centers on revelation, the sages, and Torah. Taken as a whole, *Rabbi Nathan* does not reject the importance of temple worship but rather embraces and legitimizes it in a secondary place to teaching and tradition. The compilers of the text uphold and mourn the Temple, but as a Temple that no longer exists.[19]

Commentary

Let us say that now we begin to read. We may pick up Schechter's edition, or a printed edition, or a manuscript (probably photocopied or on microfilm)—what happens? For most readers, *Rabbi Nathan* may at first appear to be just another book, but one will soon find (perhaps a few pages into a seemingly unnecessary discussion of the Garden of Eden) that the territory is quite foreign. *Rabbi Nathan* is a book of ethical teaching, but its form is not that of a manual or treatise. Rather, like many classical rabbinic texts, it is a commentary with an internal hierarchy of meaning. Its structure is given from its base text, in this case an early version of what became *The Fathers,* which sets the topical agenda for the compilers.

Through commentary, rabbis may develop, expand, modify, or adapt the basic ideas that they receive, while always working in relation to a prior structure.[20] The sages' epigrams instruct the listener or reader to act in a particular manner. The commentary develops this pedagogical discourse and needs to be read in relation to it. The interpretation of a given maxim can begin in a number of ways. One of the most common openings is the question "How so?" followed by the answer "This teaches that . . ." *(keytzad? melammed she-)*. Or, the editor may immediately introduce a verse from the Bible, introduced by "Thus it says" *(harey hu' 'omer)*.[21] These phrasings may imitate or evoke a classroom discussion in which the teacher opens with a question and then later gives the answer, or juxtaposes a maxim with biblical material.

Sometimes the interpretations of an epigram are fairly straightforward, but in many cases we find complex transformations that are similar to rabbinic exegesis of the Bible. For example, the commentary upon the instruction of the Men of the Great Assembly—"make a fence around the Torah"—is glossed as "make a fence around your words." The commentators change the focus from the Written Torah to speech, particularly speech as part of the Oral Torah. Throughout the long ensuing discussion, which is the most extensive commentary upon any maxim in *Rabbi Nathan,* the exegetical focus is upon "words" (A1,2–14; B1–3,3–14).[22]

Another example of strong "misreading" concerns the call by Yoseph ben Yohanan,[23] "Let the poor be members of your house." In both versions of *Rabbi Nathan,* the commentators reinterpret this maxim using the formula "not . . . really, but . . ." *(lo' . . . mamash 'ela' . . .):*

> Let the poor [*'aniyyim*] be members of your house. *Not* "members of your house" *really, but* let the poor speak about what they eat and drink in your house. (A7,33; emphasis added)

> Let the poor [*'aniyyim*] be members of your house. *Not* "poor" *really, but* that he be humble [*'anav*], and his wife humble, and his sons and the members of his house humble. (B14,33; emphasis added)

In both of these cases, we see an explicit rejection of the simple meaning of the maxim, what it "really" *(mamash)* means, in favor of another.[24] The second case shows a drastic change in focus, from relations with the poor to one's general comportment and inner state. The shift, though, is legitimated through a pun between "poor" *('aniyyim)* and "humble" *('anav)*.

While the commentary is structurally subordinate to the base text, in many cases it substantially changes the meaning. In addition to specific instances of exegetical transformation, by its sheer bulk the commentary can affect the emphases of *Rabbi Nathan.* For example, discussions of the opening genealogy from Moses to Hillel and Shammai make up the first third of the text. Within that, the text gives tremendous weight to the maxim of the Men of the Great Assembly—"Be patient in judgment, raise up many students, and make a fence for the Torah." In *Rabbi Nathan,* these three topics take up over one-seventh of the whole text. Furthermore, within this section, we find particular focus upon the "fence," and within that, a very long section on Adam and Eve that one would be unlikely to anticipate simply by contemplating the maxim alone. A second important expansion is an extensive analysis of the bad inclination, or *yetzer,* which contains much material that I analyze below. Other large sections in the commentary of *Rabbi Nathan* include narratives of Hillel, Rabban Yohanan ben Zakkai (discussed above in chapter 1a), Rabbi Eliezer ben Hyrcanus, and Rabbi Akiba. These accounts of sages imply a sublineage emphasizing certain figures that appear in the genealogical lists of the text: Hillel, Rabban Yohanan ben Zakkai, Rabbi Eliezer, and Rabbi Akiba.[25]

Rabbi Nathan is a commentary in another sense—much of it is made up of midrash, or exegesis of the Bible. We have to read *Rabbi Nathan* as emerging from multiple hermeneutical commitments—often a given passage emerges through the intersection of a rabbinic maxim and two or more biblical verses.[26] While the rules and boundaries of biblical exegesis are debated among the classical rabbis,[27] at least in later sources, rabbinic midrash tends to be based on the theological claim that the Bible represents God's speech as given at Sinai. This divine speech is seen as perfect (despite the many imperfections that a modern scholarly reader would find) and able to be interpreted in ways that human speech cannot. Most notably, each verse or part of a verse can be juxtaposed with verses elsewhere in the Bible to generate meanings not obvious in the local context. As the sage Hillel counsels, "Turn it, turn it, everything is in it" (A12,55; B27,55).[28] "Everything" that a rabbi needs to guide him in life is present in the Bible, if he can "turn" it correctly through midrashic interpretation.[29] The development of the maxims through midrash is another way that *Rabbi Nathan* asserts a continuity between its sages' instruction and divine revelation. At the same time, midrash is also a dimension of rabbinic culture that reveals discursive participation in a Hellenistic context, for many of the rabbis' interpretive methods parallel those of Greeks and Romans.[30]

When reading this commentary, then, we have to be aware of the epigram that is being discussed and how the commentary builds upon it. Then, with each unit of midrash, I start with the biblical verse (which often comes at the end of a teaching) and analyze the ways that the rabbinic teaching emerges from that verse. The text instructs between epigrams and biblical exegesis.[31]

Narratives

Narrative is, as Jacob Neusner argues, one of the most prominent genres in the commentary of *Rabbi Nathan*.[32] It is also a literary form that has been extensively studied as having parallels in Hellenistic literature. Specifically, scholars have compared rabbinic narrative with the *chreia*—a brief anecdote describing the actions and deeds of a wise person.[33] For both Hellenistic and rabbinic materials, epigram and narrative intertwine. In *Rabbi Nathan,* narratives develop epigrams as part of the commentary, but at the same time many narratives portray sages teaching by way of epigrams (whether the one being commented upon or others). At another level, as I discussed above, epigrams in the text are introduced by the statement, "Rabbi X said/would say . . ." As such, they can be considered mininarratives, depicting one utterance.

The pedagogical function of narratives differs from text to text. Jeffrey Rubenstein has shown, in his study of talmudic stories, that Babylonian narratives often work out tensions and express ambivalence rather than presenting sages as unambiguous exemplars. Most of the narratives of *Rabbi Nathan,* by contrast, uphold the sages. While in some cases they appear as flawed or as facing situations that reveal the limits of their virtue, generally in *Rabbi Nathan* sages define the *telos* of ethical transformation through modeling right character and action.[34] The compilers of *Rabbi Nathan* appear to have been aware of this status. We find, in a series of narratives concerning the career of Rabbi Akiba, the following gloss:

> In the future, Rabbi Akiba will make all of the poor stand guilty in judgment. If they are asked, "Why did you not study [Torah]?" and they say, "Because we were poor," they would be told, "But look, Rabbi Akiba was even poorer, and also miserable." (A6,29; B12,30)[35]

In this reflexive moment, the text of *Rabbi Nathan* tells readers how to draw upon the story of Rabbi Akiba in their lives. The sage sets a standard for right behavior. One should look at the case of Rabbi Akiba whenever considering reasons for not studying Torah. His ability to overcome obstacles such as poverty renders invalid any excuse.

A variant of the "rabbi as exemplar" is the "test" of the sage's virtue. For example, an account of two unnamed "pious ones" (*ḥasidim*) appears as commentary to the maxim, "Judge every man with the scales weighted in his favor." It both presumes, and plays upon, a test of sexual control:

Judge every man with the scales weighted in his favor. A story of a young woman who was taken captive: two pious ones *(ḥasidim)* went after her to redeem her. One of them went into a tent of prostitution. When he came out, he asked to his fellow *(ḥabeyro),* "Of what did you suspect me?"

He said, "Perhaps of learning how much money is the ransom."

He said, "By the Temple service! That is what happened."

He said, "Just as you judged me with the scales weighted in my favor, so may The Holy One, blessed be He, judge you with the scales weighted in your favor." (A8,37; see also A8,36; B19,41–42)[36]

The *ḥasidim* display three types of virtue in this story. First, they go to ransom a woman who has been kidnapped, thus carrying out the highly valued commandment of redeeming captives *(pidyon shebuyyim).*[37] Second, one of the pietists enters a place of prostitution, facing sexual temptation, and he shows his restraint. The narrator, however, plays on that test in order to depict another—a test of the second *ḥasid's* trust in his fellow. Does the second *ḥasid* "judge every man with the scales weighted in his favor?" While the first *ḥasid* appears to have committed a sexual transgression, he was gathering information in order to carry out a commandment.[38] The center of the story, then, is not the entering of the tent, but the question, "Of what did you suspect me?"—that is, did you judge me charitably, with the scales weighted in my favor, or harshly? The fellow pietist displays a third virtue through his generous assessment of his fellow *(ḥaber).*

Other stories present a sage not only as an exemplar but also as a teacher who gives instruction to his fellows or to others. In some cases, an ordinary person meets the sage in order to ask advice, to learn about rabbinic tradition, or to obtain an authoritative opinion concerning a matter of law. In these narratives of "encounter," the sage presents his knowledge, pedagogical skills, and personal virtues. One set of encounter stories focuses upon Hillel and Shammai.[39]

The narratives appear as exegesis of the maxim of Rabbi Eleazar ben Arakh, "Do not anger easily." The commentary begins, "Do not anger easily. How so? This teaches that one should be patient like Hillel the elder, and one should not be impatient like Shammai the elder" (A15,60). The editors then present a series of stories that uphold Hillel's patience in contrast with Shammai's behavior. One set of tales presents an encounter between a potential proselyte and the two sages. First, the man goes to Shammai:

What was the impatience of Shammai the Elder? They told a story of a man who stood before Shammai: He said to him, "My master, how many Torahs do you have?"

[Shammai] said, "Two, one that is written, and one that is oral."

He said, "The written one, I believe in. The oral one, I do not believe in."

[Shammai] rebuked him and sent him out in anger. (A15,61; B29,61–62)

This story turns on the rabbinic distinction between two Torahs—the Written Torah of the Hebrew Scriptures, and the Oral Torah that encompasses the entire tradition of learning that is drawn from, or grounded in, the written. In late antiquity, many religious groups affirmed the books of the Written Torah, but the Oral Torah was distinctive to rabbinic religiosity.[40] The man before Shammai accepts the Bible, but not a particular tradition of interpretation. Shammai does not consider such a man worthy of his time and sends him away.

The same man then encounters Hillel, who patiently and cunningly works with the inquirer in order to teach him the value of the Oral Torah:

He came before Hillel and said to him, "My master, how many Torahs were given?"

[Hillel] said, "Two, one that is written, and one that is oral."

He said, "For the written one, I believe you. For the oral one, I do not believe you."

[Hillel] said, "My son, sit." He wrote the alphabet for him and said, "What is this?"

He said, *"'Aleph."*

[Hillel] said, "This is not *'aleph* but *beyt*." He then said, "What is this?"

He said, *"Beyt."*

[Hillel] said, "This is not *beyt* but *gimmel*."[41] He continued, "From where do you know that this is *'aleph* and this is *beyt* and this is *gimmel*? Thus our early forefathers passed down to us [*masru*] that this is *'aleph* and this is *beyt* and this is *gimmel*. Just as you received [*qibbalta*] this in faith, so receive [*qabbel*] upon yourself that [the Oral Torah] in faith. (A15,61; B29,61–62; see also similar stories in A15,60–62; B29,60–62)[42]

We see in Hillel's pedagogy a motif that appears elsewhere in *Rabbi Nathan* and rabbinic literature: learning begins with the letters of the alphabet, and contemplating the letters reveals more than just the elements of words.[43] In this case, the story presumes that there is nothing intrinsic in an *'aleph* that makes it an *'aleph* or in a *beyt* that makes it a *beyt*. How is it that the man knows which is which, such that he can challenge Hillel's assertion that the *'aleph* is a *beyt*? The implied answer is that these correlations are fixed by convention and presumed by all who employ the system of writing.

Hillel then makes an analogy between this convention and the broader tradition of Oral Torah—just as you draw upon received opinion for basic understanding of the script of the sacred language, so should you do for other religious matters. In order to reinforce his point, Hillel employs technical terms for reception and transmission of tradition that are prominent in *Rabbi Nathan* and in *The Fathers (m.s.r.* and *q.b.l.).* This creative pedagogy stems from his patience—Hillel's willingness to work with a student who raises objections to his most strong convictions. The series of stories concludes with a remark by the now-student contrasting the two sages, stating that, in contrast with Shammai, Hillel's patience "brought me to life in this world and the next" (A15,62; B29,62).[44]

Through such tests and encounters, sages display and teach their virtues over the course of their careers. The ultimate moment for instruction, however, is upon the deathbed. After the classical rabbinic period, the concept of the "ethical will," a last teaching given by a father to his son, came to be a prominent genre of Jewish moral instruction. We see seeds of this practice in the narratives of *Rabbi Nathan*.[45] One of the most well known rabbinic deathbed scenes is that of Rabbi Eliezer ben Hyrcanus surrounded by his students. In many accounts of this moment, the controversial and charismatic teacher reveals his powers—clarifying obscure passages in the law, telling of his magical abilities, and predicting the future.[46] A small fragment, however, portrays Rabbi Eliezer as instructing in ethics and spiritual focus:

> When Rabbi Eliezer was sick, his students entered to visit him. They sat before him, saying, "Our master, teach us something from what you have taught us."[47]
> He said to them, "Let me teach you this: go forth, and each of you look out for the honor of his fellow [*ḥabeyro*]. When you pray, know before whom you stand to pray. For through this thing, you will merit life in the world to come." (A19,70)

In this story, Rabbi Eliezer offers two maxims to his students. The first concerns fellowship among his disciples—each should attend to the public standing of the others. The second directs their attentiveness during prayer toward intense focus upon the deity. Both of these teachings gain authoritative status based on their pedagogical context, the deathbed of a great sage.[48]

It is through narratives—including those of "test," "encounter," and "deathbed"—that the sage displays virtuous action. These stories provide the context in which he exemplifies right desire and emotion, skill in teaching, and knowledge of law, wisdom, and theology. Narratives, then, accompany maxims in developing the figures of the sages. The maxims present instruction and norms in general terms. The narratives show how these instructions can be carried out in practice and, in contrast with the talmudic stories analyzed by Rubenstein, how the greatest sages can fulfill such ideals without effort or struggle.

I C   Concepts and Tropes

Rabbinic thought does not provide arguments that can be characterized as philosophical. If we enter an inquiry into rabbinic ethics by way of philosophy, we not only miss the pedagogical elements discussed above, but also the distinctive features of rabbinic concepts that Max Kadushin has characterized as "organic." With certain qualifications, key elements in Kadushin's notion of organicity are extremely valuable for thinking about *Rabbi Nathan* and rabbinic thought more generally. His observations are not themselves sufficient for treating the conceptual dimensions of the text, however, for his approach does not attend sufficiently to figurative language. Tropes such as metaphor and metonymy are central to the ways that rabbis develop and define their concepts, and in fact many rabbinic concepts themselves are tropes. In this section I set out methodological tools for analyzing both the concepts and the tropes in the ethical teachings of *Rabbi Nathan*.

Diversity of Views and Value Concepts

One of the great challenges for any analysis of concepts and tropes in rabbinic literature is the diversity of opinions in a given source. Rabbinic texts in general, and *Rabbi Nathan* in particular, contain a tremendously wide range of views that differ or conflict. At the level of redaction (whatever stage of redaction we consider), rabbinic texts canonize dissent, presenting a multiplicity of viewpoints in juxtaposition. A given compiler, then, may preserve a variety of teachings. Since the text has passed through many editorial hands, conflicting ideals may also be due to the varying interests and accidents of the unknown people involved in the development of the text. One could argue, based on these features, that *Rabbi Nathan* cannot be the center of a thematic analysis—it may be just an anthology of material, either with so little editing and organization, or with so many different editorial hands, that the text cannot be treated as a whole.[1]

How, then, do we interpret *Rabbi Nathan* as a source for rabbinic ways of framing tradition and theology? The canonization of dissent itself articulates or invents a tradition that embraces a diversity of beliefs within a common debate, and this debate often reveals agreement concerning terminology and problems. At a very basic level, rabbinic sages consistently affirm certain beliefs, including the rule of one God, the value of Torah, and the significance of ancient Israel, but more specific points of agreement can be found as well.[2] In addition, while *Rabbi Nathan* is a text of diverse views, the diversity is bounded. My task, then, is to identify the terms and issues that underlie the various positions I analyze and to define the boundaries of the multiplicity in opinion within the text.

Those boundaries can be delineated inductively through collecting the range of views on a given point, which is often large but finite and able to be catalogued. Also, one can see tendencies and overall emphases in the commentary and editorial work. Like the makers of a collage, these editors shaped existing material—the structure of *The Fathers,* the midrashic and narrative sources—for their own purposes. This shaping can be seen in exegetical transformations of the base text and also in the clustering of material around certain themes and issues. In addition, comparison with parallel passages and phrases in other rabbinic texts can help specify the distinct viewpoints of *Rabbi Nathan,* particularly when *Rabbi Nathan* gives great weight to ideas that are less prominent in other texts or when it opposes concepts that appear elsewhere.

Analytically, I draw upon two categories proposed by Kadushin, "value-concepts" and "organic thinking." According to Kadushin, rabbinic concepts are distinctly dynamic and "cannot be organized into a static system, one neat proposition following upon another." He identifies four concepts as particularly complex and important for rabbinic thought: God's justice; God's mercy or compassion; Torah; and Israel (my analysis takes up two of these and treats each as central to a *cluster* of tropes and concepts). Depending on the occasion at hand and the concerns of the particular composer, one or another of the concepts will be highlighted.[3] A passage focusing on the need for right human action will emphasize God's justice, while one offering consolation in time of disaster will invoke God's compassion. *Rabbi Nathan,* for example, gives much more attention to divine justice than to divine compassion, probably because justice is the theological value concept that gives greatest significance to human action. However, this emphasis does not deny the significance of compassion; it means that it is not the concept most central for ethics. Regarding Torah, a passage exhorting one to study will highlight the joys and rewards of such practice, while another, perhaps originally directed to those immersed in the process, will emphasize difficulties and struggles.

Rabbi Nathan presents no comprehensive treatment of the relative priorities among concepts and values—no agreement or even clearly defined debate concerning what is more important under what circumstances. We are not dealing with a systematic, philosophical way of thinking. Rather, Kadushin characterizes rabbinic thought as "organic." He writes, "The organic quality of rabbinic theology accounts for that paradox, observed long ago by students, which allows differences of opinion to exist without thereby causing the basic unity of rabbinic thought to suffer. Fluid rather than crystallized thought, it gives room for differences in temperament and degree of ethical sensitivity among individuals, and even for different moods in the same individual. This is possible because on one occasion, one of the fundamental concepts may be stressed, and on another occasion, another."[4] The metaphor of an organism is problematic to the extent that it obscures human factors in the creation and transmission of the texts. Many features of rabbinic thought that Kadushin would call organic have rhetorical or ideological functions,[5] and his account has to be developed through an understanding of the text as discourse that was created, transmitted, and performed by men in particular settings. We have to be aware of the editorial hands that have shaped the "organism." Given these qualifications, Kadushin's image highlights the important point that, for rabbinic editors (and perhaps for individual sages, though we will never know for certain), concepts were often intertwined and interrelated rather than in conflict. In analyzing the use of a given concept, we should strongly consider that rhetorical aims might have been more significant than systematic reflection.[6]

As I noted in the introduction, the pedagogical discourse of *Rabbi Nathan* frames and orients the practices set out by rabbinic law.[7] There are several concepts and tropes through which the voices of *Rabbi Nathan* address the totality of their practice, but two clusters are particularly prominent and pervasive: Torah and God's justice.[8]

The word "Torah" literally means "instruction" and refers in *Rabbi Nathan* to at least three things—the five books of Moses, the Hebrew Bible (Written Torah), and the entire rabbinic tradition (Oral Torah).[9] I address all three, but the most significant is the sense of Torah as tradition. The words of Torah are encountered in public reading and worship, in personal prayer and affirmation, and in study. Rabbis call upon themselves both to study and to practice Torah, and this practice enters into most all realms of life. More specifically, Torah is central to the ways that rabbis prescribe the transformation of transgressive impulses.

I discuss rabbinic notions of God's justice in terms of divine "reward and punishment" *(śakhar va-'onesh):* God both rewards or gives payment for right action and punishes those who do wrong. Reward and punishment is the most prominent framework through which, according to *Rabbi Nathan,* God responds to human action. This theology highlights the significance of human action in the world, which is characteristic of the ethical concerns in the text. Divine justice applies to a tremendous range of activities, from actions regulated by criminal law to intentions and emotional states that may never be actualized. In the context of this theology, the compilers of *Rabbi Nathan* set out ideal motivations and emotions in relation to God.

Tropes (1)—Tension and Systematicity

Rabbinic literature generally, and ethical literature in particular, makes extensive use of tropes. I employ "trope" as a general term for a figure of speech, examples of which include metaphor (association based on similarity) and metonymy (association based on a spatial, temporal, or causal connection). Divine power may be conveyed through the metaphor, "God is a king," or the transformative power of Torah upon the person may be expressed through the figure, "Torah is fire." One important case of metonymy is the technical term for the locus of transgressive tendencies, *yetzer* (inclination). The word literally means "formation," and at least in some midrashic accounts, it represents the impulses that were placed in humans when God formed *(y.tz.r.)* Adam.[10]

The challenges in interpreting the tropes of *Rabbi Nathan* can be summarized as three related yet distinct problems. The first concerns the relations between the elements in a given trope. If metaphor, for example, juxtaposes two elements, one that is known or tangible with one that is unknown, intangible, or inchoate, how strong is that juxtaposition? When we read of God's judgment, are the actions of a human judge implied, and how so? A second problem concerns the relation between different instances of metaphoric expression. One passage may describe God as being a judge, another may depict angels as attorneys, and a third may employ the language of "guilty" and "innocent" to describe humans before God. Should these be treated as distinct, or is there some connection between them? A third problem concerns the meaning conveyed by a given trope. Once we have established the degree of vitality of a given trope and its relation to other tropes, how do we interpret its significance for rabbinic ethics? In responding to these problems, I draw upon three concepts from contemporary theory concerning metaphor—metaphoric tension, metaphoric systematicity, and cultural continua.[11]

According to Paul Ricoeur and others, a metaphor functions in two referential fields and carries degrees of tension between them. For example, the metaphor "God is a king" functions in the fields of theology and human governance, characterizing the former in terms of the latter. This trope carries tension if the juxtaposition between the two fields is strong— if the meanings associated with the known element (a king) characterize the unknown element (God). In rabbinic literature, as numerous parables comparing and contrasting divine and worldly kings make clear, the features of a human king figure prominently in this trope of divine power. However, the predication does not simply equate the deity with a worldly ruler. Rather, the rabbinic analogy serves to establish difference as well as similarity. In Ricoeur's phrasing, the metaphor "God is a king" carries tension to the extent that it asserts that God both *is and is not* a king. The rabbis' God *is* like a king in certain respects. He displays great power that is efficacious in this world and has the ability to establish laws and administer justice. But God *is not* like worldly kings in other ways. He is perfectly just, governs a realm that encompasses this world and future worlds, administers justice that is eternal, and favors his subjects, the descendants of Israel.[12]

The issues that Ricoeur addresses through the idea of tension are often discussed in terms of "living" versus "dead" tropes. I prefer Ricoeur's terminology for two reasons. First, while living/dead is a binary opposition with two extreme options, the category of tension allows us to examine degrees of intensity. Second, Ricoeur's form of analysis draws attention to the specific predication rather than the entire discursive field, which is important because tropes that lack tension can carry the possibility of having the juxtaposition renewed. For example, passages employing the term "heart" in *Rabbi Nathan* rarely show a clear reference to the internal organ, and those describing divine "pay" or "reward" rarely invoke human economics. Yet, certain cases reinvigorate the metaphoric tension for pedagogical purposes, as I show in chapters 2b and 3a.

Shifting from the features of a given trope to the relations between tropes, a question emerges—is each figurative expression distinct and solitary, or can we find associations or connections between various passages in a given text? The answer depends upon the predication. Many have to be treated individually, and the tropes that I analyze in part 2 concerning Torah are of this sort. For example, one passage presents Torah as fire, and another presents Torah as water, but this does not mean that Torah is both fire and water (which would make for either very hot water or a self-negation, as water could extinguish fire or fire can turn water into steam). Rather, in these particular cases the tropes actually indicate variants of the same point—that Torah is transformative (fire makes metal malleable, and as we have seen above, water wears away rocks).

The theological images of divine justice, in contrast, interrelate in a manner that George Lakoff and Mark Johnson characterize as "systematic" (which is not to say that the rabbis of late antiquity have a "systematic theology"). Lakoff and Johnson argue, with respect to contemporary English, that a number of expressions may interact with each other to structure a given concept or realm of experience, whether or not those who employ the concepts are aware of these interrelations. One example is the concept of argument, which often is characterized through the metaphor "argument is war":

> He *attacked* my argument.
> Your claims are *indefensible.*
> Those criticisms are *right on target.*
> I *won* that argument.
> That's a bad *strategy.*
> He *shot down* all my claims.
> That's a *powerful* assertion.

Lakoff and Johnson argue that these metaphors condition thought and action, even in cases when metaphoric tension is not present. Imagine, they say, how people would experience arguments if they were figured as dances—rather than being a matter of attack and defense, an argument would be graceful or clumsy, classical or jazzy, expressive or stilted. The cooperative and creative aspects of argumentation would be far more prominent, and the role of conflict deemphasized.[13]

Lakoff and Johnson argue that two metaphors may overlap, each describing a different aspect of the same concept. For example, in modern English an argument is often understood as being a journey:

> We have *set out* to prove that . . .
> We will *proceed in* a *step-by-step* fashion.
> We have *arrived* at a conclusion.

But an argument can also be a container:

> Your argument doesn't have much *content*. It is *vacuous*.
> That argument *has holes in it.*
> I'm tired of your *empty* arguments.
> Your argument *won't hold water.*

And some mixed metaphors employ both:

> *At this point* our argument doesn't *have much content.*
> If we keep *going* the way we're going, we'll *fit* all the facts *in*.[14]

In *Rabbi Nathan,* divine justice is usually expressed through two sets of metaphors that overlap — one from the realm of law and judgment and the other from the realm of monetary exchange.

Numerous expressions develop the imagery of God being a judge with the ministering angels as attorneys: God judges *(dan)* creatures and establishes a court *(sanhedrin)* on high, while the angels may present a legal accusation *(qosherin qaṭeygur)* against a human being. The legal imagery extends to technical language used to explain God's action in the world. Not all of these terms, however, exhibit metaphoric tension. For example, *zekhut* is a common term for religious "merit." Its root *(z.k.h.)* carries a sense of cleanliness or purity in the Bible, and in rabbinic sources it often means, "to be acquitted." Also, the root *tz.d.q.,* which has the legal sense of being just or right, is frequently used to describe righteousness, particularly in the noun *tzaddiq* (righteous one). Rarely, though, do we have evidence that these words evoke their roots in legal language.

Legal metaphors overlap with those that describe the human/divine relation as one of exchange — "God is a storekeeper" who sells goods and "God is a master (of a household)" who pays for labor. Exchange tropes can appear both in explicit theological assertions and in common technical terms. One of the most prominent technical terms is *śakhar,* which literally means "payment" but very often describes divine "reward" for action:

> When the Holy One, blessed be He, reveals his Shekhinah, he will pay [*leshallem*] a great reward [*śakhar ṭob*] to Jethro and his descendants. (A35, 105)

The same terminology, however, can appear in a mixed metaphor with legal language:

> The Holy One, blessed be He, said, "I will not judge [*dan*] them until I pay [*'ashallem*] reward [*śakhar*] to the righteous [*la- tzaddikim*]." (A32,93)

Here the terminology conveys that God both judges *(dan, tzaddiqim)* and pays reward *('ashallem śakhar).*

This overlap is part of a broader conjunction of legal and exchange metaphors through which rabbis develop the value concept of God's justice. After the talmudic period, this theology came to be known as "reward and punishment." The label itself combines one term of monetary payment (*śakhar* or reward/pay) with one of judicial action ('*onesh* or punishment). In this conjunction of metaphors, the legal imagery tends (with certain notable exceptions) to focus upon human sin and divine punishment, while the exchange motifs usually describe right action and God's reward.

Tropes (2)—Cultural Continua

How is it that tropes function in a discursive setting and convey meaning? I work with an observation that is well developed in the field of anthropology—metaphoric predications locate objects in relation to implied oppositions or continua. James Fernandez expresses this point in a manner that fits well with the discursive approach to the self that I presented in the introduction: metaphors and other tropes are predications upon inchoate nouns and pronouns that "move" them about in "quality space." That is, people employ metaphors to describe dimensions of life that are intangible and not easily apprehended through the senses—including selves and their dynamics, communities, traditions, and deities. The goal of such descriptions is to make the objects vivid and manageable so that the speaker can understand and begin to control them. Central to this control, and to the notion of quality space, are "cultural continua." Any given cultural system implies continua (or oppositions) such as inner-outer, this world–other world, static-dynamic, and soft-sharp.[15]

Fernandez gives great attention to the metaphors that people use in public discourse and ritual activity. For example, in an ethnographic study of Asturian deepsong, Fernandez analyzes a song in which an old miner describes himself as being spelt wheat, in contrast with young miners who are cherries. The metaphor of spelt wheat, in the context of the Cantabrian Mountains where the singer lives, evokes the continua of tough-sensitive, traditional-new, and mountain-maritime. The singer situates himself on the continua as tough, traditional, and from the mountains. In contrast, the young miners, as cherries, are sensitive, modern, and associated with other, maritime, regions.[16]

The similarities and differences between Fernandez's sources and rabbinic ethical literature can be illustrated through analysis of a narrative in which characters adorn and disparage through placement upon cultural continua. The story turns on the complex relations between the rabbinic movement and other Jews in Roman Palestine, criticizing members of both groups—a rabbi for his snobbish elitism, and the other man for his stubbornness. It begins with an exchange between the two:

> A story of Rabbi Simeon ben Eleazar, who was going from Migdal Edar,[17] from the house of his master, riding on his donkey and traveling along the seashore: He saw a man who was as ugly as can be. He said to him, "Idiot! Look how *ugly* you are! Are all the people of your city ugly like you?"
>
> He said to him, "What can I do? Go to the *artisan* who made me, and tell him, Look how ugly is this *vessel* you have made!"
>
> When Rabbi Simeon saw that he had *sinned (ḥaṭa')*, he went down from his donkey and *prostrated himself* before him.
>
> He said to him, "I am begging your pardon. Forgive me."
>
> He said to him, "I will not forgive you until [you go to] the artisan that made me, and say, Look how ugly is this *vessel* that you have made!" (A41,131; emphases added)

In this exchange, the first predication is adjectival—"Look how ugly you are." Rabbi Simeon situates the man on a continuum of attractive-ugly and disparages him as ugly. The man, in turn, reorients himself through the metaphor, I am a vessel. A vessel implies a maker, an artisan, and thus a second metaphor, God is an artisan. The analogy is: God created me as an artisan creates a vessel. The man removes himself from the continuum of attractive-ugly and predicates himself, along with all people, as formed by God. Both the narrator and the rabbi accept this new characterization. The narrator labels Rabbi Simeon's insult as a sin, which locates it within the realm of religious action, and then the rabbi places himself on a continuum of low-high by prostrating himself and begging for forgiveness.

As the story continues, the rabbi repeatedly asks for forgiveness, running for three miles after his critic, but the man refuses. They enter the city, and the people welcome and honor Rabbi Simeon. The stubborn man then insults him with a pun, "If this is a r̲abbi, may ones like him not multiply [yir̲bu] in Israel" (emphasis added). Finally, persuaded by the people of the city, he forgives. Then, we read a public sermon by Rabbi Simeon:

> On that same day, Rabbi Simeon entered his great house of study and expounded: Always may a man be flexible like a *reed* and not rigid like a *cedar*. What is this reed like? All the winds come and blow upon it, and it bends with them. If the winds are quiet, the reed returns and stands in its place. And what is the end of this reed? It *merits* to be taken as a pen to

write the book of the *Torah*. But a cedar does not stand in its place. Rather, when the south wind blows, it uproots it and turns it over on its head. What is the end of the cedar? Woodcutters come and cut it down. They roof their houses with it, and the rest they throw into the *fire*. From this, they say, "May a man be flexible like a reed and not rigid like a cedar." (A41,131; emphases added)[18]

The basis of this sermon is an epigram—"May a man be flexible like a reed and not rigid like a cedar"—that employs the tropes of reed and cedar. The cultural continuum is flexible-rigid, with "flexible" evaluated positively. Implicitly, the rabbi upholds himself and his flexibility in retracting his insult, and he criticizes the other man, who rigidly refuses to forgive.

The sage also gives religious significance to the continuum of flexible-rigid. A reed can be used to write the Torah. That is, God rewards flexibility with contiguity (spatial and causal) to the sacred tradition. This reed contrasts with the rigid cedar, which ultimately is burnt. Thus, Rabbi Simeon's predications are:

> I am a flexible reed and you (the other man) are a rigid cedar.
> A reed is contiguous with the Torah. A cedar is burnt in
> flames.

The images of the reed and the pen are particularly salient in the rabbinic context. Some rabbis were scribes and did in fact write the Torah. Rabbi Simeon's predication that he is a reed conveys the assertion, "I (a rabbi) create and am close to the Torah."[19]

The interaction between Rabbi Simeon and the obstinate man exemplifies the role of cultural continua in metaphoric predications. In this case, the continua include attractive-ugly, sacred-profane, high-low, and flexible-rigid. The story as a whole, though, is not an instance of rhetorical adornment or disparagement but of ethical instruction. Rabbi Simeon's snobbish insult and the man's stubbornness are both negative examples concerning virtuous action—the rabbi's action is labeled as a "sin," and the other man is criticized through the rabbi's homily. Through these characters and their exchange, the storyteller advocates both humility for rabbis and flexibility for all people. While it presumes tensions between rabbis and other Jews, the story sets out an ideal of harmonious and respectful relations between them.

How do such continua and oppositions function more generally in rabbinic ethics? They appear in the midst of pedagogical epigrams and exegesis, where the "inchoate (pro)nouns" are rabbinic value concepts such as the student (*talmid*), the sage (*ḥakham*), basic impulses or inclinations (*yetzer*), Torah, and God. Rabbis employ metaphors to specify these concepts and to place them in dynamic relation through characterization in worldly terms. For example, metaphors of soft materials (water and flesh) and hard ones (stone and iron) often appear in teachings concerning the impact of Torah upon the person. Torah may be *soft* water wearing away *hard* stone, or *hard* iron wearing away a *soft* fleshy heart, or if the inner impulses are *hard,* Torah appears on another plane, being a *hot* fiery being that *softens* iron. Each of these ways of placing Torah and the self upon the continuum of hard and soft implies a particular stance concerning the ease with which the student's impulses respond to the tradition, and concerning the power of the tradition to transform the participant. For another example, theological metaphors of law and monetary exchange characterize a person's status before God, implying oppositions such as innocent/guilty or continua based on degrees of wealth. Spiritual wealth correlates with innocence, and debt with guilt. Those who observe the commandments and follow the divine will attain divine "pay" *(śakhar),* while others live off of "credit" and are threatened by "collectors," ultimately to be declared "guilty" and punished by God.

1d The Text and Its Sages

Conclusion

We can now specify in detail how *Rabbi Nathan* hails or calls out to its potential subjects. The skeleton of the text is its epigrams, many of which employ imperatives and address the reader or listener directly as "you," implying an "I" who should respond. The commentary often echoes a scholastic setting of question and answer, opening the discussion of a given maxim by asking, "How so?" and giving an answer, or citing a biblical verse and then exploring connections between Scripture and rabbinic instruction. The commentary includes many narratives, in which sages both teach and model correct actions. A student receiving this pedagogical discourse, then, would encounter at any given moment multiple *forms* of instruction, along with a diversity of views and a wide range of concepts and tropes. In the context of rabbinic circles, this discourse was transmitted through living teachers, who may well have modeled their own behavior after the sages in the text.

The voices of *Rabbi Nathan* call out not to a universal subject but to one who locates himself as a student in a particular set of relationships and distinctions. Several features of *Rabbi Nathan* indicate participation in the broader cultural context of Roman late antiquity, including the genres of maxims and narratives, the genealogical arrangement of sages' names, the hermeneutical methods of midrash, and, more broadly, the scholastic setting. However, the text prescribes that aspiring sages distinguish and often separate themselves from those around them, including Romans, women, and many other Jews. Within the rabbinic movement, *Rabbi Nathan* presents a scholastic, politically moderate community that upholds certain figures (Hillel, Rabban Yohanan ben Zakkai, Rabbi Eliezer ben Hyrcanus, and Rabbi Akiba) and downplays the significance of others (such as the patriarchs).

As part of this community, the subject addressed by *Rabbi Nathan* is to characterize his ideal action through maxims such as, "Let your house be a meeting place for the sages, sit in the very dust of their feet, and drink with thirst their words" (A6,27; B11,27; *Fathers* 1:4) and "Appoint for yourself a teacher, acquire for yourself a fellow, and judge every man with the scales weighted in his favor" (A8,35; B19,39; *Fathers* 1:6). These instructions are developed through the commentary of *Rabbi Nathan,* such that the student should receive the sages' teachings upon himself with great reverence and intensify this reception through study, practice, and ultimately teaching. All this would be done with peers who are partners not only for study but also for dining and sleeping. What is it, though, that is taught, studied, and practiced? Rabbinic scholastic activity centers upon the tradition of Torah, and now I turn to this dimension of rabbinic ethics.

Rabbinic Tradition

The claim that something is part of a tradition implies that it was received from the past and that, as such, it carries authority in the present. People may traditionalize most anything—images, ideals, narratives, texts, designs, practices, objects, buildings, and much more. This traditional status may reflect an actual inheritance from the past, or it may be an invention. Many cases, including the rabbinic Torah, reveal an intertwining of the two, for innovation and change in a tradition often occurs through asserting a link between what is new and what was received. Traditions affect and shape selves at multiple levels, and selves in turn may have varying forms of both active and passive responses to tradition. Elites such as the rabbinic sages can encounter their traditions with high degrees of intentionality and creativity.[1]

I focus upon traditional discourse—writing and speech that is taken to be authoritative as handed down from the past. This does not necessarily imply a fixed set of beliefs or doctrines, but rather a common set of concerns, terminology, and modes of argumentation in which beliefs and doctrines are debated and elaborated. Alasdair MacIntyre invokes traditional discourse as a solution to an epistemological problem. If virtues are defined in terms of practices, how do we know that our practices and ways of orienting toward them are correct? MacIntyre's answer: they are good if they are upheld through a vital tradition.[2] These concerns are present for the compilers of *Rabbi Nathan* in that their tradition, the Torah, sets out and justifies their central practices as well as communal narratives. However, rabbis' conception of tradition is far richer than an epistemological foundation. They hold their tradition to emerge from divine revelation at Sinai, which is preserved as the Written Torah and continually renewed through the development of the Oral Torah.[3]

Rabbinic literature is filled with descriptions of the revelation at Sinai that dramatize and intensify the biblical narrative. The accounts may highlight Moses and even envision his ascent as a heroic storming of the heavens, or they may speculate upon the nature of God's utterance and the experiences of the Israelites.[4] The openings of *Rabbi Nathan* and *The Fathers* link God's revelation with human reception of tradition: Moses received *(qibbel)* the Torah at Sinai. Then large portions of the biblical record are reinterpreted as the teaching of Torah from teachers to disciples: Joshua, the elders, and all the prophets become steps in a genealogy that begins with Moses and leads to the sages (A1,1–2; B1,1–2; *Fathers* 1:1).[5] This process of transmission is to be replicated in every exchange of traditional learning—students receive from their elders, and in their maturity they pass on what they know to new generations. In *Rabbi Nathan* Moses's reception of Torah is developed and expanded in a number of ways. Moses goes through a process of sanctification and, according to one sage, receives the revelation with distinct emotions of "awe, fear, trembling, and shaking."[6] As discussed above, the latter image also appears in *Rabbi Nathan* as the ideal way for students to receive the teachings of sages.[7]

Elsewhere, *Rabbi Nathan* portrays Torah as primordial and heavenly. Through midrashic interpretation of the word *'amon* (artisan, constant, ward) in Proverbs 8:30, commentators derive that Torah confirms *('amen)* God's blessedness through singing with the angels, "Blessed be the Glory of the Lord from His Place" (Ezek. 3:12).[8] A revocalization of this word as *'uman,* or architect, likely underlies the metaphor that Torah is the "precious implement with which the world was created."[9] The tablets of Sinai were formed during the original six days of creation, but the text is independent from its inscription and can fly from its stony context in order not to be destroyed.[10] Torah is also compared to primary elements of nature such as fire and water, manufactured objects such as linen and wool, and supernatural entities like the tree of life and the "wings of the Shekhinah."[11]

The study and practice of Torah is one of the highest valued activities for the rabbinic movement.[12] The prescriptions and prohibitions of Torah encompass the entirety of rabbinic life—criminal and civil law, ritual guidelines, and ethical ideals (after all, *Rabbi Nathan* is itself part of Torah). More specifically, we find in *Rabbi Nathan* numerous lists of rabbinic curricula. Characteristically, they begin with the Hebrew Bible.[13] The simplest catalogue, which scholars attribute to tannaitic times, is Scripture, midrash, apodictic law *(halakhot)*, and nonlegal material *('aggadot)*. Other, and probably later, accounts include commentary to the Mishnah *(gemara')*, additions to the Mishnah *(tosephtot)*,[14] Aramaic translation of the Bible *(targum)*, rhetoric *(śiḥin)*, parables *(meshalim)*, subtleties of the Torah and subtleties of the scribes, and the interpretative rules of the sages.[15] We can see in these lists that the Torah, as a tradition, is not a fixed or static entity. Even within this single text there are signs of development over time, and various configurations may have represented the curricula of different disciple circles.

Torah is often contrasted with *derekh 'eretz*. Literally "the way of the world", this phrase can have a variety of meanings, including "worldly matters," "sexual activity," and "supererogatory action." In the third sense, the contrast of *derekh 'eretz* and Torah concerns the value of independent ethical action in comparison to communal study and practice of rabbinic tradition. In *Rabbi Nathan,* sages either claim that Torah is primary and *derekh 'eretz* secondary or that the two are necessary and complementary— "if there is no Torah, there is no *derekh 'eretz,* and if there is no *derekh 'eretz,* there is no Torah." Similarly, we find assertions about the complementary nature of Torah and good deeds *(ma'aśim ṭobim)*.[16] Rabbis also have various ways to denote the acts of neglecting, leaving, or nullifying the Torah (including *b.ṭ.l., p.r.sh.,* and *p.s.q.*), or of being distracted from Torah by matters that are insignificant or, worse, improperly sexual *(debarim beṭelim* or *dibrey baṭalah)*.[17]

How does a rabbi engage with Torah? The word literally means "instruction." Commonly one "studies" *(l.m.d.)* Torah or engages in the "study of Torah" *(talmud torah)*. In many cases we read that teachers or students "sit" *(y.sh.b.)* and "occupy themselves with" *('.ś.q.)* Torah, or study specifically the Mishnah *(sh.n.h.)*, or interpret the Bible homiletically *(d.r.sh.)*. "Study" may appear alone or as part of the call to study, practice, and teach. This tripartite prescription is perhaps the most crucial—an instruction to maintain both contemplative and practical immersion in the totality of tradition.[18] Intense involvement with Torah has a multifaceted effect upon the self, and the following chapters examine in great detail how the teachings of *Rabbi Nathan* describe and uphold this impact.

2a   Torah and Transgressive Tendencies

Rabbinic literature often presents three sins as central or cardinal: idolatry *('abodah zarah, 'abodat 'elilim,* or *'abodat kokhabim),* incest *(gilluy 'arayot),* and murder *(shephikhut damim).*[1] Each of these extreme manifestations is paradigmatic of a more general and often implicit category, which I label as religious transgression, sexual transgression, and misanthropy (hatred or aggression toward other humans). The three realms interact in complex ways. To give one example, a teaching of Rabbi Akiba asserts that anger (an emotion often linked with aggression) is a cause of idolatry (religious transgression).[2]

The compilers of *Rabbi Nathan* portray Torah as a restraint for transgression, and this feature of Torah is crucial for ethical transformation. In addition, however, Torah appears as both dangerous and vulnerable. Aspects of tradition may incite wrong action rather than restrain it, and a person's knowledge of Torah may be lost through incorrect behavior or emotional states. These facets of Torah can be seen in passages from the first two chapters of *Rabbi Nathan,* which comment upon the first epigram in the text: "Be patient in judgment, raise up many students, and make a fence for the Torah" (A1,2; B1,2; *Fathers* 1:1). This saying of the Great Assembly is the most extensively commented upon one in *Rabbi Nathan,* and the themes of Torah and transgression run through the material. The discussion isolates the three elements and interprets each one in multiple ways: first, "be patient in judgment," then, "make a fence for the Torah," and third, "raise up many students."[3]

My analysis responds to two tendencies in contemporary scholarship. First, many researchers approach rabbinic understandings of transgression through tracking specific terms, particularly *yetzer* (impulse, inclination) and *leb* (heart). I fully affirm the value of this project, and I do it myself below. However, I have found that concern with transgression is far more pervasive in *Rabbi Nathan* than a study of terms would indicate: the passages I examine do not employ the words *yetzer* or *leb,* though they address dimensions of human experience associated with them. If we focused only on the terms, we would not see the degree to which rabbis were concerned with this issue.

Second, scholars tend to highlight the rabbinic view that Torah has a positive impact upon the self.[4] Again, I uphold this point, but I have also found that for the compilers of *Rabbi Nathan,* the dynamics of Torah and transgression are far more complex than that. Torah can intensify wayward desire, or one may lose grasp of tradition through anger or idolatry. The text also distinguishes between Oral and Written Torah, describing different possibilities and dangers in each. I first explore the multiple ways, according to *Rabbi Nathan,* that tradition impacts the self, and this account sets the stage for discussions concerning the role of Torah in ethical transformation.

Be Patient in Judgment: The Dangers and Vulnerabilities of Torah

The compilers of *Rabbi Nathan* see their Scriptures as, among other things, dangerous. They are troubled in particular by four passages, all of which they attribute to Solomon, and quote them at length. Two of these are from the Song of Songs (7:11–13) and have explicit erotic content. One from Ecclesiastes counsels, "Go in the ways of your heart, and according to the vision of your eyes" (Eccles. 11:9). This advice conflicts with the command of Numbers 15:39, which is part of the *Shema,* not to "turn after your hearts and your eyes, that you whore after them."[5] Finally, a passage in Proverbs contrasts a seductress harlot with the female figure of Wisdom, employing the image of a prostitute to warn young men against temptation as such. This warning is itself apparently too graphic for the rabbinic successors of the Wisdom schools—it may backfire, inciting the very temptations that are condemned. Rabbis feared that these writings of Solomon would incite both improper sexual desire and religious transgression.[6]

The initial part of the maxim of the Men of the Great Assembly is usually translated into English as "be patient in judgment" or "be deliberate in judgment." Both the terms for "judgment" *(din)* and "patient/deliberate" *(metunim)* are difficult. The commentary transforms them, such that the maxim instructs one to rely upon oral tradition in the reception of dangerous Written Torah. The exegesis begins with a flurry of attempts to paraphrase the term *metunim:*

How so? It teaches that a man should take time in judgment [*mamtin bedin*], be settled in judgment [*meyushshab bedin*], as it is written, "Also these are the parables of Solomon that the men of Hezekiah, king of Judah, copied out [*he'etiqu*]" (Prov 25:1). *He'etiqu* [copied out] means *himtinu* [took time]. Abba Shaul says: *himtinu* [took time] means *peyrshu* [interpreted]. (A1,2; see also B1,2–3)

In this dense passage,[7] the commentators make a four-step bridge from the Great Assembly's term "be deliberate" to Abba Shaul's focus on interpretation, which is their real interest:

1. The Men of the Great Assembly's instruction to "be deliberate" *(metunim)*, which is in a passive form, is glossed in an active form as "take time" *(mamtin)* and also with the participle "settled" *(meyushshab);*
2. The editor cites a prooftext invoking the men of Hezekiah and the preservation of Solomon's writings, which uses the word "copied out" *(he'etiqu);*[8]
3. The editor states that "copied out" *(he'etiqu)* means "took time" *(himtinu)*, which echoes the original gloss on the maxim in (1), and;
4. The editor cites Abba Shaul, who says that "took time" *(mamtin)* means "interpreted" *(peyrshu)*.

By breaking down the chain into these steps, we can see the work done by the commentators. Their goal is to develop the relation between (2) the preservation of Solomon's writings and (4) the need for interpretation.[9] Drawing together these elements with the saying of the Great Assembly, the text continues:

At first, they would say, Proverbs, Song of Songs, and Ecclesiastes were stored away. For, they would say, these were mere parables and not among the Writings. They arose and stored them away, until the Men of the Great Assembly came and interpreted [*peyrshu*] them. (A1,2; B1,2)[10]

From here, the editors quote the problematic sections of Proverbs, Song of Songs, and Ecclesiastes. The maxim of the Great Assembly, through the exegesis of *Rabbi Nathan,* counters the dangers posed by these canonical texts. It instructs the interpreter to "be deliberate in judgment" concerning the Written Torah. The student should receive the Torah carefully and interpret it through the oral traditions of the sages. In doing so, he will maintain a settled *(meyushshab)* state. The Oral Torah is a corrective to the dangers of the Written Torah.

Immediately following this discussion, the commentators of *Rabbi Nathan* offer "another opinion," a second exegesis of the maxim. The underlying concern of this other opinion is the vulnerability of Torah—if one is angry, one may lose grasp of the Torah and forget the sacred discourse. The commentators interpret "be deliberate in judgment" as a call for emotional equilibrium.

First, they immediately transform the maxim from a focus on "judgment" to "words," stating, "This teaches that a man must be deliberate in his words [*mamtin bidbarav*]. Let him not be angry concerning his words, for all who are angry concerning their words forget their words" (A1,2–3; B1,3). How do they know this? They find hidden between the lines of the Bible a story about Moses in which he exemplifies what one should *avoid* doing. The biblical text says that Moses was angry with Israelite military leaders following the battle with the Midianites after the events of Ba'al Pe'or (Num. 31:14). The Israelites had "whored" after the Moabite women and "bowed down" to their gods (Num. 25:1–2).[11] After Moses's commands to the soldiers, Eliezer the Priest instructed them regarding the handling of the booty, citing "the laws of the Torah that the Lord commanded to Moses" (Num. 31:21). The midrashic questions are: Why did not Moses command the soldiers directly? Why did Eliezer the Priest do so?

The answer is: because Moses forgot his words in anger. The biblical shift in speaker becomes a moral teaching concerning emotion, memory, and language. Moses exemplifies the perils a sage may face if he lacks self-control.[12] Anger, in this account, negates the man's command of Torah, leading him to forget his words. The sage must maintain a state of equanimity when speaking, particularly concerning sacred matters. The instruction "Be deliberate in judgment" is interpreted as "Be calm when speaking"—restrain anger when involved in traditional discourse.

The Torah is vulnerable. One's internal state can be overwhelming, and the words of Torah can be forgotten. Other parts of *Rabbi Nathan* explore the vulnerability of tradition at the communal level, saying that it can be lost through idolatry—if people follow other gods, they will lose their access to Torah. The paradigmatic example of this is the Israelites' worship of the golden calf at Sinai leading to the tablets of revelation being destroyed.[13]

Make a Fence for the Torah

The next instruction of the Men of the Great Assembly is, "make a fence [*seyyag* or *seyag*] for the Torah." Judah Goldin has suggested that in the Second Temple period these words may have been counsel to preserve the Written Torah from corruption.[14] *Rabbi Nathan*, however, shows no concern with this issue. Rather, the commentators immediately interpret "the Torah" as "your words," and the instruction becomes, "Make a fence for your words."[15] The discussion of "make a fence for your words" includes an elaboration of eight different fences, attributed to God, Adam, the Torah, Moses, Job, the Prophets, the Writings, and the Sages (Torah, Prophets, and Writings refer to the three sections of the Hebrew Bible).[16]

The primary concept, which appears in many places in rabbinic literature, is articulated in the fence of the Sages: one should follow a stricter standard than is required by the Written Torah to insure that one does not transgress divine law. The specific example in *Rabbi Nathan* is the recitation of the evening *Shema*. If the law requires a person to say the *Shema* by dawn, the fence is to do so by midnight (A2,14; B3,14).[17] The account of Adam's fence reflects upon problems in this hermeneutic process, and I first examine this one. The fences attributed to the Torah, Moses, Job, and the Writings all extend the legal principle into the realm of self-control and set out important features of rabbinic subjectivity. In these four units, the trope of the fence has several dimensions: the extension of a law, the distancing of oneself from transgression and from sources of temptation (particularly women), and implicitly the fencing in of a man's own desire.[18]

Adam's Failed Fence: The Dangers of the Oral Torah

We saw above, in the exegesis of "Be patient in judgment," that the Written Torah may incite transgression if not interpreted properly. Interpretation also has its risks, and a number of passages in *Rabbi Nathan* stress the danger of faulty hermeneutics. The most highly developed example is the fence of Adam.[19] This fence is found through the juxtaposition of two verses: Genesis 2:17 and 3:3. The first presents God's commandment to Adam, "[A]s for the tree of knowledge of good and bad, do not eat of it. For on the day that you eat from it, you will surely die" (Gen. 2:17). The second is Eve's report to the snake of the commandment, "as for the fruit of the tree that is in the center of the garden, God said, 'Do not eat of it, *and do not touch it,* lest you die'" (Gen. 3:3; emphasis added). According to the rabbinic interpretation, the difference between the two verses represents Adam's interpretation to Eve of the divine command. Adam considers himself a good counselor, and he decides that if Eve must not *eat* of the tree, he should tell her not even to *touch* the tree—he makes a fence around God's law to prevent transgression.

The problem is that Adam's version of the law is vulnerable to falsification. The commentators of *Rabbi Nathan* do not question the validity or clarity of God's threat—"on that day that you eat of it, you will surely die." Rather, they focus on the touching forbidden by Adam, adding a narrative. The snake convinces Eve to eat the fruit by finding the space between Adam's fence and God's law. He touches the tree and does not die after doing so (in some accounts, he pushes Eve against the tree).[20] The snake has violated Adam's command to Eve, but not God's command to Adam, and only the latter is punished by death. The result: "[W]hat did Eve say in her mind? All the words that my master [*rabbi*] admonished me, from the beginning, they are a lie." Then she eats.[21] The pun between "my master" and "rabbi" emphasizes the paradigmatic status of Adam—Adam transmits the commandment to Eve as a rabbi interprets the Torah to a community (A1,4–5).

In this interpretation of Genesis, we see rabbinic reflection on the dangers of their own hermeneutic processes. The greatest transgression of all, the paradigmatic sin that brought death upon humankind, came about through oral interpretation of the law in a rabbinic fashion. An anonymous statement sums up the situation:

> What caused this touching? The fence that the first Adam made around his words. Based on this, they said: If a man makes a fence around his words, he cannot stand by his words. Based on this, they also said: A man should not add to what he hears. (A1,4–5)

In Roman late antiquity, for groups now labeled as Jews, Christians, and Gnostics, the story of Adam and Eve was a source for much exegetical thinking concerning sexuality. Often we find highly misogynistic treatments of Eve that place excessive blame upon her, and all women, for the events. *Rabbi Nathan* displays this sexism in many of its discussions concerning Adam, Eve, and the Serpent. However, we should note that in this highly prominent account, Eve may be passive and easily fooled, but Adam, as a proto-rabbi, bears the burden of responsibility.[22]

The Fence of the Torah: Torah Bounding Sexual Desire

The next three fences that I consider prescribe the bounding in of sexual desire. The concerns underlying these passages are that a man should avoid having sex with the wrong woman (a family member, another man's wife, or a prostitute) and that he should not have sex with any woman at the wrong time (a time that would compromise his standards of purity). The basic legal prohibitions address physical contact and intercourse. The fences, however, set a much higher standard, proscribing even proximity and conversation.

The first of these fences is attributed to the Torah, or the first section of the Bible, and centers upon passages in Leviticus that command, "do not come near" a woman. The compilers of *Rabbi Nathan* present two examples of this fence and then draw from them a more general principle. In the first case, the underlying issue is the minimal standard of purity for a man. A man in a pure state should not touch a woman who is impure because of her menstrual period (Lev. 15:19–24). The rabbinic commentators find a fence for this law in Leviticus 18:19: "To a women in her time of menstrual impurity, do not come near to uncover her nakedness." He should not make any advance upon a woman in her time of impurity:[23]

> Which fence did the Torah make around her words? Thus it says, "To a women in her time of menstrual impurity, do not come near to uncover her nakedness" (Lev. 18:19). Could he hug her, kiss her, and speak idle chatter [*debarim beṭelim*] with her? Scripture says, "Do not come near." Could he sleep with her, when she wears her clothes, upon a bed? Scripture says, "Do not come near." Could she wash her face, or color her eyes? Scripture says, "Concerning the woman who is unwell [*ha-davah*] in her menstrual impurity . . ." (Lev. 15:33). All the days that she is in menstrual impurity [*she-beniddah*], she shall be in isolation [*benidduy*]. From this they say: For any woman who disfigures herself in the days of menstrual impurity, the spirit of the sages is satisfied with her. For any woman who adorns herself in her days of impurity, the spirit of the sages is not satisfied with her. (A2,8; also B3,12)[24]

The rabbinic exegesis gives a very wide-sweeping interpretation of the command "do not come near to uncover her nakedness." It proscribes any action that could, in any way, lead to the arousal of sexual desire—hugging, kissing, speaking flirtatiously, or sleeping in the same bed while clothed.[25] The woman, moreover, may not wash her face or put on makeup. She must actively make herself unattractive in order not to arouse male desire.[26]

The second example of Torah's fence centers on a law concerning incest, which commands that one not "come near" a close relative "to uncover nakedness" (Lev. 18:6). The commentators again generalize this command in strong terms. They focus particularly upon the impressions one gives in public, instructing that a man should show no intimacy with a woman:[27]

> Thus it says, "For all men: to one of his own flesh, do not come near. . . ."
> (Lev. 18:6). From here they say a man should not join with any of the
> women at an inn, even with his sister or his daughter, because of public
> opinion. He should not tell stories with a woman in the market, even if
> she is his wife—and needless to say, with another woman—because of
> public suspicion. (A2,9)[28]

The commentators draw upon a verse prohibiting adultery to instruct
both men and women to fence in desires for intimacy. If a man is seen
with a woman, any woman, "public opinion" and "public suspicion" may
be aroused even if the couple is not. This must be prevented.

These passages, then, teach two distinct forms of bounding—one case
concerning a man and a menstruating woman in private and the other
concerning a man and any woman in public—both of which have their
bases in the biblical command "do not come near." The commentary then
develops this counsel in general terms:

> It is said here (Lev. 18:19), "do not come near," and it is said there (Lev.
> 18:6), "do not come near." To anything that brings one to the hands of
> transgression, do not come near. Distance yourself from that which is hid-
> eous and that which resembles something hideous. Therefore, the Sages
> said: Distance yourself from a minor sin lest it bring you to a major sin.
> Run to fulfill a minor commandment, for it will bring you to a great com-
> mandment. (A2,9)[29]

Rabbinic exegesis of legal passages here yields general principles. The commentators argue that, underlying both verses, is the anonymous maxim,
"Distance yourself from that which is hideous and that which resembles
something hideous." Then they link this maxim with another to extend
this idea to a concern with habituation—sinning leads to more sin, and
observance leads to more observance. The ultimate teaching of Torah's
fence is, "Do not come near" any sin, because an initial transgression may
lead to greater ones.[30]

The Fence of Moses: Torah Bounding
Sexual Desire

The fence of the Torah presumes a rabbinic ideal of
maintaining purity in daily activities. The fence of Moses addresses another type of purity standard, that of men striving for high levels of
sanctity and contact with the divine. This concern is expressed through

interpretation of a biblical story—the sanctification of Israelite men at Sinai in preparation for the divine revelation.[31] Again, the commentators juxtapose two verses. The first is God's command to Moses, requiring abstinence and maintenance of purity for two days: "The Lord said to Moses, 'Go to this people, and make them holy *this day and the next,* and then they will wash their garments'" (Exod. 19:10, emphasis added). The second verse is Moses's command to the people. It employs an unusual ordinal construction that I render with its awkwardness: "He said to the people, 'Be ready for *the third of days* [*lishloshet yamim*]. Do not approach a woman'" (Exod. 19:15, emphasis added). The rabbinic exegesis of "the third of days" is that Moses did not tell the men only to abstain from sex for two days in order to be ready for the third. Making a fence around divine command, Moses told them to abstain for three full days:

> Which fence did Moses make around his words? Thus it says, "The Lord said to Moses, 'Go to this people, and make them holy this day and the next, and then they will wash their garments'" (Exod. 19:10). Moses the Righteous did not want to speak to Israel exactly as the Holy One, blessed be He, spoke to him. Rather, thus he spoke to them, "He said to the people, 'Be ready for the third of days [*lishloshet yamim*]. Do not approach a woman'" (Exod. 19:15). Moses added one day for them by himself. Moses thought, "A man may go to his wife [i.e., have intercourse with her], semen may come out from her on the third day, and they will be impure. Then, Israel will be found receiving the words of Torah from Mount Sinai in impurity. Thus, I will add for them a third day, so that no man will go to his wife, no semen will come out from her on the third day, and they will be pure. They will be found receiving the Torah from Mount Sinai in purity." (A2,9; B2,9–10)

The commentary attributes to Moses a mishnaic argument: in addition to immediate impurity caused by sex, a woman risks a delayed impurity from a later outflow of semen. Because of this risk, all Israelites must abstain from sex for three full days prior to the reception of the Torah.[32] Sexual restraint is thus a necessary condition for the maintenance of sanctity. For the compilers of *Rabbi Nathan,* Moses's fence speaks to ideals that are current for the disciples of the sages; in rabbinic literature, control of sexuality is often a sign that a sage can be regarded as holy.[33]

The Fence of Job: Torah Bounding Sexual Desire

The fence of Job addresses another problematic way that a man may orient toward a woman—desiring another man's wife. The sequence opens with a passage that echoes the discussion of the Torah's fence:

> Which fence did Job make for his words? Thus it says, "[God said to the Adversary, have you noticed my servant Job. For there is none like him in the land:] a man who is blameless [*tam*] and upright, fearing God, and turning from wrong" (Job 1:8). This teaches that Job distanced himself from anything that may bring him to transgression, from that which is hideous and that which resembles something hideous. (A2,12; B2,8–9)

In the opening of the Book of Job, God says that Job is always "turning from wrong." The midrash interprets this to claim that Job exemplifies an ideal articulated earlier—one should distance oneself from all transgression.[34]

How does Job distance himself? The Decalogue prohibits both adultery and coveting another man's wife. Job's fence for these laws appears in his statement, "I made a covenant with my eyes, lest I gaze at a virgin" (Job 31:1). Job not only restrains himself from coveting another man's wife, he refuses to look at any woman who could, in the future, marry another man:

> Thus it says, "I made a covenant with my eyes, lest I gaze at a virgin" (Job 31:1). This teaches that Job was strict with himself and did not even look at a virgin. Thus we reason from the minor case to the major: if with a virgin (whom if he wanted he could marry for himself, or to his son, or to his brothers, or to his cousin) Job was strict with himself and did not look at her, how much the more so with a man's wife! Why was Job strict with himself, not even looking at a virgin? Because Job thought, "Perhaps I will stare today, and tomorrow another man will come and marry her. Then it will be found that I was looking at another man's wife." (A2,12–13)

The midrashic development turns on the "virgin" mentioned in Job 31:1, who represents a woman eligible for marriage. Job exemplifies a man who suppresses attraction for such a woman. Why? In the future another man may marry her, and Job would retroactively be guilty of lusting after another man's wife. In order to avoid this situation, Job distances himself from this transgression by fencing in his gaze.[35]

The Fence of the Writings: Torah Bounding Sexual Desire and Religious Transgression

The final fence I examine is attributed to the Writings, the third major division of the Hebrew Bible. The center of the midrash is a verse from the Book of Proverbs, spoken by an adult man to a young man, "Distance your way from her, and do not come to the doorway of her house" (Prov. 5:8). The one to avoid is the "strange" woman *(zarah).* She and other dangerous women are juxtaposed in Proverbs with the female figure of Wisdom who appears in Proverbs 8.[36]

The commentators develop "Distance your way from her" according to two interpretations—one literal and one metaphorical.[37] Literally, the strange woman is a prostitute, which continues the theme of distancing oneself from improper sexual activity. The metaphoric exegesis begins with a gloss. In the printed edition, it is, "This refers to Epicurians," and in manuscripts we find, "This refers to sectarianism" *(minut).*[38] In either case, the "strange woman" represents the wrong community of spiritual elites:

> Which fence did the Writings make for their words? Thus it is written, "Distance your way from her, and do not come to the doorway of her house" (Prov. 5:8). "Distance your way from her"—this refers to Epicurians. A man is told, "Do not go among the Epicurians or enter their midst, lest you stumble with them." He may say, "I am certain about myself, so even if I enter their midst, I will not stumble with them," [or] perhaps[39] you will say, "I will listen to their words and then return." Scripture says, "Of all who come to her, none return or attain the paths of life" (Prov. 2:19). (A2,13–14; B3,13)[40]

The fence that rabbis find preserves "distance" between the student and rival communities of religious elites. Since we have witnesses for both "Epicurians" and the multivalent *minim,* the possible rivals are many—those attracted to philosophy, Gnosticism, Christianity—and probably the instruction meant different things at different times.[41] Sages give great weight to the power of community and fellowship in shaping individuals. Teachers and colleagues are necessary for ethical transformation, and association with other communities and powerful individuals could lead a person away from the tradition. The individual is considered weak in relation to the group. Even if a man thinks he is strong enough simply to dabble in other social worlds, Scripture warns that he would neither "return" nor "attain the paths of life."[42]

Torah and Transgressive Tendencies: Conclusion

All of the material that I have discussed in this section is part of the commentary upon two imperatives attributed to the Great Assembly: "Be patient in judgment" and "Make a fence for the Torah." I have highlighted passages that describe the interrelation between rabbinic tradition and human transgression. None makes use of technical terms that are generally associated with impulses to transgress *(yetzer* and *leb)*. The study of such terms is extremely valuable, and they will be examined at length below. If we only engaged in such research, however, we would overlook this extensive and prominently placed material and probably underestimate the degree to which the compilers of *Rabbi Nathan* were concerned with the impact of tradition upon the self.

The compilers of *Rabbi Nathan* portray their tradition as a complex and ambivalent entity. The Written Torah may incite the very desires that sages find troubling, giving rise to sexual desire or counseling the reader to act in ways that conflict with commandments that appear elsewhere in the Bible. For this reason, one should be patient in judging these passages and follow the oral tradition of interpretation. However, interpretation has its own dangers, as is exemplified in grand terms through Adam's failed fence. Risks are present at all points of the hermeneutic circle.[43] Torah is also vulnerable to powerful elements internal to a person. At a personal level, Moses's anger shows that intense emotional states can lead one to forget traditional learning. To counter this, *Rabbi Nathan* again counsels patience—patience with others and equilibrium when speaking. This individual level is only one of the ways that Torah is vulnerable. At a communal level, the case of the golden calf shows that, through false observance, the entire tradition can be lost. When sages in *Rabbi Nathan* uphold Torah as transforming the self, they emphasize one aspect of the possible ways that spontaneous desire and Torah can intersect. This observation is important to keep in mind as we examine the role of Torah in ethical transformation. We will read, for example, that Torah can soften bad impulses as a fire can soften metal. Rabbis were aware, however, that Torah may heat up the very passions that they hoped to transform.

We have also seen, in the rabbinic trope of a "fence," an important concept that sages invoke in response to transgressive tendencies. Commentators transform the maxim, "Make a fence for the Torah," into ethical instruction, calling upon the rabbinic subject to make discursive fences that maintain distance between himself and transgression. Several passages focus upon male sexual desire, upholding the ideals that a man should have intercourse only with the correct woman (his wife) and only at the correct time and place (in private, when she is not menstruating and he is not striving for a high level of sanctity). In other cases, *Rabbi Nathan* counsels a man not to look at, talk to, have any kind of physical contact with, or even be near a woman. Moreover, he should avoid other spiritual communities as he would avoid these women, for they may, in another way, seduce him into transgression.

The metaphor of the fence is developed through a continuum of closeness and distance. We see this very clearly in the repeated use of verbs derived from the roots "to come near" *(q.r.b.)* and "to distance oneself" *(r.ḥ.q.)*. The Torah's fence instructs the reader "do not come near" *(lo' tiqrab)* to a menstruating woman, to any women in public, or to anything that brings one to transgression. One must also "distance" oneself *(hirḥiq)* from that which is hideous and, according to the Writings, from the "strange woman" who represents sectarianism. In quoted biblical verses, Eve is commanded not to touch the tree *(lo' tigge'u bo)*, and Moses commands the Israelite men not to "approach" *('al tiggeshu)* a woman sexually.

We should recognize that the sages articulating these tropes of distance were likely immersed in social and familial relationships. *Rabbi Nathan* portrays figures that live in the context of a broader society, not ones who leave towns and cities and go into the desert to distance themselves from temptation and transgression. The text calls for not a physical but a discursive, figurative, character-based approach to separation. While rabbis had certain spaces for study and dining that may have been solely for sages and their followers, generally we should understand the figure of the fence, and its related images, in the context of a social world in which temptations were proximate.[44] Within the discursive world of *Rabbi Nathan,* rabbinic tropes of distance contrast with the teaching of the House of Hillel that I examined at the opening of this book. In that passage, which follows immediately upon the end of the discussion of fences, early sages claim that when rebellious people are "drawn" or "brought close" *(nitqarebu)* to the study of Torah, they become righteous and pious (A3,14). In the following chapter, I examine this process of ethical transformation in detail.

2b The Heart and Its Formation

I have examined the dynamics of tradition and the self with a focus upon tradition, or Torah. Now I shift our lens to the self, particularly ways that rabbis understand the nature of basic impulses, instincts, and desires; the transformation of these through Torah; and the qualities of the sage whose being is permeated by traditional discourse.

When analyzing rabbinic texts that speak to these issues, whether in *Rabbi Nathan* or elsewhere, I have found it crucial to address three groups of questions. First, how is the self constituted in discourse? Rabbis describe or construct the self through highly figurative language. The self, or key elements within it, may be characterized as an animal needing discipline, a metal that must be formed, or a territory to be governed. The Torah, or the parts of the self engaged with the words of Torah, is then the yoke that guides the animal, the fire that softens the metal, the king that rules the territory. Each of these tropic configurations has its own implicit continua and sets out a distinct account—often with important rhetorical features—concerning the process of self-transformation. Much of my task will be to draw out and analyze these accounts.

Certain tropes appear repeatedly as technical terminology for describing what, in modern terms, would be called the psyche. The most important of these are the *yetzer* (inclination) and the *leb* (heart). The *yetzer*, in turn, often appears as a binary relation of "good" and "bad" inclinations.[1] *Yetzer* and *leb* both have metonymic associations: the *yetzer* at least in some sources recalling the causal link between God's formation *(y.tz.r.)* of Adam and impulses instilled through that formation,[2] and the *leb* conveying a spatial link between one's somatic experience of desire and the chest. In most cases, though, these terms seem to be tensionless or "dead" tropes, appearing as concepts that denote parts of the self—sometimes even hypostasized in strong terms[3]—and often they are characterized through further figurative images (such as, "the heart is a stone").

A second group of questions centers on the dynamics of spontaneous impulses, instincts, or desires. One specific problem is the relation between those impulses that lead one to affirm divine law and those that lead to transgression. Daniel Boyarin has distinguished dualistic and monistic rabbinic psychologies—the former framing the self in terms of conflicting good and bad impulses and the latter positing a single force within the self that inspires both creation and destruction.[4] Another question is whether transgressive dimensions of the self can be changed. Some rabbinic teachings portray the bad *yetzer* as a substance that can be trained, molded, worn away, or conquered, such that one can envision life without inner division. Others present negative impulses as given and always present: the sage can do his best to struggle with and subdue them over the course of his lifetime, but he can never fully be rid of them (except, in some accounts, through an eschatological act of God).

The third group of questions concerns the elements external to the self. What are the roles of Torah and of God in the process of transforming impulses, instincts, or desires? Torah and God are of course interrelated value concepts, but the nuances of the texts are lost if we collapse them. Each passage presents a particular account of the ways in which the person orients toward the Torah, God's judgment, and God's compassion. One may emphasize immersion in traditional discourse, another may highlight God's eschatological judgment, and yet another may call for prayer to invoke divine compassion. Or these elements may appear in various combinations.

The material in *Rabbi Nathan* does not present a unified stance on these questions. However, there are general tendencies within the text. For the most part, *Rabbi Nathan* portrays a dualistic picture of competing good and bad forces within the self, and it holds out the possibility that negative impulses can be fundamentally transformed, particularly through the study and practice of Torah. However, some passages counter these generalizations. Certain teachings affirm in a complex way the value of tendencies usually seen as bad, such as jealousy and lust.[5] One prominently placed teaching focuses on the role of divine compassion, and a highly developed teaching presents the bad *yetzer* as an element that one does not change but struggles with until God's ultimate judgment.[6]

The *Yetzer,* Good and Bad

Rabbis often present transgressive tendencies as emerging from the *yetzer,* a construct that has its exegetical grounding in three biblical verses from Genesis. The sense that the *yetzer* is bad *(ra')*[7] has its roots in the story of the flood. Humankind must be destroyed because "every *yetzer* of the thoughts of his heart, is only bad [*ra'*] all of the time" (Gen. 6:5). Later, a similar observation justifies the opposite response. God will never again curse the earth on account of people, "for the *yetzer* of the heart of the human is bad [*ra'*] from his youth" (Gen. 8:21). The idea that there are two inclinations, rather than just one, is linked to God's formation of Adam, for a key word has an unusual doubling of the letter *y (yod)*: "The Lord God formed [*vayyitzer*] the human [*ha-'adam*], dust from the earth" (Gen. 2:7). One midrashic interpretation of this doubling is that God's formation included both the good *yetzer* and the bad.[8] Such exegetical moves, however, are not explicit in *Rabbi Nathan;* the word *yetzer* appears as a technical term without reference to these passages.

In *Rabbi Nathan* and other rabbinic texts, the heart may also be a seat of transgressive tendencies, and some sources locate the *yetzer* in the heart. A key verse is the command that became central to the *Shema*—you should love God "with all of your heart [*lebabekha*]" (Deut. 6:5). Commentators interpret the doubled consonants in *lebabekha* as indicating two forces in the heart, which they characterize through the category of *yetzer*—you should love God "with good *yetzer* and bad *yetzer*."[9] The heart also has other roles in rabbinic psychology as the center of thought, emotion, and desire. It may be anxious *(mitpahed)*, be torn in anger *(metareph)*, contain jealousy *(qin'ah)*, and enjoy *('oheb)*. The heart can also be affected or transformed by language and images. A number of rabbinic epigrams (which I discuss in chapter 3b) instruct that one "place" the words of Torah, or certain images of God, upon it.[10]

In *Rabbi Nathan,* the most highly commented upon epigram concerning *yetzer* is attributed to the first-century Rabbi Yehoshua, who says, "The malicious eye, the bad *yetzer,* and hatred of creatures cast a man out from the world" (A16,62; B30,62; *Fathers* 2:11). The bad *yetzer* appears in a brief catalogue of misanthropic qualities—forms of hatred and ill feeling toward fellow humans. The appearance spurs, in the editorial development of *Rabbi Nathan A,* a vast compilation of teachings concerning *yetzer* and its dynamics, and this compilation is the source for much of the material that I examine in this section.[11]

How, then, does the bad *yetzer* "cast a person out from the world?" The commentary opens with an anonymous teaching that the bad *yetzer* has its origins in the mother's womb and inspires paradigmatic forms of transgressive behavior—breaking the Sabbath, murder, and adultery. The good *yetzer* emerges at age thirteen, which probably presumes the practice that at this age a boy takes on the commandments. It appears as an internal voice that quotes Torah, citing a law to counter each potential act of transgression:

> They said: The bad *yetzer* is thirteen years older than the good *yetzer*. From the belly of a person's mother it grows and comes with him. If he begins to desecrate the Sabbath, nothing in him protests. [If he begins to commit murder, nothing in him protests. If he goes to do an act of transgression, nothing in him protests].[12] After thirteen years, the good *yetzer* is born. When he begins to desecrate Sabbaths, it says to him, "You idiot! Look, it says, 'The one who desecrates it will surely die!'" (Exod. 31:14). When he goes to commit murder, it says to him, "You idiot! Look, it says, 'If a man spills the blood of another man, his blood will be spilled'" (Gen. 9:6). When he goes to do an act of sexual transgression,[13] it says to him, "You idiot! Look, it says, 'the adulterer and the adulteress will surely die'" (Lev. 20:10). (A16,62–63; compare B16,36)

The psychological dualism contrasts not body and soul, but innate tendencies to transgress and the guidance of the traditional discourse.[14] The bad *yetzer* is primordial, appearing in the infant while still in the womb. It manifests itself as an impulse to violate rabbinic law. When reading the statements describing transgression, we should not take them too literally—that the concern is with children under thirteen who actually murder and commit adultery. The list is exegetically derived from the verses quoted later as the voice of the good *yetzer*, which are biblical laws directed toward adults. The passage, I believe, posits tendencies toward transgression in children that, if not countered, can ultimately lead to these major violations.

The Hebrew text has an ambiguity that may be important for reflecting upon rabbinic selves. Who or what is the agent in transgression? In the statements describing the tendencies, the third person subject of the verb may be "he" (the child) or "it" (the *yetzer*). If the subject is the child, then the text seems to frame the bad *yetzer* as a moral blindness—children may have a wide range of desires, but they have no ability to observe themselves or to counter their impulses that lead to transgressive action. If the subject is the bad *yetzer* itself, then the teaching presents a more negative picture, positing an impulse within children that specifically drives them to violate norms.[15]

The good *yetzer* is "born" at age thirteen. Again, we should not interpret this image too literally, that at age thirteen a new voice pops into a person's head. Thirteen is both an approximation of puberty and the time at which a male is to begin observance of the commandments, but other rabbinic sources prescribe study and habituation beginning at earlier ages.[16] The good *yetzer,* then, appears when the socialization of childhood has crystallized and also when males deepen their involvement in rabbinic tradition.[17] By saying that the good *yetzer* is "born," rabbis present this cultural process as natural.

In this portrayal of the good *yetzer,* procedural reasoning and character development are interrelated. The passage sets out three moments of decision making—whether or not to violate the Sabbath, murder, or commit adultery—and three laws to guide action. At the same time, these procedural norms are set in the context of an account of the self that emphasizes the importance of an internal faculty generated by traditional formation.[18] The good *yetzer* is both a receptor of Torah, enabling one to internalize the discourse, and also an inner monitoring faculty. It counters impulses to engage in the three major forms of sin—religious, aggressive, and sexual—through criticizing the person about to transgress and citing appropriate verses from the Bible to guide action ("You idiot! Look, it says . . .").[19] The good *yetzer* is framed as reactive; it counters transgression, but it does not actively promote positive action or care for others.[20]

In addition to the pervasive concern with religious, sexual, and aggressive transgression, two passages in *Rabbi Nathan A* draw attention to self-destructive impulses. The source of one teaching is part of God's call to Cain, "Sin crouches at the opening [*la-petaḥ*]" (Gen. 4:7). The exegesis specifies the "opening" as the "openings of the heart"—reinvigorating the trope of the heart with tension through emphasizing its physicality. The bad *yetzer* is located where the heart opens to the rest of the body, directing aggression back toward the self:

> Rabbi Reuben ben Atztrobali says: How can a person distance himself from the bad *yetzer* that is in his belly, because the first drop that a man places in a women is the bad *yetzer*? The bad *yetzer* is located at the openings of the heart, as it is said, "Sin crouches at the opening [*la-petaḥ*]" (Gen. 4:7). It says to a person, at the time that the infant lies in the crib, "The man wants to kill you!" He wants to tear out his hair. An infant lies in his crib, and he places his hand on the back of a snake or a scorpion, and it stings him. Nothing but the bad *yetzer* in his belly causes him [to do this]. He puts his hand on the top of coals and is burnt. Nothing but the bad *yetzer* in his belly causes him [to do this], because the bad *yetzer* drives him headlong [*zoreqo bebat ro'sh*]. But come and see a goat or a lamb— when it sees a pit, it backs up, because there is no bad *yetzer* in cattle. (A16,63–64; compare B16,36)[21]

Rabbi Reuben ben Atztrobali places the origin of the bad *yetzer* even earlier than does the teaching discussed above—in the father's semen rather than the mother's womb.[22] Rabbinic literature presents a number of views and debates concerning the origins of the *yetzer* as well as several discussions of this verse.[23] The distinct feature of this passage is a focus upon self-destruction and particularly the detail with which self-destructive tendencies are elaborated. The characterization of the *yetzer* shows great psychological subtlety. The *yetzer* is an internal aggressor, threatening the infant with fantasies—"the man wants to kill you!"—that delude him into frenzy. His defensive response hurts none but himself.

The ensuing examples of a child putting her or his hand on a scorpion and on coal could be interpreted in a number of ways: as a lack of an instinct for self-preservation, as a child's curiosity, or as an active impulse toward self-destruction. The ambiguity, to some degree, turns on how old we imagine the child *(tinoq)* to be, and how much awareness the child would have of its surroundings—are we imagining an impulse to touch something that is dangerous out of ignorance, or an impulse to touch something despite or because of its danger? The latter interpretation is supported by passages elsewhere in *Rabbi Nathan* where being stung by a scorpion, being burnt by coal, and falling off a roof all appear as examples of careless and self-destructive behavior.[24] However we stand on this question, the sequence concludes by stating that, unlike a human child, a goat or a lamb will not engage in such actions. The struggle with the bad *yetzer* is distinctive of human life.[25]

A more radical portrait of self-destructiveness appears in a teaching of Rabbi Yehudah the Patriarch that places the bad *yetzer* in opposition to the body. The sage's parable presumes that God will ultimately judge a man's *yetzer,* condemning the bad within him.[26] This impending judgment underlies a Kafkaesque scene that opens with an unexplained seizure and criminal charge. "They" accuse a man of robbery. He could take all of the punishment upon himself, but he chooses to drag down his "friend" as well:

> Rabbi Yehudah the Patriarch says: Let me tell you a parable—to what can the bad *yetzer* be compared? To two people who entered an inn. One was seized for robbery. They said to him, "Who is with you?" He could have said, "My friend was not with me," but he thinks, "Because I will be killed, let my friend be killed with me." So thinks the bad *yetzer,* "Because I am lost to the world to come, I will make the entire body perish." (A16,64)

A man is seized for robbery (though we do not know that he is actually a robber), and he chooses to bring his fellow to jail with him. Rabbi

Yehudah glosses the man as the bad *yetzer*, presumably facing divine con-
demnation. The "friend" is reinterpreted as the body. The *yetzer*, facing
divine judgment, will cause the body to perish along with it. Once again,
self-destruction reigns.

The bad *yetzer* thus acts as an envious man, wanting to destroy what is
good because he cannot have it. The object of its envy is the body that it
inhabits and specifically the possibility of embodied resurrection and life
in the world to come. The picture is not simply that the bad *yetzer* aims
to kill the person, which appears in talmudic sources (*b. Sukk.* 52b and
b. Qidd 30b). Here, God may ultimately eliminate the negative part of the
self through divine judgment. This part of the self has cognitive dimensions and realizes what may happen. As a result, it responds maliciously,
aiming to destroy the rest of the person. An aspiring sage has within him,
then, a destructive element that fundamentally refuses to be changed or
eliminated. The very possibility of divine intervention results in this element dragging him down to "perish" in sin.[27]

Tropes for Transformation

Given such accounts of desire and transgression, how do
the compilers of *Rabbi Nathan* describe and prescribe the transformation
of negative impulses? This general question opens up a number of more
specific ones, which help sharpen our vision for examining ethical discourse. Concerning innate tendencies, one could ask, does the self have
within it all that is necessary to be good, or must it draw fundamental elements from outside? Does the self respond easily to change, or is it resistant, even actively hostile? Concerning the process of transformation, does
one focus upon increasing good tendencies or upon decreasing the bad?
Does one respond to negative impulses by trying to channel them into
positive ones, or by trying to eliminate them, or are both of these hopeless,
so one must always struggle with persisting tendencies to transgress and
destroy? What is the role of intentional action—does one actively make
change happen, or is there a passive element, such that one must let it happen? Is the process gradual and steady, or sudden and dramatic?

Sometimes ethical discourses explicitly articulate these questions, but
often the key issues are implicit. Scholars of comparative ethics have developed a number of heuristic tools for analyzing such concerns, identifying different "models" of attaining virtue. Each of these models implies a

distinct configuration of answers to the above questions. A prominent model among Hellenistic philosophers is that of therapy and medicine: the philosopher heals the soul from false belief as a doctor heals the body from disease. This imagery appears once in *Rabbi Nathan* to describe the learning of Torah but not with a specific focus upon character formation. In rabbinic literature more broadly, a teaching in both a Palestinian midrashic collection and the Babylonian Talmud states that Torah is a "remedy" *(sam)* for the *yetzer*.[28] Another important set of images among thinkers in late antiquity, which we see in *Rabbi Nathan*, is that of warfare and governance. There are conflicting forces within a person, and one has to battle with and strive to govern that which is seen as wayward or out of control.[29]

Other models, which scholars have developed for analyzing early Chinese sources, center on tropes that are similar to ones that appear in *Rabbi Nathan*. "Development" models portray a slow, steady process that is dependent both upon intentional action and upon the natural propensities of the self. These may appear in a number of variations. Some models center upon agricultural metaphors, according to which one becomes virtuous through attention to and cultivation of innate tendencies—the slow, gradual growth of something that is at first nascent within the self. Another position holds that innate or spontaneous impulses should not be trusted and require "re-formation." This would imply intentional action that shapes and channels a recalcitrant human nature, figured through tropes such as straightening a bent piece of wood, sharpening metal, and molding clay.[30]

I identify in *Rabbi Nathan* two broad visions of ethical transformation through Torah—"development" and "conflict and governance." Each type has subtypes, and I examine them in detail. Then I analyze a passage that resists the entire framework developed herein—one that foregrounds not Torah but God in the confrontation with bad impulses. One significant qualification is in order, however. Rabbinic sources do not allow us to speak of "models," only "metaphors" of transformation. A model would imply that the figurative images are linked with some form of theoretical account. We do not know that the metaphors in *Rabbi Nathan* are the outgrowth of such thought, and unlike the theological images I discuss later, tropes concerning Torah do not even interrelate in a systematic manner. However, it is possible to find the boundaries of the diversity, cluster certain types of tropes, and inquire concerning the underlying issues that drive these figurative statements.[31]

Metaphors of Development

Rabbinic metaphors of development fall into three major groups. The first group, metaphors of training and discipline, depicts farm animals. The student is a calf, lamb, or ox, and Torah may be a yoke that controls or a goad that urges from behind. The second depicts rubbing, wearing away, or shaping of a hard substance such as stone or metal. Torah, as the active force, may be soft water, hard iron, or a hot flame. The third type of development metaphor centers upon agricultural imagery—the self is a field that needs cultivation. Each of these types can set out a more or less optimistic picture, depending on where the *yetzer* and the Torah appear on the implicit cultural continua. Images of shaping, for example, imply a continuum of hard-soft. The more the Torah is portrayed as hard, and the self as soft, then the easier and faster is the process of transformation. Or in the case of agriculture, the more fertile the land, the greater are the possibilities of growth through tradition.

Training a Farm Animal

In rabbinic literature, the most prominent trope drawn from the practice of domesticating an animal is that of a "yoke," which appears in the phrase "acceptance of the yoke of the kingship of Heaven" *(qabbalat 'ol malkhut shamayim).*[32] Sages take over the term "yoke" from biblical sources, in which it was a vital metaphor.[33] *Rabbi Nathan B* preserves a maxim that employs this image, but it remains undeveloped, without tension: Nehuniah ben ha-Kanah says, "All who take upon themselves the yoke of Torah are released from the yoke of government and the yoke of worldly matters" (B32,68).[34]

A more vital and innovative metaphor of bovine discipline appears in a homily of Rabbi Eleazar ben Azariah, a late-first-century sage. He midrashically interprets Ecclesiastes 12:11—"The words of the sages are as goads, and as nails planted are the words of masters of assemblies; they are given from one shepherd"—in a rhetorically sophisticated sermon on the nature of Torah. I focus on the first metaphor, which describes Torah's impact on the person in terms of a "goad" that keeps a cow directed toward its furrow.[35] In *Rabbi Nathan,* the homily appears in a chapter that opens with statements of praise by Rabbi Yehudah the Patriarch (late second century CE) for the sages that preceded him. When the first-century

Rabbi Eleazar ben Azariah appears in the list, the commentators present a narrative in which Rabbi Yehoshua ben Hananiah asks his students to recount the preaching of Rabbi Eleazar. The students respond by reporting two homilies, and the second begins:

> They said to him, "He also interpreted exegetically [*darash*] the verse, 'The words of the sages are as goads, and as nails planted are the words of masters of assemblies; they are given from one shepherd'" (Eccles. 12:11). Just as a goad directs the cow to its furrows, so the words of Torah direct the person to the ways of life. If you say, just as a goad may be removed, so one may remove the words of Torah, Scripture says, "as nails planted . . ." (A18,68)[36]

This complex midrash atomizes the verse from Ecclesiastes, interpreting each element as a trope. I have quoted only the opening section, which presents the following metaphors:

> Torah is a goad
> a person is a cow
> the ways of life are a furrow

The third metaphor, of course, has within it another metaphor, which is that right action is a road or "way" *(derekh),* which one can follow or stray off.[37] The key analogy is that the words of Torah direct a person on the ways of life as a goad directs a cow in furrows.[38] For Rabbi Eleazar ben Azariah, Torah is first of all something that shapes a person in practical life, a spur in the back that disciplines a student and keeps him upon the right path. The student is to be receptive to this goad, which counters and trains his wild natural impulses.[39]

The animal-training motif also appears among a series of sayings that contrast studying Torah in youth and in old age. Most of these focus on the relative ease of learning Torah when one starts young. The first teaching, however, employs the metaphor of a trained calf to convey the effect of Torah upon character and action:

> [Rabbi Nehurai] would say: One who studies Torah in his youth, to what can he be compared—to a heifer that was broken [*kibbeshuha*] when she was young, as it is written, "Ephraim is a trained heifer [*'eglah melummadah*] and loves to thresh . . ." (Hosea 10:11). One who studies Torah in his old age resembles a cow who was broken only in her old age, as is written, "Like a stubborn cow, Israel was stubborn" (Hosea 4:16). (A23,76)[40]

The sage contrasts Hosea 10:11 with Hosea 4:16, setting up an opposition between a "trained heifer" and a "stubborn cow." Each of these metaphors operates in relation to two continua—young-old and receptive-stubborn—and they are located on opposite ends of each one. The young calf/student is receptive; the old cow/student is stubborn. The link between these tropes and Torah study may be inspired by the word "trained" *(melummadah)* in Hosea 10:11, which is derived from the root "to learn" *(l.m.d.)*. These predications respond to the issue: Does the self respond to tradition easily? At a young age, Rabbi Nehurai says, a student is receptive to being formed by Torah and can easily be trained, but an older person has developed dispositions that make him stubborn and resistant. The young student takes on the yoke of the Torah and commandments, and he loves to "thresh" through the *halakhah*.

A third passage employs metaphors of domestic farm animals to highlight the role of the commandments in forming a person—they are necessary in order to become a mature adult. The scene appears as part of the commentary to a maxim of the first-century Yose the Priest, "Prepare yourself to study Torah, for it is not an inheritance for you." The commentators present an account of Moses appointing Joshua to be his successor. Joshua appears as a rabbinic student attaining the role of a public leader. He becomes a translator of Torah recitation *(turgeman)* and will offer a homily in public *(yidrosh)*.[41]

At this moment, Moses describes the community to his successor. He draws upon a verse from the Song of Songs: "If you do not know, for yourself, O most beautiful of women, go for yourself in the tracks of the flock and pasture your kids at the tents of the shepherds" (Songs 1:8). According to Moses's interpretation, Joshua is the woman figure in the song, and the Israelites are her "kids." They are immature, not yet adult, because they have only just received the commandments and have not begun regularly to observe them:

> At that time, Moses said to Joshua, "Joshua, regarding this people that I pass on to you [*moser*]: I do not pass on to you goats but kids. Sheep I do not pass on to you but lambs, for they have not involved themselves with the commandments, and they have not become goats and sheep. As it is said, 'If you do not know, for yourself, O most beautiful of women, go for yourself in the tracks of the flock and pasture your kids at the tents of the shepherds'" (Songs 1:8). (A17,65)[42]

Through the contrasts of kids/goats and lambs/sheep, the passage teaches that the key transition to adulthood comes through involvement with the commandments. Without observance, people are merely "kids" and "lambs," regardless of their age. These metaphors differ from the others of farm animals in centering on biological growth rather than discipline. Here, like the image discussed above of the good *yetzer* being "born" at age thirteen, the text portrays enculturation as a natural process.

These metaphors of animal training deanthropomorphize the process of ethical transformation. The student is compared to an animal that, in rabbinic eyes, is lower than humans, and the process of education is portrayed in crude terms—putting on a yoke, prodding with a goad, breaking a heifer.[43] The metaphors present the Torah and divine commandments as powerful and coercive, and there seems to be little concern here with innate intelligence. The teachings call upon the student to be docile and receptive, receiving the guidance and habituation that the Torah provides. These scenes do, however, portray the student as a living being that can learn and grow, and also rebel. A stronger deanthropomorphizing tendency can be seen in the following group of images.

Wearing Down Stone and Forging Metal

Sages draw upon images of stone and metal to convey a similar process of transformation in which one employs an external element to re-form existing parts of the self. While the animal training metaphors apply to the self as a whole, tropes of stone and metal characterize specifically the rebellious and transgressive parts of the self that emerge from the heart and the *yetzer*. As hard, inert, passive material, these tendencies are neither active in the learning process, nor visibly hostile. One important example of these tropes is the account of Rabbi Akiba that I quoted and discussed at the very opening of the book. The sage begins by observing water wearing away stone; then he infers from this natural scene of slow erosion a more powerful image of tradition impacting the heart— Torah is strong iron upon a receptive, fleshy heart.

Later in *Rabbi Nathan,* as part of the extensive discussion of *yetzer* commenting upon the maxim of Rabbi Yehoshua, we again find the trope of iron. In this case the metaphor describes not the transforming agent but a part of the self. The late-second-century Rabbi Simeon ben Eleazar builds upon the image in Proverbs 25:21–22 of "piling up coal" upon the head of the "enemy" to teach that the words of Torah are like fire upon the metallic *yetzer*. The passage combines themes that appear throughout rabbinic literature—Torah as fire, the bad *yetzer* as metal, the image of metal being placed in fire to purify it[44]—to argue that one can re-form one's *yetzer* as an artisan shapes metal:

> Rabbi Simeon ben Eleazar says: I will tell you a parable—to what can this matter be compared? The bad *yetzer* can be compared to iron that is placed in a flame. All the time that it is in the midst of the flame, people can make from it all the utensils that they want. So too, the bad *yetzer*: its only means of reform are the words of Torah, for they are like fire, as it is written, "If your enemy is hungry, feed him bread, and if he is thirsty, give him water to drink; for you pile up coal upon his head, and the Lord will repay you [*yeshallem lakh*]" (Prov. 25:21–22). Do not read "will repay you [*yeshallem lakh*]" but "will put him at peace with you [*yashlimennu lakh*]." (A16,64)[45]

The prooftext, Proverbs 25:21–22, describes a quiet attack on an enemy through generosity—be generous to your enemy so that you will pile "coals" of shame upon him, and God will repay you. The sage draws upon the image of coals and extends it, through the parable, to describe the labor of an ironworker making utensils. The teaching is that the bad *yetzer*, being metal, resists change while in its natural state. When immersed in the flames of Torah, however, its tendencies and energies become useful. In sum, the layers of the teaching are as follows:

You pile up coal upon his head.
You place fire upon iron (in order to mold it).
You address the words of Torah to your bad *yetzer* in order to transform it.
You address the words of Torah to your destructive tendencies in order to
    transform them.

These metaphors convey a more pessimistic view of innate tendencies than we find in Rabbi Akiba's inference from the well—Rabbi Akiba's heart of flesh and blood is softer and more easily shaped than a bad *yetzer* of iron. Yet Rabbi Simeon ben Eleazar's pessimism is matched by an intensely positive stance concerning the power of Torah. While Rabbi Akiba places the Torah and the self on the same continuum of hard-soft, Rabbi Simeon locates the Torah at an entirely different plane. It is a hot element that can move the bad *yetzer* across the hard-soft continuum so that it becomes soft, molten metal. That which is otherwise unchangeable becomes responsive. Both Rabbi Akiba and Rabbi Simeon, then, envision Torah as a transformative force that is far more powerful than the *yetzer* or the heart itself. While they disagree as to the nature of innate tendencies, the two sages present distinctly optimistic visions for re-forming oneself through tradition.[46]

Cultivating a Poor Field

A homily attributed to Rabbi Simeon ben Yohai articulates a truly pessimistic view of human potential. Through use of a parable, this sage employs imagery of agricultural labor to assert that humans are like a poor piece of land. No matter how much they work on themselves, their produce will be a fraction of what they need simply to pay their rent—"rent" being the good deeds required to avoid eternal punishment. However, the sage offers hope that Israel will be able to petition for God's compassion in the future and be saved from Gehenna:

> Rabbi Simeon ben Yohai says: From here[47] we learn that Israel never sees the face of Gehenna. They made a parable. To what can this be compared—to a king of flesh and blood who had a low-lying field. People came and rented it for ten *kor* of wheat per year. They fertilized it, tilled it, irrigated it, and cleared it, but they only harvested one *kor* of wheat per year. The king said to them, "What is this?" They said to him, "Our lord, the king, you know regarding the field that you gave us, that from the beginning you harvested nothing from it. Now, we fertilized it, cleared it, and irrigated it with water, but we harvested from it only one *kor* of wheat." Thus, in the future, Israel will say before the Holy One, blessed be He, "Master of the Universe, you know that the bad *yetzer* stirs us up," as it is written, "For He knows our formation [*yitzrenu*]. [He is mindful that we are dust]" (Ps. 103:14). (A16,64; also B30,63)

Rabbi Simeon ben Yohai's agricultural imagery is linked with the second half of Ps. 103:14. From the words "we are dust," he draws out a metaphor comparing humans to a poor field.[48] The metaphor implies a continuum of fertile-infertile, and he locates humans upon it as infertile, unable to cultivate a righteous character that observes the divine commandments. No matter how much intentional action or labor one performs, humans do not have the basic potential to grow as virtuous beings; there are significant limits upon how much people can change themselves. Rabbi Simeon ben Yohai's parable protests against God regarding this deficient human nature. God is an unfair landlord, demanding "rent" in obedience that is far greater than the "land" of human potential can produce.

The sage, though, incorporates this pessimism into a homily focusing on God's compassion. He interprets the biblical statement that God "knows our formation" *(yitzrenu)* through the construct of *yetzer,* developing the verse to mean, He knows the nature and power of our *yetzer*. Because of this knowledge, God will show sympathy for human limitation and has compassion in judgment, and the descendants of Israel will not "ever see the face of Gehenna."[49]

Metaphors of Conquest and Government

In certain respects, the overarching trope of ethical transformation through Torah is that of a movement from inner division to unity.[50] The sage becomes one, after having experienced two or more forces contending within him. This general dynamic is intensified through metaphors of conquest and government. Such metaphors do not portray a slow steady process of continued labor on a day-to-day basis. Rather, the negative forces are active, defending their territory and even imprisoning the positive. Ethical transformation is figured as attack, or escape, or at least taking over territory. The process may have times of no results, like being in a prison or storming a wall, but eventually the sage experiences an inner upheaval through which a new ruler—Torah—comes to power.

Metaphors of conquest and government in *Rabbi Nathan* appear in three arrangements. All of them interweave images of space with those of power. The first is that of a warrior conquering a city, which sets out an opposition of inside/outside: the bad *yetzer* on the inside, controlling the person, and the warrior on the outside, trying to get in. The rabbinic student must be active, attacking inner forces that are defended by a protective wall. A second passage envisions a radical change of power through depicting the good and bad inclinations as competing rulers. Space is configured in a very different way. Initially the good *yetzer* is inside, imprisoned in a body controlled by the bad *yetzer* (being inside, in this case, implies lack of control). The good *yetzer* then must escape and through a coup govern the self. A third account portrays a more peaceful rise to power in which the Torah comes to inhabit an empty room. There is no focus on an opposing, hostile enemy—just the movement from outside to inside by Torah as king.

The Mighty Warrior

The sage Ben Zoma employs the metaphor of a warrior conquering a city in a maxim that echoes Stoic forms of rhetoric.[51] He asks questions that appear to address worldly achievements and goods: who is truly wise, humble, rich, and mighty? His answers, however, uphold scholastic virtues of self-control and openness to others. The fourth and last of these answers invokes the *yetzer:*

> Who is the mightiest of all mighty men? This is one who conquers his *yetzer,* as it is written, "Better is one who is slow to anger than a mighty man, and one who governs his spirit than one who conquers a city" (Prov. 16:32). (A23,75; B33,72; *Fathers* 4:1)[52]

This compact passage has an extremely rich exegetical reworking of biblical tropes. In order to clarify the hermeneutical dynamics, I map out the verse:

Better is (a) one who is slow to anger than (b) a mighty man,
    and (a′) one who governs his spirit than (b′) one who conquers a city.

The verse, then, evaluates (a) as greater than (b), and (a′) as greater than (b′). Ben Zoma maintains this assessment, but he also *reinterprets* (a) and (a′) through the images of (b) and (b′) to create a new metaphor. That is, one who is slow to anger or governs his spirit *is* a mighty man who conquers a city. The "city," however, is now an inner space inhabited by the *yetzer.*[53]

Ben Zoma's maxim makes no mention of the Torah and does not necessarily uphold tradition as central to the conquest of inner impulses. The commentary maintains and highlights the motif of battle, and also links it to the study of Torah, by citing two more verses that take up the themes of "might" and conquest of a city:[54]

> For anyone who conquers his *yetzer,* it is accounted to him as if he conquered a city filled with mighty men, as it is written, "A wise man went up to a city of mighty men, and he brought down its secure stronghold" (Prov. 21:22). "Mighty" means "mighty in Torah," as it is written, "[Bless the Lord, O his angels], mighty in strength, and doers of His word, to hear the sound of His word" (Ps. 103:20). Some say that this refers to the ministering angels, as it is written [at the beginning of the verse], "O His angels, mighty in strength" (Ps. 103:20). Some say that refers to one who makes his enemy his loved one. (A23,75)[55]

The exegesis of Proverbs 21:22 develops the spatial imagery in Ben Zoma's epigram. The wise man as warrior is below and outside, going up to the city to enter it. In terms of inner space, this means that, for those who fight their *yetzer,* the bad impulses start out on the inside and are protected by walls. The wise man must break through the barrier and enter, taking control of the inner city. So far, the midrash continues Ben Zoma's contrast between the sage and those who are "mighty" in a worldly sense—the wise man conquers a city of "mighty" men. However, an abrupt shift comes when the "mighty" men of the city are glossed as being "mighty in Torah" and as hearing the word of God (based on Ps. 103:20). Now the "mighty" are not enemies, but Torah scholars. The sequence culminates through transforming the image of inner battle into one of apprenticeship. The wise man now goes up to the city of Torah scholars in order to learn from them at the house of study.[56]

Through chaining together these verses with the maxim, the compilers of this passage link three tropes to characterize the impact of Torah upon the student—the self or key parts of it as a city, one's transformation as a battle, and the impact of Torah as a movement from outside to inside—and also uphold the study of Torah in urban or semiurban areas. According to these metaphors of conquest, both the power of a man's *yetzer* and his ability to overcome it are more pronounced than is conveyed in figures of re-formation. His desires are not just hard stone or metal, but a stony fort protecting hostile soldiers. In response, he is not an artisan, but a mighty warrior who struggles as a hero in battle. The self is at conflict with itself, with powerful forces on either side. After great struggle, eventually the stronghold is brought down, the warrior comes to rule the city, and inner division is overcome.[57]

From Prison to Rule

A very different configuration of conquest imagery appears in an anonymous passage that follows directly upon a citation from Leviticus prohibiting adultery—"the adulterer and the adulteress will surely die" (Lev. 20:10).[58] The commentators develop the concern with sexual transgression through a verse from Ecclesiastes to frame the issue in terms of self-governance. The good and bad *yetzer* are kings who vie for power over the body. In the present, the bad *yetzer* rules while the good is in prison. Sometime in the future, though, a radical change of power will occur, and the imprisoned king will emerge:

> When a man heats himself up and goes to do an act of unchastity, all of his body parts obey him, because the bad *yetzer* is king over the 248 body parts. When he goes to fulfill a commandment, all his bodily parts detain him,[59] because the bad *yetzer*, which is in his belly, is king over all 248 body parts that are in a man. The good *yetzer* resembles one who is

confined in a prison house [*beyt ha-'asurim*], as it is said, "From the prison house [*beyt hasurim*] he comes to rule . . ." (Eccles. 4:14). This is the good *yetzer.* (A16,63; compare B16,36)

The prooftext has to be understood in its broader biblical context, which compares two figures: "Better is a child poor and wise than a king old and foolish, who no longer knows to heed warning. For from the prison house he comes to rule, and even he born to kingship will become poor" (Eccles. 4:13–14). Several midrashic interpretations of Ecclesiastes 4:13 interpret the wise child as the good *yetzer* and the foolish king as the bad *yetzer.*[60] This correspondence, brought over to verse 4:14, underlies the image developed here—the bad *yetzer* now rules as king, and the good *yetzer* is in prison.

The dynamics between the good and bad *yetzer* are developed in terms of three oppositions: time (present/future), space (inside/outside), and power (imprisoned/ruling). In the present, the good *yetzer* is inside and imprisoned, while the bad *yetzer* rules. In the future, the good *yetzer* will escape and rule. This spatial imagery is very different than that in Ben Zoma's trope of the warrior. For Ben Zoma, the warrior is outside and needs to get into the city, while here the good *yetzer* is bound inside and has to get out.

The themes of power and government are linked with the body. The bad *yetzer* "is king over the 248 body parts," constraining the impulses of the good *yetzer.*[61] This account appears similar to Hellenistic dichotomies between body and soul. However, here the body is ethically neutral, able to be controlled either by bad or good impulses. Also, as we have seen above (in the passage that precedes this one in *Rabbi Nathan A*), the good *yetzer* is not the soul but the human capacity to internalize and respond to the discourse of Torah. The compilers of *Rabbi Nathan* thus present the relation between Torah and transgressive tendencies through metaphors that echo Greek and Hellenistic accounts of the body as a prison: the bad *yetzer* encloses the human receptivity to Torah as a prisoner.

The passage envisions not a process of development, or a constant battle, but a future moment of vast change that overturns the current power structure. Self-transformation comes through an inner revolution or coup. The result is a total reversal of powers. That which was confined will control, and that which ruled will be deposed. After this upheaval, the whole person, including the body, will be governed according to the good *yetzer.* The good *yetzer,* in turn, is not only a voice that speaks internally to the person. Rather, it is deeply connected with the body and its action.[62]

Filling up the Heart

A third variant of governance metaphors does not depict a battle but simply a king entering an open space and taking control. This image portrays a much more harmonious picture of ethical transformation, without hostile opposing forces within the person. Rather, the student must open up a space within himself for the words of Torah to enter and establish sovereignty. This imagery of entering empty space appears explicitly only in *Rabbi Nathan B,* but it is implied in a narrative of *Rabbi Nathan A* and arguably in other passages found in both versions.

I have discussed above the instruction of Yose ben Yoezer, "Let your house be a meeting place of the sages, sit at the dust of their feet, and drink with thirst their words" (A6,27; B11,27; *Fathers* 1:4), because the second and third elements of the epigram inspire stories of Rabbi Akiba's career. In *Rabbi Nathan B,* as commentary to "drink with thirst their words," we also find a passage depicting Torah's effect upon the heart:

> "And drink with thirst their words." For any time that the words of Torah enter and find the rooms [of the heart][63] empty, they enter and dwell within. The bad *yetzer* does not rule them, and a person cannot cast them out from inside. They told a parable—to what can this be compared? To a king who was walking on the road, and he found empty rooms and a dining room. He entered and dwelled within, and no person could cast him out from inside. Thus, any time that words of Torah enter and find the rooms of the heart empty, they enter and dwell within. The bad *yetzer* does not rule them, and a person cannot cast them out from inside. (B13,30)[64]

The "heart" usually appears in rabbinic literature as a dead or tensionless trope, not evoking the image of a physical organ. This account, however, plays on literal and figurative senses of "heart" through the image of a "room." The metaphoric transfers are:

(a) "room" as part of a house to (b) "room" as a chamber of the heart;
(b) "heart" as a physical organ with chambers to (c) "heart" as a locus of emotion and desire.

The teaching combines (c) and (a) to present the seat of emotion and desire in spatial terms, having rooms of a house. These rooms provide dwelling for either Torah or the bad *yetzer.*

The parable describes a king entering the rooms and living within, and the king is interpreted as Torah. Because Torah rules the heart, the bad *yetzer* cannot do so. Once again, a metaphor of government presumes the opposition of inside/outside. The inside is neither a city walled against a warrior nor a prison but an empty space. If the space is filled with Torah, then tradition governs and leaves no room for the bad *yetzer*. Through this exegesis of Yose ben Yoezer's maxim, the compilers of *Rabbi Nathan B* call upon the student to "drink with thirst" the words of Torah so that wayward desires cannot enter the heart.[65]

This way of understanding the relation between Torah and desire is implicit elsewhere in *Rabbi Nathan*. It may underlie calls to turn one's attention toward Torah when awaking late at night (A29,87; B34,75; B35,79), insuring that, in such a vulnerable moment, there is no space in the heart for sexual or other desires. Another example can be seen in a story of Rabbi Tzadok that appears in *Rabbi Nathan A* (which I analyze in detail below). When imprisoned by the Romans and sent a prostitute, he "placed his eyes upon the wall so that he would not see her, and he would sit and study all night" (A16,62). We see a graphic dramatization of filling one's heart with Torah to prevent the entry of sexual desire. He controls his focus of attention in order to stop himself from perceiving the woman.[66]

Divine Intervention

In *Rabbi Nathan,* most passages concerning *yetzer* appeal to Torah as the means of transformation. Divine presence is necessary, but it is mediated through the tradition. One teaching, however, states in very strong terms that life is a constant struggle with the bad *yetzer*. Only God's eschatological judgment can remove it. This motif is particularly important to consider when thinking about rabbinic ethics generally: while it is not prominent in *Rabbi Nathan,* it is developed at length elsewhere in rabbinic literature.[67]

The teaching is attributed to Rabbi Yose ha-Gelili, a contemporary of Rabbi Akiba, and parallel versions appear in *Rabbi Nathan* and the Babylonian Talmud. Let us first consider the talmudic account:

Rabbi Yose ha-Gelili says: For the righteous, the good *yetzer* rules them [*shophetan*], as it is written, "my heart is slain [*halal*][68] within me" (Ps. 109:22). For the wicked, the bad *yetzer* rules them, as it is written, "Transgression says to the wicked, 'In the midst of my heart there is no fear of

God before His eyes'" (Ps. 36:2). For those in the middle, both rule them, as it is written, "For He will stand on the right of the needy, to save from the judges of his soul" (Ps. 109:31). (*b. Ber.* 61b)

Rabbi Yose's statement presents the two inclinations as potential rulers. The good *yetzer* can rule a righteous man if he, in daily combat, "slays" the bad one (from Ps. 109:22). The wicked have only "transgression," and no fear of God, in their hearts (from Ps. 36:2). For those of average piety, two "judges" rule their souls (from Ps. 109:31).[69]

Anticipating the comparison with *Rabbi Nathan,* it is crucial to note that the talmudic passage presents a daily struggle by the individual with the bad *yetzer.* Rabbi Yose uses the verb *shophet* to describe the activity of the *yetzer.* This verb can mean "govern or rule," or more specifically "judge." Here the word carries the general meaning—the good or bad *yetzer* rules the person on an ongoing basis. Similar language and the same prooftexts appear in *Rabbi Nathan,* though Rabbi Yose describes not a daily struggle but God's eschatological judgment, and the word *shophet* denotes this judgment.

In *Rabbi Nathan,* Rabbi Yose's teaching appears among several midrashic developments of Genesis 6:3: "My spirit shall not abide [*yadon*] in humans forever." The collection gathers material that puns on the unusual term *yadon,* most often reading the word through variations of the root *d.y.n.*—"to judge" or "judgment."[70] Rabbi Yose interprets the verse as, "My spirit shall not judge man in this world." From this, he develops an account of the workings of divine compassion. According to Rabbi Yose, the reward for the righteous is God's destruction of the bad *yetzer* itself. For the purposes of reference, I divide the passage into three numbered sections:

(1) Rabbi Yose ha-Gelili says: Thus it says, "[my spirit] shall not judge [*lo' yadon*] [man in this world]." The Holy One, blessed be He, said, "I do not evaluate equally the bad *yetzer* in relation to the good *yetzer.*" When?—as long as their sentence is not signed. But once their sentence is signed, the two of them are evaluated equally in transgression.[71]

(2) He would say: For the righteous [*tzaddiqim*], He takes from them the bad *yetzer* and gives them the good *yetzer,* as it is written, "My heart is slain [*halal*][72] inside me" (Ps. 109:22). For the wicked, He takes from them the good *yetzer* and gives to them the bad *yetzer,* as it is written, "Transgression says to the wicked, 'In the midst of my heart, there is no fear of God before His eyes'" (Ps. 36:2). For those in the middle, he gives them both.

(3) As for one who comes to the bad *yetzer*, the bad *yetzer* judges him [*shopheṭo*]. One who comes to the good *yetzer*, the good *yetzer* judges him, as it is written, "For He will stand on the right of the needy, to save from the judges of his soul" (Ps. 109:31). (A32,93)[73]

Part (1) continues the discussion of divine judgment that appears in the preceding passages. Rabbi Yose interprets Genesis 6:3 to assert that God does not judge human beings in this world, only after their lifetimes—"my spirit shall not judge [*lo' yadon*] man in this world." When judgment comes, it is directed toward the good and the bad *yetzer* within a person. A difficult question is whether to interpret Rabbi Yose's *yetzer* as a hypostasized entity that can exist and be judged separately from the person, or whether the judgment concerns the actions generated by *yetzer* as an inner faculty.

Part (2) is almost the same as the parallel in the Talmud. However, in its new context the midrash has an entirely different meaning. Rather than addressing the daily struggle of a man against his *yetzer*, the passage describes God's action upon the person. In the next world, God will either slay the bad *yetzer* within or fill the heart with a double dose of it. Note also that the third prooftext, Psalm 109:31, no longer describes the status of "those in the middle." Rather, it has been reserved for another teaching.

In (3), a different midrash based on Psalm 109:31 interprets the plural "judges" not as the two inclinations within one "middle" person, but as two possibilities for eschatological judgment, one for the righteous and one for the wicked. The human faculties have been fully hypostasized as agents of divine decision. The righteous will have the benevolent good *yetzer* as their judge, and the wicked, the destructive counterpart. In this account, it appears that one's good and bad *yetzer* cannot be changed. However, one can "come to" *(ba' le-)* one or the other. The choice affects both whether one is righteous or wicked in this world, and the nature of divine judgment in the next.[74]

According to Rabbi Yose, then, students of the sages must struggle all their lives with the impulses of the bad *yetzer*, with no hope of resolution until the time of judgment. Torah is not sufficient to discipline, reform, conquer, or govern their transgressive impulses. People must do the best they can with what they have, negotiating their inclinations. Change will occur through God's action as reward for the righteous and punishment for the wicked. If the student succeeds in aligning himself with his good *yetzer*, God will reward him with a fully righteous self. If not, God will act directly upon his heart and leave him fully wicked.

Torah and the Tested Sage

What happens when a rabbi shapes his heart and *yetzer* through rabbinic tradition? One answer to this question appears in a series of sage stories compiled in *Rabbi Nathan A* (but they do not appear in version B). Each of these accounts presents a "test" of the sage in which he is threatened or tempted. In passing the test, he shows himself to be a man who has deeply internalized the discourse of Torah such that he can draw upon it when facing his fears and desires.[75] The greatest of these sages— Rabbi Akiba and Rabbi Eliezer ben Hyrcanus—show that they have fully overcome the inner division figured through the good and bad *yetzer*. In both cases, their most basic desires are channeled through the tradition, and they show no signs of an impulse toward transgression.

These stories appear in the extended discussion of *yetzer* in chapter 16 of *Rabbi Nathan A*. They follow upon the passage, discussed above, that depicts ethical transformation as a coup. It culminates in the verse, "From the prison house [*beyt hasurim*] he comes to rule" (Eccles. 4:14). The commentators then interpret this verse through four narratives of sages who are either imprisoned or under threat. The first three of these stories present tests of exemplary male figures. Each one is subjugated to powerful non-Jews, yet at the same time each is offered the possibility of sexual intercourse: they are both under threat and sexually tempted.[76] Gender and power are intertwined in complex ways, and the key point is that in all three cases, the hero withstands both the threat and the temptation. The verse "from the prison house he comes to rule" applies in two respects. The good *yetzer* "rules" the body, with its desires and fears, and the man comes to "rule" the situation through his self-control. The words of Torah are central to this governance.

Joseph the Righteous

The first story centers upon the biblical figure of Joseph and his encounter with Potiphar's wife.[77] In the account of Genesis, after she says, "Lie with me," Joseph gives reasons to refuse. First he lists the good things that Potiphar has done for him, and then he says, "How can I do this most wicked thing, and sin against the Lord" (Gen. 39:7–9). Why does Joseph shift attention, mid verse, from Potiphar to God? The commentators open up a literary space in the middle of Joseph's deliberation and insert an answer:

There are those who say: This is Joseph the Righteous.[78] When that wicked woman came, she would make him suffer with her words. She would say to him, "I will confine you in the prison house [*beyt ha-'asurin*]."

He said to her, "The Lord frees the imprisoned" (Ps. 146:7).

She said, "I will put out your eyes."

He said, "The Lord opens the eyes of the blind" (Ps. 146:8).

She said, "I will make you double over."

He said, "The Lord straightens up the bent" (Ps. 146:8).

She said, "I will make you wicked."

He said, "The Lord loves righteous men" (Ps. 146:8).

She said, "I will make you an Aramean."

He said, "The Lord protects the aliens" (Ps. 146:9).

Until he said, "How can I do this most wicked thing [and sin against the Lord]" (Gen. 39:9). (A16,63)

The narrative focuses upon and intensifies the power relations implicit in the demand of Potiphar's wife. In this rabbinic account she explicitly asserts the ability to impose force, including imprisonment (a motif that appears both in the story of Genesis and in the verse from Ecclesiastes), mutilation, and exile.[79] Joseph responds by citing words of the Written Torah, which offers a reply to each of her threats. Through drawing upon his internalized traditional discourse, he does not give into lust or fear but rather reinforces his courage and announces the immanence of divine power. Joseph is "Righteous" because his trust in God through Torah is absolute, so he does not "sin against the Lord."[80] In more analytic terms, the creators of the story interpret Psalm 146 through a narrative that frames verses 7–9 as ready-made answers for Joseph in this exchange. These verses, as uttered by Joseph, provide the bridge in the narrative between Joseph's statement of loyalty to Potiphar (Gen. 39:8–9a), and his worry concerning transgression against God (Gen. 39:9b).

James Kugel, in his extensive treatment of Joseph and Potiphar's wife in exegetical sources, presents this passage from *Rabbi Nathan* as distinct because prison appears as a threat and because it "interweaves different verses of Ps. 146." This Psalm does appear, however, in a narrative depicting Potiphar's wife threatening Joseph preserved in *Genesis Rabbah.* The setting is not when she says, "Lie with me," but later when he is prison. She taunts and threatens him, and Joseph responds by quoting Psalm 146:7–8.[81] The idiosyncratic feature of the story in *Rabbi Nathan,* then, is the combination of three elements that appear separately in other rabbinic sources: the test of his ability to control his sexual desire, the threat of prison, and Psalm 146. Each of these elements, moreover, is absolutely central to the broader themes of the unit: he overcomes sexual temptation and fear of prison through ruling himself ("from the prison house he comes to rule") by way of the psalm and more generally the words of Torah.

The story of Joseph is only the first of four narratives. Perhaps, in rabbinic eyes, he hesitates too long before affirming that he will not "sin against the Lord," for he is the lowest figure in a hierarchy of four sages. The rabbinic commentators tell the reader, "Do not be astonished at Joseph, for Rabbi Tzadok was the great one of the generation." The following story begins, "Do not be astonished at Rabbi Tzadok, for Rabbi Akiba was greater than he." And the following, "Do not be astonished at Rabbi Akiba, for thus Rabbi Eliezer the Great was greater then he." The editors thus set out each sage as being greater than the previous in "ruling" his bad *yetzer*.

Rabbi Tzadok and Rabbi Akiba

These narratives present rabbinic sages—Rabbi Tzadok and Rabbi Akiba—whose control of sexual desire is tested while they are among Romans. The two stories have the same structure: (1) opening (2) capture and temptation (3) display of self-control (4) complaint by the rejected women (5) question from a powerful Roman, and (6) explanation by the sage. I present them in parallel:

(Tz1) Do not be astonished at Joseph the Righteous, for Rabbi Tzadok was the great one of the generation.[82]

(Ak1) Do not be astonished at Rabbi Tzadok, for Rabbi Akiba was greater than he.

(Tz2) When he was taken captive [to Rome],[83] a matron took him and sent him a beautiful female slave.

(Ak2) When he went to Rome, they slandered him[84] before a general, who sent him two beautiful women. They were bathed, anointed, and adorned like brides. They fell over him all night: one saying, "Come to me," and the other saying, "Come to me."

(Tz3) When he saw her, he placed his eyes on the wall so that he would not see her, and he would sit and study[85] all night.

(Ak3) [Rabbi Akiba] would sit between them, spit, and not turn to them.

(Tz4) In the morning, she asked for a reception with her mistress and said, "Death is better for me than if you give me to that man."

(Ak4) They asked for a reception with the general and said, "Death is better for us than if you give us to that man."

(Tz5) She sent for him and said, "Why did you not do with this woman as men do?"

(Ak5) [The general] sent for him and said, "Why did you not do with these women as men do with women? Are they not beautiful? Are they not children of Adam like you? Did not the one who created you create them?"

(Tz6) He said to her, "What would I do? I am from the high priesthood, and from a great family. I said to myself, 'Perhaps I will have intercourse with her and multiply the bastards in Israel.'" When she heard his words, she commanded that he be let go in great honor (A16,63).

(Ak6) [Rabbi Akiba] said to him, "What could I do? Their odor came over me from the meat of carrion, torn animals, and creeping things" (A16,63).[86]

As in the story of Joseph, political subordination and sexual temptation are intertwined. The rabbis are either in prison (Tz2) or threatened with it (Ak2). Both are offered women for a night, and their sexual control is astonishing to the Romans (Tz4–5, Ak4–5), but it earns honor (Tz6). In refusing to join physically with the Roman women, or acting "as men do," the rabbis maintain cultural separation (Tz6, Ak6). The stories present an ambivalent picture of rabbinic relations with the Roman Empire. Rabbi Akiba, for example, has traveled a long distance from his home in the eastern Mediterranean, meeting and seeming to have no real conflict with a high-ranking Roman figure. However, we see signs of danger, and in the end, his traditionally formed character resists conformity to Roman society.

If considered apart from the broader literary context, the main focus of the stories is probably the separation and nonconformity. David Stern has argued that such narratives represent rabbinic versions of the Hellenistic "love disaster" story—a type that was widespread in the Greco-Roman world, with origins as early as Homer. The narratives "involve a character who is irresistibly attractive, not necessarily to everyone in the world but inevitably so to the one person who should not be attracted to her; and for that person, the attraction is always disastrous." Such narratives frequently have "a public, national dimension: the erotic ordeal, for example, frequently involves an act of national treason or betrayal." This ordeal is "the primary mode of contact through which their leading characters engage the larger world, a world that is explicitly represented as sexually charged and dangerous." These rabbinic love-disaster narratives, then, center upon a rabbinic sage who faces such an "erotic ordeal." They present Roman society "through the figure of a threatening, seductive gentile female."[87] In these particular stories, Roman women mediate relations between men, and their single point of strength is their aspiration to succeed as objects of male passion ("Death is better for us than if you give us to that man"). The sages resist both the threat and the seduction, asserting power through rejecting the women even though the ultimate sources of peril are actually other, powerful Romans.

Both stories culminate in a confrontation between the rabbi and the powerful Roman in which the sage has to explain his reasons for maintaining sexual and cultural separation. Rabbi Tzadok focuses on the possibility of impregnation, which would result in a "bastard" (Tz6).[88] The general poses to Rabbi Akiba difficult questions concerning Jewish separation, appealing to universalist ideals. In late ancient Rome, these queries resonate with a long history of anti-Jewish rhetoric. Specifically, allegations that Jews were xenophobic went back to the third century BCE or earlier.[89] Rabbi Akiba, like Rabbi Tzadok, asserts separation based on tradition. He does not disagree with the general's claims concerning creation, "Are they not children of Adam like you? Did not the one who created you create them?" Rather, his reply implies that tradition defines identity: the women's lack of dietary observance trumps their status as created human beings.[90]

In the context of the commentary upon "from the prison house he comes to rule," we should focus not only on the cultural separation but also on the sages' control of fear and desire. For Rabbi Tzadok, Torah furnishes the direct means through which he eludes his own sexual desire. He fills his heart and mind with the words of tradition, studying all night (perhaps reciting passages from memory) and avoiding visual apprehension of the women. Through this exercise, he makes it through the night chaste. Why is Rabbi Akiba greater than Rabbi Tzadok? He is a free man, though at risk of slander, while Rabbi Tzadok is imprisoned. Rabbi Akiba receives two beautiful "women" who are outfitted as brides, while Rabbi Tzadok is sent a single slave. Rabbi Akiba has greater freedom, greater risk to his name, and at least twice as much temptation. However, he does not need to engage in spiritual work to prevent being overcome by sexual desire. In contrast with Rabbi Tzadok, his night is not one of struggle. Rabbi Akiba has no desire for the women at all. He just spits (Ak3).

Rabbi Akiba perceives the women not as objects of sexual desire, but solely as people who violate rabbinic ideals for dietary restriction. His sense of their "odor"—from three paradigmatic types of impure flesh—overwhelms him, even though the women were bathed, anointed, and adorned. There are several rabbinic sources, particularly in the Babylonian Talmud, that compare women to food, but here it is not fully clear what is being portrayed. Perhaps he smells the rabbinically unclean food on their breath. Perhaps, in a more general sense, their bodies are fundamentally odious to him because of what they have consumed.[91] Whatever the case, a crucial point is that the sage does not *overcome* sexual desire; rather, he does not have any. He is not *obeying* a law; rather, his fundamental desires are shaped through legal categories such that he experiences no temptation toward transgression.[92] We can see this focus on character both in the narrative voice ("[Rabbi Akiba] would sit between them, spit, and not turn to them") and in the rabbi's response to the general ("What could I do? Their odor came over me.").[93] This sage appears as a being entirely permeated by his traditional discourse. He has fully internalized Torah, such that even his most fundamental instincts are channeled through its categories, and he has no desire for these "brides." In the language of virtue ethics, Rabbi Tzadok is self-controlled or continent, able to control his wayward desires, while Rabbi Akiba has tempered his impulses so that he is fully virtuous, having no inner conflict with his ideals.[94]

Rabbi Eliezer ben Hyrcanus

Rabbi Akiba may appear to represent the highest degree that one can internalize the Torah. He reveals no signs of spontaneous sexual desire, even when surrounded by two enticing women for a night. The editors of *Rabbi Nathan,* however, do not present him as the peak of ethical transformation. Rather, the ultimate account in the exegesis of "from the prison house he came to rule" is the elder Rabbi Eliezer ben Hyrcanus. This story has a parallel and probably earlier version in the Palestinian Talmud.[95] Comparison with this talmudic story will help clarify the distinct interests of *Rabbi Nathan.*

In the Palestinian Talmud, the literary context is a legal debate concerning the status of a girl who is betrothed, in which Rabbi Eliezer takes the strong stand that the action of a girl who is a minor is not legally valid.[96] The compilers then present a story attributed to Rabbi Abbahu, in which Rabbi Eliezer exemplifies his own policy:

> Rabbi Abbahu said: A story of the mother[97] of Rabbi 'Liezer, who would pressure him to marry the daughter of his sister. He would say to her, "My daughter, go and marry! My daughter, go and marry," until she said to him, "I am your maidservant, to wash the feet of the servants of my lord." Despite this, he wed her but did not touch her [*hikkirah*] until she showed two hairs. (*y. Yeb.* 13:2, 13c)[98]

Rabbi Eliezer is pressured by his mother to marry his underage niece, but he encourages the girl to marry someone else (note, though, that he does not attempt to find a husband for her himself). In response, she paraphrases Abigail's supplication to David, "Your handmaid is a maidservant, to wash the feet of the servants of my lord" (1 Sam. 25:41).[99] The rabbi responds with a compromise. He fulfills the wishes of his mother and niece by marrying, but he does not acknowledge (*hikkir*) the marriage until she reaches the age of puberty (which is marked by "two hairs").

The story in the Palestinian Talmud presents only a brief verbal exchange between Rabbi Eliezer and his niece, and it says nothing of the sage's desires. The version in *Rabbi Nathan,* in contrast, highlights three issues: the intimacy between himself and his niece, their difference in age, and the sexual act of consummating their marriage:

> Do not be astonished at Rabbi Akiba, for Rabbi Eliezer the Great[100] was greater than he. He raised his sister's daughter for thirteen years, [and she slept] with him in a bed until the signs of puberty came to her. He said, "Go and marry yourself to a man." She said, "Am I not your handmaid, a maidservant to wash the feet of your students?" He said, "My daughter, I have already grown old. Go and be married to a young man who is like you." She said, "No. Thus I said before you, is not your handmaid a maidservant to wash the feet of your students?" When he heard her words, he got her permission to betroth her, and he had intercourse with her. (A16,63)[101]

This version highlights the intimacy between Rabbi Eliezer and his niece by telling that they slept in the same bed before she showed the signs of puberty. Rabbi Eliezer's mother is not part of the story—the question of marriage is just between the sage and his niece. The niece's age is not a legal concern. She reaches puberty before she makes her declaration to her uncle, so her act would be valid, even according to Rabbi Eliezer's legal standards. Instead, the story focuses upon appropriateness and propriety. Rabbi Eliezer's objection is simply, "I have already grown old. Go and be married to a young man who is like you." Finally, the sexual dimension is emphasized. Rather then employing the legal language of "recognition," as the Palestinian Talmud does, here the story culminates by telling of their intercourse.[102]

How, then, is Rabbi Eliezer an exemplar of "from the prison house he comes to rule," and in what sense is he greater than Rabbi Akiba? Given the literary context of "test" stories, the account appears to presume the sexual attraction of an older man ("I have already grown old") toward a young girl. It upholds Rabbi Eliezer for not acting on such attraction. The details in this story concerning intimacy and sex support this point. Through this portrayal of Rabbi Eliezer, rabbis admit having sexual desire for pubescent girls, but also they uphold the ideal that a truly refined man does not have such an impulse.

But what exactly is Rabbi Eliezer's test? Are we to presume it is his restraint while sleeping in bed with his niece? Or is the key point his initial refusal to marry her, even without legal obstacle? These questions are not answered explicitly. The story does not focus on one particular point in the interaction, one moment in which Rabbi Eliezer shows his control of his bad *yetzer*. In contrast with Joseph, Rabbi Tzadok, and Rabbi Akiba, Rabbi Eliezer displays control of sexual desire both night after night and in a momentous moment. Moreover, he does so in relation to a Jewish woman, not a Roman. This display of character, in the eyes of the rabbinic editor, is the greatest of all.

For today's readers (as I have found in classrooms and conferences), this story is an odd culmination to a rabbinic hierarchy of virtue. After all, Rabbi Eliezer winds up as an older man who has intercourse with a thirteen-year-old girl. One interpretation is that he actually does not represent the ideal of a man who is fully governed by his good *yetzer*. Rather, in marrying his niece, he succumbed to his bad *yetzer*. Such a reading raises two important questions. The first concerns our scholarly hermeneutics. Given the hierarchy of sages presented by these editors—marked by the expression, "Do not be astonished at X, for thus Y was greater"—should we presume a unified account and clear pinnacle, or is it possible that the top of the hierarchy is a flawed character who reveals the limits of the sage?

The second question concerns the dynamic of *yetzer*—how deeply are the "good" and "bad" impulses tied to the rabbinic law? That is, do rabbis characterize the bad *yetzer* only in terms of those impulses that lead one to transgress the law, while the good *yetzer* is the ability to act in accord with it? If this is the case, then there is no problem with Rabbi Eliezer marrying his niece and having intercourse if she is of legal age—this would be fully in accord with the good *yetzer*, not the bad. Also, we should remember that rabbinic literature has many discussions of marriage between men and young girls, and that in Roman late antiquity such practices were not out of the ordinary. However, one may posit other norms—as evident in Rabbi Eliezer's own hesitation to marry her because of his age—and argue that rabbinic culture has extralegal reasons to see Rabbi Eliezer as less than fully virtuous.[103]

My leaning on these questions is toward the view that, in these passages, the *yetzer* is very much tied to the law, Rabbi Eliezer is presented as an exemplar, and the discomfort that contemporary readers have with the text reveals differences between modern and late ancient ethical outlooks. However, the evidence is not unequivocal.[104]

The four sage stories, then, set out a hierarchy of male figures, all of whom represent ideals of self-control. This hierarchy is clearly marked by the editors, and while its criteria are not stated explicitly, the ranking appears to be based upon two factors. First, the nature of the test differs in the four stories. The compilers are particularly concerned with sages being tempted by those who are powerless and proximate (both physically and ethnically). All of the tests portray sexual temptation, but the degree of threat by a powerful figure diminishes as the ranking on the hierarchy increases: Potiphar's wife makes a large number of significant threats against Joseph, including prison and physical punishment, Rabbi Tzadok is in prison but treated well, Rabbi Akiba is slandered but not in prison, and Rabbi Eliezer has no threat whatsoever. At the same time, the greater sages have more intimate relations with the women: while Joseph encounters Potiphar's wife, Rabbi Tzadok faces one slave woman, Rabbi Akiba spends the night with two women falling over him, and Rabbi Eliezer sleeps night after night in bed with his niece. The contrast between the least and greatest tests is striking: Potiphar's wife, a powerful foreign woman who attempts to seduce and to threaten, presents less of a test than a Jewish child sleeping at the side of a sage.

The second factor in the hierarchy of stories is the hero's response. All of the figures resist both the dangers and temptations, but the lesser ones struggle to do so, while the greatest exhibit no signs of effort or internal struggle. Joseph enters into dialogue with Potiphar's wife, hesitating and rationalizing about why he does not lie with her. Rabbi Tzadok does not negotiate but has to look at a wall and recite Torah. He controls his desires but is vulnerable, and the story implies that if he looked at the women or thought about anything but Torah, he would be overcome. Rabbi Akiba, by contrast, can look at the women all he wants. They touch and fall over him, but he is disgusted by their very scent. Finally, Rabbi Eliezer shows the control that Rabbi Akiba does, not in a unique situation but rather every night in his own bed.[105]

2c   Rabbinic Tradition

Conclusion

My central argument concerning tradition and rabbinic
ethics is that, according to the prescriptions of *Rabbi Nathan,* a rabbinic
student becomes a sage through a process of subordination to, and internalization of, the Torah. Now, after a detailed study of the text, I can specify
the dynamics of this elected subjection. Let us begin with internalization.

As I discussed in the introduction, the category "internalization" itself
turns on a trope of space: that which is outside is brought inside. At a most
general level, the rabbinic teachings portray internalization in that the traditional discourse becomes part of the self. The good *yetzer,* an inner faculty, speaks verses of the Bible to the larger self. Joseph quotes the Written
Torah in a time of fear, Rabbi Tzadok recites Oral Torah to keep himself
from arousal, and Rabbi Akiba encounters seductive women solely in terms
of legal categories. In all of these cases, the language of Torah has become a
central part of the self, interacting with and controlling other impulses.

This interaction and control is detailed through many tropes that portray the dynamics of Torah and the self. In this material, the spatial relations vary. Sometimes Torah gains control through being "inside," as in
Ben Zoma's image of a warrior conquering a city or that of a king entering
a room. In other cases, the power of Torah is figured as "outside" the self—
a goad that prods, a yoke around the neck, iron that wears away flesh, fire
that heats up metal. The most complex image is the good *yetzer* being a
king who must escape prison to rule the body. The good *yetzer* is a part of
the self, but it is confined in some deep location where it is ineffective and
must flee that realm in order to govern. While the category of internalization captures the general dynamic of the self constituting itself as a subject
through a discourse that originates elsewhere, we have to give a nuance to
the spatial imagery. Within the general category of "internalization," there
are multiple visions of internal and external control. (A further complexity
concerning rabbinic tropes is that they do not have fixed referents. A

"king" could be the bad *yetzer,* the good *yetzer,* or the Torah. In part 3 I discuss the most common use of the royal trope—God is a king.)

How does the self internalize the tradition? *Rabbi Nathan* presents this process as centering on relations of subordination. These relations are most clear in the metaphors of development. The student places himself before the Torah as an animal under a yoke or before a goad, as flesh worn away by iron, or as metal shaped in fire by a smith. In each case, the self enters a relationship in which it is formed by an external, powerful force. Rabbi Simeon ben Yohai's figure of agricultural cultivation could imply a different orientation—one of self-tending and care—but he employs the image to argue that humans do not have the ethical fertility for such a process.[1]

Metaphors of conquest and governance portray a more complex dynamic of subordination. They resonate with, and may be drawn from, Hellenistic ideals of an elite man governing himself as he would a community.[2] In *Rabbi Nathan* the ruling agent is the tradition, as internalized by the rabbi. This move is most explicit in the account of Torah entering the space of the heart, for clearly the student's inner desires become subjects of Torah as king. The maxim of Ben Zoma concerning the mighty man does not, in its shortest form, make mention of Torah. However, the exegesis in *Rabbi Nathan* transforms his imagery into a teaching that Torah study enables internal conquest. The most complex image is again the escape and coup by the good *yetzer.* What does it mean to say that the good *yetzer* is king of the self? If we understand the good *yetzer* to be an internal receptor of Torah, which is evident elsewhere in *Rabbi Nathan* (in fact, in the preceding passage), then we again see the tradition governing the self. Finally, Rabbi Yose's account of divine judgment portrays a very different image of subordination—to God as judge—which I explore at length below.

Comparative and Theoretical Points

Both groups of tropes inspire possibilities for comparative study. Metaphors of conflict and government probably enter rabbinic thought by diffusion from Greek and Hellenistic thought. This initial observation of similarity and borrowing can be developed through an examination of difference. In the rabbinic case, the conquering element is not reason or another inborn part of the self but Torah or an internal receptor of it. Another point of comparison could be the status of the body. Rabbinic teachings show no consistent evaluation of the body as intrinsically good or bad. In one passage the bad *yetzer* initially governs the body; in another the bad *yetzer* aims to destroy it; and in others, the body appears to indicate or display the degree of one's cultivation. A well-formed sage, such as Rabbi Akiba, responds in immediate somatic ways to his surroundings and shows only disgust, not arousal, when facing temptations deemed forbidden by his tradition.[3]

In addition to this realm of comparison, rabbinic metaphors of development are provocatively similar to those employed by early Confucians to describe the dynamics of their tradition. Similarity does not necessarily imply cultural contiguity. With vast historical and geographical separation, no evidence of cultural contact, and very different theological/metaphysical outlooks, these two groups share certain views concerning self-transformation. One hypothesis is that certain constellations of features—such as scholasticism, a strong orientation toward a sage and a tradition, and maybe a pessimistic view of human nature—lend themselves to certain tropic configurations, but this would have to be investigated much further. Differences between the ethics of the two groups would also be valuable to explore, particularly concerning the relation between their relatively similar views concerning the sage and tradition and their very different views at the level of theology or metaphysics.[4]

At a theoretical level, the category of "tradition" is now a central one in virtue ethics. A highly sophisticated and influential account is offered by MacIntyre. He argues that one cultivates virtues through practices as framed by narratives. Tradition provides the social and conceptual grounding for this process, setting out appropriate practices as well as narratives that frame and uphold those practices. Tradition, then, is a "moral starting point," and it is also an "inheritance" that is received from the past. His well-known definition is, "A living tradition then is an historically extended, socially embodied argument, and an argument precisely in part about the goods which constitute that tradition." A key element in sustaining traditions is "the exercise or lack of exercise of the relevant virtues." In later works, he provides extensive analyses of specific traditions and their dynamics, focusing upon the "rationality" of traditions as they face both internal tensions and confrontations with rivals.[5]

MacIntyre's definition captures important features of the rabbinic Torah, and it is a central element in my opening formulation of tradition. However, study of *Rabbi Nathan* draws attention to other ways that tradition can play a role in ethical transformation. First, MacIntyre emphasizes argumentation that is distinctly philosophical. The rabbinic tradition, by contrast, is to a large degree generated through intellectual processes that are much more associative and imaginative than philosophical. It centers upon midrash, the exegesis of a set of writings that are considered divinely given and authorized. Notions of revelation, canon, exegesis, and intertextuality are thus necessary for understanding the modes of reasoning that underlie rabbinic ethics.[6]

Second, Torah provides a foundation for rabbinic ethical thinking, but rabbis also see it as having a direct impact upon the person. Through tropes of development and governance, rabbis portray tradition as having an immediate role in self-formation. MacIntyre does not consider anything like this. Third, the compilers of *Rabbi Nathan* were well aware that tradition is an ambivalent phenomenon that can incite transgression, but this complexity has not made its way into contemporary ethical theory. Finally, MacIntyre downplays the role of authority in the social functioning of tradition. A key element in rabbinic comportment toward tradition is subordination to the discourse. As I discussed above in the introduction, MacIntyre and others have noted the significance of subordination for character formation, but generally virtue ethicists have not addressed it fully.[7]

MacIntyre's account of tradition remains an extremely valuable starting point for analysis. Consideration of the rabbinic case reveals its limitations for comparative study and ways that it can be developed. Moreover, the traditions that MacIntyre studies may exhibit features similar to the rabbis' Torah that he himself does not identify. MacIntyre's own analyses of, say, medieval Christian scholasticism could be rethought with new attention to the dynamics of exegesis, the immediate impact of tradition upon the self, the ways that tradition may spur as well as remedy transgression, and the roles of authority and subordination in forming ideal selves.

Rabbinic Theology

Rabbinic sages assert that divine activity is manifest in the world, appearing by way of measured, though not necessitated, response to what humans are and do. Their understandings of human action, as well as their ideals for the motivations that generate actions, center upon their relation with God. One cannot study rabbinic ethics, then, without studying rabbinic theology. Contemporary historical and philosophical accounts of ethics, however, do not give us adequate conceptual tools for analyzing this dimension of rabbinic thought.[1] They have tended to downplay the theological elements of past outlooks, perhaps because of the great differences between ancient theologies and a modern or postmodern outlook. My challenge, then, is to find ways within a scholarly framework to describe this foreign worldview.

When discussing rabbinic "theology," I employ the word in its most literal sense—as discourse about God—and not in ways that imply systematic thought influenced by philosophical methods. Rabbinic theology centers upon concrete images that are often derived through exegesis. The material is diverse, sometimes emphasizing God's mercy and compassion, sometimes God's justice, sometimes God's saving power, sometimes God's mysterious absence. Often rabbis portray God in anthropomorphic terms. In *Rabbi Nathan* God appears as a warrior fighting both supernatural creatures and the political enemies of Israel, as a mourner weeping over the nation's state of exile, and as a lover meeting the sage with a kiss.[2] The theological motifs that give most significance to human activity, and which are most prominent in *Rabbi Nathan,* are those that center on God's justice, or divine reward and punishment *(śakhar va'onesh).* Sages portray divine evaluation of and response to human beings through predicating God as a king and judge decreeing judgment, an employer giving payment for service, or a storekeeper selling goods on credit.[3]

The modern or postmodern reader likely will have difficulty finding sympathy for a theology heavily focused upon justice. Such an outlook presumes a stern deity and human self-interest (fear of punishment and desire for reward). Moreover, it can easily legitimate inequality and blame victims of oppression and disaster, for one can assert that those who are well-off deserve their status as divine payment and that those who suffer are being punished. All of these criticisms are appropriate, though as we will see, many are anticipated and addressed within the rabbinic sources themselves.

It is perhaps best to approach rabbinic notions of reward and punishment as implying a broad trope of order[4]: an interrelated set of images and concepts that envision a world in which God's presence insures a stable and just accounting. Regardless of appearances to the contrary, ultimately the good are rewarded and the bad punished. Attempts to construct through theology or ontology an ordered and just world appear in many religious traditions—a notable example is the widespread notion of karma in South and Southeast Asia.[5] One of the great distinguishing features of modernity is the break with ideals of cosmic or divine justice.[6] However, fragments or survivals of such outlooks appear in the contemporary world. In English, examples include the expression, "What did I do to deserve this?" (implying that some wrong action in the past is the cause of misfortune in the present) or "They will get what is coming to them!" (asserting that the universe will work to punish someone in the future for a wrong done now).

Theologies of reward and punishment are remarkable for the immense respect they imply for human activity. We see a highly developed sense of causality. Human action occurs and then reverberates through divine accounting, affecting the future self, other individuals, the community, and sometimes the entire cosmos. When sages wish to highlight the significance of the human acting before God, they focus on God's justice. When they want to highlight God as the center of meaningful action, then they draw upon other motifs. In this part of the book, I examine three interrelated questions: How does *Rabbi Nathan* conceptualize God's response to human action? What is the nature of a human action before God? How does *Rabbi Nathan* instruct the rabbinic subject to comport himself before God?[7]

A brief textual note is necessary before moving to the analyses. I stated in chapter 1a that I take the printed edition of *Rabbi Nathan A* as my base text, though I aim to account for all variants in the sources for *Rabbi Nathan* as well as *The Fathers*. In my chapter on rabbinic tradition, this was less difficult, for *Rabbi Nathan A* generally has a richer collection of material on Torah than *Rabbi Nathan B*. With regard to reward and punishment, however, much of the most interesting material appears only in manuscripts of *Rabbi Nathan A* or in *Rabbi Nathan B*. Though I still base my central arguments on the printed edition of *Rabbi Nathan A,* in this chapter I give much more attention to passages that appear in the other sources, and I note when I am doing so.[8]

3a   Divine Reward and Punishment

A sage, anonymous in *Rabbi Nathan A*, expresses in a concise epigram the fundamental tropes of divine reward and punishment:

> He would say,
> All [*ha-kol*] is given on pledge.
> A net is cast[1] over all that live [*kol ha-ḥayyim*].
> The store is open.
> The storekeeper sells on credit.
> The ledger is open.
> The judge sits.
> The collectors continue to collect payment from the person—
>   always, every day [*bekhol yom*], whether he knows or not.
>   (A39,116–17; B44,123; *Fathers* 3:16)[2]

This passage employs two powerful metaphors to describe God: a storekeeper with a ledger and a judge in charge of collectors. God sells goods on credit, implying that physical and material benefits come with an account, and humans have to pay for them through right action. For those in debt, God acts as a judge who decrees judgment and sends out collectors to mete out punishment. The repeated use of the word "all" *(kol)* emphasizes the encompassing nature of God's presence—all is given on pledge *(ha-kol)*, this process concerns all that live *(kol ha-ḥayyim),* and the collectors come every day *(bekhol yom).*

In more general terms, this passage combines two sets of tropes in describing God's action—those of law and those of monetary exchange—which I examine in detail. I turn first to the legal imagery.

Legal Tropes

The sages of *Rabbi Nathan* often employ the metaphor of a king to convey their sense of divine power and governance. Royal tropes have a long history in biblical and later Jewish theology, and God's sovereignty is developed through images that include royal qualities and trappings (such as a throne), a court, and involvement in affairs of the kingdom. Often the metaphor of a king overlaps with that of a judge—one of God's roles as a king is to be a fair and just judge—though in many cases the two images appear independently.[3]

Perhaps the most powerful account of divine power and judgment in *Rabbi Nathan* appears in a narrative about the legendary founder of rabbinic Judaism, Rabban Yohanan ben Zakkai. At the moment of his death, the great sage is in tears.[4] When asked by his students why he cries, he draws an analogy between a human king and God, the divine king:

> If I were going to greet a king of flesh and blood—if he would become angry with me, his anger is only in this world. If he would chastise me, his chastisement is only in this world.[5] If he would kill me, his death penalty is only in this world. Not only that, but I could persuade him with words or bribe him with money. But, I am going to meet none but the King of the kings of kings, the Holy One, blessed be He. If He becomes angry with me, His anger is in this world and in the world to come. I cannot persuade Him with words or bribe Him with money. He has two paths, one to the Garden of Eden and one to Gehenna. I do not know if He will sentence me to Gehenna, or if He will have me enter the Garden of Eden. About Him Scripture says, "Before Him shall kneel all that go down to dust" (Ps. 22:30). (A25,79)[6]

Divine power (God is a king) is manifest through divine judgment (God is a judge).[7] Rabban Yohanan ben Zakkai's theological teaching turns on the metaphoric tension in the predication "God is a king" and highlights two aspects of a subject's interaction with a ruler. God can give a sentence, including a death penalty, as a human judge would do. The person standing before God, in turn, can try persuasion or bribery as one might with a judge.[8] Given this similarity, the sage emphasizes a difference: the immensity of divine judgment at death. God's punishment is not only in this world but also in the world to come.

In addition, God is a perfect judge, with whom persuasion and bribes are futile. This point is developed in other teachings as well. In *Rabbi Nathan B,* an epigram in the name of Rabbi Eliezer, son of Rabbi Eleazar ha-Kappar,[9] states:

> Those who are created are to die, and those who are dead are to be brought to life, and those who are brought to life are to be judged—to know and make known that He is a witness and the one who knows and in the future will judge. There is, in His presence, neither iniquity, nor

forgetfulness, nor favoring of persons, nor taking of bribes. (B34,76–77; also *Fathers* 4:22)

This maxim focuses specifically upon judgment after the resurrection of the dead. God fulfills more than one role in the legal process, being both a witness and a judge. The sage asserts that God is perfectly just and shows no favoritism, lapse of memory, or susceptibility to bribery.[10]

In other passages, the metaphor "God is a judge" is developed through terms that have Greek etymologies—"court" *(sanhedrin* from Greek *synedrion), "defender" or "advocate" *(senigur* from Greek *synēgoros),* and "accuser" *(qaṭeygur* from Greek *katēgoros).*[11] These figures are interpreted into biblical accounts. For example, in a discussion of Noah, the flood, and divine justice, Rabbi Yehudah the Patriarch states that God sentenced Noah's generation because there was no judicial order on earth. His comments are based upon a midrash to Genesis 6:3—"My spirit shall not abide [*yadon*] in humans forever"—in which he interprets the *yadon* as referring to judgment *(d.y.n.):*

> Rabbi said: Thus it says, "shall not judge [*yadon*]." The Holy One, blessed be He, said, "If they do not establish a court [*sanhedrin*] on earth, I will establish a court [*sanhedrin*] for them on high." (A33,93)[12]

This short comment describes the origin of divine justice: God created the heavenly court as a response to the lack of such an institution on earth.[13]

The legal dualism of a defending attorney *(senigur)* and a prosecutor *(qaṭeygur)* appears in *Rabbi Nathan B* and *The Fathers* in an epigram that has no explicit exegetical features:

> Rabbi Eliezer ben Yaakov says: Anyone who fulfills a commandment acquires for himself a defending attorney [*senigur*], and anyone who does an act of transgression acquires for himself a prosecutor [*qaṭeygur*]. Repentance and good deeds are crowns[14] before retribution. (B35,80–81; *Fathers* 4:11)

The heavenly court of justice has advocates for and against the defendant. Each side can be strengthened by human action—observance strengthens the advocacy and transgression adds to the prosecution.[15]

In *Rabbi Nathan A,* we do not see this pairing, but the figure of the prosecutor appears in an account of Moses's ascent on high to receive the tablets of the covenant. Developing the common rabbinic motif that the ministering angels oppose Moses, the compilers present a rationalized challenge in the form of a legal accusation:

> At that time, the ministering angels presented an accusation [*qosherin qaṭeygur*] against Moses: Master of the Universe, "What is man that You are mindful of him, the child of Adam that You take notice of him. You have made him a little less than divine and crowned him with glory and majesty. You placed him as ruler over the works of your hands. You set all under his feet: sheep and oxen, all of them, and also the beasts of the fields, birds of the heavens, and fish of the sea" (Ps. 8:5). (A2,10)[16]

The angelic challenge is based on a psalm. In the biblical context, the psalmist writes as a human, expressing his humility while praising God. In the rabbinic rereading, these words are placed in the mouth of the angels, who ask: "What is" so great about humans such that they have a special status on earth, being nearly divine and ruling other creatures? The commentator frames this question using a legal term of accusation— *qaṭeygur*—portraying the angels as taking part in a heavenly court.

Interrelated legal tropes extend far beyond accounts of the heavenly realms. Much technical terminology employed in epigrams and exegesis is drawn from legal and judicial discourse.[17] Sometimes in *Rabbi Nathan,* these terms are used specifically for human, not theological activity. For example, maxims of the early-first-century BCE Yehudah ben Tabbai and Simeon ben Shetah are directed toward judges. The first cautions:

> Yehudah ben Tabbai says: Do not place yourself in the role of the chief justice ['*orekhey ha-dayyanin*].[18] When the litigants [*baʿaley ha-dinim*] stand before you, let them be in your eyes as guilty ones [*reshaʿim*]. When they leave your presence, let them be in your eyes as innocent ones [*zakkaʾim*], as soon as they accepted upon themselves the judgment [*ha-din*]. (A10,42; B20,22; *Fathers* 1:8)[19]

Several terms are derived from the Hebrew root meaning "to judge, judgment" *(d.y.n.):* "chief justice" *('orekhey ha-dayyanin),* "litigants" *(baʿaley ha-dinim),* and "judgment" *(ha-din).* We have already seen, though, that many other passages employ this root in a theological sense to describe divine judgment.[20] Similarly, the sage contrasts the "guilty" *(reshaʿim,* from the root *r.sh.ʿ.)* with the "innocent" *(zakkaʾim,* from the root *z.k.h.).*[21] The root *r.sh.ʿ.* often appears in *Rabbi Nathan* with a more general sense of "wicked." Often the binary opposite of "wicked" is "righteous" *(tzaddiq),* which itself is derived from a root for "just" or "justice" *(tz.d.q.).*[22] The root *z.k.h.,* moreover, is the basis of the common term *zekhut,* which denotes "merit" before God based on right action.[23]

A short passage that employs three of these terms appears as commentary to a maxim of Hillel, "If I am not for myself, who is for me?" As I discuss at length later in this chapter, the commentators of *Rabbi Nathan* interpret this maxim in terms of the accumulation of merit *(zekhut)* before God. One of the teachings interprets a verse from Ecclesiastes:

> Thus it says, "Yes, a living dog is better than a dead lion" (Eccles. 9:4). . . . Another opinion: "Yes, a living dog is better." This is the wicked one [*rasha'*] who endures in this world. If he repents, The Holy One, blessed be He, receives it. But a righteous one [*tzaddiq*], when he dies, he can no longer add merit [*zekhut*]. (A12,54; also see B27,54)[24]

The terms "wicked" *(rasha')*, "righteous" *(tzaddiq)*, and "merit" *(zekhut)* are technical terms whose bases are metaphoric; they are words derived from legal language that describe human behavior before and in relation to God. These are not the only such terms, and others are based upon the roots *ḥ.v.b.* ("guilt" or "debt"), *g.z.r.* ("decree"), and "punish" *('.n.sh.)*.[25] In most of these cases, the metaphoric tension is minimal, for generally there is no explicit sense that the terms evoke their etymological origins. If they appeared in isolation, they aptly would be described as "dead" metaphors. However, since they are used in conjunction with other legal terms, and in the same text that develops images of God as a judge, they are more accurately characterized as the most pervasive, and the least "tense," instances of legal/judicial metaphors in rabbinic theology.[26]

Generally, *Rabbi Nathan* employs legal language to describe divine punishment: "judge" *(d.y.n.)*, "wicked" *(r.sh.')*, "guilt" *(ḥ.v.b.)*, "decree" *(g.z.r.)*, and "punish" *('.n.sh.)* all describe the negative dimensions of divine sentencing. Certain legal terms are important for reflection upon right action before God, particularly "merit" *(zekhut, from z.k.h.)* and "righteous" *(tzaddiq, from tz.d.q.)*. However, when rabbis discuss God's reward or payment for right action, they usually draw upon another metaphor—that of monetary exchange.

Exchange Tropes

In manuscripts of *Rabbi Nathan A,* as well as in *Rabbi Nathan B* and *The Fathers,* a compact statement attributed to Rabbi Tarfon portrays a lifetime before God as a workday:

> The day is short.
> The work multiplies.
> The workers are lazy.

> The pay [*ha-śakhar*] is great.
> Know that the payment of the righteous is in the future to
>   come.[27]

The sage never makes a direct predication concerning the deity, but God is implied as an employer. The epigram emphasizes human finitude by stating that life, like a full workday, is short. It also presents a pessimistic vision of human motivation, for "the workers are lazy." These aspects of the self contrast with the immense nature of divine reward. For those who work, "the pay is great," even if deferred to the world to come. The sage's term for "pay"—*śakhar*—occurs throughout *Rabbi Nathan,* and elsewhere in rabbinic literature, to express the concept of divine reward or payment.[28]

Usually the metaphor of divine "pay" appears without tension, with no explicit allusion to its origin in human exchange relations. However, one notable story plays upon analogy and disjunction between human and divine payment as the basis of a comic account. The narrative appears as part of an extended exposition of the epigrams attributed to Hillel the Elder, much of which concerns the themes of divine justice and human merit. One of Hillel's maxims is the concise Aramaic statement, "According to the suffering is the reward" *(lephum tza'ara' 'agra').*[29] As commentary to this maxim, the compilers of *Rabbi Nathan* present a story of Hillel. In *Rabbi Nathan A,* Hillel encounters people who apply the logic of the maxim to their material goods:

> A story of Hillel the Elder, who was walking on the road and ran into people carrying wheat: He said to them, "How much is a *se'ah?*"
> They said, "Two *dinar.*"[30]
> He met other ones, and he said to them, "How much is a *se'ah?*"
> They said, "Three *dinar.*"
> He said, "But the first ones said two!"
> They said, "You stupid Babylonian, do you not know that 'According to the suffering is the reward!'"
> He said, "Stupid empty-headed people! When I speak to you, you answer me like this?!" What did Hillel the Elder do with them? He brought them to correct understanding. (A12,55)

The wheat sellers interpret the epigram—"According to the suffering is the reward"—in a literal manner. The second group wants to charge more than the first, apparently based on their greater suffering. The implicit point of the narrative, which is the "correct understanding," is that the epigram is a figurative, theological assertion and not a guide for human monetary exchange. The sages do not assert that market prices should reflect difficulty in production and distribution. Rather, the principle is strictly for divine reckoning, describing the ways that God pays those who suffer in divine service. Application of the maxim to the human realm is "stupid" and "empty-headed."

In *Rabbi Nathan A,* the story employs an Aramaic word for "payment," "wages," or "reward" *('agar),* and the Hebrew *sakhar* does not appear. In *Rabbi Nathan B,* however, the parallel narrative about Hillel centers upon the Hebrew term. Here, Hillel encounters a donkey driver who reasons in strictly economic terms. It is the sage who states the maxim—"According to the suffering is the reward"—to highlight that he lives according to a supernatural conception of accounting:

> Ben He He says: According to the suffering is the reward.
>
> A story of a donkey driver who came to Hillel the Elder:
>
> [The donkey driver] said to him, "Sir, see how we are better off than you [Babylonians]. You trouble yourselves all this way when you go up from Babylonia to Jerusalem. I go out from the entrance of my house and lodge at the entrance to Jerusalem."
>
> [Hillel] waited some time, and said to him, "For how much will you rent [*maskir*] me your donkey from here to Emmaus?"
>
> "For a *dinar.*"
>
> "To Lod, for how much?"
>
> [The donkey driver] said to him, "For two."
>
> "To Cesaerea, for how much?"
>
> [The donkey driver] said, "For three."
>
> [Hillel] said, "I see that as much as I increase the distance, you increase the payment [*ha-sakhar*]."
>
> [The donkey driver] said, "Yes, according to the distance is the payment [*ha-sakhar*]."
>
> [Hillel] said, "Is not the payment [*sekhar-*] for my legs like the payment [*sekhar-*] for the legs of this animal?"
>
> Thus Hillel maintained the doctrine, "According to the suffering is the reward." (B27,55–56)

In this story, Hillel is the one whose logic makes no sense in human economic terms. The donkey driver compares himself to Hillel, claiming superiority because his life entails less difficulty. Hillel rejects this assertion by reframing the comparison and asserting that his own situation is analogous to that of the donkey, and the response centers on the term *sakhar.* He asks to rent *(maskir)* the donkey and inquires concerning the fee *(ha-śakhar).* After the donkey driver asserts that, "according to the distance is the payment [*ha-śakhar*]," Hillel retorts, "Is not the payment [*śekhar-*] for my legs like the payment [*śekhar-*] for the legs of this animal?"

What does Hillel mean by this simile? The driver rents out his donkey, charging according to the distance. Hillel claims that when he walks from Babylonia to Jerusalem for religious purposes, God rewards him according to his distance traveled—according to his suffering. The implicit analogy is:

> Just as a renter pays for the donkey's effort, so God pays Hillel for his effort (though Hillel, unlike the donkey, gets to keep the "pay" that he earns).

The metaphoric tension in the word *śakhar* corresponds to the tension between human and theological reasoning. Hillel's economic logic is absurd by purely human standards and only makes sense given a theological perspective. The term is a point of continuity from which the discontinuity is most clearly evident. This narrative, like its parallel, reveals that metaphors of exchange—God is an employer who gives reward/pay *('agar* or *śakhar)*—were living and dynamic tropes in the discursive world of *Rabbi Nathan.*

Metaphors of monetary exchange are imbedded in various other terms. Two key distinctions allow sages to reflect upon the relation between payment in this world and in the world to come: (a) direct payment *(sh.l.m.)* and credit *(maqqiph* and *ma'aleh 'al),* and (b) capital *(qeren)* and interest *(peyrot).* For example, one passage contrasts the wicked and the righteous in monetary terms:[31]

> The wicked are paid [*meshallemin*] and the righteous are given credit [*maqqiphin*]. The wicked are paid as people who observe the Torah with bad intention and nothing good is ever found in them. The righteous are given credit as people who observe the Torah with good intention and nothing bad is ever found in them.[32] Each one receives a little, and the rest is set aside for them, multiplying. (A39,118; also B44,123)[33]

In this case, being "paid" *(sh.l.m.)* is an immediate event, while receiving "credit" *(n.q.p.)* means that payment is deferred to the world to come.[34] Underlying this epigram is the challenge of theodicy, which in one rabbinic formulation is framed: Why is it that the wicked are at ease while the righteous suffer? These metaphors of exchange express a common rabbinic response to this problem. The righteous suffer now but will be rewarded in the world to come, while the wicked ultimately will be punished.[35] Specifically, the wicked receive their payment from God (whatever they have earned through good deeds) immediately and in this world. The righteous may have much larger accounts with God, but rather than receiving the benefits now, they have credit for the world to come.

This teaching raises a number of questions. What of the righteous who prosper? If someone is successful and well-off in this world, does that necessarily mean that the person will perish in the world to come? Is it possible that right action before God could be rewarded in this world? A passage that opens the next chapter of *Rabbi Nathan A* partially addresses this problem through a distinction between capital and interest:

> Four things, if a person does them, he eats their fruits [*peyrot*] in this world, and the capital [*ha-qeren*] remains in the world to come. These are: honor of father and mother, deeds of loving-kindness, bringing peace between a person and his fellow, and the study of Torah is as great as all of them. (A40,119; also A40,120)[36]

The tropes have complex layers of meaning. Not only is human exchange a metaphor for God's payment, but the monetary terms are themselves metaphoric. The word for "capital" *(qeren)* is most literally a "horn" or a "handle," and the word for "interest" is the plural "fruits" *(peyrot)*. The underlying image seems to be a plant whose produce can be harvested, but its base remains and will generate more in the future.[37] The passage employs these tropes to teach that there are four ways of acting for which one is rewarded both in this world and the next. Prosperity in this world does not necessarily mean that all merit is being exhausted—it may be the "fruit" of these good forms of behavior.

In addition to these images of payment/credit and capital/interest, terms such as "inherit" *(n.ḥ.l.)*, "redeem" *(p.d.h.)*, and "accounts to" *(ma'aleh 'al)* also describe the process of receiving divine reward.[38] The most common of these—"accounts to" *(ma'aleh 'al)*—is based on a word that means "raise up." By extension, it can take on the monetary sense of "credit or account to," probably implying the image of "raising up" on a scale. In *Rabbi Nathan B,* the term is used to describe the government giving a pension to a man *(ma'aleh lo saleyra')*.[39] However, the metaphoric tension between this human sense and the theological sense of divine credit usually is not present.

One example of divine credit appears in the commentary upon a list of the ten divine utterances that are the source of creation:

With ten utterances the world was created. What need do inhabitants of the world have of this? It is to teach you that,[40] for anyone who practices one commandment, and anyone who observes one Sabbath, and anyone who preserves one life, Scripture accounts it to him as if [*ma'aleh 'alav ha-katub ke'ilu*] he preserved the entire world that was created with ten utterances. (A31,90–91; B36,90; *Fathers* 5:1)

In this passage, as in others, the words "Scripture accounts it to him as if" mark a divine response that appears to be disproportionate to a human action: great reward for small or indirect good actions and great punishment for small or indirect bad actions. The term "as if" *(ke'ilu)* is crucial, for it indicates that the minor act simulates or substitutes for the major.[41] Rabbis make use of the expression to emphasize the significance of apparently minor actions. One receives credit for the observance of a single commandment or Sabbath, or the preservation of one life, as if one had preserved the extent of divine creation.

The metaphor of God as an employer or storekeeper who engages with humans in monetary terms is thus developed through technical terms that include "pay/reward" *(śakhar)*, "to pay" *(sh.l.m.)*, "to extend credit" *(n.q.p.)*, "capital" *(qeren)*, "interest" *(peyrot)*, "inherit" *(n.ḥ.l.)*, "redeem" *(p.d.h.)*, and "accounts to" *(ma'aleh 'al)*. This set of interrelated metaphors overlaps with the legal metaphors described above to elaborate rabbinic thought concerning divine reward and punishment. There are also cases of individual words that have both legal and monetary resonances, such as the root *p.r.'*, which has a basic sense of owing or paying off a debt, yet it also is the basis of a term for divine retribution or punishment *(pur'anut)*.[42] These theological images assert that humans exist in relation to a deity that evaluates and responds to human states and actions. Of the many tropes and value concepts in rabbinic theology, those of divine reward and punishment give the greatest weight to what humans are and do. An individual act can have immense significance (for the individual, for the community, and for the cosmos), and events in the world can be interpreted as divine response to prior human behavior. Let us now turn from the theological to the human side of this relationship.

Human Action and Divine Response

Given the theological tropes that I have examined, what does it mean to act in relation to God? Such action does not consist of single, discrete events. Rather, a given act or state of character is part of a complex interrelation between human behavior and God's response: the person acts, God responds with reward or punishment, and in between, there are various possibilities for intervention in divine reckoning. My focus is upon the first two elements.[43]

Before entering into that discussion, however, I must confront a problem. While *Rabbi Nathan* contains numerous images and terms for God's justice and payment, descriptions of human action often do not employ them. Many passages depict a causal connection between an act and a consequence with no explicit mention of divine activity. Do we have reason to consider these to imply a theological framework or simply the view that actions have built-in, worldly consequences that bring the results described? We cannot be sure, but it is worth noting that there is no assertion of a worldly causality whose results differ from the judgments that God would make. Passages that do not mention divine judgment neither depict a competing way of conceiving the consequences for actions, nor counter the general rabbinic belief in God's ultimate power. For this reason, it seems that in the world presented by *Rabbi Nathan,* God's judgment includes and subsumes natural causality.[44] In the discussion below, I give most weight to passages that explicitly describe God's involvement in the world. However, I draw upon and cite all materials that express — explicitly or implicitly — causality based upon normative evaluation of human action.

Human Actions and Character

What aspects of human life are subject to divine accounting? As discussed in the introduction, *Rabbi Nathan* presumes and frames rabbinic law but does not itself elaborate it. The text contains some discussion of actions governed by criminal, civil, and ritual laws, particularly the paradigmatic sins of idolatry, incest, and murder.[45] We also find much material concerning God's command to Adam and Eve and their transgression. Generally speaking, however, the compilers of *Rabbi Nathan* draw upon images of divine reward and punishment in setting out ideals for activities that are not specified by law but that are crucial for a scholastic religiosity: teaching and study, interpersonal relations, and inner states. Often sages employ hyperbole to emphasize dimensions of life that their audience may take to be minor, stating that an apparently small sin is more grave than a well-known and major transgression, or that God's response to small actions is far greater than one might think.

The significance of study is upheld, for example, in commentary upon a maxim of Hillel, "If you come to my house, I will come to your house":

> How is this so? These are people who early in the morning and in the evening go to the synagogues and study houses. The Holy One, blessed be He, blesses them for the world to come, as in the matter where it is said, "In every place where I cause My name to be mentioned [*'azkir 'et shemi*], I will come to you and bless you" (Exod. 20:21). (A12,55; compare B27,55)[46]

In its biblical context, Exodus 20:21 refers to sacrificial acts upon an altar, stating that one can sacrifice "in any site where I [God] shall pronounce my name [*'azkir 'et shemi*]." In the rabbinic interpretation, the sacrificial site or "place" becomes the synagogues and study houses, and the verb *'azkir* is not specifically the act of pronouncing the divine name but a more diffuse sense of invoking and recalling God's presence through study and worship. Finally, the commentators interpret the biblical promise for a blessing as being deferred to the next world. The teaching instructs the student to go to the synagogues and study houses—"come to My [God's] house"—with the promise that God will "come" to those sacred spaces and reward such action with next-worldly blessing.[47]

Sages also exhort diligence in study through threats of divine punishment. For example, in a list of epigrams attributed to Rabbi Akiba, we find the following dramatic statement:

> He would say: Why do students of the sages die when they are young? Not because they are adulterers, and not because they steal, but rather because they break from the words of Torah and occupy themselves with words of conversation—and moreover, because they do not begin again at the place where they broke off. (A26,82; B35,81; also A29,88)

If a person who strives to become a sage dies when he is young, what is the cause? Rabbi Akiba presumes it is a matter of divine punishment and first suggests two legally prohibited actions (adultery, theft) but states that the reason for the death is failure in concentration: turning from the distinct, sacred speech of the study house (the words of Torah) to that of everyday life (words of conversation). Loss of intellectual focus is worse than major sins. The consequence is, figuratively speaking, death.[48]

The scholastic ideals upheld by the sages extend beyond teaching and study. Interpersonal relations, particularly the control of speech, are central to their community. For example, a number of passages employ strong hyperbole to convey the dangers of "malicious speech" *(lashon ha-ra')*. A numerical catalogue cites the cardinal sins of idolatry, incest, and murder, only to place malicious speech as greater in transgression:

> Four things for which the person who does them will be punished in this world and in the world to come: idolatry, incest, and murder. Yet malicious speech [*lashon ha-raʿ*] is greater than all of them. (A40,120)

In this passage, we see the figurative, exhortative nature of rabbinic epigrams in stark terms. The anonymous statement lists the greatest sins of the rabbinic legal and moral world as a means of highlighting the dangers of improper speech. Malicious speech, above even the cardinal sins, will engender divine punishment.[49]

Finally, a number of passages emphasize the significance of internal states in divine accounting. For example, commentators interpret a saying of Shammai—"Receive all people with a cheerful countenance"—in terms of gift giving and cordiality among colleagues:

> How so? This teaches that if a person gives his colleague all the good gifts of the world, yet his face is downcast, Scripture accounts it to him as if [*maʿaleh ʿalav ha-katub keʾilu*] he did not give him anything. But if one receives his colleague with a cheerful countenance, even if he did not give him anything, Scripture accounts it to him as if [*maʿaleh ʿalav ha-katub keʾilu*] he gave him all the good gifts of the world. (A13,57; B23,48)

The facial expression is not just a social convention, but a visible testimony of willingness both to give and to receive. Such willingness is valued as central to the process of gift exchange with greater significance than the action itself. If one follows the instruction of Shammai and receives "all people with a cheerful countenance," then divine accounting records this act as if a gift had actually been given.[50]

According to *Rabbi Nathan,* then, God does not only judge a certain realm of life that can be designated as "legal" or "religious." Rather, actions that are framed in terms of divine reward and punishment range from those addressed by rabbinic law—including paradigmatic sins—to the common activities of the student. Sages and later commentators go to great rhetorical lengths to emphasize the significance of everyday life. The apparently small dynamics of the scholastic environment—teaching, study, and interpersonal relations—are central for the rabbinic community as well as for an individual's ethical transformation, and *Rabbi Nathan* emphasizes that they are crucial for receiving God's payment.

Divine Response

Many passages in *Rabbi Nathan* promise but do not spec-
ify divine rewards and punishments.[51] When the text names particular rewards and punishments, they may be either physical or spiritual. Physical
blessings appear in this world, but the spiritual may be received in this
world, at or just after death, or in the world to come.[52]

The promise of physical rewards, even monetary wealth, may seem
striking given my earlier discussions of teachings that place the reward for
the righteous in a future world. Rabbinic thought on this issue is not consistent. Often *Rabbi Nathan* will unabashedly uphold rabbinic ideals through
promises of worldly benefit, though in these passages God's presence tends
to be implicit. For example:

> Rabbi Natan ben Yoseph says: Anyone who neglects the words of Torah
> in wealth, his end will be to neglect them in poverty. Anyone who fulfills
> the words of Torah in poverty, his end will be to fulfill them in wealth.
> (A30,89; also B35,82; *Fathers* 4:9)[53]

The sage's rhetorical goals are to uphold the study and practice of Torah
and to counter any excuse based on economic circumstances. He asserts
that observance will result, eventually, in wealth. A similar stance appears
in narratives of Rabbi Akiba's and Rabbi Eliezer ben Hyrcanus's careers.
Both figures face great obstacles in their study, and Rabbi Akiba in particular is said to struggle with poverty. However, both stories culminate with
the man attaining great wealth. For Rabbi Akiba:

> They said: Before he passed from the world, he had tables of silver and
> gold, and he went up to his bed on ladders of gold. (A6,29–30; also
> B12,30)

The sagely life presented in *Rabbi Nathan,* then, includes the possibility of
material prosperity. While nothing in the text affirms that one should
make money directly from the teaching of Torah, many passages assert that
a great man will not only be distinguished in character, but that God's
favor will appear in concrete, worldly forms. A rabbi can, and should, wind
up rich.[54]

Along with these physical consequences for action, *Rabbi Nathan*
presents spiritual rewards and punishments. There is more material on
spiritual rewards than spiritual punishments, and the punishments tend to
be described in very general terms—people may be sent to Gehenna (the
rabbinic "Hell"), or they may simply "perish" from both this world and the

world to come.[55] By contrast, many accounts of spiritual rewards during life and at death are vivid and complex. When we consider these rewards, we encounter an important link between ethics and mysticism: one of the central ways that rabbis strive for intense encounter with God is through right character and action.[56]

Spiritual rewards in this world often involve God's indwelling presence, the Shekhinah, that can be earned through study. Some teachings portray this experience as reserved for the greatest of the sages in the greatest of generations:

> Rabban Yohanan ben Zakkai received from Hillel and from Shammai. Hillel the Elder had eighty students. Thirty of them were fit for the Shekhinah to rest upon them like Moses our Rabbi, but their generation was not fit for this. (A14,57; B28,57; also *Fathers* 2:8)[57]

According to this passage, not only must a sage be "fit" to experience the Shekhinah, but the whole generation also has to be ready. By contrast, in *Rabbi Nathan B* we find an everyday or normal mysticism: any time that students study together, the Shekhinah is present.[58] For example, in the commentary to the maxim "acquire for yourself a fellow [*ḥaber*]," we read:

> Students of the sages who sit and study repeatedly—the Shekhinah goes from one to the other and blesses them, as it is said, "I will walk among you" (Lev. 26:12). (B18,40; also *Fathers* 3:2 and 3:6)

The midrash is based on a passage from Leviticus that concludes a list of promises to those who follow the divine commandments. The interpretation shifts the context to study, specifying the divine presence—"I will walk among you"—as the activity of the Shekhinah. According to the new teaching, all students who study in a focused manner encounter God and receive divine blessing.[59]

Perhaps the most powerful mystical images in *Rabbi Nathan* surround the moment of death. Reward for the righteous at death is elaborated through a collection of stories concerning Moses, and a key scene combines the powerful motifs of God's kiss, the storage of souls, and the Throne of God's Glory *(kabod)*:[60]

> The Holy One, blessed be He, took Moses's soul and stored it under the Throne of Glory, as it is said, "the soul of my lord [*nephesh 'adoni*] will be bundled [*tzerurah*] in the bundle of life [*tzeror ha-ḥayyim*] with the Lord your God" (I Sam. 25:29).[61] When He took it, he did so with a kiss, as it is said, "[Moses the servant of the Lord died there, in the land of Moab,] by

> the mouth of [*'al pi*] the Lord" (Deut. 34:5). Not only is the soul of Moses
> stored under the Throne of Glory [*kise' ha-kabod*], but also the souls of
> the righteous are stored under the Throne of Glory, as it is said, "the soul
> of my lord [*nephesh 'adoni*] will be bundled [*tzerurah*] in the bundle of life
> [*tzeror ha-ḥayyim*] with the Lord your God" (1 Sam. 25:29). (A12,50; also
> B25,51)

According to this midrash on Deuteronomy 34:5, Moses dies literally "by
the mouth" of God—not by a command, but by a kiss. In talmudic literature, this form of death marks the highest sign of divine favor.

Death is followed by storage of the righteous souls—a motif derived
from Abigail's blessing to David, which affirms that God will protect "the
life of my lord" *(nephesh 'adoni)* (1 Sam. 25:29). The exegesis centers on
interpreting *nephesh* ("life") in the sense of a "soul" that exists apart from
the body and on taking the epithet *'adoni* ("my lord") to mean not David
but "the Lord." Moses and the righteous are souls "of my Lord." They are
wholly devoted to God, and because of this, they will be stored ("bundled")
with God in the "bundle of life." In this passage, the "bundle" is interpreted as the Throne of God's Glory *(kise' ha-kabod)*. This throne is the
center of much mystical speculation, and proximity to it is one of the great
rewards for the righteous. At the intersection of Abigail's blessing to David
(1 Sam. 25:29) and the biblical account of Moses's death (Deut. 34:5), rabbinic commentators find the promise that the righteous will be rewarded
with continued proximity to God after an erotic mystical death.[62]

In addition to consequences for action during life or at death, many
teachings emphasize divine response in the world to come, though these
rewards and punishments are not specified. The contrast between "this
world" and "the world to come" occurs numerous times throughout *Rabbi
Nathan*.[63] The distinction has several functions in rabbinic thought. We
have seen that it can be central to demonstrations of God's justice given
worldly injustice—the righteous suffer in this world but will be rewarded
in the world to come, when the wicked receive their punishment.[64] More
generally, it introduces a tremendous flexibility in thinking about divine
reward and punishment, for ultimate rewards may have little to do with,
and may in fact be the reverse of, the present situation.

I have given particular attention to divine reward (more than punishment), in part because of its prominence in *Rabbi Nathan* as a whole, but
also because such reward is crucial to rabbinic ideals for the sage: a great
sage should receive material and spiritual benefits from God. This reward
may not appear during a sage's lifetime, but ideally he attains worldly success and mystical experiences. A corollary to this point is that the theology

of reward and punishment, along with the conception of human action that I am examining, underlies many accounts of rabbinic mysticism. Proximity to God through a kiss or at the Throne of Glory is understood, at least in some passages, as the consequence of right character and action.

The Recipient

Who receives the reward or punishment for a given action? Often God responds to the person who does the act, but not necessarily. Teachings in *Rabbi Nathan* vary as to whether divine justice addresses specific people or a community or nation as a whole. Rabbinic interpretations of biblical accounts often focus on the latter, such as the corporate punishment of Sodom for their sins and corporate rewards or punishments for Israel. Adam and Eve's transgression, however, is a dramatic case in which the acts of individuals bring punishments for many—the curses upon Adam for all humanity, those upon Eve for all women.[65] When sages instruct their students and peers, they give great weight to the mutual influence of individual and group. Some state that the individual is rewarded or punished along with the immediate community, while others emphasize the ability of the sage to bring merit or demerit to those around him.[66]

A second issue concerning the recipient of divine reward and punishment is merit transfer. We have seen that God's response is not necessarily immediate, and that actions may be recorded in a divine accounting. The most common technical terms used to describe these dynamics are *śakhar* ("pay or reward") and *zekhut* ("merit," from the root *z.k.h.,* which originally meant "clear, clean, or pure," and later took on the sense of legal acquittal).[67] One may accumulate or lose credit, and credit or debt may transfer between persons or groups.

There are some passages in *Rabbi Nathan,* though, that deny in explicit terms the possibility of merit transfer, asserting that each individual earns merit for her- or himself.[68] One such statement appears as commentary to a statement by Hillel:

> He would say: If I am not for me, who is for me? When I am for myself, what am I? If not now, when? (A12,48; B27,54; *Fathers* 1:14)[69]

In *Rabbi Nathan* this maxim is interpreted atomistically, using terms denoting the acquisition of merit and also midrashic interpretation of a verse from Ecclesiastes:

He would say: If I am not for me, who is for me? If I do not earn merit [*'ezkeh*] in my lifetime, who will transfer merit to me [*yizkeh bi*]?[70] When I am for myself, what am I? If I do not earn merit [*zokheh*] for myself, who will transfer merit to me [*yizkeh bi*] for myself?[71] If not now, when? If I do not earn merit [*zokheh*] in my lifetime, who will transfer merit to me [*yizkeh bi*] after my death? Thus it says, "Yes, a living dog is better than a dead lion" (Eccles. 9:4). "Yes, a living dog is better"—this is the wicked one who endures in this world. "Than a dead lion"—even than Abraham, Isaac, and Jacob, for they sleep in dust. Another opinion: "Yes, a living dog is better." This is the wicked one [*rasha'*] who endures in this world. If he repents, The Holy One, blessed be He, receives it. But a righteous one [*tzaddiq*], when he dies, he can no longer add merit [*zekhut*]. (A12,54; also see a significantly more developed parallel in B27,54)[72]

Ecclesiastes 9:4 contrasts a smaller, despised animal that lives (a dog) with a larger, more powerful, and better esteemed one who is dead (a lion). The verse affirms life through asserting that the dog is in a superior state.[73] The rabbinic midrash interprets this contrast in moral terms—the dog represents the wicked, who are not well-off in relation to God. If they are alive, though, their prospects are better than the righteous (the lion) who are dead. Why?—because the wicked while alive can still earn merit.[74]

The commentators of *Rabbi Nathan* interpret Hillel's maxim by way of this midrash. The laconic expression of being "for myself" *(li)* becomes a process of "earning merit" for myself. Only I can earn merit for myself, and I must do so during my lifetime. If I do not do so, no one can transfer merit to me, whether during my lifetime or after death.[75] While numerous passages in *Rabbi Nathan* imply that the person who acts is not identical with the recipient of the ensuing divine reward or punishment, this passage stands against the idea that merit can transfer among the living or between the living and the dead.

Correspondence between Act and Response

I stated above that a theology of reward and punishment is, in many respects, a broad trope of order, envisioning a world in which people experience appropriate consequences for their ways of living. This sense of order is strongest when rabbis assert a close correspondence between action and divine response—when the results of an action are measured precisely, in form and degree, to the act itself. Three issues arise in studying the poetics of such correspondence. First, does correspondence appear in the content of the act and the response, the literary style through which they are formulated, or both? Second, is the correspondence one of similarity or of contiguity? That is, does the response resemble the act, or is it linked through a physical, temporal, or causal connection? Third, how precise is the correspondence? Correspondence may admit of degrees, with sometimes an exact fit between act and response, sometimes a loose connection, and sometimes an explicit disjunction. The rabbinic phrase for a strong correspondence is "measure for measure" *(middah keneged middah),* but it does not appear in *Rabbi Nathan.*[76]

A stark example of a sage asserting strong correspondence between act and punishment, both in style and in content, is a brief anecdote about Hillel:

> He saw a skull that floated on the surface of the water and said to it, "Since you drowned others, they drowned you. And those who drowned you, others will drown." (A12,55; B27,56; *Fathers* 2:6)[77]

As elsewhere in *Rabbi Nathan,* the theology of reward and punishment provides the basis for interpreting events that have already occurred. Hillel has no information concerning the identity of the skull, but he infers that the person has been killed. Then he interprets, in a manner that seems spontaneous and ad hoc, the significance of the presumed murder. Hillel asserts a direct correspondence between the consequence (being killed) and an assumed prior act (the person had killed someone else). Throughout, he employs the same terminology—the verb "to drown" or "to make float," from the root *ṭ.v.p.*[78]

Another example of strong correspondence between act and response is a blessing that appears at the end of a "test" narrative of two pious ones *(ḥasidim),* which appears as commentary to the epigram, "Judge every man with the scales weighted in his favor." I discussed several features of this story above in chapter 1b, and here I want to focus on the concluding blessing. After the second *ḥasid* succeeds in his test by showing his generous judgment, his fellow blesses him:

> Judge every man with the scales weighted in his favor. A story of a young woman who was taken captive: Two pious ones [*ḥasidim*] went after her to redeem her. One of them went into a tent of prostitution. When he came out, he asked to his fellow [*ḥabeyro*], "Of what did you suspect me?"
> He said, "Perhaps of learning how much money is the ransom."
> He said, "By the Temple service! That is what happened."
> *He said, "Just as [keshem she-] you judged me with the scales weighted in*

my favor, so [kakh] may The Holy One, blessed be He, judge you with the scales weighted in your favor." (A8,37, emphasis added)[79]

The correspondence in meaning is reinforced by exact correspondence in language. The *ḥasid* "judged me with the scales [weighted in] my favor," and the blessing is that God will "judge you with the scales [weighted in] your favor." Moreover, the syntactic construction of "just as . . . so . . ." [*keshem she-* . . . *kakh* . . .] strengthens the point further—it appears often in rabbinic Hebrew syntax to draw analogies and can, on its own, convey divine response that is measure for measure.[80]

A complex interrelation of similarity and contiguity can be seen in a teaching of Rabbi Akiba. It appears as part of the commentary upon the Great Assembly's call to "raise up many students":[81]

> [Rabbi Akiba] would say: One who lays his eyes upon his wife, [wanting] that she die and he inherit from her, or that she die and he marry her sister, and anyone who lays his eyes on his brother, [wanting] that he die and he marry his wife—in the end they will bury him during their lives. About him, Scripture says, "One who digs a pit will fall into it, and one who breaks a fence, a snake will bite him" (Eccles. 10:8). (A3,15; also B4,16)

In the prooftext from Ecclesiastes, the correspondence between act and consequence is most explicitly one of contiguity, both spatial and causal. The pit that one digs is the place of the fall. The fence that is broken is the locale of the snake.[82] Rabbi Akiba's midrash, however, draws from this verse a teaching that asserts a correspondence of similarity rather than contiguity and focuses on desire rather than action—wanting that one's wife or brother die results in one's own death.[83]

A number of teachings in *Rabbi Nathan* employ a very different rhetorical move, portraying a blatant noncorrespondence between act and result. Generally, an apparently minor deed brings a strikingly harsh consequence. I have discussed several such cases above, such as when a sage says that distraction from study causes death.[84] These passages emphasize the importance of apparently small dimensions of life. They may also convey that, at least for the great sages, every action and inner state is spiritually and ethically significant. The life of a sage is fragile, and even the smallest slip in attentiveness can mean disaster.[85]

An example of such a teaching is another maxim attributed to Rabbi Akiba (appearing in the same cluster of material as the previous one). The sage depicts a case of extreme punishment for an act of greed or theft:

Rabbi Akiba says: Anyone who takes a *peruṭah* from the public fund when he is not in need [*'eyno tzarikh*] will not pass [*niphṭar*] from the world until he is in need [*yitztarekh*] [of charity] from his fellow. (A3,15)

This passage builds upon one in the Mishnah that presents an act of greed (taking money when not in need) as having large consequences (being in significant financial need of others).[86] Here there is a disjunction between content and style. At the level of content, a minor sin brings large consequences. By naming a *peruṭah,* the smallest unit of currency in rabbinic literature, Rabbi Akiba specifies an almost insignificant amount of money. Taking this tiny sum, though, leads to significant financial need. Stylistically, however, the punishment corresponds to the action at the level of consonants. The offender "will not depart [*niphṭar*] from the world until he is in need" because of taking a "coin"—a *peruṭah.* Also, he will be in need *(yitztarekh)* of support because he has taken money that he does not need *(tzarikh).*[87] Content and style, then, may be mutually reinforcing as in the blessing of the *ḥasid,* but here they are layered in a more complex manner: the style conveys similarity between act and result, but the content plays with and disrupts the expectation of order and predictability.

Divine Reward and Punishment—Conclusion

The rabbinic theology of reward and punishment consists of interrelated concepts and tropes through which the compilers of *Rabbi Nathan* frame the totality of their practice and set it in relation to normative ideals. The theology has, at its conceptual basis, a very simple claim. God is just, rewarding good action and character and punishing bad action and character. This claim is elaborated in a manner that provides tremendous flexibility and variation. The relation between human action and divine response is in no way fixed. Reward or punishment may appear immediately, later in one's lifetime, after death, in the next world, or addressed toward other people. The response may also have various degrees and forms of correspondence (or lack thereof) with the action that generates it. This flexibility allows the sages and their followers to address a tremendous range of life situations and rhetorical concerns.

I have aimed to convey the full diversity of views present in the text. However, some rabbinic concepts—such as the role of divine compassion *(raḥamim)* and the notion that humans cannot understand God's involvement in the world—appear in *Rabbi Nathan* but are not developed at length.[88] Generally speaking, the editors present a world in which God's action is comprehensible and responsive to human character and action.

3b   Motivation and Emotion

As I have presented the material, divine response follows human action, but this sequence is only part of the rhetorical dynamic in rabbinic ethical instruction. In important ways, accounts of divine response are prior to human behavior, for the sagely voices emphasize God's judgment in order to shape and influence what people do. Teachings concerning divine reward and punishment are not only descriptive or theoretical. They are part of a pedagogical text that aims to shape motivation, emotion, and ultimately the way that the readers and listeners act in the world. What are the features of an ideal subject before God as king, judge, employer, or shopkeeper? At one level, the dual system of rewards and punishments appeals to a fairly simple psychology of self-interest centered upon desire and fear. Rabbis link this self-interest to norms for right action. If one acts according to the prescriptions of Torah and the words of the sages, one's desires and fears will be relieved.

These desires and fears are compounded by the distinct quality of God's judgment, which is omnipresent, momentous, and unpredictable. Divine reward and punishment concerns not only one sphere of human life, one area of ritual or religious activity. Rather, the omnipresent deity judges action and intent, practice as well as the state of character. The full range of life (from the dictates of civil and criminal law, to ritual requirements and temple sacrifice, to the most mundane aspects of everyday activities, even to emotions and mental states) falls under the realm of reward and punishment. A moment of arrogance, distraction during a lesson, speaking badly about a fellow student, forgetting to light the Sabbath candles, openly defying Sabbath laws, committing murder or adultery—all of these are factored in divine accounting. The momentous nature of divine justice is most prominent after death. The righteous may die in a moment of erotic mystical experience and then their souls might stay at the Throne of God's Glory until the world to come. In contrast, punishment for the wicked can be eternal banishment from God's presence. Finally, certain passages emphasize that, as a bottom line, even the sages do not know their status in God's accounting.[1]

The complex and intense nature of divine judgment should intensify basic desires and fears. God's observation and recording of all intentions and deeds, leading to judgment that is certain and momentous, mean that a rabbi must be vigilant at all times. He must attend to multiple levels of action and internal states, always maintaining awareness of God's presence and of the tremendous significance that God's presence brings to every moment of life. Moreover, he is always to be anxious, never certain that he has credit before his deity.[2]

So far, I am drawing out aspects of rabbinic views concerning motivation that are implicit in what I have examined. There are, however, instructions in *Rabbi Nathan* that explicitly prescribe certain motivations and emotions in relation to God. They center upon the tropes of law and exchange, calling upon the subject to focus upon God as a judge and as an employer in order to cultivate states such as humility, divine-directed anxiety, love, and reverence.

Directing Attention

The most widespread of these instructions appears in two forms: one centering on the verb *histakkel,* indicating observation, intellectual reflection, or attention;[3] the other on "giving" something to one's "heart" (or giving one's heart to something).[4] For both, the object of attention can be God, Torah, or the body. Consider the teaching of the first century Akabya ben Mahalalel as presented by three sources:[5]

> Akabya [ben] Mahalalel says: Anyone who gives [*noten*] four things to his heart [*'el libbo*] will sin no more. (A19,69)[6]

> Akabya ben Mahalalel says: Let a person attend to [*yistakkel*] four things, and he will not come into the hands of transgression. (B32,69)[7]

> Akabya ben Mahalalel says: Attend to [*histakkel*] three things, and you will not come into the hands of transgression. (*Fathers* 3:1)[8]

Both expressions—"attend to" and "give" to one's "heart"—appear in the transmission of this instruction. In all cases, the goal of such attention is to avoid sin or transgression through an intense focus upon "four" or "three" things.

These "things" set out a contrast between God's power and judgment as a king and judge, and human existence as finite and embodied. According to *Rabbi Nathan A:*

> Akabya ben Mahalalel says: Anyone who gives four things to his heart will sin no more: from where he comes, to where he goes, what in the future he will be, and who is his judge.
> From where he comes—from a place of darkness.
> To where he goes—to a place of darkness and gloom.
> What in the future he will be—dust and worm and maggot.
> Who is his judge—the King of the kings of kings, the Holy One, blessed be He. (A19,69–70; B32,69; *Fathers* 3:1)[9]

The "four things" that one must "give" to the heart set out the permanent boundaries of human existence: origin (from where he comes), end (to where he goes and what in the future he will be), and divine judgment. Then each of the "things" is glossed to frame human worldly existence as moving from darkness to darkness, ultimately ending in nothing but "dust and worm and maggot."[10]

These tropes intensify the contrast between the person and God, setting out a dualism between the embodied human and the all-powerful divine judge.[11] Human origin and end are lowly, marked by finitude, boundaries, and contingency. The implied contrast is God as infinite, unbounded, and permanent. Then the teaching predicates God in more specific imagery: God is a judge as well as "the King of the kings of kings." The links between divine sovereignty and judgment appear in stark, concise terms. These theological images, in turn, imply that humans are subject to divine rule and judgment. The salient oppositions, then, are finite/infinite, mortal/immortal, contingent/permanent, subject/sovereign, and judged/judging. Akabya ben Mahalalel's instruction calls for constant attention to these predications, which devalue embodied existence except as oriented to divine judgment. God and God's judgment should be at the center of one's consciousness, with all worldly concerns reduced to darkness and dust. The aim of this exercise is practical—the person "will sin no more."[12]

In the commentary of *Rabbi Nathan B* to Akabya ben Mahalalel's instruction, we find a number of teachings attributed to Rabbi Yehudah the Patriarch. One of these employs the same instruction for attention, but with different theological imagery:

> Attend to [*histakkel be-*] three things, and you will not come into the hands of transgression. Know what is above you [*lema'alah*]: an eye

sees, an ear hears, and all of your deeds are written in a book. (B32,70; *Fathers* 2:1)[13]

This maxim is striking given that it is attributed to the redactor of the Mishnah. In *Mishnah Ḥagigah* we read that there are four things that one should *not* "attend to" *(mistakkel),* and one of them is "what is above" *(mah lema'alah)* (*m. Ḥag.* 2:1).[14] While the passage in *Ḥagigah* proscribes certain forms of mystical or philosophical speculations, this instruction prescribes attention to anthropomorphic features of God's presence on high: an eye and an ear, as well as a book in which human deeds are written. These concrete images imply God's omnipresent perception and recording of all actions, providing the basis for divine judgment.[15] Attention to these features of the divine body reinforces an image of God's hierarchical observation: one is seen and heard from above by a deity who is not Himself seen. Again, the goal is that one will not transgress.[16]

While the passages I have discussed call for attention to God's presence, two epigrams employ similar terminology but focus upon the "words of Torah." Both are attributed to sages who flourished in the first century CE, and they may be variants of a common original.[17] The shorter passage appears in *Rabbi Nathan B:*

> Rabbi Nehuniah ben ha-Kanah says: . . . One who gives his heart to [*ha-noten libbo le-*] words of Torah[18] eliminates from it words of foolishness. And one who gives his heart to [*ha-noten libbo le-*] words of foolishness eliminates from it words of Torah. (B32,68)

The sage prescribes that one direct the heart to the words of Torah in order to keep it filled with the appropriate discourse.[19] In *Rabbi Nathan A,* we find a more developed account:

> Rabbi Hananiah, Deputy of the Priests, says: Anyone who places the words of Torah upon his heart [*kol ha-noten dibrey torah 'al libbo*] cancels [*mebaṭṭelim*] from it desires of a sword [*hirhurey ḥereb*],[20] desires of hunger, desires of foolishness, desires of prostitution, desires of the bad *yetzer* and desires of a bad wife,[21] desires of meaningless words [*debarim beṭelim*], and desires of the yoke of flesh and blood. For thus it is written in the Book of Psalms by David, king of Israel, "The precepts of the Lord are upright, making happy the heart. The commandment of the Lord is pure, enlightening the eyes" (Ps. 19:9). (A20,70)[22]

This unit develops the instruction through a midrash and a list. Let us start with the midrash. Rabbi Hananiah cites a verse from the Psalms: "The precepts of the Lord are upright, making happy the heart. The commandment of the Lord is pure, enlightening the eyes" (Ps. 19:9). The psalm states that divine precepts affect the heart, and the previous verse mentions the *torah* (instruction) of the Lord (Ps. 19:8): The midrashic interpretation draws these images together to assert that "the words of Torah" *(dibrey torah)*, if placed upon the heart, will make it "happy" through eliminating its problematic desires.

The word I translate as "desires" *(hirhurim)* is clearly difficult. It can denote desires, thoughts, or anxieties. In this passage, it probably should be translated in a number of ways: desires "for" things (prostitution), desires that emerge "from" things (the bad *yetzer*), anxieties (of a sword?), and states (of foolishness).[23] This list of desires is long, and it indicates the intended audience. Some elements are universal aspects of somatic existence (hunger), some are male (prostitution, a bad wife, and arguably the bad *yetzer*), and one is a problem for rabbinic ideals of intellectual focus (meaningless words). The sage affirms that a man can rid himself of all these distractions through proper attention, saying that the words of Torah actually "cancel" *(mebaṭṭelim)* them.[24]

If attributions of rabbinic names have any historical value, then we may infer that this concern with attention was influential among sages in the first century CE—Akabya ben Mahalalel, Rabbi Hananiah, and Rabbi Nehuniah ben ha-Kanah. Later, it appears through the voice of Rabbi Yehudah the Patriarch, of the late second century. From the perspective of literary composition and juxtaposition, we can see that the expressions were noted by the compilers of both *Rabbi Nathan A* and *B,* who in different ways clustered them together (A19–20,68–71; B32, 68–71).

Internal Speech

Another set of instructions calls for selves to internalize speech. They are to "say" particular words to themselves in order to create, at all times, the experience of facing God's ultimate judgment.[25] In fact, people are to imagine that they stand before God without any merit. The goal is a state of constant anxiety, in which every moment and every action feel momentous. The stakes are high—eternal blessing or punishment. This material appears as commentary to the maxim of Nittai ha-Arbeli, a sage of the Second Temple period:

> Distance yourself from an evil neighbor, do not befriend the wicked, and do not give up [*'al titya'esh min*] [the idea of] retribution [*ha-pur'anut*]. (A9,38; B16,35; *Fathers* 1:7)

His maxim is difficult and allusive in a number of respects, but I focus upon the third element. What does it mean to "give up" retribution?[26]

The commentary interprets the "retribution" as divine retribution and "do not give up" in a very strong sense. One must not give up the awareness of divine retribution at any moment:

> And do not give up the idea of divine retribution. How is this so? It teaches that a person's heart should be in a state of anxiety [*mitpahed*] every day. He should say, "Woe is me [*'oi li*], perhaps retribution will come upon me today, or perhaps tomorrow." He is found to be in a state of fear every day, as it is said of Job, "I feared something fearful [*pahad pahadti*] [and it has overtaken me. What I dreaded has come upon me]" (Job 3:25). (A9,42)

The anonymous teaching builds upon a verse from the Book of Job. The doubling of the root *p.h.d.* (fear) in Job's statement inspires the midrash that one must be anxious *(mitpahed)* at all times. Then, the text says that one must memorize and speak a distinct phrase to oneself—"Woe is me [*'oi li*], perhaps retribution will come upon me today, or perhaps tomorrow."[27] The possibility of God's judgment is to be the center of attention, constantly, "every day."

This passage is immediately followed by "another opinion," a second interpretation of the maxim. In order to understand the conceptual and metaphoric underpinnings of this teaching, however, we have to revisit two passages that I examined in chapter 3a. The first responds to the challenge of theodicy by contrasting God's responses to the wicked and to the righteous in monetary terms:

> The wicked are paid [*meshallemin*] and the righteous are given credit [*maqqiphin*]. (A39,118; also B44,123)

The wicked receive their reward from God immediately, in this world. The righteous may have much larger accounts with God, but their reward will only come in the world to come. As I noted above, this solution raises another problem. According to the logic of divine accounting in this passage, what will happen to a person who intends and acts well yet also prospers in this world? Will that person receive reward in the world to come? One possible answer to this question appears in a numerical catalogue that draws upon the tropes of capital and interest:

> Four things, if a person does them, he eats their fruits [*peyrot*] in this world, and the capital [*ha-qeren*] remains in the world to come. (A40,119; also A40,120)

For at least certain actions, the righteous person can prosper in this world and still gain life in the world to come. To do so, one must live off the "fruits" in this world, and "the capital remains in the world to come."

With these issues and terms in mind, let us turn to the second opinion concerning "do not give up [the idea of] retribution:"

> Another opinion. Do not give up the idea of divine retribution. How is this so? When a person sees what is at his hand succeed, he should not say, "Because I merited it [*zakhiti*], the Omnipresent[28] has given me food and drink in this world, and the capital [*qeren*] remains for the world to come." Rather, he should say, "Woe is me ['*oi li*]. Perhaps there remains to me, before Him, only one merit [*zekhut*]. He has given me food and drink in this world, in order that he make me perish in the world to come!" (A9,42)

The passage presumes that, if "a person sees what is at his hand succeed," a question would arise regarding God's judgment in the world to come—does this success mean that all credit is used up in the present? One answer is, "the capital [*qeren*] remains for me in the world to come." This response, however, could lead to a complacent sense that one has been good enough, or worse, that success necessarily implies God's favor and fortune. To counter such a response, the commentary teaches that one must "not give up" attention to God's punishment, especially in times of success. In fact, it is necessary to presume the worst possible case and say internally, "Woe is me"—this may be my only merit before God, and I must strive all the harder for righteousness.[29]

According to these two passages, one "should say" specific things to oneself, countering any sense of complacency or self-righteousness. In the first, this focus should be maintained "every day," and the second concerns moments when "a person sees what is at his hand succeed." The internal voices interpret events in the world through divine accounting. God's judgment and power are to be at the forefront of consciousness, and people should attend to the next world, anxious that they will perish for lack of merit.

"Be" a Servant before the Master

So far I have addressed instructions for attention to God's power and judgment. What of God's reward? If a deity gives payment, then questions arise concerning ideal human motivation. Given the promise of reward for right character and action, what is the normative status of desire for that reward? That is, what is the role of self-interest in the spiritual path—should a person act in order to benefit through God's payment, whether material or spiritual?

These questions underlie the maxim attributed to Antigonus of Sokho, who probably lived in the second century BCE:[30]

> Antigonus of Sokho received from Simeon the Righteous. He would say: Do not be like slaves [*'abadim*] who serve the master for the sake of receiving a food allowance [*'al menat leqabbel peras*]. Rather, be like slaves who serve the master not for the sake of receiving a food allowance, and let the fear of Heaven [*mora' shamayim*] be upon you. (*Fathers* 1:3)

What tropes are operating here? Scholars have debated the translation and imagery. The key term is equivocal: *'abadim* may refer to "slaves" or to free "servants." The next question is, what is *peras*? A common translation is "reward," but Elias Bickerman has argued that it refers to a "daily food allowance" that masters were expected to give slaves in the Hellenistic world.[31] The problem, then, is that we do not know whether Antigonus refers to slaves before a master or free servants before an employer. The complexities multiply when we consider the tremendous diversity in the status and power of slaves in the Hellenistic period and late antiquity. Scholars have only begun the difficult project of reconstructing their everyday lives. Generally speaking, though, the figure of a slave before a master would imply a stronger assertion of both divine power and human servitude than would a free servant before an employer.[32]

The instruction for attention centers on the simple imperative, "be." Antigonus calls upon others to "be" like the slave/servant, and to "let" a sense of fear or reverence "be" upon them. He does not specify when and where such imitation and fear should happen, implying that these foci should be present at all times. Whether we follow the strong reading of a master/slave, or the softer one of master/free servant, the passage commands that people *not* take God's response to be their motivation for action. God has the power to provide for human beings, and perhaps should do so, but the individual must not act in order to attain those benefits. Rather, Antigonus instructs, "[L]et the fear of Heaven [*mora' shamayim*] be upon you." The term *mora'*, from the root *y.r.'.*, denotes a divine-oriented fear, awe, or reverence (not a worldly, self-centered fear). "Heaven" *(shamayim)* is often an epithet for God. For this Second Temple sage, constant reverence toward and fear of God is the ideal condition for appropriate service. He rejects any form of self-interested action.[33]

This epigram is particularly valuable for identifying the interests of the editorial stream that developed *Rabbi Nathan,* for disjunction between the maxim and the commentary reveals their concerns. The commentary differs with Antigonus on two points: the radical rejection of self-interest and the theological tropes of a master and a slave. The editors both preserve the past material and bring it in line with their outlook, creating a much more moderate and complex set of ideals for motivation. The most simple and dramatic transformation appears in the initial glosses upon the maxim itself:

> Antigonus of Sokho received from Simeon the Righteous. He would say: Do not be like slaves/servants [*'abadim*] who serve the master for the sake of receiving a food allowance [*'al menat leqabbel peras*]. Rather, be like slaves/servants who serve the master not for the sake of receiving a food allowance, and let the fear of Heaven [*mora' shamayim*] be upon you, *so that your payment [śekharkhem] will be doubled in the world to come.* (A5,25–26; also B10,25–26; emphasis added)[34]

If we read the passage as a whole, the maxim, with its unusual reference to a *peras,* is now brought in line with standard rabbinic terminology and tropes, particularly the notion of "pay" *(śakhar).* As the recipients of this payment, *'abadim* would be free servants: the fundamental dichotomy in the passage being that of employer/worker rather than master/slave.[35] The editorial addition also modifies Antigonus's rejection of self-interest. Now the end of the statement is in tension with the beginning: act without concern for reward, but know that if you do so, you will in fact receive reward in the world to come. The new form of the maxim appears to allow for a deferred self-interest. One can act for the sake of reward, but only reward in the world to come.[36]

Rabbi Nathan stakes out a middle ground regarding the role of self-interest in ideal motivation. The editors call upon the individual to orient toward God not as a master of slaves but as an employer of servants. They soften Antigonus of Sokho's claim that one should not act for any reward, maintaining that one should not act based on desire for reward in this world, but also implying that it is acceptable to maintain a limited and deferred self-interest, in which hopes for "pay" are postponed until the next world. In this context, the notion of "the world to come" is not just a theological image concerning existence after death, but a motivational concept that influences desire.[37]

Exegetical Developments in *Rabbi Nathan B*

The compilers of *Rabbi Nathan* steer between two poles concerning motivation—full elimination of self-interest and desire for reward in this world. In both *Rabbi Nathan A* and *B*, editorial glosses imply an acceptance of a deferred self-interest. In *Rabbi Nathan B*, the commentary to Antigonus's maxim also includes a more specific and contentious engagement with the idea that one can attain reward in this world.[38] Rabbinic narratives of the *ḥasidim ri'shonim* and the late midrashic text *Seder Eliyahu* present strong imagery conveying that intense piety brings mystical and miraculous responses from God.[39] In *Seder Eliyahu*, we find an extensive discussion of the idea that "some of" *(mi-qetzat)* the reward of the world to come is present for the righteous *(tzaddiqim)* in this world *(ba-'olam ha-zeh)*. The compiler of *Seder Eliyahu* elaborates upon this doctrine at length with an extended essay describing various rewards: sitting and studying with God, radiance of the face, life without suffering or the bad *yetzer*, honor and strength, the power to resurrect the dead, destruction of enemies, and festive dining.[40]

The commentary of *Rabbi Nathan B* to Antigonus's maxim includes a passage that is not paralleled in *Rabbi Nathan A*. The passage is difficult to interpret, in part because of the line, *mi-qetzat śekhar ha-tzaddiqim ba-'olam ha-zeh*. This phrase, I believe, refers to the view articulated in *Seder Eliyahu*, and it can be rendered, "some of the reward for the righteous [in the world to come] is present in this world."[41] I translate as follows:

> One should have expected that they would say: Some of the reward for the righteous [in the world to come] is present in this world. But, for those who lack faith,[42] Scripture says, "Turn your eyes from me, for they distance me" (Songs 6:5). They have caused me to have it said: That portion of the gift of reward for the righteous [will be deferred] to the world to come. (B10,26)[43]

This anonymous midrash transforms the male voice of the Song of Songs into the voice of God. The male's statement about his lover's strikingly beautiful eyes becomes God's comment concerning the effect of desire upon divine presence—turn your greedy eyes from me, for such motivation distances me from you.

According to *Rabbi Nathan B,* strong promises such as those found in *Seder Eliyahu* are problematic because they would engender improper motivation among "those who lack faith." Such people would act with desire for immediate tangible reward, not with the deferred self-interest upheld in *Rabbi Nathan.* For this reason, reward for the righteous will be postponed to the next world. This passage may represent a fragment of theological contention between mainstream and pietistic strands of Judaism in late antiquity or the early medieval period. The middle ground advocated by *Rabbi Nathan B* is not just a conceptual space between radical rejection of self-interest and acceptance of self-interested desire but also a response to positions that likely were taken by other Jewish intellectual and religious elites.

Let us return to the maxim of Antigonus of Sokho and focus on the last element, which prescribes a particular emotional or affective orientation toward God:

> Antigonus of Sokho received from Simeon the Righteous. He would say: Do not be like slaves/servants [*'abadim*] who serve the master for the sake of receiving a food allowance [*'al menat leqabbel peras*]. Rather, be like slaves/servants who serve the master not for the sake of receiving a food allowance, and *let the fear of Heaven* [*mora' shamayim*] *be upon you.* (A5,25–26; B10,25–26; *Fathers* 1:3; emphasis added)

The phrase "fear of Heaven" *(mora' shamayim)* denotes a response to the deity of fear, reverence, trembling, or awe. According to the sage, one should not only avoid self-interest, but also strive to cultivate a constant state of heavenly directed fear. In *Rabbi Nathan* and rabbinic literature generally, the highest forms of comportment toward God are love *('ahabah)* and fear or reverence (usually *yir'ah,* from the same root as *mora'—y.r.'*). They are paired in a number of places in both *Rabbi Nathan A* and *B.* The most common rabbinic assessment of the two emotions is that love is greater than fear. However, as Louis Finkelstein has observed, several passages in *Rabbi Nathan* uphold fear over love.[44] Antigonus's maxim was probably formulated before this duality developed, and it only mentions fear.

In *Rabbi Nathan A,* there is no commentary to this last element. For the compilers of *Rabbi Nathan B,* however, the words "fear of Heaven" inspire a discussion concerning the two poles of ideal human response to

God. For the purposes of reference, I divide the passage into four sections and highlight the varying evaluations of love and fear. The third section appears in two significantly different manuscript recensions, and I present them in parallel:

> (1) A parable. [To what can this be compared?] To a man who does the will of his master, yet his heart is haughty against the will of his master. [Or to a man who does the will of his father] and his heart is haughty against the will of his father.[45]

> (2) One who acts from *love* is not like one who acts from *awe and fear* [*'eymah veyir'ah*].

> | (3a) One who acts from *love* inherits life in the world to come. | (3b) One who acts from *love* inherits life in this world *and does not* inherit life in the world to come. |
> | --- | --- |
> | One who serves in *awe and fear* inherits life in this world *and does not* inherit life in the world to come (MS R). | One who serves in *awe and fear* inherits life in this world and life in the world to come (MS H).[46] |

> (4) Thus we find regarding the early fathers that they served in *awe and fear,* and they inherited both life in this world and life in the world to come. Of Abraham, what does Scripture say? "For now I know that you are one who fears God" (Gen. 22:12). Of Joseph, what does it say? "I fear God" (Gen. 42:18). What does it say about Jonah? "I fear God" (Jonah 1:9).[47] (B10,26; emphasis added)

This passage presents a number of difficulties. First of all, the parable in (1) is not completed, and its relation to the rest of the passage is unclear. Second, our two recensions of (3) differ on the crucial issue—which is greater, love or awe and fear? One asserts that awe and fear are the greater, for they bring life in this world and the world to come (3b). The other states, in contrast, that serving in love will lead to life in the world to come (3a). What do we make of this difference? Scholars have responded to this discrepancy in a number of ways, some saying that the primacy of "awe and fear" is "late" or "strange," and some that it is "early."[48]

I believe that the wording of MS H (3b), which upholds awe and fear, best fits the literary context. The discussion of the patriarchs and Jonah (4) centers on fear. This is particularly striking given that often in rabbinic literature Abraham is the great exemplar of serving God in love; he is upheld over Job, who is said to stand in fear.[49] The statement in (2)—"One who acts from love is not like one who acts from awe and fear"—appears to be setting up the evaluation that fear is greater. One can very well imagine that the parable in (1) would finish by saying that fear is greater, for a haughty servant or son would serve out of fear even if not out of love. Finally, since the exegetical context is an epigram that advocates maintaining "fear of Heaven," we have all the more reason to think that the commentators would highlight this emotion.[50]

Study of manuscript variants is one way to identify tensions that existed over the course of the transmission of the text. We see here an example of editorial hands at work. The poles of love and awe are given, and their relative value is contested. Textual "corruption" can reveal such contention. It is likely that an early version of the passage upheld "awe and fear" over "love." Yet some transmitter, or school of transmission, disagreed with this position and consciously or unconsciously changed a crucial statement concerning the hierarchy of affects. What is at stake? The poles of fear and love not only denote the two highest, yet very different, rabbinic modes of orienting toward God and the commandments; they also indicate, in different times and contexts, distinct strands of elite Jewish religiosity. Finkelstein connects the primacy of fear in *Rabbi Nathan* with the first century CE school of Shammai, which has a stringent and conservative approach to legal thought. Fear is also a central term for the *ḥasidim ri'shonim*.[51] The dominant and more moderate rabbinic position is to uphold love, and love is also central to erotic dimensions of rabbinic mysticism as well as to martyrological ideals.[52]

The maxim of Antigonus of Sokho and its commentary in *Rabbi Nathan* provide answers to the question, What is the role of self-interest in the lives of religious elites? On one hand, rabbis have a theology that links service of God and self-interest through the promise that the righteous will be rewarded. On the other hand, certain figures in *Rabbi Nathan* reject this self-interest, the most prominent being Antigonus of Sokho. He calls for a mode of attention structured in terms of similes: "be like" a slave before God as "master" and serve this master in fear and reverence, with no expectation of payment or even basic support for life. The commentators soften the dichotomies implicit in the tropes and allow for a deferred self-interest. In addition, in *Rabbi Nathan B* we see the assertion that one must serve the employer out of both fear and love—one manuscript highlighting fear, another love.

We can identify, then, three different modes of comportment before a deity that rewards and punishes: (1) serving God to receive payment (self-interest); (2) serving God to receive payment not in this world but in the next (deferred self-interest); (3) serving God only through love and fear. The text does not arrange these types as such, but implicit in the material may be a hierarchy moving from self-interest to deferred self-interest to consciousness in which motivation and emotion are centered on the deity and not on reward.

3c   Rabbinic Theology
Conclusion

My central thesis regarding rabbinic theology is that, according to *Rabbi Nathan,* the rabbinic student becomes a sage through subordination to God, as understood through internalized figurative language. Once again, the material leads to nuances in the broad category of internalization. The images of God become internal in a very different way than does the traditional discourse of Torah. For the tradition, we encountered various tropes describing the interaction of Torah and the self as well as narratives portraying sages permeated with the words of Torah. In the case of the deity, I have identified instructions that direct the self to focus attention upon certain images. Through constant or regular exercise, God's presence is always to be in the consciousness, giving rise to distinct emotions. These instructions appear in three variations. The first is most explicitly a form of attention: the call to "attend to" or "place" upon the "heart" particular tropes depicting God and divine involvement in the world. The second is an internal voicing: the prescription to "say" certain statements to oneself, either all the time or at crucial moments. And the third is a form of simulation: one should "be like" a servant before God as master.

What is internalized?[1] At a most basic level, the object of attention is a sentence or image that employs tropes of divine reward and punishment.[2] Each instruction for attention has a distinct set of continua and/or oppositions. Akabya ben Mahalalel's teaching sets out a contrast between God as a judge and king, and humans as embodied, finite, and mortal. The implicit oppositions are:

God	human
judge	judged
sovereign	subject
permanent	contingent
infinite	finite
immortal	mortal

The commentary to the maxim of Nittai ha-Arbeli also employs the figure of God as a judge, but the fundamental issue is not human finitude but rather whether one has sufficient "capital" or "merit." People are to place themselves on continua of debt-credit and guilt-innocence, always considering themselves to be in debt, guilty, and facing divine retribution. Finally, the maxim of Antigonus of Sokho centers on tropes of exchange rather than law. The fundamental opposition is slave/master or servant/ master, and people are to locate themselves as eager servants. The sage focuses on the economic dimension of the relation — the master's act of giving a food allowance or wages. However, the divine economy works in a different manner than does the human economy. According to the glosses in *Rabbi Nathan,* an individual earns next-worldly "pay" *(sakhar)* through *not* seeking remuneration for service.

All of these tropes intensify the human status of subordination that runs throughout the imagery of divine reward and punishment. The theology generally implies that humans are subjects before a king, defendants before a judge, and employees before an employer. In all of these relations, God has the full power to judge and to pay. The instructions for attention intensify this dynamic. They highlight one's finitude in comparison to God's power, one's indebtedness and guilt before God's judgment, and one's servitude and dependence in relation to God as a master. Through these instructions, God's presence is always to be at the center of awareness. The ideal result is that the rabbinic subject moves from a self-interested orientation centered on worldly desire and fear, to a God-centered consciousness characterized by spiritual anxiety, love, and reverence.

It is striking to what degree contemporary scholars of ethics analyze and draw upon ancient thought and practice that is heavily theological — and moreover theologies that differ greatly from modern ones — without addressing the role of God. Perhaps this reflects a fear that direct discussion of God would entail an inappropriate theologizing within academic discourse. Or, it may reveal a piety that does not want to encompass God in an academic framework, perhaps even wanting to sneak theological accounts into a secular debate. Or a scholar may not want to confront the radical difference of ancient theologies, hoping to draw only upon the parts of ancient thought that moderns and postmoderns can believe.

In any case, we cannot describe rabbinic ethics without describing the workings of their deity. Large portions of the tradition are based on exegetical methods that take the Bible to be a written record of divine speech. Without an understanding of the theological basis for midrash, the process of justification makes no sense. More directly, I have shown that rabbinic notions of human action are deeply connected with their understanding of God's action in the world, so we cannot study rabbinic ethics without studying rabbinic theology. This does not mean that descriptive ethics should itself be theological. Specifically, my analysis of figurative language does not imply claims concerning the referent of these tropes—my analysis is not meant to assert that rabbinic views concerning God are either true or false.

Comparative and Theoretical Points

Rabbinic instructions for attention can be juxtaposed in provocative ways with material from Greco-Roman philosophical schools that Pierre Hadot conceptualizes as "spiritual exercises." Hadot writes that the well-known exercises of Ignatius of Loyola are part of an older and broader tradition that has its roots in Greco-Roman and Hellenistic schools of philosophy. His research centers upon the Greek *askēsis* and *meletē,* which he translates as "spiritual exercise," as well as the Latin *exercitium spirituale.* However, his study goes beyond occurrences of those particular terms, and he aims to develop a category that can be used in comparative and theoretical reflection.[3]

Hadot employs "spiritual exercise" in both very general and more particular senses. At the general level, Hadot writes that "exercise" is a way that Stoics and other philosophical schools would characterize philosophy, framing it as central to an "art of living" or "therapeutic of the passions" that encompasses all of life and many different activities.[4] This spiritual exercise may be seen as similar to physical exercise: "[J]ust as, by dint of repeated physical exercises, athletes give new form and strength to their bodies, so the philosopher develops his strength of soul, modifies his inner climate, transforms his vision of the world, and finally, his entire being."[5] Through contemplating nature, universal reason, or totality, philosophers of various schools identify with some other in order to free themselves from ordinary concerns and desires.[6] Spiritual exercises, then, are central to a vision of self-formation modeled after therapy or medicine: the philosopher heals the soul from false belief as a doctor heals the body from disease.

Rabbis also set out scholastic activity, particularly Torah study, as an exercise in the broad sense that the process is not only intellectual but also central to the transformation of a student into a sage.[7] *Rabbi Nathan* differs from Hadot's account in the significant respect that, as I noted in chapter 2b, the medical or therapeutic model is not prominent. Also, there are no parallels made between physical and spiritual exercise, and the text describes no specific practices or meditations—elaborated in terms of frequency, timing, location, or body position—that one should do as part of self-formation.[8]

In addition to this general account of philosophy as a way of life, Hadot discusses specific Greco-Roman exercises. For example, drawing upon two lists of Philo of Alexandria, Hadot categorizes Stoic practices as including "first attention, then meditations and 'remembrances of good things,' then the more intellectual exercises: reading, listening, research, and investigation, and finally the more active exercises: self-mastery, accomplishment of duties, and indifference to indifferent things."[9] Hadot also examines a number of other intellectual pursuits in the Greco-Roman world as being spiritual exercises, including physics, Socratic dialogue, and comportment toward death.[10]

The first form of exercise in the list—attention—is most important in relation to *Rabbi Nathan*.[11] Hadot writes that these exercises often are indicated by the Greek word *prosochē,* which is a "continuous vigilance and presence of mind, self consciousness which never sleeps, and constant tension of the spirit." He also quotes a passage from Marcus Aurelius's *Meditations* that centers on attention to the present moment:

> Everywhere and at all times, it is up to you to rejoice piously at what is occurring at the present moment, to conduct yourself with justice toward the people who are present here and now, and to apply the rules of discernment to your present representations, so that nothing slips in that is not objective.[12]

Hadot writes that this attention to the present moment can be "equivalent to the continuous exercise of the presence of God. In the words of Plotinus' disciple Porphyry: 'Let God be present as overseer and guardian of every action, deed, and word!'"[13]

This focus upon attention has notable similarities with the rabbinic instructions for maintaining focus upon divine reward and punishment (and the words of Torah) that I have discussed. We see a common concern with the general orientation that one maintains during all activity. The rabbinic teachings, like the Greco-Roman exercises, aim to move the person away from a focus on the day-to-day and from a self-centered perspective to a focus on an external other. Hadot's theoretical formulation of spiritual exercises, as well as his research on Hellenistic philosophical schools, provides a lens through which we can consider the practical significance of certain well-known maxims and their commentaries in *Rabbi Nathan*.

   At the same time, a full comparison of rabbinic and philosophical exercises would likely lead to an exploration of difference within this similarity. As with other features of *Rabbi Nathan* (including its maxims, genealogical lists, and narratives), rabbinic forms of expression and underlying concerns have similarities with the writings of philosophical schools, yet the content differs dramatically. Rabbis attend not to nature, reason, or the immediate moment but to Torah and divine justice.[14] Some rabbinic teachings centered upon Torah call for the elimination of certain but not all passions (arguably the teaching of Rabbi Hananiah, and perhaps also the "test" narratives sages discussed in chapter 2b). Instructions centered upon God, in contrast, call for the development of particular emotional states, including distinct forms of anxiety, love, and fear or reverence. This difference also appears in comparing philosophic and rabbinic orientations toward death. Hadot discusses various forms of "training for death," ranging in time from Socrates to Plotinus, in which one contemplates a universal perspective or totality in order to transcend states of subjectivity or individuality.[15] Contrast the deathbed scene of Rabban Yohanan ben Zakkai, in which the sage is overwhelmed with God's presence as king and as judge. In this moment, his senses both of the divine and of his subjectivity are greatly intensified. The result is an intense emotional expression—crying.[16]

   What historical claims, if any, can be drawn from these observations? My minimal claim, which I most strongly assert, is heuristic rather than historical: Hadot's formulation of spiritual exercises provides a valuable scholarly tool through which we can examine certain passages in rabbinic literature. These teachings not only present rabbinic beliefs and concepts as part of instruction to guide a person's action, but also they are exercises of attention in the specific sense that I have presented. A more maximal set of claims, however, could be developed. The broad yet very important characterization of rabbinic Judaism as "part of the general 'discursive space' of the Hellenistic culture in Late Antiquity" opens up the challenge and possibility of specifying the relations within that space. Such a project would involve a reexamination of Hadot's descriptive work, detailed research into the dating of the rabbinic teachings I have examined, and close comparative analysis between specific passages in rabbinic and Greco-Roman philosophical sources.[17]

Conclusion

In my analysis of *The Fathers According to Rabbi Nathan,* I have aimed to draw out both that which is specific and distinctive as well as that which is general and exemplary. Within the text, I have worked inductively, examining individual teachings and their nuances, but I have also identified broad themes and concerns that run throughout this entire corpus. As a result, I have both argued the general claim that diverse teachings in *Rabbi Nathan* prescribe a process of ethical transformation centered on chosen relations of subordination to, and internalization of, three central external others, and I have shown the tremendous variety of ways that these dynamics of subordination and internalization are portrayed.[1]

This dual commitment to the distinctive and the exemplary is also present in my treatment of the text in relation to other sources. On one hand, within the rabbinic movement, *Rabbi Nathan* upholds a particular set of ideals focused on a compelling sage who guides disciples in the study and practice of Torah. The text presents a scholastic community set in Roman Palestine that is politically moderate and separate from the institution of the patriarch. Such interests are intertwined with its ethics, including the extensive concerns with the control of speech and the strong focus on Torah as the means of transforming the *yetzer.* As I have often pointed out in the footnotes, consideration of additional sources will reveal ethical outlooks that are not prominent in *Rabbi Nathan.* These include concepts (such as divine compassion), tropes (such as biological metaphors for Torah as nourishing), and configurations (such as the *yetzer* being set primarily in relation to divine justice rather than Torah).

On the other hand, I chose *Rabbi Nathan* as an exemplary source for the study of rabbinic character ethics. It is a large compilation, created over several hundred years, with numerous parallel sources elsewhere in rabbinic literature. My analysis concerns a significant stream of rabbinic thought, and the research questions and methods that I have articulated should have an even wider resonance. My conceptual tools for the descriptive study of ethics, attention to pedagogical features of the text, and focus upon the sage, tradition, and deity as key external others, all can be starting points for inquiry into other ethical outlooks—in rabbinic literature, in late antiquity, and beyond.[2]

In the introduction, I presented my theoretical framing of ethics in two stages: first a general account of character ethics and then a more detailed treatment of ethical transformation as willed or chosen subjection. I would like to conclude by examining two sets of issues that emerge from the study. One concerns character ethics and the interrelation of concepts, and the other concerns subjection and the relation between pedagogical discourse and the social world.

The Interrelation of Value Concepts in Rabbinic Character Ethics

My initial framing of character ethics has been a tripartite question: How does a person or group understand (a) what people are at origin or by nature (b) what ideal people are and do, and (c) processes of transformation from the given to the ideal? In my examinations of Torah and divine judgment in *Rabbi Nathan,* I identified two sets of responses to this question.

The first set frames the natural or spontaneous elements of human beings in terms of transgressive tendencies, often though not always linked with the categories of *yetzer* and the heart. The ideal sage is a man who is fully constituted through the Torah such that his most basic impulses are structured in accord with rabbinic laws and ideals. He attains this state by allowing himself to be trained, molded, planted, conquered, or governed by the tradition. The second set of responses presumes basic desires for reward and fears of punishment. The theology of God's justice appeals to these desires and fears, steering the self toward right action. The ideal, though, is orientation toward God not out of self-interest but with love and divine-directed reverence, and one attains this state through exercises of attention focusing upon the divine.

What connections can we find between these two ways of framing character ethics? Or in broader terms, how do the tradition and deity interrelate? Kadushin's notion of organicity is useful, for it draws attention to ways that rabbinic value concepts interweave with one another. Torah has its roots in God's speech, one learns about God's action through Torah, and the study and practice of Torah can bring God's reward. More specifically, we have seen points of overlap—one passage in which the struggle with *yetzer* is framed in relation to God and not Torah, another in which the bad *yetzer* fears divine judgment and attempts to destroy the body, and yet another in which a sage appeals to God for compassion given limits in human potential for cultivating the *yetzer*. However, deeper issues remain concerning the interrelation of value concepts in rabbinic ethics, such as the problem of whether or not a concept can be implicit in a passage when relevant terminology does not appear. For example, if a teaching describes a wicked person sinning before God, and no mention is made of his *yetzer*, can we infer that the text presumes such a person to be governed by his bad *yetzer*? I would be cautious about making such a claim, but if we are going to move from textual analysis to considering rabbinic thought, such inferences could be important.

A more complex aspect of the organic relations between value concepts emerges through considering a specific problem in the material on *yetzer*, a problem that appears for many ethical outlooks that have pessimistic views of human nature. The most common understanding of transgression in *Rabbi Nathan* appears to be that humans are born with the bad *yetzer* or some equivalent, and that its transformation comes through cultural processes centered upon Torah. People have a good *yetzer*, but if we put weight upon its "birth" being the age of thirteen, which is a social category marking legal responsibility, and upon its being a receptor of Torah, then good impulses appear not to be innate parts of the self but rather products of tradition. If this is the case, then rabbis lack an account of why someone would follow the path of Torah in the first place. What draws a young man governed by the bad *yetzer* to take on the commandments, immerse himself in Torah, and work to change his desires?[3]

Several answers can be given,[4] but the strongest reply would be to interpret accounts of *yetzer* as organically related in a strong sense with those of divine justice. The tropes of reward and punishment presume a self-interested desiring and fearing person, and they offer motivation for such a person to follow God's commandments. One could say, then, that this self-interest—gaining payment for right character and action, and avoiding divine punishment—would be the initial incentive for transforming the *yetzer*.[5] This answer does not appear in the text, though, and a danger is that such a discussion may be more akin to the work of later traditional commentators interpreting the text than the scholarly project of describing rabbinic thought in late antiquity. At the same time, we scholars may have to face such dangers if we want to move forward in addressing the subtleties of rabbinic ethics.[6]

Pedagogical Discourse and the Social World

I have emphasized that concepts such as Torah and divine justice are embedded in a range of rhetorical forms, including narratives, parables, midrashic exegesis, and of course maxims. Each form instructs the recipient in its own ways: maxims often address the subject directly, sage stories present exemplary models of men who have, to one degree or another, successfully cultivated themselves, and so on. Scholars have noted for a long time that rabbinic texts do not accurately describe the social world but rather present idealized accounts whose purpose is in part to change and transform that world. My study has given great weight to this point, both examining in detail the pedagogical features of the text and working to imagine the function of that text in the formation of ideal selves and communities. The maxims and their commentary call out to and instruct a subject who, ideally, would respond to the instruction in the affirmative and appropriate it in guiding his action and shaping his character.[7]

The pedagogical nature of *Rabbi Nathan* is an important factor in interpreting the imagery that depicts the impact of others upon the self. *Rabbi Nathan* generally portrays the sages, Torah, and God as powerful, able to liberate their subjects from other dangerous or oppressive authorities, most notably Rome but also competing religious elites. The text also tends to frame the student as weak and the authorities as imposing themselves upon him—as iron on flesh, fire upon iron, a warrior upon a city, or a king upon a subject. These tropes are among the many strategies in *Rabbi Nathan* that aim to persuade, entice, and guide followers along the rabbinic path, and sages clearly considered subordination to be a key element in the relationships that facilitate the transformation of the self.

The imagery, though, does not necessarily reflect material power relations. In late antiquity the subordinate relations of a rabbinic student to the sage, tradition, and God were not imbedded in a strong institutional setting or upheld by significant ability to inflict force. Throughout much of the period, moreover, the rabbinic sages may have been marginal figures in Roman Palestine, their tradition embraced by relatively few.[8] Even within the text, reading against the grain, there is evidence that the community is fragile, the tradition disputed, and divine support lacking. We read of Jews who challenge the sages or who have their own legal traditions, students with varying degrees of diligence and talent, and renowned sages who do not begin to study until they are twenty-one or even forty years old. The Torah is vulnerable both to individual volatility and communal lapses in commitment.

The larger political picture is bleak. While *Rabbi Nathan* generally avoids or omits the events of history, we find extensive discussions of Romans destroying the Jerusalem Temple in 70 CE and some portrayals of martyrdom after the Bar Kokhba rebellions in the early second century. History appears, then, in the form of disaster and oppression; it gives testimony not to the presence but to the apparent absence of God. These observations, I believe, set out a dark background to the picture painted in *Rabbi Nathan,* against which its bright and strong accounts of rabbinic authorities show all the more intensely—accounts that are central to an impressive project of trying to create, through pedagogical discourse, a world that is stable and ordered in accord with rabbinic ideals.

Notes

Bibliography

Indexes

Notes

Introduction

1. Catherine Hezser characterizes the rabbinic movement as a network "in which each rabbi had direct contacts to a limited number of colleagues and through them indirect contact to other rabbis whom he could consult in case of need." See *The Social Structure of the Rabbinic Movement in Roman Palestine*, 228–39. For the designation of the rabbis as a "class" (not in the Marxist sense), see Lee Levine, *The Rabbinic Class of Roman Palestine in Late Antiquity*. An important recent study of both Palestinian and Babylonian sages in relation to their social contexts is Richard Kalmin, *The Sage in Jewish Society of Late Antiquity*. Seth Schwartz makes a strong argument for the lack of rabbinic influence among Jews during the classical rabbinic period, particularly from 135 to 350 CE but also from 350 to 640 CE. See *Imperialism and Jewish Society, 200 BCE to 640 CE*, 175–76, 199–202, 238–39, and generally 101–289. The "elite" status of the rabbis is then complex: they were clearly elites in terms of education, they aspired to attain roles of influence and leadership in Jewish communities, and at times they were successful.

2. Marc Hirshman presents key issues in an articulate fashion, writing that the rabbinic sages of the first centuries of the common era "turned debate and dissent into their very trademark. Whether in matters legal, ethical, or theological, differing and even contradictory opinions were the norm. A natural result of this rabbinic posture is that the entire rabbinic corpus is anthological. We do not possess individual works of the rabbis, great as they might have been. We have instead catenae or collections of statements. Sometimes they present real conversations between sages, but other times they reflect an editorial juxtaposition of opposing views. These characteristics of rabbinic literature create a formidable challenge for those who wish to treat rabbinic thought systematically" ("Rabbinic Universalism in the Second and Third Centuries," 101).

3. The current critical edition of the text is Solomon Schechter and Menahem Kister, *Aboth de Rabbi Nathan: Solomon Schechter Edition*. Major textual studies include Louis Finkelstein, *Introduction to the Treatises Abot and Abot of Rabbi Nathan* (Hebrew with an English summary) and "Introductory Study to *Pirke Abot*." A recent and crucial study is Menahem Kister, *Studies in Avot de-Rabbi Nathan:*

Text, Redaction, and Interpretation (Hebrew). All translations of Hebrew and Aramaic texts in this book are my own. Both versions A and B of *Rabbi Nathan* appear in reliable English translations that have excellent notes and scholarly commentary: Judah Goldin, *The Fathers According to Rabbi Nathan;* Anthony Saldarini, *The Fathers According to Rabbi Nathan (Abot de Rabbi Nathan) Version B;* Eli Coshdan, *'Aboth d'Rabbi Nathan;* Jacob Neusner, *The Fathers According to Rabbi Nathan: An Analytical Translation and Explanation.* Very important studies include Goldin, *Studies in Midrash and Related Literature,* 3–117; Saldarini, *Scholastic Rabbinism: A Literary Study of the Fathers According to Rabbi Nathan;* Neusner, *Judaism and Story* and *Form-Analytical Comparison in Rabbinic Judaism: Structure and Form in The Fathers and The Fathers According to Rabbi Nathan.*

4. I use "rabbinic ethical literature" to refer to texts including *The Fathers, Rabbi Nathan, Derekh Eretz Rabbah, Derekh Eretz Zuṭa,* parts of *Kallah Rabbati,* and arguably *Seder Eliyahu Rabbah* and *Zuṭa.* Daniel Sperber labels similar material as "Rabbinic wisdom literature." See his *Commentary on Derech Erez Zuṭa, Chapters Five to Eight.* He describes collections of epigrams as manuals in his "Manuals of Rabbinic Conduct," 9–26. Note also the category "ethical midrashim" employed by H. L. Strack and Günter Stemberger in *Introduction to the Talmud and Midrash,* 340–43.

5. There are complex textual and literary issues concerning whether this passage does in fact comment upon "raise up many disciples." In the printed editions and manuscripts, this passage is at the end of chapter 2, where it would be part of the commentary to another statement of the Great Assembly, "make a fence for the Torah." Solomon Schechter emends the text such that it opens chapter 3 and comments upon "raise up many disciples." Louis Finkelstein disagrees with this change, but Goldin offers an analysis of all of *Rabbi Nathan A,* chapter 3, that supports Schechter. See A3,14–15 and nn.1, 4; Finkelstein, *Introduction,* 26–28; Goldin, "The Third Chapter of *'Abot de-Rabbi Natan,*" in *Studies in Midrash,* 101–16; also Kister, *Studies,* 130.

6. The image of proximity conveyed by the Hebrew *nitqarebu* is among a cluster of spatial tropes within *Rabbi Nathan.* Passages that comment upon the instruction to "make a fence for the Torah," which I discuss in chapter 2a, counsel that people should not come near *(q.r.b.)* or should distance themselves *(r.ḥ.q.)* from a menstruating or seductive woman, from competing religious groups, and from transgression in general. Here, in the passage that follows that material, the House of Hillel calls for proximity—one should bring people close *(q.r.b.)* to the study of Torah.

7. Solomon Schechter, *Aspects of Rabbinic Theology: Major Concepts of the Talmud,* 136.

8. Most stories and fragments focus on his late start, how he becomes rich, and his relation with Rachel his wife—both her devotion to him, and his study and his gifts to her after attaining success; see *b. Shabb.* 59a–b; *b. Ned.* 50a–b; *b. Ketub.* 62b–63a; *y. Shabb.* 6:1, 7d; *Siphre Deut.* 357; Finkelstein, ed., *Sifre on Deuteronomy,*

429. Tal Ilan discusses this opening to the story of Rabbi Akiba as part of her extensive treatment of material concerning Rachel, his wife. See *Mine and Yours Are Hers: Retrieving Women's History from Rabbinic Literature*, 274–77. This story and parallels are discussed in Shmuel Safrai's "Tales of the Sages in the Palestinian Tradition and the Babylonian Talmud," 220–29. For an analysis of this set of stories as setting out rabbinic ideals for relations between rabbis and their wives, see Daniel Boyarin, *Carnal Israel: Reading Sex in Talmudic Culture*, 134–66. Also note Neusner, *Judaism and Story*, 79–86, 118, 134, 147–49.

9. In the commentary to Yose ben Yoezer's maxim, the compilers present the story of Rabbi Akiba along with one of Rabbi Eliezer ben Hyrcanus. In *Rabbi Nathan A,* the narrative of Rabbi Akiba is told as commentary upon the third element of the maxim; in *Rabbi Nathan B,* the second (A6,27–33; B11–13,27–33). The stories are parallel in that each has the five qualities listed above (begins study late, goes to the sages, and so on). Given this basic picture, each story contains features of the legends that surround the particular rabbi—including Rabbi Eliezer's asceticism and his skeptical father, and Rabbi Akiba's diligence and his supportive wife. For a full analysis of the story concerning Rabbi Eliezer, addressing various recensions in rabbinic literature, see Zipporah Kagen, "Divergent Tendencies and Their Literary Moulding in the Aggadah," 151–70; also Neusner, *Judaism and Story*, 79–86, 119–22, 134, 147–49. I examine other elements of the stories at various points in this book.

10. Reading *shahaqu* (carved) as *she-ḥiqqequ* (chiseled). This prooftext appears in a different teaching (attributed to the school of Rabbi Ishmael) concerning the bad *yetzer* that also employs the metaphor of a rock, but the agent that transforms the *yetzer* is the study house (*b. Qidd.* 30b and *b. Sukk.* 52b).

11. The motif of a well has been studied extensively. See Michael Fishbane, "The Well of Living Water: A Biblical Motif and Its Ancient Transformations," 3–16; David Flusser and Shmuel Safrai, "The Essene Doctrine of Hypostasis and Rabbi Meir," 306–16; Steven D. Fraade, *From Tradition to Commentary*, 111, 254–55 n.182. Another case of water as a motif in *Rabbi Nathan* appears on A11,47–48; B22,47; *Fathers* 1:11. In a later version of this account of Rabbi Akiba, the image has strong mystical resonance. See Moshe Idel, *Kabbalah: New Perspectives*, 77–78, and Fishbane, "Well," 14–15. In the Book of Ezekiel, the figure of a "heart of stone" is employed to describe human rebelliousness that requires a divine act of transformation (Ezek. 36:26; also see *b. Sukk.* 52a; *Lev. Rab.* 17:6). In the parallel story of Rabbi Akiba in *Rabbi Nathan B,* he comments upon seeing the well that "my heart is hard like a stone" (B12,29). Also see Alon Goshen-Gottstein, *The Sinner and the Amnesiac: The Rabbinic Invention of Elisha ben Abuya and Eleazar ben Arach,* 238–40 and notes.

12. Ivan Marcus offers a different and very insightful analysis of this passage. He states that the metaphor describes "mental enlargement." Focusing on the sense of heart as "mind," he writes, "[T]he study of Torah will enlarge the heart, that is, expand the mind's capacity to contain Torah. This metaphor is very similar to the mishnaic image of the mind as a cistern to be filled up with Torah traditions

before it can ever become a self-sustaining 'fountain' of independent understanding" (*Rituals of Childhood: Jewish Acculturation in Medieval Europe*, 49–50). This interpretation gives weight to the many intellectual applications of the well/fountain/cistern motif. However, there are three reasons to situate the story of Rabbi Akiba in the context of more holistic ethical transformation. First, the motif of water often conveys features of character as well as intellect (see, for example, the saying of Rabbi Meir in *Fathers* 6:1; for analysis and parallels, see Flusser and Safrai, "The Essene Doctrine," and Fishbane, "Well"). Second, the particular prooftext of Job 14:19 appears in the Talmud in relation to the transformation of the bad *yetzer* (*b. Qidd.* 30b and *b. Sukk.* 52b). Third, as I show in part 2, in the literary context of *Rabbi Nathan,* the "heart" is a seat of desire and emotion, and Torah affects the student not only intellectually but also at the level of emotion and desire.

13. I discuss at length my definitions of sage, tradition, and deity, and the significance of these terms for ethics, in each of the relevant chapters. For now, though, I note that charismatic, authoritative individuals such as sages, teachers, and saviors can be crucial both for teaching and for modeling ways of living, particularly in religious contexts. On the figure of the sage in ancient Greek literature, see Pierre Hadot, "The Figure of Socrates," in *Philosophy as a Way of Life: Spiritual Exercises from Socrates to Foucault,* 147–78. On teachers and saviors as religious types, see Lee Yearley, "Teachers and Saviors," 225–43. Traditions—discourses and practices that have been handed down over time, or at least which certain people claim have been handed down over time—can be important elements in defining selves, both because of intrinsic persuasiveness and because of the legitimacy that people claim for them. See Alasdair C. MacIntyre, *After Virtue: A Study in Moral Theory,* especially 220–23; Hans-Georg Gadamer, *Truth and Method,* part 2, especially 277–85, 358–62; Edward Shils, *Tradition;* Eric Hobsbawm and Terence Ranger, eds., *The Invention of Tradition.* Finally, even if the scholar's orientation precludes belief in supernatural beings, ethical development in a given culture may center upon spirits, angels, demons, deities, ultimate principles, or the very absence of these. A deity, for example, may be understood to have direct impact upon the self, and it may legitimate and ground any of the above transforming elements—a teacher, a tradition, and so on.

14. This work is not one of modern ethical reflection but of historically distanced descriptive analysis, even though I draw upon conceptual tools from contemporary ethics. I am aware that I examine the classical sources of what has become a major world religion. I believe that the tension between the importance of rabbinic sources for Judaism in the present day, and the striking differences between rabbinic worldviews and those of modernity, make the project of examining this ancient material particularly fruitful. My descriptive study, though, is a very different project than the important field of modern Jewish ethics, which draws upon rabbinic materials and places them in relation to contemporary ethical problems and frameworks. The goal of this other approach, however, is not to describe fully the ethics of earlier historical periods. On the modern study of ethics,

both prescriptive and descriptive, see Louis Newman, *Past Imperatives: Studies in the History and Theory of Jewish Ethics,* 1–14. Recent works of modern Jewish ethics include Marvin Fox, ed., *Modern Jewish Ethics: Theory and Practice;* Elliot Dorff and Louis Newman, eds., *Contemporary Jewish Ethics and Morality: A Reader.* A recent modern formulation of traditional Jewish ethical terms is Eugene Borowitz and Frances Schwartz, *The Jewish Moral Virtues.* My account also should not be conflated with the construction of Judaism as "ethical monotheism" that emerged in the nineteenth century, and my focus upon ethics should not downplay the significance of law *(halakhah)* in rabbinic thought. Rather, as I discuss further in the introduction, I see rabbinic ethics as deeply intertwined with or encompassing rabbinic law. I thank Jerome Copulsky for raising these issues, and see David Novak, *Natural Law in Judaism,* especially 82–91 on the modern equation of Judaism and ethics. Finally, perhaps the most prominent figure in Jewish ethics today is Emmanuel Lévinas. Examining the similarities and differences between my account of rabbinic ethics and his phenomenology as well as textual interpretations could yield important insights but is beyond what I attempt in this book. In general terms, though, I have found him to be an exciting interpreter of ancient sources for a modern or postmodern audience, but I have been wary of drawing upon his studies for this descriptive project.

15. The Mishnah was completed in the early third century in Roman Palestine, though *The Fathers* was likely reworked and edited over a much longer period. One sign that it is a late addition to the Mishnah is that different manuscripts contain the text in different parts of the canon. On the tractate, see M. B. Lerner, "The Tractate *Avot,*" 263–81.

16. These points have been explored at length in the scholarly literature. See especially Finkelstein, *Introduction;* Goldin, *Studies in Midrash,* 3–117; and my discussion in chapter 1a.

17. I employ "discourse" to denote language as spoken or written by people and directed toward other people, in contrast with language treated as a system or structure. See the account in Paul Ricoeur, *Interpretation Theory: Discourse and the Surplus of Meaning.* The term is particularly valuable for my analysis because discourse includes both oral and written instances of language, and *Rabbi Nathan* preserves in writing much material that, in the context of late antiquity, likely was oral or at least taught and studied orally. In addition, scholars of discourse attend to the social function of language and its relation to both practices (such as self-transformation) and institutions (such as the rabbinic movement). I develop the concept of discourse further later in the introduction and throughout. I draw the important term "pedagogic discourse" from Steven Fraade's valuable study of rabbinic midrash, *From Tradition,* especially 163–64; see also Elizabeth Shanks Alexander's work on pedagogical aspects of the Mishnah in "Casuistic Elements in Mishnaic Law: Examples from Mishnah Shevu'ot," 232–43. My use of "pedagogical discourse" has some overlap with Michael Satlow's use of "rhetoric" in his study of rabbinic sexuality, *Tasting the Dish: Rabbinic Rhetorics of Sexuality,* 7–11 and

throughout. Persuasion is certainly a strong element in pedagogy, though my ter-minology emphasizes the scholastic context presented and presumed by *Rabbi Na-than* (see my discussion in part 1).

18. Key works of Max Kadushin include *The Theology of Seder Eliahu: A Study in Organic Thinking, Organic Thinking: A Study in Rabbinic Thought,* and *The Rabbinic Mind,* second edition. Classic studies of rabbinic thought include Solo-mon Schechter, *Aspects of Rabbinic Theology;* Adolph Büchler, *Studies in Sin and Atonement in the Rabbinic Literature of the First Century;* George Foot Moore, *Ju-daism in the First Centuries of the Christian Era;* Ephraim Urbach, *The Sages: Their Concepts and Beliefs.* An exemplary recent work that attends to many of the topics that I examine is Fraade, *From Tradition.* Hava Tirosh-Samuelson's recent exten-sive study of Jewish virtue ethics includes a chapter on late ancient rabbis (*Happi-ness in Premodern Judaism: Virtue, Knowledge, and Well-Being,* 101–42).

19. In writing "thought and culture," I generally agree with Boyarin's account of rabbinic literature as discourse. He writes that he moves beyond "rabbinic thought" to culture "as a set of complexly related practices both textual and em-bodied"; see *Carnal Israel,* 10–18. I differ in that I do not set out a contrast between studying "thought" and "culture," but rather I examine thought as it arises in and through discourse and as it relates to practice. On one hand, I draw upon the con-ceptual tools of discourse analysis, yet at the same time I hold that *Rabbi Nathan* represents sophisticated thought about ethics, theology, and other matters that is comparable to the conceptual work done by other intellectual elites of late ancient Rome as well as ancient Greece, China, and other regions. For this reason, I attend far more than Boyarin does to genres, tropes, and concepts. I thank Charlotte Fon-robert for her suggestions regarding these points.

20. The problem of historically contextualizing *Rabbi Nathan* is a thorny one. I address the issues in chapter 1a, but in brief, *Rabbi Nathan* presents a discursive world depicting Roman Palestine primarily in the first and second centuries CE. There is a strong consensus among scholars, however, that the text was compiled and edited over a period that extended far beyond that time.

21. For a brief list of terms that were coined or gained new significance in the classical rabbinic period, see Urbach, *Sages,* 4. The observation that elites in late antiquity were particularly concerned with the self or person goes back at least to Marcel Mauss's essay, "A Category of the Human Mind: The Notion of Person; the Notion of Self." For a recent translation by W. D. Halls and valuable essays criti-cally developing Mauss's observation, see Michael Carrithers, Steven Collins, and Steven Lukes, eds., *The Category of the Person: Anthropology, Philosophy, History.* Michel Foucault has made very strong and controversial statements concerning the "care of the self" in late antiquity. For historical purposes, his research is valu-able to the extent that, as Arnold Davidson writes, "the manner in which Foucault conceptualized issues showed clear resonance with" the work of historians such as Paul Veyne, Pierre Hadot, and Jean-Pierre Vernant. For Davidson's examination of

Foucault in relation to these scholars, see "Ethics as Ascetics: Foucault, the History of Ethics, and Ancient Thought," 63–80. Foucault's key writings on the "care of the self" are *The Use of Pleasure; The Care of the Self,* and Luther H. Martin, Huck Gutman, and Patrick H. Hutton, eds., *Technologies of the Self: A Seminar with Michel Foucault.* Foucault highlights the intensification of these dynamics during late antiquity in *Care of the Self,* 39–68. Paul Veyne uses the category "care of the self" in a section of his history of private life, *The Roman Empire,* 229–32. He places this discussion within a larger section that is provocatively entitled "Tranquilizers" (207–33). On "spiritual exercises," see Pierre Hadot, *Philosophy as a Way of Life* and *The Inner Citadel: The Meditations of Marcus Aurelius.* Also on Roman elites, see Maude Gleason, *Making Men: Sophists and Self-Presentation in Ancient Rome,* especially xi, xxv. On early Christianity, see Peter Brown, *The Body and Society: Men, Women, and Sexual Renunciation in Early Christianity* (note Brown's comment about his debt to Foucault on xvii–xviii); David Brakke, *Athanasius and Asceticism,* who draws upon Foucault on 142–200; Virginia Burrus, *"Begotten, not Made": Conceiving Manhood in Late Antiquity,* who very explicitly responds to Brown's research; also Jennifer Hevelone-Harper, "Spiritual Direction," in *Late Antiquity: A Guide to the Postclassical World,* ed. G. W. Bowersock et al., 704–5 with references. The work of both Foucault and Brown has influenced Boyarin's studies of rabbinic Judaism, including *Carnal Israel.* Martha Nussbaum's important research addresses similar topics, though she makes strong distinctions between philosophical and nonphilosophical materials that Foucault does not. See *The Therapy of Desire: Theory and Practice in Hellenistic Ethics,* especially 5–6, 353–54 on Foucault, Hadot, and Davidson.

22. See Paul Ricoeur, *Oneself as Another.*

23. On this point I am inspired by Charles Taylor's distinction between "procedural" and "substantive" rationalities and by Ricoeur's discussion of "morality" and "ethics"; see Taylor, *Sources of the Self: The Making of the Modern Identity,* 85–90 and throughout; Ricoeur, *Oneself as Another,* 170–71; also MacIntyre, *After Virtue,* 118.

24. Among virtue ethicists, my work is particularly inspired by Taylor, *Sources of the Self;* MacIntyre, *After Virtue, Whose Justice? Which Rationality?,* and *Three Rival Versions of Moral Inquiry: Encyclopedia, Genealogy, and History;* Lee Yearley, *Mencius and Aquinas: Theories of Virtue and Conceptions of Courage;* Philip J. Ivanhoe, *Ethics in the Confucian Tradition: The Thought of Mencius and Wang Yang-ming,* and *Confucian Moral Self-Cultivation,* 17–30. For other works on virtue ethics, see the review article of Lee Yearley, "Recent Work on Virtue"; and the important articles collected in Roger Crisp and Michael Slote, eds., *Virtue Ethics.* On subject formation, a few central works include Foucault's *Use of Pleasure* and *Care of the Self;* Martin, Gutman, and Hutton, *Technologies of the Self;* Arnold Davidson, "Ethics as Ascetics"; Talal Asad, *Genealogies of Religion: Discipline and Reasons of Power in Christianity and Islam;* Judith Butler, *The Psychic Life of Power: Theories in Subjection.*

25. Ricoeur, for example, writes that ethics (what I am calling character ethics) encompasses but does not take the place of morality (or deontology) (*Oneself as Another*, 170).

26. This concern with character does not mean that the law is reduced in importance to being instrumental, only a means for developing oneself. Rather, rabbis uphold observance of the law as intrinsically valuable. An examination of character ethics does not have to begin with nonlegal sources; a character ethic could likely be drawn out from the law, and a valuable book for such an inquiry is Howard Eilberg-Schwartz, *The Human Will in Judaism: The Mishnah's Philosophy of Intention*. On the modern debates concerning ethics and law in Jewish ethics, see Newman, *Past Imperatives*, 45–62. I thank Thomas Lewis for his insightful comments concerning the relation between procedural- and character-based approaches to ethics.

27. Compare MacIntyre, *After Virtue*, 52–53. In relation to Foucault's ethics (a) would be similar to his "ethical substance," (b) to his *"telos,"* and (c) to his "mode of subjection" and "ethical work." See Foucault, *Use of Pleasure*, 25–30 and the more extensive analysis in 38–92.

28. Here and throughout I use these terms synonymously to describe this third element of ethics. Each one has problems. In thinking about rabbinic terminology, I find "transformation" to be the most accurate, since it conveys that one works with and changes God's "formation" *(yetzer)* within the person (I will discuss the concept of *yetzer* at length in chapter 2b).

29. My distinction between discourse and practice as two elements of the process of transformation aims to capture, in somewhat broader terms, Foucault's "mode of subjection" and "ethical work" (*Use of Pleasure*, 26–27, 53–77). Asad emphasizes the importance of the distinction between analyzing (a) practice and communal structure and (b) a symbol system (see *Genealogies of Religion*, 36). As thought that reflects upon or frames practice, rabbinic ethical literature can also be categorized as a form of metapraxis. Thomas Kasulis writes that metapraxis is "the development of a philosophical theory about the nature of a particular praxis, in this case, religious praxis. It theorizes about what lies behind or beyond the practices of a religious tradition" ("Philosophy as Metapraxis," 169–95). Rabbinic *'aggadah,* however, is a variant of metapraxis in that it does not present a "philosophical theory." For a study of character formation that centers on practices, see Asad's exemplary work on medieval Christian monasticism. He addresses the "disciplined formation of the Christian self," particularly the programs for forming moral dispositions, in monastic communities organized according to the Rule of Saint Benedict. He focuses upon the roles of surveillance, hierarchy, set schedules of activities, and the infliction of pain in the cultivation of virtue. See his articles "Pain and Truth in Medieval Christian Ritual" and "Discipline and Humility in Christian Monasticism," in *Genealogies of Religion*, 130, 136, and generally 83–167. See also Saba Mahmood, *Women's Piety and Embodied Discipline: The Islamic Resurgence in*

Contemporary Egypt; and Jason David BeDuhn, *The Manichaean Body in Discipline and Ritual,* especially 66–68.

30. This oblique approach to ethics, by way of other cultural forms, is somewhat similar to Foucault's study of ethics by way of diet, marriage, erotic relations, and love. See his *Use of Pleasure* and *Care of the Self.* Regarding the three rabbinic authorities of sage, Torah, and God, note Schwartz's argument that in the first century CE, "the three pillars of ancient Judaism" were God, Torah, and Temple (*Imperialism and Jewish Society,* 49–87). The triad I identify in *Rabbi Nathan,* then, shows a post-70 CE outlook that centers on the continuation of the first two with the sage present rather than the (destroyed) Temple.

31. MacIntyre, *After Virtue,* 216–19 and generally 204–20. See also Emile Benveniste's comments concerning psychoanalysis and discourse in "Remarks on the Function of Language in Freudian Theory," in *Problems in General Linguistics,* 65 and generally 65–75.

32. I refer to his key sentence, "A living tradition then is an historically extended, socially embodied argument, and an argument precisely in part about the goods which constitute that tradition" (*After Virtue,* 222). I discuss the concept of tradition at length in part 2, including an examination of MacIntyre's definition in chapter 2c.

33. David Harvey, *Justice, Nature, and the Geography of Difference,* 53–54, also 83. In the intellectual world of early rabbis, a similar dynamic of reception and creativity can be seen in the focus upon "receiving" *(q.b.l.)* as well as "passing on" *(m.s.r.)* the Torah, or in the focus upon a tripartite call to study, practice, and teach the commandments.

34. Both Harvey and Ricoeur draw attention to the body as a key starting point for inquiry, since it is a physical and tangible center point of human existence. Harvey writes that the body "is an unfinished product, historically and geographically malleable in certain ways"—not infinitely malleable, but evolving and changing based both on internal and external processes. It "is not a closed and sealed entity but a relational 'thing' that is created, bounded, sustained, and ultimately dissolved in a spatiotemporal flux of multiple processes." In an apt metaphor, Harvey characterizes the body as "porous"—internalizing elements from the natural world (oxygen, food, liquid) as well as the social (including, but not only, discourse). See his *Spaces of Hope,* 98–99; also *Justice, Nature, and the Geography of Difference,* 51–54. Ricoeur also addresses the internalization of social processes that exist outside oneself (*Oneself as Another,* 33–35; 122, 150, 319–29). In reading *Rabbi Nathan,* this attention to the body is a valuable reminder for today's readers to attend, in our scholarly imagination, to the embodied persons who spoke, heard, wrote down, read, disseminated, or otherwise engaged with the text. There is also a different but related question of how the body is portrayed within the discourse of *Rabbi Nathan,* which is a topic I address in my article, "The Beastly Body in Rabbinic Self-Formation."

35. Harvey, *Justice, Nature, and the Geography of Difference,* 79–80 (emphasis in the original).

36. Ibid., 80, 87.

37. Ricoeur, *Oneself as Another,* 113–14, 158–59. This account builds upon his extended discussion of narrative and temporality in *Time and Narrative.*

38. Ricoeur, *Oneself as Another,* 158–63.

39. More generally, we do not have access into the "paths of appropriation" used by those who encountered rabbinic discourse in late antiquity. At certain points the text itself gives prescriptions for ways that the recipient is to respond to its own discourse, and I address these whenever possible.

40. There is a cluster of scholars, extending back at least to Marcel Mauss, which does not treat the self as an ahistorical essence that transcends culture but as something that is shaped by particular social and cultural contexts. Mauss argued long ago that the relative prominence of the self *(moi)* in relation to person or persona *(personne)* varies according to cultural context. See his "A Category of the Human Mind"; also Hans Kippenberg et al., eds., *Concepts of Person in Religion and Thought;* and George Levine, ed., *Constructions of the Self.* A significant philosophical treatment of the self in modern Western philosophy is Taylor, *Sources of the Self.*

41. More generally, even in materials that have no explicit discussion concerning what humans are, no explicit discussion of selfhood, the scholar can search for what is presumed or invoked in pronominal expressions. From this minimal level, more complex accounts can be developed or analyzed, including constructions of not-self. See the elegant treatment of Buddhist thought by Steven Collins in *Selfless Persons,* especially 71–84; also "What Are Buddhists *Doing* When They Deny the Self?" 59–86.

42. Ricoeur highlights that the word "self" is itself a pronoun in many European languages, one that is often reflexive and intensifying (that which makes "him" into "himself"). See *Oneself as Another,* 1–2, 45–46, 192–93. As Thomas Lewis has pointed out to me, "reflexive" and "intensifying" can be problematic overtones. On the general topic of pronouns, see Benveniste, "The Nature of Pronouns," in *Problems in General Linguistics,* 217–22. Also, I find provocative the observation that several great twentieth-century thinkers build their understandings of the self/person/anthropos using pronouns—Sigmund Freud (I and it), Martin Buber (I, you, and it), Mauss, and, in his own way, Louis Althusser (you and I)— so we can situate their thought as complex variations on this linguistic analogy. See Mauss, "A Category of the Human Mind"; and Martin Buber, *I and Thou.* On the significance of Freud's use of pronouns and the issue of translation, see Bruno Bettelheim, *Freud and Man's Soul.* Note Althusser's use of the call, "Hey, you there!" in "Ideology and Ideological State Apparatuses (Notes Towards an Investigation)," 174. Also see Charles Winquest, "Person," 225–38.

43. As I discuss in chapter 1a and throughout, the discourse of *Rabbi Nathan* is not directed toward a universal and autonomous self but toward a male located

in specific scholastic and traditional relationships. In addition, Elaine Pagels has emphasized to me that *'adam* often does not refer to all persons and can exclude, for example, those who are female or enslaved. On the other hand, modern and postmodern Jewish interpreters have held that, in a society in which the text is read and responded to by a broader community than the original audience, there are possibilities for appropriation by selves not addressed by the text.

44. Ricoeur writes, "'I' and 'you,' to be sure, stand out from the group [of indicators] as interlocutors, subjects of utterance" (*Oneself as Another,* 30). Elsewhere he states, "Related to the act of utterance, the 'I' becomes first and foremost among the indicators; it indicates the one who designates himself in every utterance containing the word 'I'" (*Oneself as Another,* 45). The pronouns "I" and "you" are deeply intertwined and even "reversible," meaning that, "when I say 'you' to someone else, that person understands 'I' for himself or herself. When another addresses me in the second person, I feel I am implicated in the first person" (*Oneself as Another,* 192–93, and, generally 18, 40–46). Benveniste, "The Nature of Pronouns" and "Subjectivity in Language," in *Problems in General Linguistics,* 217–30. John Dunne has pointed out to me that this point must concern the reference of an utterance, not the grammatical person, since in many languages third-person pronouns may be used to address a person as "you." Also, we should be aware that, especially in literary works, "I" and "you" often indicate ideal or model authors and readers but not necessarily actual ones.

45. Ricoeur recognizes this disjunction, and in analyzing the self-designation of subjects, he devotes separate but related studies to discourse, action, narrative, and ethical commitment. See for example, *Oneself as Another,* 22, 93, 96, 98–102, 319, 335. Consider also the differing views of Benveniste, Butler, and Asad. Benveniste asserts a link between speaking, consciousness, and temporality. Individuals frame themselves as subjects when they refer to themselves as "I" in discourse, and subjectivity is "the psychic unity that transcends the totality of the actual experiences it assembles and that makes the permanence of the consciousness" (Benveniste, "Subjectivity," *Problems in General Linguistics,* 224–27). Butler's account of the subject centers on agency, but her goal is to theorize "the theory of power together with a theory of the psyche." Central to the psychic dynamics of the subject is self-reflection, which occurs through the conscience and which is intertwined with desire and melancholia (Butler, *Psychic Life,* 3, 22–30; her extended analysis of melancholia appears on 133–98). Asad, in contrast, argues that, "*agent* and *subject* (where the former is the principle of effectivity and the latter of consciousness) do not belong to the same theoretical universe and should not, therefore, be coupled." He emphasizes that consciousness is only a part of agency, for "instinctive reaction, the docile body, and the unconscious work, in their different ways, more pervasively and continuously than consciousness does" (Asad, *Genealogies of Religion,* 15–16, emphasis in the original). I agree with Asad that we should not assume a tight connection between consciousness and agency, that there are strong grounds for situating the category of the subject in relation to consciousness, and

that he is correct to emphasize the importance of "instinctive reaction, the docile body, and the unconscious." However, I agree with Butler that, as a contemporary concept, the link between power and the psyche is important to develop, and we should not equate the psyche with consciousness. Butler writes, "the subject emerges in tandem with the unconscious" because of the tendency to repress subordination or dependency (*Psychic Life,* 7). More generally, Freud argues that a large portion of the psyche, including much of the ego itself, is unconscious. See "Dissection of the Psychical Personality," 69–72.

46. Yearley stresses this point throughout his analysis in *Mencius and Aquinas.* Butler varies on this issue. In one place she describes the subject as both a "place holder" and a "structure" (*Psychic Life,* 10).

47. Power has been theorized as both a substance and a relation, and Foucault argues for the latter. His analyses have been extremely influential, and while many have looked to his work for a *theory* of power, at his most nuanced he emphasizes that the particular modalities of power are specific to a given situation. His major study of power examines three ways of organizing punishment in early modern Europe represented by monarchical law, reforming jurists, and the prison institution (*Discipline and Punish: The Birth of the Prison,* especially his summary on 130–31).

48. Foucault himself tended to separate his analyses, so much so that his paradigmatic works seem to set out ideal types (which is one of several ways that his work is Weberian). In his late work Foucault writes or says that his research concerns these three "axes." See *Use of Pleasure,* 3–7; also his essays "What Is Enlightenment?" and "On the Genealogy of Ethics," in *The Foucault Reader,* ed. P. Rabinow, especially 48, 351–52. A very important treatment of these three dimensions of Foucault's work is Arnold Davidson, "Archaeology, Genealogy, Ethics," 221–40; also "Ethics as Ascetics," 63–80. Gilles Deleuze offers a powerful reading of Foucault's ethics in relation to his earlier thought in "Foldings, or the Inside of Thought (Subjectivation)," in *Foucault,* 94–123. Brakke draws upon Foucault's studies of both power and ethics in his *Athanasius and Asceticism,* especially 142–200. Many of the weaknesses that people attribute to any one of the three approaches can be corrected by seeing them as parts of a larger project. Those who criticize Foucault's account of power for not attending to agency should note that his real study of the latter is in his work on ethics. Those who say that his study of ethics lacks attention to dynamics of authority should look back to his analysis of power. The image of "axis" implies a graph, of which the axes are the pure elements—x, y, and z—and phenomena can be mapped as functions of these elements. For example, along the axis of power, a study of prisons would need to draw upon tools set out in *Discipline and Punish.* However, subject formation in such contexts may also involve a significant dimension of self-creation, or ethics, within the structure of disciplinary power relations. Famous examples include Nelson Mandela's daily exercises while in South African prisons, or Pramoedya Ananta Toer's unsent letters to his daughter while in Buru. For these cases, concepts that

Foucault draws from elites of late antiquity such as "exercise" *(askēsis)* and "writing the self" could yield insight. For Pramoedya Ananta Toer's letters, see *The Mute's Soliloquy.*

49. There are other ways to come at these issues. For example, Pierre Bourdieu's work on the formation of dispositions in relation to social structures could be a valuable complement to a virtue ethicist's work on the formation of dispositions through the will and practical reason. On G. W. F. Hegel's ethics, I have learned much from Thomas Lewis. On Bourdieu's notion of *habitus,* a key precursor is Mauss's presentation of the concept in "Body Techniques," in *Sociology and Psychology,* 95–123. Bourdieu develops this term in a number of writings, including *The Logic of Practice.* More recently, see June Nash, *Mayan Visions: The Quest for Autonomy in an Age of Globalization,* 219–54.

50. Midrash is a distinct form of biblical exegesis practiced by the rabbinic movement. Mishnah denotes both a form of study and a particular corpus of rabbinic law. Gemara is the commentary to the Mishnah preserved in the Talmud. For a broad argument along these lines, see David Weiss Halivni, *Midrash, Mishnah, and Gemara: The Jewish Predilection for Justified Law.* Joseph Dan remarks that, during this period, rabbinic ethical thinking occurs entirely within these forms of literature. See *Hebrew Ethical and Homiletical Literature* (Hebrew), 8–11 and generally 1–25. The regularities that mark this period have similarities to what Foucault calls an *episteme,* though his formulation specifically addresses scientific knowledge. One definition of *episteme* is "the totality of relations that can be discovered, for a given period, between the sciences when one analyzes them at the level of discursive regularities." See Foucault, *The Archaeology of Knowledge and the Discourse on Language,* 191–92. The term is also important in his *The Order of Things: An Archaeology of the Human Sciences.*

51. Rabbinic literature does not have extensive discussions of children's education, but key examples include *Siphre Deut.* 46 (Finkelstein, *Sifre on Deuteronomy,* 104); *t. Ḥag.* 1:2 in Saul Lieberman, *Tosefta Ki-fshutah: A Comprehensive Commentary on the Tosefta,* part 5 (Hebrew), 375; *b. Sukk.* 42a–b; *b. Erub.* 82a; *b. Ket.* 50a; *b. B. Bat.* 32a; Marcus, *Rituals of Childhood,* especially 42–44.

52. By "nation," I do not mean the modern sense of the term but a more general understanding of a "people" (Hebrew: *'am*) claiming common language, culture, and in the case of Jews, ancestry.

53. He defines ethics as "the elaboration of a form of relation to self that enables an individual to fashion himself into a subject of ethical conduct." Foucault, *Use of Pleasure,* 251, also 25–32, and *Care of the Self,* 41. As Aaron Stalnaker has pointed out to me, the definition is circular, defining ethics ultimately in terms of ethics. This circularity leaves the exact content or nature of ethics open for further descriptive or constructive analysis. Note that Foucault's four concepts for guiding a study of ethics may be an extension of the four classical causes: the ethical substance as the material, the *telos* as the end, the mode of subjection as the formal, and the ethical work as the efficient. Deleuze also appeals to the four causes in

interpreting this aspect of Foucault's thought, but he does so in a different way. See Foucault, *Use of Pleasure,* 25–30 and the more extensive analysis in 38–92; Deleuze, *Foucault,* 104.

54. On Foucault's "mode of subjection," see *Use of Pleasure,* 27 and 53–62. My innovation in relation to Foucault, then, is to read his work on ethics back in relation to his work on power in order to highlight the role of subordination in ethics, the third axis of subject formation. Ricoeur, *Oneself as Another,* 156–57. MacIntyre discusses "craft" in *Three Rival Versions,* especially 61–68; references to "authority" and "obedient trust" in a teacher appear on 82–104 (Bryan Van Norden pointed out to me the importance of the latter section). Note also that modern claims of autonomy are often inappropriate for understanding such processes. Conversations with Paul Kollman, Valentina Izmirlieva, and Willis Johnson have been very important for my thinking on these issues.

55. Judith Butler expresses this dynamic in elegant terms, writing, "'Subjection' signifies the process of becoming subordinated by power as well as the process of becoming a subject." More specifically, "power that at first appears as external, pressed upon the subject, pressing the subject into subordination, assumes a psychic form that constitutes the subject's self-identity." There is, therefore, "an ambivalence at the site where the subject emerges." Writing as a feminist concerning patriarchy, she is concerned with "dependency on a discourse *we never chose,* but that, paradoxically, initiates and sustains our agency" (*Psychic Life,* 2–3, 7 [emphasis added], and generally 1–18). She traces a line of thought concerning subjection from Hegel, through Nietzsche and Freud, Foucault and Althusser, to recent psychoanalytic theorists. The category has its roots in the phenomenology of Hegel, particularly the lord-bondsman dialectic of his *Phenomenology of Spirit.* See Hegel's *Phenomenology of Spirit,* especially 104–38; and Alexandre Kojève, *Introduction to the Reading of Hegel,* especially 30–70. I agree with Butler that all subjects are formed through subordination to discourses that are not chosen (the second axis in Foucault's analysis), but Foucault's ethics (his third axis) reminds us that this is not the only dimension of subjection formation.

56. One objection to the category of chosen or elected subjection runs as follows. All forms of subject formation occur through power relations in which we find both the exercise of choice and external influences. The category of subjection itself captures that complex process, and distinguishing chosen subjection is unnecessary and misses the subtleties in "subjection" as such. Models for studying subjection, then, would be Foucault's *Discipline and Punish* and *History of Sexuality: Part 1, An Introduction.* Such a position represents a subtle reading of these two books, and it highlights the important point that in many cases the strands of subjection may be deeply intertwined. There are cases in which this connection is particularly prominent, particularly in women's ethical transformation through patriarchal traditions and institutions, and very possibly in all subject formation in the disciplinary constellation of power that emerged in Europe in the eighteenth century. However, I hold to the distinction for three reasons. First and most

generally, I believe that we should analytically distinguish dynamics that are chosen or cultivated from those that are forced or unconscious, even if we cannot presume a free will unaffected by socialization and relations of power. Second, for a description of rabbinic subject formation, the category of willed subjection enables a distinction between the affirmed subjection to God, for example, and the unwanted subjection to Rome. Third, in interpreting Foucault's work, as noted above I focus upon his late interviews in which he frames the study of the subject in terms of three axes, which he labeled as knowledge, power, and ethics. These axes can define a grid to help us analyze various configurations of external and internal shaping. This being said, a very interesting project could begin by reading *Discipline and Punish* with a focus on Foucault's many references to monastic models for disciplinary time and space (for example, see pages 135–56). Given Foucault's later interest in ethics and Christian self-formation, which led to his formulating the axes of subjection, one could rethink his work in terms of the ways that the axes of power and ethics intersect in eighteenth-century Europe.

57. See for example Butler's interpretation of Hegel in *Psychic Life,* 32–62. More generally, a key influence is Kojève, *Introduction to the Reading of Hegel,* especially 30–70. Thomas Lewis has helped me with these points.

58. See Asad, *Genealogies of Religion,* 83–167; Sarah Coakley, *Power and Submissions: Spirituality, Philosophy, and Gender,* especially xii–xx; Mahmood, *Women's Piety and Embodied Discipline;* Mahmood, "Feminist Theory, Embodiment, and the Docile Agent: Some Reflections on the Egyptian Islamic Revival"; BeDuhn, *The Manichaean Body.* I have also learned much from Jeremy Manheim's research on the *Bodhicaryāvatāra.* I discuss possibilities for comparative study of subjection in ethics more fully in "Self, Subject and Chosen Subjection: Rabbinic Ethics and Comparative Possibilities."

59. This is a descriptive point, meaning that my inductive analysis in the body of this book will show that imagery of subordination and internalization are both central to prescriptions for ethical transformation in *Rabbi Nathan.* I have not been able to find a way to delineate more fully the relation between subordination and internalization in the process.

60. Harvey, *Justice, Nature, and the Geography of Difference,* 48–57; *Spaces of Hope,* 98–101; see also my discussion and notes earlier in the introduction.

61. Ricoeur, *Oneself as Another,* 122, 156, and also on Kant, 208–9.

62. See also Butler's questions concerning internalization in *Psychic Life,* 19–20.

63. Althusser distinguishes the "(Repressive) State Apparatus," which exists in the public domain and functions by violence, from "Ideological State Apparatuses," which exist in the private domain and function by ideology. As examples of ideological state apparatuses he lists churches, parties, trade unions, families, schools, and newspapers. For Althusser, "ideology" is central to the functioning of the "Ideological State Apparatuses." One of his definitions of the term is that "all ideology represents in its necessarily imaginary distortion not the existing relations of production (and the other relations that derive from them) but above all the

(imaginary) relationship of individuals to the relations of production and the relations that derive from them." Ideology actively transforms individuals into subjects, or recruits subjects among individuals, through "interpellation" or "hailing." This hail "can be imagined along the lines of the most commonplace everyday police (or other) hailing: 'Hey, you there!'" At the same time, the subject as a governing and governed part of the self is always present. There is no presubjected, pre-ideological state. He writes, "Assuming that the theoretical scene I have imagined takes place on the street, the hailed individual will turn round. By this mere one-hundred-and-eighty-degree physical conversion, he becomes a *subject*. Why? Because he has recognized the hail that was 'really' addressed to him, and that 'it was *really him* who was hailed' (and not someone else)." In other words, ideological formation is a primary aspect of the self. The act of "turning" to the hail intensifies and reinforces that subjection. However, Althusser's image is skewed by his reference to police. This figure can convey the threat of violence and repression, which according to Althusser's own framework does not exemplify the workings of ideology. Rather, the hails of ideology come from literature, media, unions, politicians, lawyers, parents, teachers, and religious leaders. As he himself argues in his analysis of Christian symbolism, a hail may also come from a deity. Althusser, "Ideology and Ideological State Apparatuses," 140–48, 164–65, 170–83.

64. Ricoeur, *Oneself as Another,* 317 and throughout; my discussion of relations between self and other summarizes key points from 165, 317–56. The great twentieth-century scholar of the other in ethics, and specifically Jewish ethics, is of course Lévinas, and Ricoeur draws upon his writings extensively.

65. On the significance of Feuerbach in the development of the modern hermeneutics of suspicion, see Van Harvey, *Feuerbach and the Interpretation of Religion,* 1–14. Ricoeur summarizes this issue by writing, after a discussion of Lévinas's thought, "Perhaps the philosopher as philosopher has to admit that one does not know and cannot say whether this Other, the source of the injunction, is another person whom I can look in the face or who can stare at me, or my ancestors for whom there is no representation, to so great an extent does my debt to them constitute my very self, or God—living God, absent God—or an empty place. With this aporia of the Other, philosophical discourse comes to an end" (*Oneself as Another,* 355). While philosophical study may not be able to move beyond this point, the paths of descriptive and comparative study remain quite open, and perhaps they will open up new possibilities for philosophical reflection as well.

Part 1. The Text and Its Sages

1. Many twentieth-century scholars have examined rabbinic thought as a whole, drawing together materials from the midrash, Mishnah, and Talmuds. See Schechter, *Aspects of Rabbinic Theology;* Büchler, *Studies in Sin and Atonement;* Moore, *Judaism in the First Centuries;* Urbach, *Sages.* This method has been highly criticized by Jacob Neusner, who argues in numerous publications that one must

analyze one text at a time, taking each one as expressing a particular viewpoint. One example is his study of *Rabbi Nathan* entitled *Judaism and Story.* He often overemphasizes the work of rabbinic editors and overparticularizes. Important critiques of Neusner's strong stances include Boyarin, "On the Status of the Tannaitic Midrashim"; Shaye Cohen, ed., *The Synoptic Problem in Rabbinic Literature.* Max Kadushin's early work focuses on *Seder Eliyahu,* which he takes to be characteristic of rabbinic thought generally. See *The Theology of Seder Eliahu* and *Organic Thinking.* Despite the many merits of Kadushin's work, one of the few things that contemporary scholars agree on concerning *Seder Eliyahu* is that the text is not representative of rabbinic thought but rather stands on the side of midrashic and talmudic literature.

2. A number of studies that were published in the early 1990s examined a feature of rabbinic culture through focusing on one text as exemplary but not comprehensive. Perhaps most crucial for my work is Steven Fraade's study of rabbinic commentary and the figure of the sage, *From Tradition,* which addresses *Siphre Deuteronomy.* Daniel Boyarin's theory of intertextuality in midrash focuses upon the *Mekhilta of Rabbi Ishmael* in *Intertextuality and the Reading of Midrash.* David Stern's analysis of parables centers on *Lamentations Rabbah* in *Parables in Midrash;* also see Galit Hasan-Rokem's treatment of that text in *Web of Life: Folklore and Midrash in Rabbinic Literature.* It is also valuable to note that, while studying a single text sets certain boundaries for the study, it also has led me to expand the analysis. For example, I have found certain limits in centering a thematic study upon technical terms. An important category for rabbinic ethics is *yetzer* (inclination, impulse). I soon learned in gathering my material for this project that much discussion concerning impulses and their transformation in *Rabbi Nathan* appears without use of that word. My treatment of these topics in part 2, then, tracks the use of *yetzer* but also collects and analyzes many passages in which the word does not appear. This general point, as well as much rich material, may not have come to my attention had I structured my analysis around terms rather than a text.

1a. *Rabbi Nathan* and Its Contexts

1. Schechter and Kister, *Rabbi Nathan.* Kister is currently working on a new critical edition. His valuable introduction to the reprint of Schechter's volume discusses the achievements and problems of the work.

2. Finkelstein, *Introduction* and "Introductory Study"; Kister, *Studies,* especially 225–37. On the early, pre-ninth-century fragment, see Marc Bregman, "An Early Fragment of *Abot de Rabbi Natan* from a Scroll" (Hebrew). For a summary of the textual witnesses, dating, and scholarship, see Strack and Stemberger, *Introduction to the Talmud and Midrash,* 225–27.

3. Kister has argued that *Rabbi Nathan A* itself has two "branches" of manuscript transmission, one represented by MS N and the other by MS O and the printed edition (*Studies,* 6–7). Bregman claims that he has identified, in addition

to versions A and B, another strand in a *genizah* fragment. See "An Early Fragment," 201–22. Kister rejects this claim in *Studies,* 72–79. The state of the manuscript witnesses and printed editions is reminiscent of stories by Jorge Luis Borges or Umberto Eco in which the erudite fictional elaboration of what is known about a text actually marks that its origins are obscure and key historical questions are impossible to answer with certainty. For these writers, though, the ironic use of the scholarly voice opens up literary space for creativity, while the project at hand actually is scholarship, and this complex situation has to be addressed methodologically. Borges often uses such a voice in opening his stories. See his "Tlön, Uqbar, Orbis Tertius," "The Approach to Al-Mu'tasim," "Pierre Menard, Author of Don Quixote," and "The Works of Herbert Quain," in *Ficciones;* also Umberto Eco, *The Name of the Rose,* 1–5.

4. Since there was more than one printed edition, even this choice is problematic (see Kister, *Studies,* 227). I have not found differences among printed editions to be significant for my arguments, but when I have found variants, I note them.

5. Dominick LaCapra, *Rethinking Intellectual History: Texts, Contexts, Language,* 35–61. Also see the analysis by David Perkins, who presents a particularly skeptical stance. For example, he writes, "We experience the text as a nexus of meanings, and which ones are in the text and which derive from context cannot be strictly determined. In any act of interpretation, the borders between the textual and the contextual are drawn by convention" (*Is Literary History Possible?,* 122 and generally 121–52).

6. Daniel Boyarin makes a similar point when he states that one cannot write a book like Peter Brown's *Body and Society* for rabbinic culture, for *Body and Society* "is dependent on analyzing bodies of doctrine produced by given individuals whose biographies, life situations, social and political context, philosophical backgrounds, etc., are to some extent known to us, and we have no such information regarding late-antique rabbinic Jewish literature." Boyarin, however, attempts "to write of rabbinic culture as a whole" (*Carnal Israel,* 25–26), while I focus on one cluster of thought preserved in *Rabbi Nathan.* Fraade's comments about *Sifre Deuteronomy* also hold for *Rabbi Nathan,* that the text "presents itself, implicitly to be sure, as the *collective* and *cumulative* teachings of the class of rabbinic sages" (*From Tradition,* 17). On statues honoring intellectuals, see Gleason, *Making Men,* especially 3–54.

7. For these features of the author as a function of discourse, see Foucault, "What Is an Author?" 101–20. On the general issue, with references, see Donald Pease, "Author," in *Critical Terms for Literary Study,* ed. Frank Lentricchia and Thomas McLaughlin, 105–17.

8. Medieval compilations refer to the text in various ways. Kister discusses the sources and speculates about the significance of the name, emphasizing the point that "Rabbi Nathan" appears on the first page (*Studies,* 15–17).

9. Saul Lieberman, "The Martyrs of Caesarea," 395 and generally 395–446. See also the valuable studies presented in Peter Schäfer and Catherine Hezser, eds., *The Talmud Yerushalmi and Graeco-Roman Culture.*

10. Contemporary scholars both treat talmudic sources as literary creations and attempt to situate them in historical contexts. Some emphasize literary and hermeneutic features, such as Jeffrey L. Rubenstein, *Talmudic Stories: Narrative Art, Composition, and Culture,* 3–15, 265–82; Christine Hayes, *Between the Babylonian and Palestinian Talmuds: Accounting for Halakhic Difference in Selected Sugyot from Tractate Avodah Zarah,* 3–30. Others center on the challenge of making historical claims, such as Kalmin, *Sage in Jewish Society,* 1–5 and throughout.

11. Schechter states that one cannot date the text of *Rabbi Nathan* as it exists now (*Rabbi Nathan,* xxvi); see also the discussions in Saldarini, *Scholastic Rabbinism,* 138–43, and Kister, *Studies,* especially 5–7, 213–22. Kister notes phrases that appear to be post-Talmudic ("Introduction" to Schechter and Kister, *Rabbi Nathan,* 13). *Rabbi Nathan,* then, has a pseudepigraphic quality—not in the strong sense of being a full composition attributed to an earlier author but in a weaker sense that centuries of editors developed the text without making their work explicit. Kister's emphasis on the "metamorphosis" of traditions, which pervades his study, exemplify this dynamic, and I have benefited from conversations with Marc Bregman concerning pseudepigraphic features of rabbinic literature. See his article "Pseudepigraphy in Rabbinic Literature," though in that study he focuses on individual attributions rather than entire texts. Hayes discusses the differences between nonlegal and legal sources on these issues in *Between the Babylonian and Palestinian Talmuds,* 14–17.

12. The lateness of *The Fathers* is especially clear if we include chapter 6. But, even in the first five chapters, there are signs of late editing, and there were likely influences between *The Fathers* and *Rabbi Nathan* over the time of their compilation. Attempts to recover the earliest versions of maxims in *The Fathers* and *Rabbi Nathan* can be seen in Finkelstein, *Introduction,* and Goldin, *Studies in Midrash.* An extensive treatment of these complex issues is in Kister, *Studies,* 117–38, 193–217.

13. For the dates and character of textual witnesses, see Kister, *Studies,* 225–37. On the early fragment, see Bregman, "An Early Fragment," 201–22.

14. Robert Brody writes that the Geonic period began, "strictly speaking," in the second half of the sixth century, but his analysis begins after the Muslim conquest of Babylonia and the rise of the Abbasid dynasty in the eighth century. My comment applies to the world that he studies, and it is very possible that important elements in the compilation of *Rabbi Nathan* occurred during the early Geonic period. Brody comments that "knowledge of events in that portion of the Geonic period which preceded the Muslim conquest is virtually nil" and "sources for the first Muslim century are very limited, so that direct knowledge of the Geonate and related institutions is essentially restricted to the period following

the rise of the Abbasid dynasty in 750." See *The Geonim of Babylonia and the Shaping of Medieval Jewish Culture,* xix and generally xix–xxi, 3–18.

15. See, for example, Elias Bickerman, "The Maxim of Antigonus of Socho," reprinted in *Studies in Jewish Christian History,* 270–89; Goldin, "The End of Ecclesiastes: Literal Exegesis and Its Transformation" and "The Three Pillars of Simeon the Righteous," in *Studies in Midrash,* 3–38; also Finkelstein, *Introduction* and "Introductory Study."

16. Kister, *Studies,* ix, 7, 220, and also 193–217 on the relations between *Rabbi Nathan* and other sources. Regarding Babylonian influences on *Rabbi Nathan A,* see Kister, *Studies,* 206–12; Saldarini, *Scholastic Rabbinism,* 121–42, and *Fathers According to Rabbi Nathan B,* 12–16; and Strack and Stemberger, *Introduction to the Talmud and Midrash,* 227.

17. Fernand Braudel, *On History,* 74–76 and throughout. I thank Charles Hallisey for pointing out this discussion to me.

18. A question worthy of further examination is the status of "events" in rabbinic Judaism as compared with other groups in late antiquity. In *Rabbi Nathan* the major historical events of late antiquity are the destruction of the Jerusalem Temple and later persecutions after the Bar Kokhba rebellions (A4,22–25; A17,65; B6–7,19–22; A38,114–15; B41,114–15). These events stretch the limits of the compilers' resources for responding to the challenge of theodicy, and the accounts reveal a struggle to imagine God's role in the world. In early Christianity, by contrast, reflection centered on Jesus's life and death as evidence of divine presence and on the hope for its return. See, for example, Anthony Kemp, *The Estrangement of the Past: A Study in the Origins of Modern Historical Consciousness,* 3–34; R. A. Markus, *The End of Ancient Christianity,* 85–95. Charles Mathewes has helped me develop my thoughts on these points.

19. For comparisons with Christian sources, see Naomi Koltun-Fromm, "Zippora's Complaint: Moses Is Not Conscientious in the Deed! Exegetical Traditions of Moses' Celibacy," 283–306; Hayim Lapin, "Hegemony and Its Discontents: Rabbis as a Late Antique Provincial Population." On Babylonian influence upon *Rabbi Nathan,* see note 16 above.

20. On the figure of the sage and its significance for ethics, see Davidson, "Ethics as Ascetics," 74–77 and generally 63–80. Davidson's treatment is inspired by the work of Pierre Hadot, especially *Philosophy as a Way of Life,* 147–78. On rabbinic sages as literary figures, see Fraade, *From Tradition,* 18–19, 69–121; Kalmin, *Sage in Jewish Society,* 1–5; Rubenstein, *Talmudic Stories,* 1–15, 281–82; Boyarin, *Carnal Israel,* 15–16; Bregman, "Pseudepigraphy in Rabbinic Literature," 27–41. Earlier important studies include Yonah Fränkel, *Studies in the Spiritual World of the Sages* (Hebrew); William Scott Green, "What's in a Name? The Problematic of Rabbinic Biography," 77–96.

21. Even if it were present in written form, the social life of the material was most likely in disciple circles, where students met with teachers and encountered

their verbal instruction. Saul Lieberman has made an influential argument that the Mishnah was published through memorization and public oral recitation. See Lieberman, "The Publication of the Mishnah," in *Hellenism in Jewish Palestine,* 83–99. For an extended discussion of the relation between oral performance and writing among the rabbis, see Martin Jaffee, *Torah in the Mouth: Writing and Oral Tradition in Palestinian Judaism 200 BCE–400 CE,* especially 5–8. See also the reflections by Gleason in *Making Men,* xxiv, xxvii, 27. Charlotte Fonrobert has given me helpful comments on this issue.

22. Saldarini, *Scholastic Rabbinism,* 79–84 and throughout. On the category of "scholasticism" in a comparative perspective, see José Ignacio Cabezón, "Introduction," in *Scholasticism: Cross-Cultural and Comparative Perspectives,* 4–6; also *Buddhism and Language: A Study of Indo-Tibetan Scholasticism.* Michael Swartz has discussed the applicability of Cabezón's formulation to rabbinic Judaism. See his "Scholasticism as a Comparative Category and the Study of Judaism," in Cabezón, ed., *Scholasticism,* 91–114. Note that Swartz draws on Saldarini, *Scholastic Rabbinism.* On the term "disciple circle" in contrast with "school," see David Goodblatt, *Rabbinic Instruction in Sasanian Babylonia,* 267–85. Shaye Cohen has argued that while most rabbinic study communities were disciple circles, there is evidence that the patriarchs of Roman Palestine had a more institutionalized school. See "Patriarchs and Scholars." Hezser, in summarizing her analysis of whether or not the rabbinic movement was institutionalized, writes, "Study houses in tannaitic and amoraic Palestine were not rabbinic academies in the sense of schools with a fixed curriculum, appointed officials, and a succession of teachers. They were convenient places where some rabbis and others occasionally went to occupy themselves with Scripture" (*Social Structure of the Rabbinic Movement,* 226 and generally 184–227).

23. Various individual comparisons appear in Judah Goldin's essays on *The Fathers* and *Rabbi Nathan.* See his *Studies in Midrash.* Henry Fischel has argued that the stories of Hillel, including those in *Rabbi Nathan,* have strong resonance with Greek tales of sagely virtue, the *chreia.* See his "Story and History," in *Essays in Greco-Roman and Related Talmudic Literature,* 443–72. The book as a whole addresses the relation between Greco-Roman and rabbinic literature. For a comparison of a maxim in *Rabbi Nathan* to Stoic rhetoric, see Fischel, *Rabbinic Literature and Greco-Roman Philosophy,* 70–73 and notes. On the genealogical list, see Elias Bickerman, "La Chaîne de la Tradition Pharisienne." On the trope of the "fence" in Jewish, Greek, and Latin literature, see Siegfried Stein, "The Concept of the 'Fence': Observations on Its Origin and Development," 301–29; also my discussion in chapter 2a. On reading rabbinic literature as evidence of a multilingual context, see, Steven D. Fraade, "Rabbinic Views on the Practice of Targum, and Multilingualism in the Jewish Galilee of the Third-Sixth Centuries," 253–86. On the general issue of Hellenism and the rabbis, see the overview and programmatic statement by Schäfer, "Introduction," in Schäfer and Hezser, eds., *The Talmud Yerushalmi and Graeco-Roman Culture,* vol. 1, 14–16 and generally 1–23; Jaffee,

Torah in the Mouth, 126–52; and Lieberman, *Greek in Jewish Palestine* and *Hellenism in Jewish Palestine.* On problems in the contemporary use of the term "hellenization," see Schwartz, *Imperialism and Jewish Society,* 22–25.

24. Schwartz, *Imperialism and Jewish Society,* 162–63. David Stern writes, along these lines, "The attitude of Rabbinic Judaism toward Greco-Roman culture was many-sided, and the full significance of its complexity is still debated by scholars. . . . The fact that the Rabbis hated the Romans for destroying the Temple and for their blatant cruelty and corruption did not mean that they consciously rejected every aspect of Hellenism or of Greco-Roman culture; their unmitigated opposition to idolatry certainly did not make them immune to unconscious influence by many aspects of pagan culture" ("The Captive Woman: Hellenization, Greco-Roman Erotic Narrative, and Rabbinic Literature," 104–5). Tirosh-Samuelson compares rabbis to philosophers in *Happiness in Premodern Judaism,* 106–8. For one approach to comparative study through analogy, examining cases with no historical or geographical connection, see Yearley, *Mencius and Aquinas,* especially 169–203.

25. Saldarini's arguments for the scholastic nature of *Rabbi Nathan* run through *Scholastic Rabbinism,* but see especially 79–92, 135–42; I quote from page 82. On education in second century CE Galilee, see Martin Goodman, *State and Society in Roman Galilee, AD 132–212,* 71–81. On the sages as a small, urban community, see Levine, *Rabbinic Class,* 66–69; Hezser, *Social Structure of the Rabbinic Movement,* 157–65; Seth Schwartz, "Gamaliel in Aphrodite's Bath: Palestinian Judaism and Urban Culture in the Third and Fourth Centuries," in Schäfer and Hezser, eds., *The Talmud Yerushalmi and Graeco-Roman Culture,* vol. 1, 203–17; Hayim Lapin, "Rabbis and Cities: Some Aspects of the Rabbinic Movement in its Graeco-Roman Environment," in Schäfer and Hezser, eds., *The Talmud Yerushalmi and Graeco-Roman Culture,* vol. 2, 58–80. Also on the sages as historical figures, see Kalmin, *Sage in Jewish Society.*

26. On the idea that study can be a "way of life," see Hadot, *Philosophy as a Way of Life,* 264–76. I discuss Hadot's work at length in chapter 3c. Note also the comments by Schechter in *Aspects of Rabbinic Theology,* 136; Saldarini, *Scholastic Rabbinism,* 82–84; Levine, *Rabbinic Class,* 43–66. Goldin argues, based on passages in *The Fathers* and *Rabbi Nathan,* that rabbis not only studied Torah but also had philosophical discussion (*Studies in Midrash,* 58–76). On humility, see A7,33–34; B14,33–34; A15,60–62; B29,60–62. Note also the late addition to a story depicting the martyrdom of Rabbi Ishmael and Rabbi Simeon that shifts the focus from "delay [*'inuy*] of justice," to arrogance and the need for humility; A38,114; B41,114; Menahem Kister, "Metamorphoses of Aggadic Traditions" (Hebrew), 213–20. And on the broader concern with humility in rabbinic culture, see Tirosh-Samuelson, *Happiness in Premodern Judaism,* 127–29. On the control of speech, see A1,3–A2,14; B1,3–B3,14; A9,39–42; B16,36; A40,120.

27. On raising up students, see A1,2; A3,14–17; B1,2; B4,14–17; *Fathers* 1:1. On being careful with words, see the maxim of Abtelion in A11,47–48; B22,49; *Fathers*

1:11; Finkelstein, *Introduction,* 150; and Kister, *Studies,* 67. On praise for teachers, see A18,67–68; and praise for students, A14,58. On the general topic of teachers' functions in relation to their students, see Hezser, *Social Structure of the Rabbinic Movement,* 335–39, and on status differences among students, drawing upon these lists, 347–50.

28. This parallel between the student and Moses is made explicit in MS E, which adds, "Just as our fathers received [the Torah] on Mount Sinai with awe, fear, trembling, and shaking, so too, he will receive upon himself every word that emerges from your mouth with awe, fear, trembling, and shaking" (A6,27 n.9). Also see A6,27–28; A17,84; B10,26; B11,28; *Fathers* 4:12; Kister, *Studies,* 140–42. Regarding the comparison between emperors' edicts and sages' teachings, note that the student is to "receive" upon himself the instruction with these emotions, though the people only "read" the letters of the emperors. For the material concerning responses to emperors, see Lieberman, "Roman Legal Institutions in Early Rabbinics and in the Acta Martyrum," 7–9; also Goldin, *Rabbi Nathan,* 175 n.5. Finkelstein argues that these passages in *Rabbi Nathan* are signs of Shammaitic redaction in early stages of the text (*Introduction,* 29–32); also Saldarini, *Fathers According to Rabbi Nathan B,* 90. Also important is the commentary by Goldin, "The First Chapter of *Abot de Rabbi Nathan,*" 278–80. On the relations between teachers and students among Palestinian rabbis, see Hezser, *Social Structure of the Rabbinic Movement,* 339–446; also, on the house as a "meeting place" in the maxim, 209–10.

29. On the four utensils, see A40,127; B45,127; *Fathers* 5:15 and generally A40,126–27. Other passages compare the student to a stone that may be chiseled and formed to varying degrees; A28,86; B46,129. For an elaborate account of the student's comportment in the classroom, see "Seven qualities of the clod [*golem*] and seven of the sage" (A37,110–12; B40,110–12; *Fathers* 5:7; Schechter, *Rabbi Nathan,* 148–49). I discuss numerical catalogues in chapter 1b. For an overview of students' functions in relation to their teachers among Palestinian rabbis, see Hezser, *Social Structure of the Rabbinic Movement,* 332–35.

30. In *Rabbi Nathan B,* the maxim is attributed to the other member of the pair, Nittai ha-Arbeli.

31. Lieberman, "The Discipline of the So-Called Dead Sea Manual of Discipline."

32. Hezser, "Rabbis and Other Friends," in Schäfer and Hezser, eds., *The Talmud Yerushalmi and Graeco-Roman Culture,* vol. 2, 202 and generally 189–254.

33. A similar list appears in *Siphre Deut.* 305 (Finkelstein, *Sifre on Deuteronomy,* 323–24). See also Kister, *Studies,* 132–33; Hezser, *Social Structure of the Rabbinic Movement,* 351–52 (she quotes this passage along with others outside of *Rabbi Nathan* that present students fulfilling some of these ideals). Daniel Boyarin and Catherine Hezser both discuss this intimacy and its relation to sexual practices. Neither one equates homosocial ideals with homosexuality, but Boyarin's analysis gives greater weight to the possibility of there being erotic dimensions. See Boyarin,

Unheroic Conduct: The Rise of Heterosexuality and the Invention of the Jewish Man, 16–17; Hezser, "Rabbis and Other Friends," 2: 245–47. On the "secrets of Torah," see Moshe Idel, "Secrecy, Binah, and Derishah," 311–43. The final gloss—"secrets of Torah and secrets of *derekh 'eretz*"—may be a later addition. I discuss the phrase *derekh 'eretz* in chapter 2a. See also A29,88 and A29,89 on standards for how the *ḥaberim* should interact with each other. Intense intimacy among students was also a feature of late ancient Roman schools, as Edward Watts argues in, "The Student Self in Late Antiquity," in Brakke, et al., *Self-Revelations.*

34. Note, though, that the word "Jew" rarely appears in *Rabbi Nathan* (but see B19,42 as an exception). More often we see the name "Israel" or more specific designations such as "students of the sages."

35. Narratives depict the Roman destruction of Jerusalem and the Second Temple in 70 CE (A4,22–25; A6,32–33; A17,65; B6–7,19–22) as well as persecutions following the Bar Kokhba revolt (A38,114–15; B41,114–15). On rabbinic suspicion of Roman rule, see also A11,46–48. On Roman rule in Galilee in the second century, which was likely the setting for the early formation of *Rabbi Nathan,* see Goodman, *State and Society,* 135–39.

36. The story of Rabban Yohanan ben Zakkai's escape from Jerusalem and encounter with Vespasian appears in A4,22–25; B6,19; *Lam. R.* 1.5.31; and *b. Gitt.* 55b–56b. On the history of the scholarship concerning these stories, see Ilan, *Mine and Yours,* 3–16. Recent studies addressing *Rabbi Nathan* include Neusner, *A Life of Yohanan ben Zakkai,* 157–66, and *Development of a Legend: Studies on the Traditions Concerning Yohanan ben Zakkai,* 114–19 (and generally on *Rabbi Nathan* 113–32), 146–51, 162–67, 228–34; Saldarini, *Fathers According to Rabbi Nathan B,* 60–73 and notes, and "Johanan ben Zakkai's Escape from Jerusalem: Origin and Development of a Rabbinic Story"; Peter Schäfer, "Die Flucht Johanan ben Zakkais aus Jerusalem und die Gründung des 'Lehrhauses' in Jabne," 43–101, especially 57–60; Boyarin, "Masada or Yavneh? Gender and the Arts of Jewish Resistance," 306–29. Rubenstein presents a full analysis of the story in the Babylonian Talmud, with several pages translating and discussing the version of *Rabbi Nathan A,* in *Talmudic Stories,* 139–75. Hezser discusses this story several times in *Social Structure of the Rabbinic Movement,* including 66–67 (overview), 171–80 (on how many rabbis went to Yavneh), 195–214 (on what was established there), 294–95 (on prophetic aspects of the story).

37. A4,18–25; B5–9,18–25; *Fathers* 1:2. On the maxim itself, see Goldin, *Studies in Midrash,* 27–38. The dual assertion is made with a dialectic structure. In *Rabbi Nathan A,* the commentary upon "Torah" upholds Torah as more valuable to God than sacrifice (citing Hos. 6:6), then the commentary upon "service" says that the Temple is necessary for the maintenance of the world, and then that upon "good deeds" tells of the Temple being destroyed and rabbinic study and deeds taking its place (again citing Hos. 6:6) (A4,18–25; B5–9,18–25).

38. Version B has a more extended account of Roman violence. One passage describes the general Titus having sex with a prostitute in the Holy of Holies, and

in one manuscript, he does so on a Torah scroll (B7,20–21; Finkelstein, *Introduction*, 203; Saldarini, *Fathers According to Rabbi Nathan B*, 66–70 and notes). On early accounts of hostile forces desecrating the Temple with pigs, see Peter Schäfer, *Judeophobia: Attitudes Towards Jews in the Ancient World*, 66–69.

39. Note that, when Rabban Yohanan ben Zakkai is being carried out of the city in a coffin, in *Rabbi Nathan* the guards do not appear to be Jewish, and the disciples carrying the coffin make an appeal to Jewish burial practices. In the talmudic version, however, the guards are Jewish rebels.

40. The use of *sh.n.h.* for "teach" may indicate materials that eventually became the Mishnah. The word for "prayer" may also refer specifically to the Amidah. Other manuscript variants include "phylacteries" and "house of prayer." See Schechter's comments in A4,22 n.62 and Goldin's in *Rabbi Nathan*, 183 n.29. Goldin also argues that Rabban Yohanan ben Zakkai's three goals are post-70 CE transformations of the three pillars of Simeon the Righteous (*Studies in Midrash*, 33).

41. Generally, the sages of *Rabbi Nathan* remember the Temple cult with some ambivalence, honoring sacrificial practices and festivals but emphasizing that rabbinic practice can substitute for the centralized worship; see the full accounts in A4,18–24; B5–9,18–24; also my discussion in chapter 1b concerning the "arrangement" of maxims in the text.

42. Here I differ, to some degree, with Rubenstein's claim that *Rabbi Nathan A* "expresses absolutely no criticism or ambivalence" toward Rabban Yohanan ben Zakkai. I generally agree with Rubenstein's analysis of the narrative as well as his larger point that Babylonian narratives tend to present ambivalences and work out tensions, while the ones in *Rabbi Nathan* tend to uphold particular ideals through the figures of the sages (*Talmudic Stories*, 169–72 and throughout). See my discussion of narratives in chapter 1b.

43. The same language and similar thematic dynamics appear elsewhere in *Rabbi Nathan*. A story of the prominent and wealthy Jewish man, Kalba Sabua, begins, "When Vespasian the Caesar came to destroy Jerusalem, the Zealots wanted [*biqqeshu*] to burn in fire all of the provisions" (literally: "the good"). Kalba Sabua said to them, "Why do you destroy this city and want [*mebaqqeshim*] to burn in fire all the provisions?" The narrator again states that Vespasian is the agent of Jerusalem's destruction, but the same voice now asserts that radical rebels (the Zealots) "want" (again from the root *b.q.sh.*) to burn all the food that had been stored away. The hero of this story, Kalba Sabua, places blame upon the Zealots. This politically moderate friend of the rabbinic sages, like Rabban Yohanan ben Zakkai in the other narrative, is the only figure who seeks a path other than destruction. Again, the compilers of *Rabbi Nathan* present the events of 70 CE in a way that condemns Roman aggression but asserts the need to respond in ways that are pragmatic and sustainable (A6,32). Kister points out the similarities between this story and that of Yohanan ben Zakkai in *Studies*, 71–72.

44. See especially A38,114–15; B41,114–15; also B7,20–21. On this issue in other

rabbinic sources, see Boyarin, *Dying for God: Martyrdom and the Making of Christianity and Judaism,* 22–41.

45. Charlotte Fonrobert writes, "On a most basic level, an androcentric perspective on the world and human culture is one in which the literary subject as the projecting center of perceiving is gendered male, explicitly or not. In other words, we are not merely dealing with a textual culture that creates explicit hierarchies, but one that imagines a certain directionality of perceiving. The male subject may be qualified in multiple ways, but in an androcentric body of literature the imagining, perceiving, speaking, and knowing subject is predominantly marked as male. Often, this marking is hidden or only implied, which may make it much more powerful and convincing" (*Menstrual Purity: Rabbinic and Christian Reconstructions of Biblical Gender,* 8). Boyarin has argued that talmudic accounts of masculinity have significant features that, in the context of late ancient Rome, would be categorized as "feminine." See "Masada or Yavneh?" as well as *Unheroic Conduct,* 127–50. This observation may be most salient in relation to the tropes that appear in *Rabbi Nathan* concerning the relation of Torah to the self, for they often portray the self as receptive, allowing itself to be penetrated or guided by the words of tradition (for example, Torah may be a king that enters an empty room within the self, or a yoke or goad that guides from outside). I examine these tropes in full in part 2.

46. On Eve, see A1,6; B1,6–8; B9,24–25; B42,116–17. On Miriam, see A9,39–41. On women as distracting from Torah or inciting gossip, see the commentary to Yoseph ben Yohanan's maxim, "Do not talk overmuch with your wife [*ha-'ishah*]" in A7,35; B34–35; *Fathers* 1:4. The commentary to this maxim in *Rabbi Nathan B* includes a passage that raises the issue of sexual temptation. Generally, on rabbinic and other Jewish interpretations of Eve, see Boyarin, *Carnal Israel,* 84–88, 77–106; Judith Plaskow, *Standing Again at Sinai: Judaism from a Feminist Perspective,* 38–39; Elaine Pagels, *Adam, Eve, and the Serpent.*

47. An exception may be one story in *Rabbi Nathan A* of a strong woman who challenges the sages and their understanding of divine justice. Her voice, however, is quickly silenced by Elijah; A2,8–9; also *Seder Eliyahu Rabbah* 15/16 (Friedmann, *Seder Eliahu Rabba, Seder Eliahu Zuṭa, and Pseudo-Seder Eliahu Zuṭa,* 76); Schofer, "Protest or Pedagogy?"

48. On menstrual laws, with a specific focus on the tractate *Niddah* of the Babylonian Talmud, see Fonrobert, *Menstrual Purity;* on marriage, Michael Satlow, *Jewish Marriage in Antiquity;* another important recent study with a strong attention to gender is Aryeh Cohen, *Rereading Talmud: Gender, Law, and the Poetics of Sugyot,* especially 153–219.

49. See Boyarin, *Carnal Israel,* 167–96. Boyarin argues that some Palestinian sources consider the possibility that women may study Torah, but Babylonian ones reject this idea. Note by contrast that in some Christian circles upper-class women with ascetic practices became influential, and their lives were the center of popular narratives: these include Macrina, Melania the Elder, and Olympias of

Constantinople. Also, convents provided a setting where women studied Scripture (Brown, *Body and Society,* 259–84). There is archeological evidence that women had roles in Jewish worship that are not preserved in the elite literature. See Bernadette Brooten, *Women Leaders of the Ancient Synagogue: Inscriptional Evidence and Background Issues.*

50. On Eve, compare A1,4–8 with B1,4–8; B8,23–24; B9,24–25; and B42,116–17. More specifically, both A and B present a parable that alludes to the story of Pandora: a woman is told by her husband not to open a jar, but she does. In A, compilers state that the parable describes Adam in relation to God, portraying the events as Adam's transgression of God's command. In B, the parable is linked to Eve in relation to Adam, framing the issues as Eve's transgression of Adam's command (A1,6; B1,6–8; Boyarin, *Carnal Israel,* 84–88). Also, in B but not A we find passages that present women's commandments (menstrual separation, separation of the dough offering, and lighting the Sabbath candle) as punishments for Eve's actions in Eden. See B9,25; B42,117; Boyarin, *Carnal Israel,* 90–94; also *m. Shabb.* 2:6; *b. Shabb.* 32b and generally 31b–34a; Urbach, *Sages,* 437. Version B also contains passages not found in A that emphasize differences between men and women, often disparaging women. See B9,24–25; B45,126; B48,131; Boyarin, *Carnal Israel,* 89; also *Gen. Rab.* 17:8 (J. Theodor and Ch. Albeck, *Midrash Bereshit Rabba,* 158–59); *Gen. Rab.* 18:2 (Theodor and Albeck, *Bereshit Rabba,* 162–63); *Gen. Rab.* 45:5 (Theodor and Albeck, *Bereshit Rabba,* 452–53); *Deut. Rab.* 6:11; Saldarini, *Fathers According to Rabbi Nathan B,* 286 n.38.

51. Based on *Rabbi Nathan B,* Fonrobert states that *Rabbi Nathan* is "one of the more misogynist texts in rabbinic literature" (*Menstrual Purity,* 31, 229 n.41). See also the references to *Rabbi Nathan B* in Boyarin, *Carnal Israel,* 84–94.

52. On the commandment to "be fertile and increase," see the extensive study by Jeremy Cohen, *"Be Fertile and Increase, Fill the Earth and Master It,"* especially 133–40 on the importance of marriage for rabbis. Cohen points out that most rabbinic sources follow the anonymous position in the Mishnah stating, "A man is bound by the duty of procreation but not a woman." However, in the Mishnah and elsewhere there are dissenting opinions with more inclusive positions (140–44; also *m. Yeb.* 6:6). On hospitality, see A7,33–34; B14,33–34. The ideal of women earning money so their husbands could study appears in the story of Rabbi Akiba and his wife Rachel. In *Rabbi Nathan,* we see only a fragment that presumes something like longer versions that appear elsewhere in rabbinic literature. See A6,30; Ilan, *Mine and Yours,* 38–48, 78–82, 274–77, and 292–96; Boyarin, *Carnal Israel,* 136–38 and generally 134–66; and Judith Abrams, *The Women of the Talmud,* 65–83. The text also contains negative views toward marriage. For example, in a numerical catalogue, one of three kinds of men for whom "their lives are not lives" is "anyone whose wife rules over him" (A25,82; see also B48,131). Peter Brown writes concerning the time needed for study, "The study of Torah assumed the precious privilege of free males in ancient society—the freedom to dispose of their time. For a woman, the duties of childbearing occurred in precisely those years when

their spouses, as late adolescent males, were free to serve their long apprenticeship at the feet of the Sages" (*Body and Society,* 145).

53. I discuss Adam's faulty counsel to Eve in chapter 2a; see A1,4–5; B1,4–6. On women as exemplifying communal suffering, see A17,65.

54. On criticism of marrying young girls, see B8,24; B48,131; also Saldarini, *Fathers According to Rabbi Nathan B,* 80–81 n.31, 298 n.11. On the list of four characteristics and Rabbi Yose's response, B45,126; Saldarini, *Fathers According to Rabbi Nathan B,* 286 and notes. Also, one story in *Rabbi Nathan A* portrays a strong woman who challenges the sages but is quickly silenced by Elijah (see page 200, note 47).

55. Wealthy men of Jerusalem are associated with the rabbis through the figures of Nakdimon ben Gurion and Kalba Sabua (A6,28–33; B11–12, 28–33). Note also that in these narratives, Rabbi Akiba and Rabbi Eliezer become wealthy. A story about Rabban Yohanan ben Zakkai, depicting events after the destruction of Jerusalem, portrays him as observing the poverty of others but does not state that he himself suffers (A17,65).

56. On *q.b.l.,* see Lieberman, "Discipline," 199–200; on raising thin cattle, Goldin, *Rabbi Nathan,* 219 n.18. On the *'am ha-'aretz,* see A40,126; B45,126; *Fathers* 5:10; also *m. Dem.* 2:2–3 and *t. Dem* 2; *m. Kil.* 2:3 and *b. Kil.* 9b; Levine, *Rabbinic Class,* 112–27; Kalmin, *Sage in Jewish Society,* 27–50; Hezser, *Social Structure of the Rabbinic Movement,* 353–404 (she discusses rabbis teaching in people's homes on page 356, focusing on A6,27; B11,27–28); Goodman, *State and Society,* 93–118.

57. Textual witnesses may vary as to the competitor that is named: some employ *minim* while others name different competitors, such as "Epicurians." See for example A2,13–14 and Schechter's note 72; Finkelstein, *Introduction,* 128–30. Christine Hayes writes that *minim* "is an indeterminate term for all those who questioned rabbinic Judaism. It serves as a catch-all word that denotes heretics and sectarians of various types: Jewish Christians, Gentile Christians, gnostics, pagans, apostates, Samaritans, and even Sadducees depending on context" ("Displaced Self-Perception: The Deployment of *Minim* and Romans in *B. Sanhedrin* 90b–91a," 260–61 n.29 and generally 249–89). Also see Kalmin, *Sage in Jewish Society,* 68–74; Boyarin, *Dying for God,* 22–41 and notes. Reuven Kimelman argues that the word *min* in rabbinic literature denotes deviant Jews, Jewish sectarians, or Jewish Christians, but not gentiles; see "*Birkat Ha-Minim* and the Lack of Evidence for an Anti-Christian Jewish Prayer in Late Antiquity," 226–44. See also Goodman, *State and Society,* 104–7.

58. Rabbinic literature contains few legal rulings of the *ḥasidim* but preserves and develops their maxims and stories. There is a significant scholarly literature on the *ḥasidim.* See, for example, articles by Shmuel Safrai collected in *In Times of Temple and Mishnah: Studies in Jewish History* (Hebrew), especially vol. 2, 518–39. He discusses material from *Rabbi Nathan* in vol. 2, 521–523. In English, key studies by Safrai are "Teaching of Pietists in Mishnaic Literature" and "Jesus and the Hasidim." See also Menahem Hirshman, "Towards a Clarification of the

Term 'Fear of Sin'" (Hebrew), 155–62. On Honi the Circle Drawer, see William Scott Green, "Palestinian Holy Men: Charismatic Leadership and Rabbinic Tradition," 619–47; and Goldin, "On Honi the Circle-Maker: A Demanding Prayer."

59. On *ḥasidim* as exemplars, see A8,37; B19,41–42; I quote and analyze elements of these stories in chapter 1b and in chapter 3a.

60. See A12,56; B27,56–57. Version B has two notable differences: it states directly that the man is a *ḥasid* who "would practice the laws of the *ḥasidim*," and the examiner is named as Rabbi Yehoshua, who was one of the students of Rabban Yohanan ben Zakkai. This passage is discussed by Safrai in his essays on the *ḥasidim*. See *Temple and Mishnah*, 2: 521–23; also Jaffee, *Torah in the Mouth*, 69–70. Some passages in *Rabbi Nathan* convey the rabbinic ambivalence toward such figures by embracing them but presenting them as subordinate to rabbis. In one narrative, a *ḥasid* has a profound experience that brings extended life as well as knowledge. The narrative affirms such experience but places the *ḥasid* as subordinate to Rabbi Akiba, who offers the authoritative interpretation of the event (A3,17).

61. See Safrai, *Temple and Mishnah*, 2: 534–36, and "Jesus and the Hasidim," 13.

62. For the genealogy in *The Fathers*, see *Fathers* 1:17–2:7. Finkelstein makes a great deal of this point, supposing that *Rabbi Nathan*'s initial formation began in opposition to the patriarchate. As is often the case with his research, Finkelstein's strong claim is excessive, but his textual observation is valuable. See Finkelstein, "Introductory Study," 26–29. On the name "Rabbi Nathan," see *b. B. Metz.* 86a; Goldin, *Rabbi Nathan*, xx–xxi; Finkelstein, "Introductory Study," 16 and throughout; Strack and Stemberger, *Introduction to the Talmud and Midrash*, 80; but note Kister, *Studies*, 15–17. There is currently a scholarly debate concerning the origin, authority, and institutionalization of the patriarchate. One position is that the patriarchy was an office that was "the major political force within Jewish society throughout the talmudic period." It was supported by the Roman Empire as early as the time of Rabban Gamaliel II at Yavneh, and Rabbi Yehudah the Patriarch "was the first to be granted extensive power and authority." See Levine, *Rabbinic Class*, 134 and generally 134–91; also "The Jewish Patriarch (Nasi) in Third Century Palestine," 649–88. A second position, with a more limited portrait of authority and institutionalization, is that the patriarchy began to develop only in the third century CE, and "the individual patriarchs were powerful not because they occupied the patriarchal office, but because as individuals they painstakingly acquired authority, which they held at first only informally, mainly as powerful patrons, and which only gradually, mainly in the fourth century, came to be institutionalized" (Seth Schwartz, "The Patriarchs and the Diaspora"). An intermediate stance and a discussion of the debates can be found in Hezser, *Social Structure of the Rabbinic Movement*, 405–49.

63. Marc Hirshman argues for "the existence and vitality of a school of rabbinic universalism in the second and early third centuries." He defines universalism as the idea that the Torah "was intended for all people." See his "Rabbinic Universalism in the Second and Third Centuries," 102, 115.

64. Lee Yearley distinguishes "open" religions, in which "fulfillment occurs when people transcend any particular culture" and "locative" religions, where "fulfillment occurs when people locate themselves within a complex social order that is thought to be sacred" (*Mencius and Aquinas,* 42). Both rabbinic Judaism and classical Confucianism are examples of such locative traditions. Yearley develops the distinction of Jonathan Z. Smith, who characterizes locative religions as affirming and celebrating a cosmic order that is created by bounding the chaotic. Such religions charge humans with finding a "place" that harmonizes with that order. See Jonathan Z. Smith, "The Influence of Symbols on Social Change," in *Map Is Not Territory: Studies in the History of Religions,* 129–46; also MacIntyre, *Three Rival Versions,* 196–203. Other examples in *Rabbi Nathan* of people going to study with sages appear on A15,60–62; B29,60–62. For the rabbinic legend concerning the origin of the study house, see my discussion earlier in chapter 1a of Rabban Yohanan ben Zakkai and the destruction of Jerusalem.

1b. The Text Instructs

1. Ephraim Urbach has emphasized both the need to attend to literary form and the distinctiveness of rabbinic epigrams (*Sages,* 3). However, Urbach's work as a whole does not provide a model for the integration of literary analysis and the study of rabbinic texts. Perhaps the greatest flaw of *The Sages* is that he rarely addresses literary issues—such as the interrelation of form and content, or the literary context of a given tradition—and to the degree he does, he offers the reader no justification, or even criteria, for his reasoning. On this point, I follow Urbach in word and not in action.

2. I draw in large part upon the analysis by Yonah Fränkel, who calls this the "classic" form. See his *The Ways of the Aggadah and the Midrash* (Hebrew), 396–410. Also see Fritz Maass, *Formgeschichte der Mischna,* and Neusner, *Form-Analytical Comparison.* In this section, I discuss the formal features of the epigram itself, and in the following I examine the framing elements, which in this case are, "The Men of the Great Assembly received [the Torah] from Haggai, Zechariah, and Malachi, and they said . . ."

3. Judah Goldin writes that "the three-clause structure of almost all the early sayings preserved in *Abot* (say, at least down to the disciples of Yohanan ben Zakkai) is not intended to suggest individual and independent clauses, but clauses directed towards a single thought" (*Studies in Midrash,* 16 n.21, 18 n.84). See also Saldarini, *Scholastic Rabbinism,* 10.

4. This is the wording in A12,48; A12,56 has *pased* and *Fathers* 1:13 has *yesuph.*

5. Fränkel, *Ways,* 396–402. Fränkel suggests here, based on language and phrasing, that Hillel's epigrams were closer to popular expressions than those of earlier sages and, as such, had a unique appeal.

6. Fränkel discusses this pattern in *Ways,* 406–8.

7. A14,58; B29,59; *Fathers* 2:9. This statement and the ensuing answers have received much scholarly attention. David Flusser shows that the concept of the "good way" appears to draw upon the notion of two "ways"—the way of good and the way of evil—that is present in the opening of the *Didache* as well as in the Damascus Covenant. See his "Which Is the Right Way that a Man Should Choose for Himself?" (Hebrew). Also see Shmuel Safrai, "The Term *Derekh Erez*" (Hebrew). Goldin suggests that the exchange between teacher and student here has similarities to Hellenistic philosophical discussion. See Goldin, *Studies in Midrash,* 57–76 and his expanded version of the same article, "Something Concerning the Study House of Rabban Yohanan Ben Zakkai," 69–92. Note also the maxim of Ben Zoma (A23,75; B33,72; *Fathers* 4:1; *Midr. Prov.* 15 to Prov. 15:18); Fischel, *Rabbinic Literature,* 70–73 and notes; and Saldarini, *Scholastic Rabbinism,* 98.

8. Lists appear in major clusters at the end of *Rabbi Nathan* (A31–41; B36–48; *Fathers* 5) and also within other exegetical sections (see for example B1,1). The lists in *Rabbi Nathan* deserve a full study. Saldarini lists six categories of lists: commonsense analysis of an individual text, hermeneutical analogy, lexical analogy, syntactical analogy, legal analogy, and technical exegetical analogy (*Scholastic Rabbinism,* 111 and generally 109–19). Finkelstein provides an insightful overview in *Introduction,* 81–114. A broad study of lists in rabbinic literature is Wayne Sibley Towner, *The Rabbinic "Enumeration of Scriptural Examples."* A highly sophisticated theoretical and comparative study of lists is Valentina Izmirlieva, *The Christian Art of Listing: Naming God in Slavia Orthodoxa.* On the homiletic exegesis of lists in *Rabbi Nathan,* see A31,90; A32,92; A33,93; *Fathers* 5:1–2; Kister, *Studies,* 42; also Towner, *Enumeration,* 246. On lists concerning divine reward and punishment, see the extensive commentary upon the maxim, "Seven kinds of punishment come to the world because of seven kinds of transgression" (A38,113–15; B41,113–16; *Fathers* 5:8).

9. Here I differ with Urbach, who contrasts such sayings with *other* rabbinic literary forms that have a "rhetorical homiletic tendency" and "artistic aspiration" (*Sages,* 3). My account emphasizes that such tendencies and aspirations are present in the maxims as well.

10. Collections of epigrams include *The Fathers, Derekh Eretz Rabbah,* and *Derekh Eretz Zuṭa.* On this process, see Sperber, "Manuals of Rabbinic Conduct," 9–26; see also my references on "rabbinic ethical literature" in note 4 of the introduction.

11. Note, though, Moshe Kline's provocative argument, based on the commentary to *The Fathers* by the Maharal of Prague (Rabbi Judah Leow ben Bezalel, ca. 1525–1609), that the opening genealogy is "a literary and philosophical composition" with five levels of meaning. See "The Art of Writing the Oral Tradition: Leo Strauss, The Maharal of Prague, and Rabbi Judah the Prince." I tend to see these insightful interpretations as the result of the Maharal's (and Kline's own) exegesis, rather than compositional features that can be ascribed to the second century CE.

12. Alon Goshen-Gottstein observes that including a sage's name in a text is a way of honoring him (*The Sinner and the Amnesiac*, 39–42). On the general issue of attributions to sages, see the discussion and extensive footnotes by Bregman in "Pseudepigraphy in Rabbinic Literature," 34–41.

13. A recent and subtle treatment of these groupings appears in Devora Steinmetz, "Distancing and Bringing Near: A New Look at Mishnah Tractates *'Eduyyot* and *'Abot*," 68–78. For an earlier and very influential examination, see Finkelstein, *Introduction*, ix, 4–5, and throughout; also Finkelstein, "Introductory Study," 14–15. Finkelstein makes strong claims about the dating of these sections, attributing each to a specific time and faction. We do not have to follow him on these points. He is still an astute observer of the details of *Rabbi Nathan*, particularly the disjunctive points that distinguish the sections, and these observations have value whether or not one agrees with his dating. See also Saldarini's account of the literary structure, which nuances that of Finkelstein, in *Scholastic Rabbinism*, 25–34. On the influence of the genealogical sections in mystical circles, see Michael Swartz, *Scholastic Magic: Ritual and Revelation in Early Jewish Mysticism*, 173–96.

14. See Bickerman, "La Chaîne de la Tradition Pharisienne," 256–69; also the discussion by Saldarini in *Scholastic Rabbinism*, 17–21, 74–78, and generally 9–78. Saldarini summarizes the themes in this section of *Rabbi Nathan A* in *Scholastic Rabbinism*, 9–10, 54–55. Finkelstein argues among other points that the chain of tradition is part of a much older document, and *Rabbi Nathan* preserves earlier elements than does *The Fathers;* see *Introduction*, xxvii–xlviii, 5–39. The rabbinic chain is notable, Finkelstein argues, for its use of fourteen figures—an auspicious number in the Gospel of Matthew (Matt. 1:17), but also for the priestly writers of the Books of Ezra, Nehemiah, and Chronicles. While the latter books focus on a familial genealogy of priests beginning with Aaron, *Rabbi Nathan* and *The Fathers* present a genealogy of teachers and students that begins with Moses, excludes most priests, and culminates in the early sages. See Finkelstein, *Introduction*, x–xi, 6–10, drawing upon 1 Chron. 5:29–41; Neh. 12:10; and Ezra 7:1; note, though, Saldarini's doubts in *Scholastic Rabbinism*, 76–78. Stuart Cohen has analyzed the social function of the chain of transmission, which he situates after the destruction of the Second Temple. He argues that the purpose of the material "was to stress the hegemony of the *keter torah* [crown of Torah] over the Jewish world and the supremacy within it of the early rabbinic facet of constitutional interpretation." See *The Three Crowns*, 59–60; also the discussions in Fraade, *From Tradition*, 70–71; Hezser, *Social Structure of the Rabbinic Movement*, 65–66; and the important comments by Martin Jaffee in "The Oral-Cultural Context of the Talmud Yerushalmi: Greco-Roman Paideia, Discipleship, and the Concept of Oral Torah," 53–54.

15. It is provocative to contrast the rabbinic genealogy centered on Sinai, prophecy, and teaching with the one that opens the Gospel of Matthew. The writer of the gospel presents a genealogy of birth, used in the Bible for priestly and royal lineages, to legitimate Jesus as a new king. It opens with the broad covenant of Abraham that promises a great nation, not the more specific covenant of Sinai

that includes strong legal components. Rather than highlighting prophets, it gives great weight to David as the head of the royal line and to the Babylonian Exile (this period, after the destruction of the First Temple in 586 BCE, was probably the best corollary in ancient Israel for a community living after the destruction of the Second Temple). Thus, in contrast with a focus on Sinai, prophecy, and sages, the Gospel of Matthew opens by highlighting a promise of a great nation, a king, and a time in exile. See Matt. 1, especially 1:17.

16. *Fathers* 1:16–2:7; Finkelstein, "Introductory Study," 26–29; Anthony Saldarini, "The End of the Rabbinic Chain of Tradition"; L. Levine, "The Jewish Patriarch" and *Rabbinic Class,* 134–91.

17. Finkelstein argues that group one was originally a Shammaitic document, and that group three was a continuation of it. Then followers of Rabban Yohanan ben Zakkai inserted group two to link their teacher with the genealogy and to shift the emphasis of the document from Shammai to Hillel. See *Introduction,* 52–64. He is more optimistic about the possibility of recovering early stages of *Rabbi Nathan* than I am, but his observations are provocative nonetheless.

18. See the treatment of this material by Alon Goshen-Gottstein in *The Sinner and the Amnesiac,* 39–42, 54–61. "The Four Who Entered the Garden" are four rabbis who are the center of a story told in *t. Ḥag.* 2:3; *j. Ḥag.* 2:1; *b. Ḥag.* 14b; and *Songs Rab.* 1:4. The story developed as one concerning mystical experience, but Henry Fischel argues that it may have originated as a response to Epicureanism; see *Rabbinic Literature,* 1–34. Saul Lieberman, in his notes to *t. Ḥag.* 2:3, lists many parallels in rabbinic literature with mystical and gnostic themes (see *Tosefta Ki-fshutah,* 1286–96). For a brief survey of the versions and later developments of this story, with many references, see Mark Bregman's "Introduction" to Howard Schwartz, *The Four Who Entered Paradise,* xiii–xxxiii and 209–13. *Rabbi Nathan* gives no explicit indication of what the story or the grouping means for the editors. See Finkelstein, *Introduction,* 74–100; "Introductory Study," 22–24.

19. See my comments on pages 34 and 198, note 37 concerning a similar strategy in the exegesis of the maxim of Simeon the Righteous.

20. Not all of *Rabbi Nathan,* though, is exegetical. In some places, the compilation is a nonhierarchical anthology, such that maxims appear one after another with no evident primary and secondary texts (Saldarini compares these sections to the *Tosephta;* see his introduction to his translation, *Fathers According to Rabbi Nathan B,* 5–6).

21. These expressions are very common in *Rabbi Nathan.* They have been collected and discussed by Goldin (*Studies in Midrash,* 78–79) and Neusner (*Judaism and Story,* 21–29, 209–10). On uses of *keytzad* in the Mishnah, see the recent discussion in Alexander, "Casuistic Elements," 202–3 and notes.

22. Finkelstein argues that "words" is the earlier meaning and that a later editor changed the maxim to "Torah" (*Introduction,* vii, 23–28). Goldin holds that the original term is "Torah" and that it refers specifically to the Written Torah (*Studies in Midrash,* 3–25).

23. His name appears as Yoseph in A7,33 and B14,33 but as Yose in *Fathers* 1:5.

24. Raphael Loewe writes that *mamash*, "what is tactile, sensible, and therefore real, occurs quite often to distinguish actuality from imaginative interpretation" ("The 'Plain' Meaning of Scripture in Early Jewish Exegesis," 170).

25. For the commentary to the maxim of the Great Assembly, see A1,2–A3,17; B1,2–B4,17. For additional material on Adam and Eve, B8,22–B9,25; B42,116–17. On the siege of Jerusalem, A4,22–25; B6,19–22. On Hillel, the base text records a number of maxims in his name, but we also find a series of narratives about him as commentary to a maxim of Eleazar ben Arakh (A15,60–62; B29,60–62). On Rabban Yohanan ben Zakkai, see A4,22–25; A14,57–59; A17,65; A25,79; B6,19–7,22; B28,57–58. On Rabbi Eliezer, A6,30–31; A16,63; A19,70; A25,80; B13,30–33; also Kagen, "Divergent Tendencies," 151–70. On Rabbi Akiba, A3,14–17; A6,28–30; A16,63; B12,29–30; B26,53; and Goldin, *Studies in Midrash*, 101–17. On the bad *yetzer*, A16,62–64; I have analyzed the features of this unit in my article, "The Redaction of Desire: Structure and Editing of Rabbinic Teachings Concerning *Yeṣer* (Inclination)." These large expansions thus have the features of anthology as well as commentary, for in many respects they are not secondary text but primary compositions in their own right. For an overview of the thematic differences between *Rabbi Nathan* and *The Fathers*, see Neusner, *Judaism and Story*, 30–39.

26. "Midrash" refers to three related elements of rabbinic culture: (1) a process of interpreting Scripture (2) a rhetorical and literary form, emerging from and representing this process, that can appear in various texts, and (3) a type of text that was produced starting in late antiquity and continuing into the medieval period. *Rabbi Nathan* has many examples of midrash in the second sense. However, *Rabbi Nathan* is not strictly a "midrashic text" because the basic structure is commentary upon rabbinic statements (as the Talmud to the Mishnah), not upon the Bible. See Strack and Stemberger, *Introduction to the Talmud and Midrash*, 233–314, for a survey of the various midrashic texts. There is also evidence that at least some of the epigrams in *Rabbi Nathan* were the products of biblical interpretation. For example, Goldin discusses the relation of the maxim of the Men of the Great Assembly and Ecclesiastes 12:12 in *Studies in Midrash*, 13 and generally 3–25.

27. Azzan Yadin has done extensive research on such debates, working to recover the interpretive practices and underlying hermeneutic assumptions of the legal exegesis in the Rabbi Ishmael midrashim; see "Hammer on the Rock: Mekhilta Deuteronomy and the Question of Rabbinic Polysemy"; "*Shnei Ketuvim* and Rabbinic Intermediation"; and *Scripture as Logos: Rabbi Ishmael and the Origins of Midrash*.

28. The parallel in *Fathers* 5:22 is attributed to Ben Bag Bag. Azzan Yadin had pointed out to me that, in a tannaitic context, this maxim would have had a more specific significance than the gloss I give here.

29. Scholars have used varying terminology to describe this process. Both Daniel Boyarin and Michael Fishbane draw upon the Saussurean distinction of *langue/parole*. Fishbane also explicates midrash as "opening" divine speech "from

within"—that is, expanding and developing the teachings of the Bible through linking parts with other parts. See Fishbane, *The Exegetical Imagination: On Jewish Thought and Theology,* 12–13 and generally 9–13; Boyarin, *Intertextuality,* 26–38. In Second Temple and early Rabbinic periods, midrash tended to focus upon the problems and possibilities of one verse, while later interpreters found meaning in the intersection of two verses. On early midrash focused on one verse, see James Kugel, *In Potiphar's House: The Interpretive Life of Biblical Texts.* On the linking of verses, see Boyarin, *Intertextuality.* Kugel notes the difference between earlier and later midrash (*Potiphar's House,* 259–66); also Fraade, *From Tradition;* David Stern, *Midrash and Theory: Ancient Jewish Exegesis and Contemporary Literary Studies.* Midrash contrasts with allegorical interpretation in having no explicit code or framework external to the interpretation itself. See Boyarin, *Intertextuality* and also *A Radical Jew: Paul and the Politics of Identity.* There are, though, certain codes implicit in midrash. For example, in rabbinic interpretation of the Song of Songs, the male figure is almost always God and the female either Israel or the rabbi. Some boundaries of midrashic interpretation can be seen through comparison with other traditions. A rabbi could not say that the woman in the Song of Songs is the church, nor could he say that there are "two powers in heaven," nor that the snake in the Garden of Eden represents Wisdom. These exegetical moves would place him outside of rabbinic tradition. See for example Alan Segal, *Two Powers in Heaven.* Parables are prominent in midrashic literature, both as steps in the linking of verses and as having rhetorical force in their own right. Boyarin examines parables as steps in midrashic interpretation (*Intertextuality,* 105–16), while David Stern focuses on their rhetorical force *(Parables in Midrash).* Midrashic compositions have their own rhetorical forms, often reflecting the life setting of a public sermon upon a verse of the Torah. See Joseph Heinemann, "The Proem in the Aggadic Midrashim," 100–122; Norman Cohen, "Leviticus Rabbah, Parashah 3: An Example of a Classic Rabbinic Homily," and "Structure and Editing in the Homiletic Midrashim"; Abraham Goldberg, "Form-Analysis of Midrashic Literature as a Method of Description."

30. A now classic treatment of this topic is by David Daube, whose comparison focuses largely on methods attributed to Hillel and to Cicero. See "Rabbinic Methods of Interpretation and Hellenistic Rhetoric"; also Loewe, "The 'Plain' Meaning of Scripture"; and the important essays in Lieberman, *Greek in Jewish Palestine* and *Hellenism in Jewish Palestine.*

31. Michael Fishbane suggested this phrasing to me.

32. Neusner highlights sage stories as the distinctive feature of *Rabbi Nathan,* arguing that this text has a greater concentration of such stories than other rabbinic sources (*Judaism and Story,* xi, 143). He identifies four types of narrative in *Rabbi Nathan:* (1) parable (2) formal setting for a saying (3) exemplum, in which the sage is not named, and (4) story, which describes a particular person and incident (46–60, 210) and in turn includes two types—scriptural story and sage story (61–71, 78–106). In an insightful moment of intrarabbinic comparison, Neusner

notes that *Rabbi Nathan* selects a fairly narrow range of topics for its stories and emphasizes Torah study, exemplary ethical action, and certain origins and ends of the sage's career. He writes that many topics appear in other texts but are neglected in *Rabbi Nathan,* including, "the sage's childhood and wonderful precociousness in Torah study, the sage's supernatural deeds, the sage's everyday administration of the community's affairs, the sage's life with other sages and with disciples" (78). Neusner overstates the point a bit, for *Rabbi Nathan* does have examples of each of these types—a precocious child (A8,36–37), supernatural acts by the rabbis (A25,80; and note also A6,32), and some discussions of life among the sages (A1,1; A4,18–19; B8,22)—but his overall insight holds.

33. Henry Fischel has argued that the stories of Hillel have strong resonance with the Greek tale of sagely virtue, the *chreia* ("Story and History," 443–72; note especially 467–72 on the means of rabbinic adaptation of the Greek rhetorical forms). More general arguments extending Fischel's arguments to rabbinic narratives appear in Rubenstein, *Talmudic Stories,* 5–8; Jaffee, *Torah in the Mouth,* 126–40. Jaffee draws primarily from Ronald F. Hock and Edward O'Neil, *The Chreia in Ancient Rhetoric, Volume I: The Progymnasmata.*

34. See Rubenstein, *Talmudic Stories,* 279–82 and throughout (also my comments in chapter 1a, note 42, concerning his analysis of the story of Rabban Yohanan ben Zakkai and the destruction of Jerusalem).

35. Schechter suggests the addition of "Torah" based on the Epstein manuscript (A6,29 n.27). The following passage is a similar teaching concerning one's children being a hindrance to study. The textual witnesses there vary significantly. See Kister, *Studies,* 49, and the important analysis of parallels, manuscript variants, and their cultural significance in Ilan, *Mine and Yours,* 78–82; also Safrai, "Tales of the Sages," 220–22.

36. A parallel to this maxim and story appears in *b. Shabb.* 127b; I analyze this story again in chapter 3a, with a focus on the final blessing.

37. One talmudic teaching states that *pidyon shebuyyim* is a "great commandment" *(mitzvah rabbah hi')* (*b. B. Bat.* 8a–b). Elsewhere, a narrative of Rabbi Pinhas ben Yair, who often expresses ideals characteristic of the *ḥasidim,* portrays him as going to redeem captives (*b. Ḥul.* 7a–7b; Safrai, *Temple and Mishnah,* 518–39); also see *b. Ta'an.* 22a; *b. B. Qam.* 17b; *b. B. Bat.* 3b.

38. The story thus plays on the legal principle of *mar'it ha'ayin,* according to which, for the sake of appearances and propriety, one should not do actions that appear to transgress the law. The phrase and principle appear often in rabbinic literature, particularly in the Palestinian Talmud. In the Mishnah, see *m. Kil.* 3:5 and 9:2; *m. Sheb.* 3:4; *m. Shabb.* 19:6; *m. Bik.* 7:3 and 7:5; also *b. Kil.* 9b; *b. Betza* 9a.

39. Other forms of encounter are when a student goes to the centers of learning to begin his training (A6,27–33; B11,28–33) or when people call upon a sage to settle a dispute (A3,15; Goldin, *Studies in Midrash,* 101–17).

40. I discuss the concept of "Oral Torah" later in this chapter and also in part 2. For a full treatment, see Jaffee, *Torah in the Mouth,* especially 84 and notes.

41. The first three letters of the Hebrew alphabet are *'aleph, beyt,* and *gimmel*—they correspond to *alpha, beta,* and *gamma* of Greek.

42. A parallel version of this story appears in *b. Shabb.* 30b–31a; see also the analysis in Neusner, *Judaism and Story,* 122–25.

43. In stories of Rabbi Akiba's early career, his learning and contemplation of the alphabet is portrayed as a significant point in his education. See A6,28–29; B12,29; Marcus, *Rituals of Childhood,* 35–36.

44. In *Rabbi Nathan B,* this remark comes immediately after the parallel to the story quoted herein. In *Rabbi Nathan A,* another story (also exemplifying Hillel's patience in contrast with Shammai) follows the one quoted, and then we read this comment by the student.

45. For an overall survey and typology of deathbed scenes in rabbinic literature, see Saldarini, "Last Words and Deathbed Scenes in Rabbinic Literature"; also Shaye Cohen, "Patriarchs and Scholars." On spiritual and mystical themes in such narratives, see Michael Fishbane, *The Kiss of God: Spiritual and Mystical Death in Judaism,* especially 51–86. On ethical wills in Judaism, see Israel Abrahams, *Hebrew Ethical Wills.*

46. A25,80; in A19,70 a teaching of Rabbi Eleazar ben Azariah lists Rabbi Eliezer's legal decisions; see the discussions in Finkelstein, *Introduction,* 193, and Kister, *Studies,* 42. See also *b. Sanh.* 68a; *t. Sanh.* 11:5; *y. San.* 7:13; *y. Shabb.* 2:7; and Abrahams, *Wills,* 5–7.

47. Schechter suggests omitting "from what you have taught us" (A19,70 n.11). Goldin includes the phrase in parentheses, translating "teach us (at least) one thing (more)" (*Rabbi Nathan,* 94, 195 n.6).

48. The instruction to focus upon the deity in prayer seems to be the reason that the story is placed as part of the exegesis upon the maxim of Akabya ben Mahalalel, which concludes that a person should attend to "who is his Judge" (A19,69). I discuss this epigram in chapter 3b. See also deathbed scenes of Rabban Yohanan ben Zakkai and Rabbi Eliezer in A25,79–81; *b. Ber.* 28b; Neusner, *Legend,* 221–24; *Judaism and Story,* 130–31.

Ic. Concepts and Tropes

1. Neusner makes the striking claim that he intended to study *Rabbi Nathan* as a collection without editorial arrangement, but then he found that he was wrong (*Rabbi Nathan,* ix). In his later study he argues that the distinctive formal quality of *Rabbi Nathan* is a focus on narrative, particularly the sage story, and that the distinctive message is an "eschatological" teleology focusing on the nation and the age rather than the individual (*Judaism and Story*). The complexities in the transmission of the text are brought out most intensively in Kister's *Studies.*

2. Daniel Boyarin emphasizes the idea that dissent was canonized in rabbinic literature (*Carnal Israel,* 27–30). David Stern, in discussing the multiplicity of meanings in rabbinic collections of midrash, states, "[T]he citation of multiple

interpretations in midrash is an attempt to represent in textual terms an idealized academy of Rabbinic tradition where all the opinions of the sages are recorded equally as part of a single divine conversation" ("Midrash and Indeterminacy," 155–56, revised and reprinted in *Midrash and Theory*, 33–34). See also Boyarin's use of "intertextuality" in "On the Status of the Tannaitic Midrashim," 456. I present my account of "tradition" in part 2. The idea that tradition centers on common debate rather than belief is articulated by MacIntyre, particularly *After Virtue*, especially 220–23, but also *Whose Justice? Which Rationality?* and *Three Rival Versions;* see the comments by Ivanhoe in *Confucian Moral Self-Cultivation*, 29–30, 38–39 nn.4, 10. For a study emphasizing the "invented" aspect of traditions, see Eric Hobsbawm and Terence Ranger, *The Invention of Tradition*, especially 1–14.

3. See Kadushin, *The Rabbinic Mind*, 1–26. For a more extended discussion of these fundamental concepts, see *Organic Thinking*, 6–12, and *The Theology of Seder Eliahu*, 33–34. See also the valuable study and critique of Kadushin's "value-concepts" by Richard Sarason, "Kadushin's Study of Midrash: Value Concepts and Their Literary Embodiment," 45–72. Note especially Sarason's observations concerning Kadushin's "apologetic and polemic concerns directed at the Protestant theological—and scholarly—animus against Judaism" (52–53). Another valuable survey of Kadushin's work is Avraham Holtz, *Rabbinic Thought: An Introduction to the Works of M. Kadushin* (Hebrew), especially 23–44. On divine compassion, see Fishbane, *Exegetical Imagination*, 22–85.

4. Kadushin, *The Theology of Seder Eliahu*, 24–25.

5. Sarason has addressed this problem in Kadushin's formulation at length in "Midrash," 51–54. In support of Kadushin's work, note that Kadushin's early research centers on *Seder Eliyahu*, which is distinctive for its strong editorial hand and relative coherence. Many of his statements concerning organicity may be more accurate for this text than for *Rabbi Nathan*. See also the comments by Sarason in "Midrash," 63–68.

6. At a broad level, the clusters of concepts and tropes centered on Torah and on God's justice interrelate with each other in an organic manner. While distinctive in key respects, they also "are constitutive of each other, inextricably weaving with one another" (Kadushin, *The Theology of Seder Eliahu*, 24). I discuss this point further in the conclusion.

7. See Kasulis, "Philosophy as Metapraxis," and my comments on this article in note 29 of the introduction.

8. Over the course of my research for this project, I tried to develop chapters based upon other concepts, but I found Torah and divine justice to be by far the most prominent in *Rabbi Nathan*. A very important topic is the body, for which key discussions include the of care of the body in B30,66 and B33,72; a homology between the body and the cosmos in A31,91–92; a contrast between beastly and angelic elements of the person in A37,109; a contrast between human embodiedness and God's power in the maxim of Akabya ben Mahalalel and ensuing exegesis

(A19,69–70; B32,69–71; B34,74; *Fathers* 3:1); and divination based on the position of the body at death in A25,79–80. The significance of the body appears throughout passages that comment upon Adam, Eve, and the curses placed upon them (A1, 4–8; B1,4–8; B8–9, 22–25; B42,116–117). I examine many of these sources in "The Beastly Body in Rabbinic Self-Formation." Another relevant set of concepts centers upon purity and sacrifice. See Fishbane's analysis of substitutes for sacrifices as well as covenantal virtues as two modes of ethical thinking in *Rabbi Nathan* (*Exegetical Imagination,* 67–70 and 123–35). A recent study of purity in rabbinic Judaism is Jonathan Klawans, *Impurity and Sin in Ancient Judaism,* 92–135. On the general topic of substitutes for sacrifice in Judaism, see also Jeffrey Rubenstein, *The History of Sukkot in the Second Temple and Rabbinic Periods,* especially 125–31. Note the comments by Moshe Idel concerning rabbinic traditions of the *ma'amadot* in *Kabbalah,* 170–72. A dated but still valuable study, which anticipates many current stances is Raphael Patai, *Man and Temple in Ancient Jewish Myth and Ritual.* In *Rabbi Nathan,* the most explicit statements concerning substitution for sacrifice appear in the commentary to the maxim of Simeon the Righteous, "The world rests upon three things: upon the Torah, upon the [Temple] service, and upon good deeds" (A4,18–21; B5,18–19; *Fathers* 1:2). This motif is also implied in the commentary to the numerical catalogue, "Seven kinds of punishment come to the world because of seven types of transgression" (A38,113–15; B41,113–15; *Fathers* 5:8; Urbach, *Sages,* 438).

9. Jaffee translates "Oral Torah" more literally as "Torah in the Mouth." He examines the development of the concept, which was not universal among rabbis as late as the third century CE. He acknowledges, though, that the concept appears in *Rabbi Nathan* (see the narratives in A15,60; B29,61–62 quoted in chapter 1b). Jaffee notes that there were likely written versions of the Oral Torah in the third century (*Torah in the Mouth,* especially 5, 11).

10. I discuss the concept of *yetzer* at length in chapter 2b.

11. For metaphoric tension, I draw upon the synthetic account of Paul Ricoeur. See his *The Rule of Metaphor: Multi-Disciplinary Studies of the Creation of Meaning in Language.* The notion of "metaphorical systematicity" is articulated by George Lakoff and Mark Johnson in *Metaphors We Live By;* also, George Lakoff, *Women, Fire, and Dangerous Things: What Categories Reveal about the Mind.* On cultural continua, I draw upon James Fernandez, ed., *Persuasions and Performances: The Play of Tropes in Culture;* his major theoretical statements can be found on 3–70. The literature on metaphor is tremendous, and I have selected the works most helpful for my analysis. Ricoeur surveys the philosophical literature in *Rule of Metaphor.* See also Janite Soskice, *Metaphor and Religious Language.* For a review of anthropological studies focusing on metaphor, see James Fernandez, "Introduction," in *Beyond Metaphor: The Theory of Tropes in Anthropology,* ed. James W. Fernandez, 1–13. Scholars of rabbinic literature have already drawn attention to the significance of metaphors. See especially Fraade's treatment of metaphors for

Torah in *From Tradition,* 18–19, 45–49, 57–58, 105–20; and Fonrobert's analysis of metaphors for women in *Menstrual Purity,* 40–67. Ivan Marcus has drawn upon metaphor theory for his account of medieval Jewish rituals in *Rituals of Childhood.* David J. Williams has compiled a tremendous collection of metaphors in the New Testament writings of Paul, including discussion of their historical context, in *Paul's Metaphors: Their Context and Character.*

12. Note that the issue of X being "like and not like" Y is salient even if one wants to claim that rabbis thought God literally had royal attributes. I employ tools from metaphor theory as useful for analyzing certain features of rabbinic pedagogical discourse, but I am not focusing on the question of whether rabbinic imagery is literal or figurative, mythic or metaphoric. On this set of issues, see Michael Fishbane, *Biblical Myth and Rabbinic Mythmaking,* 3–12, 81–82; on biblical metaphors, a recent discussion is David Aaron, *Biblical Ambiguities.* A classic study of the royal metaphor in the Bible is Martin Buber, *Kingship of God.* More recently, Mark Brettler presents an extensive analysis in *God Is King: Understanding an Israelite Metaphor;* and on rabbinic theology, see the analysis of parables by David Stern in *Parables in Midrash,* especially 19–21, and *Midrash and Theory,* 82–83. For a study of the royal metaphor in Jewish mysticism, including discussion of rabbinic materials, see Arthur Green, *Keter: The Crown of God in Early Jewish Mysticism.*

13. Often systematic tropes are our primary way of understanding dimensions of experience that are not easily apprehended through the senses, such as time ("time is money"), ideas ("ideas are objects"), communication ("communication is sending"), and emotions ("love is a journey"). Lakoff and Johnson, *Metaphors We Live By,* 14, 54–55, 77, 85, 112; on the ways that these metaphors condition thought and action, see 5, 10; on the issue of "dead" and "live" metaphors, 55.

14. The mixed metaphor in part turns on the commonality that both the "journey" and "container" metaphors distinguish the form of the argument (the path, the interior surface of the container) and the content (the ground covered in the journey, the substance in the container). As Lakoff and Johnson summarize, "The overlap between the two metaphors is the progressive creation of a surface. As the argument covers more ground (via the journey surface), it gets more content (via the container surface)" (*Metaphors We Live By,* 93 and generally 89–96).

15. See Fernandez, *Persuasions,* 3–70, especially 39–41. For a fruitful and provocative application of metaphor theory to ritual activity in the Bible, see Howard Eilberg-Schwartz, *The Savage in Judaism: An Anthropology of Israelite Religion and Ancient Judaism,* especially 25–26, 115–40. Note that at the level of analyzing meaning, I prefer Fernandez's anthropological methods to those that Lakoff and Johnson draw from cognitive science, as the former are more flexible and adaptable to specific contexts.

16. Fernandez, *Persuasions,* 115–20.

17. This place-name appears in Gen. 35:21.

18. A parallel account appears in *b. Ta'an.* 20a–b. See also Neusner, *Judaism and Story,* 125–26.

19. On scribes and rabbis, see Hezser, *Social Structure of the Rabbinic Movement,* 466–75. An extensive treatment of scribal activity in the creation of biblical materials appears in Michael Fishbane, *Biblical Interpretation in Ancient Israel,* 23–43. A further resonance, which may be implicit here, is the common rabbinic metaphor that Torah is fire (I discuss this trope further in chapter 2b). To the extent that this image is present for Rabbi Simeon and his audience, the rabbi claims that while the flexible man is close to Torah, the rigid one burns in the flames of the tradition. Rabbi Simeon's sermon would then culminate with the assertions: I create and am close to the Torah. You are destroyed by it. In addition, Michael Lyons has pointed out to me that the image of cedar (and its burning) could evoke Isa. 44:14–17, which concerns the making of idols. I have also learned much from discussions with Katherine Bishop about this passage.

Part 2. Rabbinic Tradition

1. This account of tradition draws from a number of sources, including Shils, *Tradition;* Gadamer, *Truth and Method,* part 2, especially 277–85, 358–62; Hobsbawm and Ranger, *The Invention of Tradition,* especially 1–14; Jonathan Z. Smith, "Sacred Persistence: Toward a Redescription of Canon," in *Imagining Religion: From Babylon to Jonestown,* 36–52; Nancy Caciola, "The Body of Tradition," presented at the annual meeting of the American Academy of Religion, Nashville, 2000. Also, I have learned much from discussions with Richard Weiss, Joshua Holo, and Mark Berkson.

2. See MacIntyre, *After Virtue,* especially 220–23, *Whose Justice? Which Rationality?,* and *Three Rival Versions;* and Ivanhoe, *Confucian Moral Self-Cultivation,* 29–30, 38–39 nn.4, 10.

3. Gershom Scholem, "Revelation and Tradition as Religious Categories in Judaism," 282–303. Kadushin presents an extensive discussion of Torah in *Organic Thinking,* 16–177. Schechter describes the scope and significance of Torah for the rabbis in *Aspects of Rabbinic Theology,* 127. In *Rabbi Nathan,* as I have discussed in chapter 1b, the distinction between Oral and Written Torah appears in narratives of Hillel and Shammai (A15,61–62; B29,61–62; also see A6,28–29 and *b. Shabb.* 31a). More generally, see Jaffee, *Torah in the Mouth,* "The Oral-Cultural Context of the Talmud Yerushalmi," and "A Rabbinic Ontology of the Written and Spoken Word: On Discipleship, Transformative Knowledge, and the Living Texts of the Oral Torah." See also Urbach, *Sages,* 286–314; Kadushin, *Organic Thinking,* 33–41; and on the Dead Sea Scrolls, Fishbane, *Biblical Interpretation,* 527–28.

4. On mystical interpretations, see Swartz, *Scholastic Magic,* 166–70 and references; Fishbane, *Kiss of God,* especially 14–17. For a large collection of midrashic passages concerning Sinai, see S. Y. Agnon, *Present at Sinai;* also Louis Ginzberg,

The Legends of the Jews, vol. 3, 107–19. For a recent article on Sinai in biblical, rabbinic, and modern theology, see Benjamin Sommer, "Revelation at Sinai in the Hebrew Bible and Jewish Theology."

5. See my discussion of genealogical lists structuring *The Fathers* and *Rabbi Nathan* in chapter 1b.

6. See A1,1. In the Book of Exodus, the concern with sanctity (and the term *q.d.sh.*) appears in Exod. 19:10–25, when Moses orders the people to "make yourselves holy" before the divine revelation. The Bible portrays a process of purification for the whole community, and according to *Rabbi Nathan* Moses goes through another ritual of initiation, a supernatural sanctification, while at Sinai. On this account of Moses, see Goldin, "The First Chapter of *Abot de Rabbi Nathan,*" 263–80; also Finkelstein, *Introduction,* xxix n.4; and my analysis in *The Making of a Sage: The Rabbinic Ethics of Abot de Rabbi Natan,* 128–31. *Rabbi Nathan B* has a much longer opening, emphasizing God's presence to a greater degree (see B1,1 and note the associations with A11,46 and B22,46). For a discussion of Moses as an intermediary, and the relation of this section to Gal. 3:19, see Goldin, "Not By Means of an Angel and Not by Means of a Messenger," 412–24. B1,2 has a more direct response to Paul's letter (see Saldarini, *Fathers According to Rabbi Nathan B,* 25 n.13). On holiness/sanctity *(q.d.sh.)* in rabbinic thought, see Fine, *This Holy Place: On the Sanctity of the Synagogue during the Greco-Roman Period,* 10–23; Eliezer Diamond, *Holy Men and Hunger Artists,* 75–85.

7. See A6,27–28; B10,26; B11,28; Lieberman, "Roman Legal Institutions," 7–9; Goldin, *Rabbi Nathan,* 175 n.5; Finkelstein, *Introduction,* 29–32; and my discussion in chapter 1a.

8. A31,91; see Goldin, *Rabbi Nathan,* 67, 126–27, 189 n.21, 204 nn.11–12. For parallels to this passage, see Ginzberg, *Legends,* vol. 5, 3–4 n.5, 132–33 n.2; also note *Sed. El. Rab.,* chapters 2, 6/7, 13/14 (Friedmann, *Seder Eliahu,* 9, 33, 68; 9 n.19 also lists parallels); Kadushin, *Organic Thinking,* 17–18. On the meaning of *'amon* in Proverbs, see Michael Fox, *Proverbs 1–9: A New Translation with Introduction and Commentary,* 285–87.

9. A39,118; B44,124. The motif appears in *Rabbi Nathan* without its midrashic source, but the derivation is in numerous places in rabbinic literature. See *Gen. Rab.* 1:1 (parallels are listed in Theodor and Albeck, *Bereshit Rabba,* 1–2); Schechter, *Aspects of Rabbinic Theology,* 127–28; Urbach, *Sages,* 287.

10. On creation during the six days, see A2,10; on the text flying off the tablets, A2,11; A41,133; B47,130. Towner analyzes B47,130 in relation to the *Mekhilta* to Exod. 17:8 (H. S. Horovitz and I. A. Rabin, *Mechilta d'Rabbi Ishmael,* 178). See also his *Enumeration,* 131–35. For other parallels, see Saldarini, *Fathers According to Rabbi Nathan B,* 294 n.4. The motif of the text returning to heaven also appears in accounts of the martyrdom of R. Hanina ben Taradion. See *Siphre Deut.* 307 (Finkelstein, *Sifre on Deuteronomy,* 346); *Semaḥot* 8:12 (Dov Zlotnick, *The Tractate "Mourning"* [*Regulations Relating to Death, Burial, and Mourning*], 60–61, 141–42, Hebrew 22); also note the version of the story in *b. 'Abod. Zar.* 17b–18a.

11. On Torah as fire, see A16,64; B43,121; Fraade, *From Tradition,* 46–48; Fishbane, *Exegetical,* 9; Dalia Hoshen, "The Fire Symbol in Talmudic-Aggadic Exegesis." On the tree of life, see A34,103; B43,121–22, based on Prov. 3:18. On water, see Fishbane, " Well," 3–16; also Flusser and Safrai, "The Essene Doctrine," 306–16. On linen and wool, see A28,35; B31,68; and on "wings of the Shekhinah," A12,53 and B26,54; and also comparisons to gold and glass on B31,68. The Torah also protects one from the angel of death (see B25,52, which cites Ps. 19:8). Elsewhere in rabbinic literature, Ps. 19:8 is the basis of a teaching that the Torah returned the souls of the Israelites to their bodies after they had been overcome by the first utterance of the divine revelation at Sinai; see *Songs Rab.* 5:16; *Exod. Rab.* 29:4; and generally on this motif, Fishbane, *Kiss of God.* In one interpretation, Torah takes the speaking position of God: rabbis interpret God's words to Eli the priest, recorded in 1 Sam. 2:30, as the words of Torah (A27,83; Goldin, *Rabbi Nathan,* 201 n.2).

12. On the "crown" of Torah being greater than that of priesthood or government, see A41,130; B48,130–31; *Fathers* 4:13; Stuart Cohen, *Three Crowns,* 14–18 and generally 7–28; also Tirosh-Samuelson, *Happiness in Premodern Judaism,* 116–17.

13. The Book of Leviticus was the first part of the Torah to be taught (for examples in *Rabbi Nathan,* see A6,29; A15,61). See also Marcus, *Rituals of Childhood,* 38–39.

14. Or "supplements" *(tosephot),* which may refer to aggadic midrash. See Schechter, *Rabbi Nathan,* 143, notes to A14; Goldin, *Rabbi Nathan,* 191 n.6.

15. In a brief and intensive study of the subject, Kister argues that the basic tannaitic list for Oral Torah is midrash, *halakhot,* and *aggadot,* but this list began to be expanded already in the tannaitic period, and more so later (*Studies,* 42–45); also see Goldin, "The Freedom and Restraint of Haggadah," 57–76; Fraade, *From Tradition,* 97, 244 n.111; and Kadushin, *Organic Thinking,* 40. Some of the longest lists of *Rabbi Nathan* appear in accounts of Rabban Yohanan ben Zakkai that include, in addition to the basic elements: *gemara, tosephtot,* subtleties of the Torah and subtleties of the scribes, and all the interpretative rules of the sages (A14,57). The list in *Rabbi Nathan B* includes *targum,* rhetoric *(siḥin),* and parables *(meshalim)* (B28,58). MS N of *Rabbi Nathan A* adds that Rabban Yohanan ben Zakkai had mystical understanding of the chariot *(ma'aśeh merkabah;* see Kister, *Studies,* 66). On Rabban Yohanan ben Zakkai's learning, see also Goldin, *Rabbi Nathan,* 191 nn.6–8; Saldarini, *Fathers According to Rabbi Nathan B,* 166 n.5. For other examples of these lists, see A8,35; A14,57; A14,59; A18,67; A28,86; A29,89; A40,127; B12,29–30; B13,30; B18,39; B28,58; B45,127; also Saldarini, *Fathers According to Rabbi Nathan B,* 94–95; 99–100 n.10; *b. Sukk.* 28a; *b. B. Bat.* 134a; Jaffee, *Torah in the Mouth,* 88.

16. For "worldly matters," see, for example, A1,1; also A25,80 for the contrast of Torah and business *(seḥorah);* for "sex," A37,109. For supererogatory action, see A22,75; B34,75; B32,70; *Fathers* 2:2, 3:17. For Torah as primary, A28,86; B35,70. On *derekh 'eretz,* see Marcus van Loopik, *The Ways of the Sages and the Ways of the World,* especially 2–6; Safrai "The Term *Derekh 'Erez,*" 147–62; Flusser, "Which Is

the Right Way," 163–78; Kadushin, *Organic Thinking*, 68–69, 117–30; Tirosh-Samuelson, *Happiness in Premodern Judaism*, 113–15. In other texts, we find the rabbinic phrase *darkah shel Torah* (the way of the Torah), but not in *Rabbi Nathan;* see *Lam. Rab.* 1; *Midr. Ps.* 2; *Midr. Prov.* 19; *Sed. El. Zuṭ.* 17. On Torah and good deeds *(maʿasim ṭobim),* see A22,75; A24,77–78; B32,68–69. Note that in two cases the parallels in *Rabbi Nathan B* use "wisdom" *(ḥokhmah)* in place of Torah, B34,75–76 (and A22,75); B34,76 (and A24,77). This is in accord with Goldin's thesis that *Rabbi Nathan A* emphasizes Torah more than *Rabbi Nathan B* (*Studies in Midrash*, 83–100). Note also my discussion in chapter 1a, with references, on the *ḥasidim.*

17. Verbal forms from *b.ṭ.l.* can mean simply "to leave (Torah) to do something else of value," such as in a debate whether it is valuable to stop studying in order to attend to a bridal procession. See A4,18; the parallel in B8,22 uses *p.s.q.* More often, the term means, "to neglect" the words of Torah or even "to nullify" a covenant. For "neglect," see A7,35; A29,87; A30,89; B5,18; B33,73; B35,82; and especially A21,72–73, where *Fathers* 3:11 is reinterpreted in terms of a concern with *b.ṭ.l. torah* (Hayim Lapin has emphasized to me the importance of this unit). For "nullify," see A9,41. In these cases, I see no difference between *paʿal* and *piʿel* forms. Compare, for example, A29,87 *(kol ha-boṭel mi-dibrey torah)* with A30,89 *(kol ha-mebaṭṭel dibrey torah).* Goldin's translation shows no attention to this difference. For examples of *debarim beṭelim* or *dibrey baṭṭalah,* see A1,3; A8,37; A11,45; A41,130; B31,66; B34,75. For an example of *debarim beṭelim* as flirtation, see A2,8. Note also the similar use of *dibrey sheṭut* (words of folly) on B32,68. On *p.r.sh.* and *p.s.q.,* for "getting up from study," see A1,1; A26,82; B8,22; B35,81. For the break with "Torah" as tradition, see A5,26; A36,109; B10,26.

18. For an extensive study of verbs used with *torah* in rabbinic literature, see S. Abramson, "From the Language of the Sages" (Hebrew), 61–65. On the biblical meanings of *torah,* see Michael Fishbane, "Torah," vol. 8, 469–83. For *y.sh.b.* and *ʿ.s.q.,* see A1,1; A4,18; A8,36–7; B33,73. Elsewhere in rabbinic literature, the term *ʿ.s.q.* has strong resonance with sacrificial practices (for example *Lev. Rab.* 7:3). Note in *Rabbi Nathan B* the use of "toil" *(ʿ.m.l.)* in B15,34–35 and "establish" *(q.v.m.)* in B7,21. On *sh.n.h.,* see A21,74; A41,133. Other uses of *sh.n.h.* include A4,23; A36,109. In the narrative of R. Eliezer's death, we see the verb as part of a threefold practice centered upon study of Scripture, study of Mishnah, and service to the sages (A25,81). On *d.r.sh.,* see A35,105; B13,32. The verb *d.r.sh.* refers to oracular inquiry in Exod. 18:15, but in the later Books of Deuteronomy and Ezra, it denotes rational legal investigation (Fishbane, *Biblical Interpretation*, 245). In the rabbinic period, the term generally denotes homiletic or midrashic interpretation, often in public (see my discussion of midrash in chapter 1b and the references cited there). On the triad of study, practice, and teaching, examples include A13,56; A27,84; B32,68; *Fathers* 4:5; Goldin, *Studies in Midrash*, 83–100; Kister, *Studies*, 45. Similar issues can be seen in A40,126; B46,129. See also Kadushin, *Organic Thinking*, 28–30. Note that the ritual recitation of Torah in synagogue is not

discussed in *Rabbi Nathan,* except for a brief mention of the practice of "pointing out the words of Torah" *(mar'in dibrey torah),* which may refer to the use of a pointer while reading from the scroll (A40, 128; Goldin, *Rabbi Nathan,* 218 n.35). Finally, an epigram attributed to Rabbi Nathan begins, "There is no love like the love of Torah" (A28,85). On the stronger image of lusting after study, see Boyarin, *Carnal Israel,* 134–66.

2a. Torah and Transgressive Tendencies

1. Outside of *Rabbi Nathan,* one teaching interprets verses of priestly material in the Bible to argue that these three sins are distinctive in being labeled as *ţum'ot*—causes of impurity (it draws upon Lev. 18:30, 20:3, and Num. 35:30–34; see *Siphra* to Lev. 16:16 and *b. Sheb.* 7b, but note also challenges to this teaching; also Moore, *Judaism in the First Centuries,* vol. 2, 58). A historically significant rabbinic ideal is that one must die rather than commit these sins: "For every transgression that is in the Torah, if a man is told, 'Transgress, and you will not be killed,' let him transgress and not be killed, except for idolatry [*'abodat kokhabim*], incest [*gilluy 'arayot*], and murder [*shephikhut damim*]" (*b. Sanh.* 74a). See the discussions in Schechter, *Aspects of Rabbinic Theology,* 219–30; also Urbach, *Sages,* 351–53 and his notes discussing sources. The three sins appear in *b. Shabb.* 33a and similar teachings in A38,115; B41,115; *Fathers* 5:9; also A36,106; A40,120; and mishnaic lists of crimes for which the criminal is stoned and burned on *m. Sanh.* 7:4 and *m. Sanh.* 9:1.

2. A3,15; B4,16–17; *b. Shabb.* 105b; and F. C. Porter, "The *Yeçer Hara:* A Study in the Jewish Doctrine of Sin," 113; Ishay Rosen-Zvi, "Evil Desire and Sexuality: A Chapter in Talmudic Anthropology" (Hebrew). In other cases, rabbis depict anger as an internal idol (Fishbane, *Exegetical,* 111–14). Sexual and religious transgression often have complex links. Moshe Halbertal and Avishai Margalit observe, "if sexual sins in the sphere of the family are permitted, then idolatry in the sphere of the relationship between human beings and God will also be permitted, and vice versa" (*Idolatry,* 24 and, generally on the topic, 9–36).

3. In the exegesis of *Rabbi Nathan,* the elements appear in a different order than in *The Fathers,* and *Rabbi Nathan* may preserve the original order and sense of the statement. See the argument by Goldin, who also claims that *Rabbi Nathan* shows no evidence of the commentators' understanding, or trying to understand, the maxim in its historical sense (*Studies in Midrash,* 3–25).

4. In his study of *Seder Eliyahu,* Kadushin writes, "[T]o the Rabbis Torah was *the* character-forming agency. By means of the study of Torah, as we have seen, a man not only learns to do what is right but becomes so tempered as to find it natural to do good and to avoid evil" (*Organic Thinking,* 75–76). Urbach discusses the significance of the commandments as a means of "refining mankind" in *Sages,* 366–67. Also see Michael Satlow, "'And on the Earth You Shall Sleep': *Talmud Torah* and Rabbinic Asceticism."

5. The *Shema* is the affirmation of faith that was and is central to rabbinic liturgy, to be recited by observant Jews when going to bed and when rising (see *m. Ber.* 1). The Song of Songs and the Book of Ecclesiastes were two of the last books to be canonized as part of the Bible, and rabbinic literature preserves debates by early rabbis about whether or not they were inspired; see for example *m. Yad.* 3:5. Saldarini summarizes the issues and lists sources in *Fathers According to Rabbi Nathan B,* 27–28 n.20. For a full study of the rabbinic material on this topic, see Shnayer Leiman, *The Canonization of Hebrew Scripture: The Talmudic and Midrashic Evidence,* especially 114–15, and 104–13 for the sources. Leiman develops the argument of Solomon Zeitlin, "An Historical Study of the Canonization of the Hebrew Scriptures," in *The Canon and the Masorah of the Hebrew Bible,* 164–201, especially 173–74, and see 172–78 on the "Writings."

6. Several other passages in *Rabbi Nathan,* particularly numerical catalogues, address biblical passages whose interpretation concerned the rabbis. See A34,100–101; B37,94; B37,96–97.

7. The manuscript issues are also very difficult. See Finkelstein, *Introduction,* 125–26 for a discussion of the variants; also Saldarini, *Fathers According to Rabbi Nathan B,* 26–28 and his notes for similar issues that arise in *Rabbi Nathan B.*

8. Fishbane writes concerning this verse that it is "a valuable witness to court-sponsored activity in ancient Israel, although it is not certain whether the verb . . . indicates the transmission or transcription of literary sources" (*Biblical Interpretation,* 33).

9. The concept of the Torah as an interpreted *(mephorash)* text is present within the Bible itself in Neh. 8:8.

10. The syntax of the Hebrew is a bit difficult in what I translate as the first two sentences. See A1,2 nn.20–21 and Schechter, *Rabbi Nathan,* 150; Goldin, *Rabbi Nathan,* 5 and 176 nn.20–21. Schechter suggests substituting the "Men of Hezekiah" for "Men of the Great Assembly" (A1,2 n.22). Goldin agrees (*Rabbi Nathan,* 5 and 176 n.22). Saldarini notes that the rabbis confused the two (*Fathers According to Rabbi Nathan B,* 27 n.20), following the argument of Saul Lieberman, "Notes on the First Chapter of Qoheleth Rabbah," 163–67.

11. A passage in *Rabbi Nathan* links these events with the prophecies of Bilaam (A1,3; Goldin, *Rabbi Nathan,* 176 n.26).

12. This teaching about Moses's anger appears in a number of variations. In *Leviticus Rabbah,* it is the third of a series of three cases in which Moses forgets the law because of anger (*Lev. Rab.* 13:1; Margulies, *Midrash Wayyikra Rabbah,* 269–70). In *b. Pesaḥ.* 66b, a parallel of this teaching appears as commentary to a maxim of the Palestinian amora, Resh Lakish, who says, "Anyone who is angry, if he is a sage [*ḥakham*], his wisdom leaves him." The text then presents Moses as an example of such a "sage," citing the same prooftext that we find in *Rabbi Nathan.*

13. This material appears in the commentary to Moses's fence, amidst a discussion of three times that "Moses' judgment agreed with God's judgment." The third case is Moses's destruction of the tablets in response to Israel's worship of the

golden calf—the nation's religious transgression negates their reception of the Torah. Moreover, the case of breaking the tablets is elaborated through a parable that portrays this transgression in sexual terms. The tablets of the covenant are a marriage contract between Israel and other Gods, but before they are given, Israel "whores" after other gods (A2,9–11; see the discussion of textual issues in A2,11 n.48 and Goldin, *Rabbi Nathan,* 179 n.27, both based on the text of the Gaon Rabbi Elijah of Vilna; compare B2,10–11; *b. Shabb.* 86a–87a; *b. Yeb.* 62a; and the discussion in Saldarini, *Fathers According to Rabbi Nathan B,* 41–42 n.10).

14. Goldin argues that the Great Assembly calls for a version of the Masoretic commentary. This technical fence insures "the proper protection and preservation of the text of the Torah (almost certainly the Five Books of Moses) lest it be corrupted by false or inferior readings" (*Studies in Midrash,* 9 and generally 3–25). He also cites a maxim of Rabbi Akiba saying, "*Masoret* is a fence for the Torah" (*Fathers* 3:13; also B33,71; this phrase does not appear in the parallel in A26,82). Johann Cook has argued that late Second Temple period sources, specifically Septuagint Proverbs and the *Letter of Aristeas,* present Torah as a "fence" for the righteous. See "Towards the Dating of the Tradition 'The Torah as a Surrounding Fence.'" Siegfried Stein presents an extensive discussion of the trope in Jewish, Greek, and Roman literatures in "The Concept of the 'Fence.'"

15. On this point, I do not follow Finkelstein, who argues that "words" rather than "Torah" represents the earlier teaching. See Finkelstein, *Introduction,* 28, 234–35 and notes; also his article in English, "The Maxim of the *Anshe Keneset Ha-Gedolah*"; Stein, "The Concept of the 'Fence,'" 314; Urbach, *Sages,* 567. Note that the shift to "words" also appears in the commentary to "Be deliberate in judgment" (A1,2–3; B1,3; discussed earlier in this chapter).

16. My list follows the order of *Rabbi Nathan A. Rabbi Nathan B* has Job/Moses/Torah rather than Torah/Moses/Job. The order in B is likely chronological, given the common rabbinic view that Job lived at the time of the patriarchs of Genesis. Saldarini suggests that the order in A fits with its overall emphasis on the importance of Torah. See Schechter's notes in B2,9–10 n.7; Saldarini, *Fathers According to Rabbi Nathan B,* 38 n.1; and on the emphasis upon Torah in *Rabbi Nathan A,* Goldin, *Studies in Midrash,* 83–100. The creators of the fences include several very different beings: God (specifically "The Holy One, blessed be He"), biblical characters (Adam, Moses, Job, perhaps the prophets), texts (Torah, Prophets, Writings), and then the postbiblical sages.

17. Also see *m. Ber.* 1:1; *b. Ber.* 4b. The discussion in *Rabbi Nathan* does not present prooftexts, though parallel sources link the principle to biblical passages; see *Mek. R. Ishmael,* 6 (Horowitz and Rabin, *Mechilta d'Rabbi Ishmael,* 18–19); *Siphre Deut.* 16 (Finkelstein, *Sifre on Deuteronomy,* 25 and notes); *Num. Rab.* 10:8; *b. Yeb.* 90b; *b. Sanh.* 46a; *b. Nid.* 3b and 4b; *y. Nid.* 1:1, 48d; also the discussion in Goldin, *Studies in Midrash,* 20–22 and notes; Urbach, *Sages,* 334; Moore, *Judaism in the First Centuries,* vol. 1, 33, 258–59.

18. *Rabbi Nathan* thus includes both the late Second Temple sense of the

Torah as a fence around the righteous (see Cook, "The Torah as a Surrounding Fence") and the sense of the fence as an extension of biblical law. On the idea of distancing oneself from transgression, see also Rabbi Yitzhak Twersky, "Make a Fence for the Torah," 26–27. The other two fences—attributed to God and the prophets—address important but different issues concerning the communication of God's power to humans. God's fence concerns warning preceding divine punishment (A1,3; B1,3–4), and the prophets' fence describes God's accommodation to human capacity (A2,13; B3,13; also *Midr. Prov.* 20).

19. Saldarini calls this fence "the archtypical incident of a hedge leading to evil" (*Fathers According to Rabbi Nathan B*, 29–30 n.30). The concern appears also in the saying of the first-century-BCE sage Abtelion, "Sages, be careful with your words, lest you teach something that is not in accord with the [appropriate] study of Torah [*she-lo' ketalmud torah*], and you are guilty of exile." (A11,46–47; B22,47; *Fathers* 1:11; Finkelstein lists the manuscript variants in *Introduction,* 150–51). Also, in the exegesis of the maxim of Antigonus of Sokho, we read that the origins of the Sadducees and Boethusians, rival sects of the Pharisees, lay in faulty transmission of tradition (this interpretation is explicit in B10,26; see also A5,26).

20. On the snake pushing Eve, see MS H of *Rabbi Nathan B* and *Midr. Psalms* 1:9 (Solomon Buber, *Midrash Psalms,* 9–10). A valuable discussion of all the versions can be found in Saldarini, *Fathers According to Rabbi Nathan B,* 33–34 n.41.

21. This issue is also taken up in *Genesis Rabbah,* though it is not the only interpretation of the relevant verses. Compare similar statements in B1,3 and Rabbi Hiyya in *Gen. Rab.* 19:3 (Theodor and Albeck, *Bereshit Rabba,* 172 and notes); the teaching of Rabbi Hiyya is a midrash linking Prov. 30:6 with Gen. 3:3. See also *Midr. Psalms* 1:9 (Buber, *Midrash Psalms,* 9–10) and *Pirqe R. El.* 13.

22. On interpretations of Adam and Eve in late antiquity, see Brown, *Body and Society,* especially 57–58 and 92–96; Pagels, *Adam, Eve, and the Serpent;* Boyarin, *Carnal Israel,* 77–106; and also my comments and notes in chapter 1a concerning the presentation of women in *Rabbi Nathan.* The full discussion in *Rabbi Nathan A* of Adam's fence includes an extended elaboration of the events in Eden and the ensuing punishments (A1,4–8). The material has many features related to the themes of sex, religious transgression, and Torah. The account of the snake touching the tree says that it "stood and touched the tree with its arms and its legs and shook it until its fruit fell to the ground," which appears to be a sexual image. A following digression, depicting Titus at the moment of entering the Holy of Holies, says that he cursed the altar quoting from the Book of Isaiah—the Written Torah becomes a tool for the paradigmatic desecration of Jewish life by the Romans. Also, building on the account in Genesis, according to *Rabbi Nathan* most of God's curses upon Eve concern reproduction, gender relations, and sexual desire. There is one passage in *Rabbi Nathan* that transmitters apparently changed because of its sexual explicitness. (Just as the Book of Proverbs had moral teachings that were too sexually explicit for the rabbis and had to be "interpreted," *Rabbi Nathan* itself had teachings that later Jews felt they needed to cover over. See

A1,6; Goldin, *Rabbi Nathan,* 177 n.56). The editors touch on other issues that are important to the scholastic ethos of the text, such as the concern to control speech. For example, one comment states that the snake "talked much with her," which paraphrases and shows the snake to violate the maxim of Yoseph ben Yohanan, "Do not talk overmuch with your wife [*'al tarbeh śiḥah 'im ha-'ishah*]." See A1,4; A7,34–35; B15,34–35, especially B15,35; *Fathers* 1:4. This collection of teachings in *Rabbi Nathan A* is made up of material that appears in disparate parts of *Rabbi Nathan B* (B1,4–8; B8,22–B9,25; B42,116–17). The editors of *Rabbi Nathan A* may have had before them something like what is found in *Rabbi Nathan B,* and then arranged the material into a distinct composition. A similar process likely underlies *Rabbi Nathan A,* chapter 16, which I address in my article, "The Redaction of Desire."

23. Goodman writes that in second-century Galilee, *niddah* was the most common source of impurity for rabbis (*State and Society,* 95). For a full treatment of this topic, see Fonrobert, *Menstrual Purity.* The Hebrew word for "come near" *(q.r.b.)* has a range of meanings, including sexual advance. In the Bible, the root can also refer to approaches in kindness, for war, and for sacrificial purposes. For examples: Gen. 20:4 and Lev. 18:6,14,19 (sexual advance); 1 Kings 2:7 (kindness); Exod. 14:20 (war); Exod. 29:3,8 (sacrifice). For a more full treatment, see Francis Brown, et al., *The Brown-Driver-Briggs Hebrew and English Lexicon* (BDB), 897–98. In rabbinic exegesis, when the phrase "do not come near" appears in cases concerning women, the dual sense of proximity and sexual advance are present. See for example *b. Shabb.* 13a–b; *b. Sheb.* 18b; *b. 'Abod. Zar.* 17a; *b. Ker.* 2b; and *Num. Rab.* 10:8; also *b. Pesaḥ.* 40b; *b. B. Bat.* 92a; *b. 'Abod. Zar.* 58b–59a; *b. Yeb.* 46a.

24. See Finkelstein, *Introduction,* 127, for a discussion of manuscript variants; also see Judith Baskin, *Midrashic Women: Formations of the Feminine in Rabbinic Literature,* 25–26. Parallels appear in *Num. Rab.* 10:8, 19:3, 46:3; see also *b. Shabb.* 13a.

25. Finkelstein links this stance concerning the menstruating woman with the opinions of the House of Shammai, and he sees this passage as evidence for Shammaitic editing of early strata in *Rabbi Nathan.* See *b. Shabb.* 64b and Finkelstein, *Introduction,* 23–24. The phrase "idle chatter" *(debarim beṭelim),* as noted earlier in part 2, can appear as a binary opposite to "words of Torah" *(dibrey Torah),* and it often has an overtone of sexual, flirtatious conversation. See also Goldin, *Rabbi Nathan,* 178 n.2. In *Rabbi Nathan B,* we find a teaching that softens the restriction to allow that the woman serve her husband by cooking for, and waiting on, him (B3,12; also Saldarini, *Fathers According to Rabbi Nathan B,* 44–45 and notes).

26. The commentators reinforce these points by seizing upon a biblical case of the word "sick" or "unwell" being used for a menstruant *(ha-davah).* In the Babylonian Talmud, this point and the midrashic interpretation of *ha-davah* are debated. A teaching in the name of the "early elders" says that she must make herself unattractive, but Rabbi Akiba disagrees (*b. Ber.* 64b). In *Rabbi Nathan A,* following this passage, the issue of a man's proximity to a menstruating woman is developed

further through a narrative of a woman whose husband dies at a young age, although he was a virtuous man. She talks with the prophet Elijah, who interprets the death in relation to this fence and concepts of divine reward and punishment. Parallel versions of this story appear in *b. Shabb.* 13a–b, introduced as a *baraita* from the school of Elijah, and in *Sed. El. Rab.* 15/16 (Friedmann, *Seder Eliahu*, 76). For a full discussion of these materials, see Schofer, "Protest or Pedagogy? Trivial Sin and Divine Justice in Rabbinic Narrative."

27. The underlying principle here is that of appearances, or *mar'it ha-'ayin*—not only must a person avoid transgression, but also one should not do actions that appear to violate the commandments, even if they do not. See my discussion in chapter 1b concerning a narrative of two *hasidim,* which plays on this principle in a very different way.

28. A parallel appears in *Num. Rab.* 10:8; also *b. Sanh.* 21b; *b. 'Abod. Zar.* 36b; *b. Qidd.* 80b. The same concept is articulated through midrash of a different verse in *b. Ber.* 43b; *b. 'Erub.* 18b.

29. See the parallel in *Num. Rab.* 10:8; also *Fathers* 4:2; *b.Hul.* 44b; *Der. Er. Zut.* 1:13; Kister, *Studies,* 124.

30. On habituation, compare a maxim of Ben Azzai, "The reward of a commandment [observed] is a commandment [observed]. The reward of a transgression is a transgression" (A25,81; B33,72; *Fathers* 4:2). The sequence on Torah's fence culminates, as rabbinic homilies often do, not with a negative but with a positive inspiration. The editors exhort the reader: While we have been talking all this time of prohibition, do not forget the benefits of observance. Now that the issue of habituation has been introduced, remember that it works on both sides—the reward for fulfilling a commandment is another commandment, and in this case, fulfilling minor commandments leads to the fulfillment of more important and difficult ones. The editors then draw this discussion toward eschatology by way of a verse from the Song of Songs, concluding the passage with the promise of reward in the world to come. Light or minor commandments are like "lilies" (Songs 7:3), which when fulfilled bring Israel to life in the world to come (A2,9). *Rabbi Nathan B* has a very different interpretation of this same verse, focusing on the "hedge" of Songs 7:3—"your belly is a heap of wheat, hedged in *(sugah)* with lilies." This "hedge" is the rabbinic "fence" *(seyyag),* and the commandments are like lilies. See also the discussion in Saldarini, *Fathers According to Rabbi Nathan B,* 45–46 nn.6–8.

31. On the gender-specific nature of this sanctification, see Plaskow, *Standing Again at Sinai* as well as "Standing Again at Sinai: Jewish Memory from a Feminist Perspective."

32. According to *m. Shabb.* 9:3, a woman who discharges semen on the third day is impure. The verse supporting this law is Exod. 19:15. The Mishnah and the narrative here, then, are mutually reinforcing. See the commentary to the mishnaic law in *b. Shabb.* 86a–87a; *Pirqe R. El.* 41; and the discussion in Saldarini, *Fathers According to Rabbi Nathan B,* 39–40 nn.8–9. Also see Ginzberg, *Legends,* vol. 3, 107 n.239; vol. 6, 33 n.191; and vol. 6, 44 n.239. In his commentary to the

Book of Exodus, Umberto Cassuto responds implicitly to this teaching by commenting to Exod. 19:15 that, "Moses further adds, not as a thematic supplement of his own, but as a detailed instruction in elucidation of the concept of sanctification: *do not go near a woman*" (*A Commentary on the Book of Exodus,* 230).

33. On this issue, and on sanctity in rabbinic literature generally, see Fine, *This Holy Place,* 10–23. The account of Moses's fence does not end here. The commentators present three times that "Moses's judgment agreed with God's judgment" (A2,9–10; B2,10–11; also *b. Shabb.* 86a–87a; *b. Yeb.* 62a; and the discussion in Saldarini, *Fathers According to Rabbi Nathan B,* 41–42 n.10). These are cases in which Moses appears to act independently of God's will, but rabbis claim that in fact he did not. Rather, his human decision corresponded with the divine. The three cases are separating from his wife (that is, not having sexual intercourse for all the time that he received prophecy from God), separating from the tent of the meeting, and breaking the tablets. In the first case, Moses exemplifies extreme control of sexual desire, abstaining from the one woman who is permitted to him. Later in *Rabbi Nathan A,* a narrative portrays Aaron and Miriam as criticizing Moses for this practice as being excessive; see A9,40. For other parallels, see Ginzberg, *Legends,* vol. 3, 107 n.239; vol. 6, 33 n.191; and vol. 6, 44 n.239. On the motif of Moses's abstinence in Philo and in Christian sources, see Koltun-Fromm, "Zippora's Complaint"; Brown, *Body and Society,* 31–32, 67.

34. In rabbinic thought, Job is considered to be contemporary with the patriarchs. Often he is portrayed as a virtuous man who does not quite measure up to Abraham. Both men are tested by God, but Abraham maintains a higher level of observance, serving God out of love at all times (see Urbach, *Sages,* 401–15). In *Rabbi Nathan,* we find Abraham and Job compared regarding hospitality. In commenting upon the maxim of Yoseph ben Yohanan to "Let your house be opened wide," the editors first cite Job as exemplifying such action and then say that Abraham is all the more generous and hospitable (A7,32–33; B14,32–33). Here in the discussion of fences, Job stands as the exemplar of chaste eyes, and Abraham does not appear. There is, though, a talmudic teaching that once again shows Abraham to be more pious on this issue (*b. B. Bat.* 16a; the passage is part of a long discussion of Job in *b. B. Bat.* 15b–16a). In *Rabbi Nathan A,* following the passage I have quoted, we find an insertion that develops the word *tam* (blameless) in another thematic direction, as meaning "born circumcised"; it lists a variety of teachings concerning Job and others with that condition (A2,12–13). This material is not found in the parallel passage of B2,8–9.

35. Compare Matt. 5:27–30. Moore may have had this passage from *Rabbi Nathan* in mind when he wrote, "When Jesus said: 'You have heard that it was said, "Thou shalt not commit adultery," but I say to you that whoever gazes at a women with desire has already debauched her in his mind,' he was not only uttering a Jewish commonplace, but with a familiar figure, 'adultery of the eyes.' Job said, 'I made a covenant with my eyes; how then should I look upon a virgin?'" (*Judaism in the First Centuries,* vol. 2, 267–68). It may be worthy of note that the word

"look" *(histakkel),* which appears five times in the short section, is elsewhere in *Rabbi Nathan* a technical term for focus, attention, or contemplation directed toward the body and various aspects of God. See my discussion in chapter 3b.

36. The framing as counsel from an adult man to a young man appears at the opening of the chapter, "My son *[beni],* listen to my wisdom" (Prov. 5:1). On the strange woman, see Fox, *Proverbs 1–9,* 118–19. Another example of a dangerous woman appears in Prov. 7:6–27. In rabbinic exegesis, the female Wisdom of Prov. 8 (especially 8:22) is commonly interpreted as Torah. See for example *Gen. Rab.* 1:1 (Theodor and Albeck, *Bereshit Rabba,* 2).

37. In *Rabbi Nathan A,* the metaphorical interpretation appears first. In *Rabbi Nathan B,* the first is literal and the second metaphorical (B3,13).

38. Schechter corrects the printed edition according to manuscripts (A2,14 n.72), and Goldin follows him in his translation (*Rabbi Nathan,* 25). Finkelstein quotes manuscript variants in *Introduction,* 128–29; note also Kister, *Studies,* 244–45, 256; also the parallel teachings in B3,13–14; *b. 'Abod. Zar.* 17a. Finkelstein suggests reading "to the house of" *(beyt)* rather than "among" *(beyn)* (*Introduction,* 128–31).

39. Goldin reads this as a doublet of the preceeding (*Rabbi Nathan,* 181 n.60).

40. Parallels appear in *b. Shabb.* 116a and *b. 'Abod. Zar.* 17a; see also Boyarin, *Dying for God,* 26–41 and 67–73.

41. On the term *min,* see my discussion in chapter 1a. Finkelstein interprets the use of *minut* and *minim* in manuscripts as specifically referring to Christians (*Introduction,* 128–31). This reading is highly plausible, particularly if one situates *Rabbi Nathan* in the fourth century or later. On the association of prostitutes and sectarians, note that for rabbis the "strange woman" *(zarah)* likely resonates with their term for idolatry, "strange worship" *('abodah zarah).* More generally, Boyarin writes when analyzing parallel material in *b. 'Abod. Zar.* 17a, "Sectarian heresy, prostitution, and collaboration with Roman power had become associated in the cultural 'unconscious' of rabbinic Judaism, no doubt at least in part simply because all three are seductive and dangerous" (*Dying for God,* 68). Note, though, that the compilers of *Rabbi Nathan* do not interpret Prov. 2:19 in relation to Roman power, and while the text reveals tensions between rabbis and the empire, the story of Rabban Yohanan ben Zakkai and Vespasian presents collaboration as problematic but necessary (see my discussion in chapter 1a). On biblical and rabbinic sexual metaphors for idolatry, see also Halbertal and Margolit, *Idolatry,* 9–36.

42. Compare a maxim of Rabbi Akiba, "Anyone who clings to transgressors, even if he does not act according to their deeds, receives punishment along with them. Anyone who clings to those who do observe commandments, even if he does not act according to their deeds, receives reward along with them" (A30,89).

43. The concern with Torah or the sages' words being dangerous appears in *Fathers* 2:10. See also Fraade, *From Tradition,* 46–48. He discusses *Siphre Deut.* 343

to Deut. 33:2 (Finkelstein, *Sifre on Deuteronomy,* 399–400) and parallels. I thank Lisa Shine for her comments on this point.

44. Hayim Lapin has made compelling arguments that rabbis in Roman Palestine were located primarily in cities ("Rabbis and Cities"). At various points in late antiquity, there were Jewish and then Christian elites in the area surrounding the Dead Sea and southwest of Roman Palestine in Egypt. For an overview addressing the significance of the Egyptian desert for Christian ascetics striving to renounce or transform sexual desire, see Brown, *Body and Society,* 213–58. Brown emphasizes, though, that many Christian leaders in towns and cities faced challenges concerning associations with women and the broader society (143 and generally 140–59). The tropes of distance and proximity have a range of uses in rabbinic discussions of community, as Steinmetz emphasizes in "Distancing and Bringing Near," 58–62.

2b. The Heart and Its Formation

1. A number of significant works have compiled material concerning *yetzer* from rabbinic literature as a whole, often with great attention to the relation of *yetzer* to Greco-Roman and Christian dualisms of body and soul. See especially Porter, "*Yeçer,*" 93–156. Solomon Schechter, G. F. Moore, and Ephraim Urbach have written important chapters on *yetzer* as part of their comprehensive studies of rabbinic theology. See Schechter, *Aspects of Rabbinic Theology,* 242–92; Moore, *Judaism in the First Centuries,* vol. 1, 479–96; and Urbach, *Sages,* 471–83. Emero Steigman discusses the topic as part of his essay, "Rabbinic Anthropology," 525–29 (on *yetzer*), 537–45 (on Torah), and generally 488–579. For a comprehensive historical study of the term "the bad *yetzer*" in Second Temple and tannaitic literature, including a number of passages from *Rabbi Nathan,* see G. H. Cohen-Stuart, *The Struggle in Man Between Good and Evil.* Daniel Boyarin has offered a provocative analysis of select passages from rabbinic and earlier Jewish literature, focusing on positive rabbinic assessments of these "evil" tendencies, in *Carnal Israel,* 61–76. Satlow discusses links between *yetzer* and sexual desire in *Tasting the Dish,* 159–67. Two recent and very important discussions are Rosen-Zvi, "Evil Desire," and Elizabeth Shanks Alexander, "Art, Argument and Ambiguity in the Talmud: Conflicting Conceptions of the Evil Impulse in *b. Sukkah* 51b–52a." The role of the *yetzer* in rabbinic ethics is also discussed in Tirosh-Samuelson, *Happiness in Premodern Judaism,* 119–21.

2. See *Gen Rab.* 34 to Gen. 8:21 (Theodor and Albeck, *Bereshit Rabba,* 320–21) and parallels listed there; Porter, "*Yeçer,*" 108 and generally 93–156.

3. See for example the teaching of Rabbi Yose ha-Gelili concerning *yetzer* on A32,93 that I discuss later in this chapter; Ishay Rosen-Zvi has emphasized this point to me.

4. See Boyarin, *Carnal Israel,* 64–65 and generally 61–76. For the monistic view, he analyzes a teaching of Abbaye in *b. Sukk.* 52a; also see Porter, "*Yeçer,*" 115,

120; and Alexander, "Art, Argument and Ambiguity." Note also a very different affirmation of the bad *yetzer* in *Sed. El. Rab.* chapter 15 (Friedmann, *Seder Eliahu,* 81).

5. For example, a passage that parodies the maxim of Simeon the Righteous appears in *Rabbi Nathan B:* "Rabbi Yehudah says: Upon three things the world rests: jealousy, desire [*ta'avah*], and compassion" (B4,17). Compare A4,25; B31,67; and of course A4,18; B5,18; *Fathers* 1:2. Contrast *Fathers* 4:21; Kister, *Studies,* 62; Finkelstein, *Introduction,* 72.

6. Compare *b. Sukk.* 51a–52b, where the compilers highlight to a much greater degree the role of God in creating and destroying the *yetzer.* In that unit, there is also less of a sense that *yetzer* can be molded or changed and more development of dualistic portrayals. Other talmudic passages give weight to prayer, such as *b. Ber.* 17a; *b. Ber.* 60b.

7. Often the Hebrew *ra'* is translated as "evil," and scholars write of "the evil inclination." However, rabbinic sources tend not to portray the *yetzer* as a part of the self that actively takes pleasure in doing what is wrong or transgressive. For this reason, I characterize it as "bad" rather than "evil." On the importance of this distinction, see the discussions in T. C. Kline and Philip J. Ivanhoe, eds., *Virtue, Nature, and Moral Agency in the Xunzi.*

8. For key examples, see *Gen. Rab.* 14 to Gen. 2:7 (Theodor and Albeck, *Bereshit Rabba,* 126–29); *Gen Rab.* 34 to Gen. 8:21 (Theodor and Albeck, *Bereshit Rabba,* 320–21) and parallels listed there. These features of rabbinic thought led F. C. Porter to write almost a century ago, "In order to understand the Jewish doctrine of the *yeçer* we must remember that it is not at all a speculative but wholly an exegetical product" (*"Yeçer,"* 108 and generally 93–156; also Schechter, *Aspects,* 242).

9. See *Siphre Deut.* 32 (Finkelstein, *Sifre on Deuteronomy,* 55), and note that here the definite article does not appear; also *m. Ber.* 9:5; Fishbane, *Kiss of God,* 3–8.

10. On thought, see A8,36; on demand, A1,4; on fear A7,34–35; on anger A12,48–49; on jealousy, A12,49; on enjoyment, A12,55; on the idea of "giving" to the heart, A19,68; A20,70; B32,68–70; *Fathers* 2:1, 3:1, and 3:5; and my discussions of these passages in chapter 3b. Note also a passage that presents the heart as adapting easily and smoothly to action on A29,87. Fishbane discusses the heart in rabbinic literature generally (*Kiss of God,* 4–5); also Flusser, "Which Is the Right Way." Porter discusses the connection between *yetzer* and *leb* and quotes several more cases of rabbinic exegesis upon biblical uses of *leb* (*"Yeçer,"* 110–11). Moore also states, "the word 'heart' itself is often used in a sense entirely equivalent to *yeser,* especially when the text of Scripture suggests a bad connotation" (*Judaism in the First Centuries,* vol. 1, 486). Another organ of the human body that appears as a seat of psychological processes is the kidney. In biblical literature, the heart and the kidneys are often paired. See Jer. 11:20; Jer. 17:10; Jer. 20:12; Ps. 7:10; Julius Preuss, *Biblical and Talmudic Medicine,* 102–8. The kidneys figure far less prominently than the heart in *Rabbi Nathan.* When they appear, they are associated with "advice" or "counsel." See A31,91–92 and Schechter's note 27; A33,94; and *Gen. Rab.* 61:1 (Theodor and Albeck, *Bereshit Rabba,* 657–58, including their listing of

sources). The intersection of kidneys and heart may be implied when we read of the snake in Eden that he "took advice [*'etzah*] in his heart" (A1,4). Note also *b. Ber.* 61a–b and Porter's comments in "*Yeçer,*" 101–2.

11. The arrangement of this compilation itself is a form of ethical teaching; see my "The Redaction of Desire," 47.

12. MS O lists only desecration of the Sabbath in the discussion of the bad *yetzer.* The other two appear as a correction in the printed edition, and Schechter includes them in his text. MS N lists all three, with the second being "obscene act" *(debar zimmah)* rather than "act of transgression" *(debar 'abeyrah),* and the third being murder.

13. The printed edition has "transgression" *(debar 'abeyrah).* MS V and MS N have "obscene act" *(debar zimmah).* See Schechter, *Rabbi Nathan,* 166 and also 144.

14. On this point more generally, see Porter, "*Yeçer,*" 134–35; Moore, *Judaism in the First Centuries,* vol. 1, 485; Urbach, *Sages,* 472. On dualism in rabbinic psychology, see Nissan Rubin, "The Sages' Conception of Body and Soul," 47–103; also Boyarin, *Carnal Israel* and *A Radical Jew.*

15. Both Jonathan Malamy and Jeff Estrin have pointed out to me this ambiguity and its significance.

16. *Eccl. R.* 4:13,1 has a parallel teaching that the good *yetzer* is born at age thirteen. Itzchak Gilath has analyzed material concerning the age thirteen in *halakhah* and its relation to the physical event of puberty and the growing of "two hairs." See "Thirteen Years-Old: The Age of Commandments?" in *Studies in the Development of the Halakhah* (Hebrew), 19–31; also Marcus, *Rituals of Childhood,* 43–44 and notes (both Gilath and Marcus discuss the important and difficult case of *Fathers* 5:21). For an example of children starting partial observance of commandments before puberty, see *m. Yoma* 8:4.

17. On the rabbinic focus on puberty as a key point of character formation, contrast the Freudian emphasis on earlier ages as crucial for the development of internal faculties of monitoring and criticism (see for example, Freud, "The Dissection of the Psychical Personality," 58–68).

18. Charles Hirschkind pointed out this aspect of the passage to me.

19. In *Pesiqta Rabbati* we find a passage very similar to the one I have just analyzed, but the correcting entity is named as Torah. Torah counters tendencies to desecrate the Sabbath, to murder, and to commit adultery. The passage is in the context of a section on Hanukkah, and this particular unit interprets Ps. 119:105 to understand Torah through the metaphor of light (*Pesiq. R.* 9; Friedmann, *Pesiqta Rabbati,* 30a).

20. Students in my classes have been particularly attentive to this point, and it also came up in discussion when I presented this material at the Annual Meeting of the Association for Jewish Studies, Washington, D.C., 2002. An interesting juxtaposition can be made between this account of the good *yetzer* and rabbinic passages in other texts stating that the bad *yetzer* is "very good" (see Boyarin, *Carnal Israel,* 61–76); here, the good *yetzer* is not really all that good.

21. The passage as a whole is difficult. In my translation I keep the ambiguities present in the Hebrew concerning the antecedents of pronouns. See also Schechter's translation in *Aspects of Rabbinic Theology*, 252, and parallels and related passages in B16,36; B30,63; *b. Sanh.* 91b. Finkelstein lists and discusses variants of the opening lines in *Introduction*, 138. Kister writes that the phrase *zoreqo bebat ro'sh* is not a talmudic expression and cites it in arguing for the post-talmudic dating of *Rabbi Nathan A.* See his "Introduction" in Schechter and Kister, *Rabbi Nathan*, 13; also Kister, *Studies*, 218–20. The expression also appears in A24,77; see Schechter's comments in A16,64 nn.22, 23.

22. Perhaps the underlying logic is that ejaculation is the result of sexual desire, and this desire is then carried forward through the semen to inhabit the infant.

23. One example is a dialogue between Antoninus and Rabbi Yehudah the Patriarch over whether the bad *yetzer* has its origin in conception or birth. The rabbi first says conception, then Antoninus objects, and the rabbi agrees that the bad *yetzer* has its origin at birth. He grounds the opinion in Gen. 4:7, interpreting the "opening" as the opening of the womb, when the baby emerges. See *b. Sanh.* 91b; *Gen. Rab.* 34 to Gen. 8:21 (Theodor and Albeck, *Bereshit Rabba*, 320). Rabbi Reuben ben Atztrobali and Rabbi Yehudah the Patriarch, then, draw upon the same biblical verse for different positions: the former interpreting it to justify the origin of the bad *yetzer* at conception and the latter justifying the origin at birth. Other interpretations of Genesis 4:7 and its imagery in relation to *yetzer* include B16,36; *Gen. Rab.* 22 to Gen. 4:7 (Theodor and Albeck, *Bereshit Rabba*, 210–12 and notes); and *Targum Pseudo-Jonathan* to the same verse. An additional resonance of "opening" is the association of this term and the womb—as in the Book of Genesis, when God "opens" the wombs of Rachel and Leah (29:31; 30:22), enabling them to be impregnated by their husbands' semen. On "opening the heart" in mystical practice, see Swartz, *Scholastic Magic*, 43–47.

24. For the scorpion, see A1,6; coal, A9,41; falling off roof, A11,45. Interestingly, most students who encounter this passage in my courses interpret it as concerning curiosity.

25. This is part of a broader tendency in rabbinic thought to define the distinctive characteristics of humans in relation to those of animals and angels. In a passage of *Rabbi Nathan B*, we read of the other pole, that the ministering angels also do not have the bad *yetzer* (B26,52; also B34,74 and B42,116 for *yetzer* being a uniquely human feature). For comparisons of humans to animals and angels in general, see A37,109; also *Gen. Rab.* 8 to Gen. 1:27 (Theodor and Albeck, *Bereshit Rabba*, 64–65 and notes).

26. See the teaching of Rabbi Yose ha-Gelili in A32,93, which I quote and analyze later in this chapter.

27. A striking symbolic substitution in the intertext of *Rabbi Nathan* occurs between the qualities that the rabbis attribute to the bad *yetzer* and to Eve. In two cases, Eve acts with the very same (self-)destructive tendencies that the rabbis attribute to *yetzer*. First, rabbis attribute to Eve the envious desire to draw another

into death, which (according to Rabbi Yehudah the Patriarch) the bad *yetzer* has of the body. An anonymous teaching in *Rabbi Nathan B* states that when Eve eats of the tree, she sees the angel of death, realizes she will die, and fears that God will create another woman in her place. She thinks, "What should I do? I will cause him to eat with me [*'immi*], as it is written, 'She took from its fruit, ate, and gave it also to her husband with her [*'mmah*], and he ate' (Gen. 3:6)" (B1,6). The midrash develops the apparently extraneous "with her" of Gen. 3:6, emphasizing that she gets him to eat so that he will be mortal *with her*. Note also that "another woman in her place" reveals a trace of Lillith traditions. For parallel sources, see *Gen. Rab.* 19 to Gen. 3:6 (Theodor and Albeck, *Bereshit Rabba*, 174 notes to line 6); also *Pirqe R. El.* 3. A second example of the conjunction between *yetzer* as a self-destructive impulse and Eve can be seen in the passage discussed earlier in this chapter, "An infant lies in his crib, and he places his hand on the back of a snake or a scorpion, and it stings him. Nothing but the bad *yetzer* in his belly causes him [to do this]" (A16, 63–64). Eve also reaches out her hand, in violation of a command, and is stung. The scene is conveyed through a parable in which a man commands his wife not to open a box. When (like Pandora) she does so, a scorpion stings her (B1,6–7; contrast the parallel in A1,6; on the general topic of Eve and Pandora, see Boyarin, *Carnal Israel*, 84–88).

28. See Nussbaum, *Therapy of Desire*, especially 13–77, 484–510. On the comparison of Torah study and medicine in *Rabbi Nathan*, see A23,76–77. The trope that Torah is a "remedy" *(sam)* for basic impulses or *yetzer* appears through an early midrash punning on Deut. 11:18 (*Siphre Deut.* 45 to 11:18, Finkelstein, *Sifre on Deuteronomy*, 103–4; also *b. Qidd.* 30b; *b. Sukk.* 52a; *b. B. Bat.* 16a). The topic of medical models and metaphors in ethics is related to, but not the same as, the interrelation of ancient medicine and the care of the self. On rabbinic sources, see Preuss, *Biblical and Talmudic Medicine*, 447–581. I address key passages in "The Beastly Body." On medical texts as sources for Greek and Roman ethics, see Foucault, *Use of Pleasure*, 97–139, and *Care of the Self*, 99–144.

29. See, for example, the material gathered in Foucault, *Use of Pleasure*, 63–72, and *Care of the Self*, 81–95; Brown, *Body and Society*, 34.

30. The idea of "development" models has emerged primarily through the study of Confucian and neo-Confucian thought, starting with Angus C. Graham, *Two Chinese Philosophers*, 54. Graham's observation has been expanded in Yearley, *Mencius and Aquinas*, 58–62; Ivanhoe, *Ethics in the Confucian Tradition;* Schofer, "Virtues in Xunzi's Thought," reprinted in Kline and Ivanhoe, *Virtue, Nature, and Moral Agency*, 69–88. The most extensive treatment is Ivanhoe's *Confucian Moral Self-Cultivation*, which distinguishes seven such models. One significant contrast to a "development" model is a "discovery" or "recovery" model, which presupposes a fully formed ideal self within that is somehow obscured. The goal here is to eliminate false perceptions or desires, as one would clean dust off a mirror or as the sun bursts through clouds that block it.

31. I do not deny that systematic thought may underlie material we find in

Rabbi Nathan, but my analysis will not presume or argue for it. Some accounts appear to have originally been homilies, especially the teachings of Rabbi Eleazar ben Azariah in A18,66–68, and of Rabbi Simeon ben Yohai in A16,64, both of which I discuss later in this chapter. On the lack of systematic thinking and imagery in *Rabbi Nathan,* contrast the thinkers discussed in Ivanhoe, *Self-Cultivation.* Note that the complex debates concerning the relation between metaphor and model, and whether or not one is a form of the other, are not the same as the point I am discussing. On those debates, see Max Black, *Models and Metaphors,* and Soskice, *Metaphor,* 97–117.

32. Adolph Büchler examines the trope of a "yoke" in *Studies in Sin and Atonement,* 63–118. See also Schechter, *Aspects of Rabbinic Theology,* 65–79; Urbach, *Sages,* 400–419.

33. In the Bible, the image of carrying a yoke conveys loyalty, and that of breaking a yoke is used to describe disloyalty and disobedience (for example, Jer. 2:20; 5:5; also 30:8–9). Moshe Weinfeld writes that the rabbinic phrase has its roots in "covenantal terms expressing loyalty to a sovereign" from the ancient Near East. In the El-Amarna letters, statements appear such as, "the yoke of the king my lord is upon my neck and I carry it." Also, "In the neo-Assyrian inscriptions we also find the idea of carrying the yoke of God explicitly expressed" (*Deuteronomy and the Deuteronomic School,* 84 n.4). On Paul's use of the trope, see Williams, *Paul's Metaphors,* 32–33.

34. See also *Fathers* 3:5. Several scholars see this teaching as parallel to the maxim of Rabbi Hananiah, Deputy of the Priests, in A20,70 (which I analyze in chapter 3b). Saldarini, *Fathers According to Rabbi Nathan B,* 187 n.1; Finkelstein, *Introduction,* 53, 67–70, 73, 122–24; and *Sed. El. Zut.* 16 (Friedmann, *Seder Eliahu,* appendix 2). Schechter quotes other parallel sources in *Rabbi Nathan,* 145.

35. This homily is attested in a number of texts. On the different recensions, see Shraga Abramson, "Four Topics in Midrash Halakhah" (Hebrew). It has recently been analyzed in two perceptive though differing studies: Menachem Fisch, *Rational Rabbis: Science and Talmudic Culture,* 88–96; and David Stern, "Midrash and Indeterminacy," 137–41. Also see Williams, *Paul's Metaphors,* 32.

36. The homily continues by addressing the nature of legal interpretation among the community of sages, advocating a pluralism that is grounded in affirming the divine nature of Scripture. David Stern has analyzed this pluralism and labeled it "polysemy" ("Midrash and Indeterminacy," 141), while Menachem Fisch situates the homily in relation to other narratives of the generation of Yabneh, calling Rabbi Eleazar ben Azariah's midrash an "antitraditionalist manifesto" (*Rational,* 88–89). Fisch observes, concerning Rabbi Eleazar's midrashic technique, that he interprets the verse "as a structured and ordered whole by ascribing to each of its claims, metaphors, and images both a constructive and an eliminative role." Each image contributes "in turn a positive analogy to Torah-study which serves at the same time also to eliminate the unwanted connotation implied by the previous image." In the first metaphor, the goad is movable, yet this "unwanted analogy

to the fruits of Torah-study is eliminated by the additional metaphor of the irremovable well-pounded nail" (90). I have also learned much from discussions with Steven Fraade concerning this passage.

37. On this image in rabbinic and early Christian literature and in the Dead Sea Scrolls, see Flusser, "Which Is the Right Way."

38. Regarding the rhetorical form "just as . . . so . . ."—note that similar fixed terms appear in inner-biblical exegesis to establish typologies (Fishbane, *Biblical Interpretation,* 352).

39. The parallel sources have a number of variations; see Abramson, "Four Topics," 1–7. Most relevant is an expansion in *Numbers Rabbah,* where teachings in the name of Rabbi Tanhuma ben Abba develop further the metaphor, "Torah is a goad" (*Num. Rab.* 14:4 to Num. 7:48). Also, in *b. Ḥag.* 3a–b, in place of "the ways of life," we read that the Torah directs a person "from the ways of death to the ways of life." On this dualistic image, see Flusser, "Which Is the Right Way"; also *t. Soṭa* 7:9–12; *Mek. R. Ishmael* to Exod. 13:2; *Pesiq. R.* 3 (Friedmann, *Pesiqta Rabbati,* 8a–b); *Soph.* 17:1.

40. For manuscript and other variants, see Finkelstein, *Introduction,* 155–56. Not all manuscripts have this material; see Schechter's notes in *Rabbi Nathan,* especially A23,76 n.12. These sayings appear in a sequence that begins with a maxim of Rabbi Nehurai instructing the student to "be exiled to a place of Torah" (A23,75). The passage I have quoted does not appear to be exegesis of the first epigram so much as another in a sequence that is also on the topic of Torah. The editors then follow this statement of Rabbi Nehurai with others of similar structure and topic, contrasting one who begins Torah study in youth with one who begins in old age. The sequence is not present in the parallel section of *Rabbi Nathan B* (B23,73). See also *Fathers* 4:20.

41. The maxim appears on A17,65; B30,65; *Fathers* 2:12; Yose the Priest was a student of Rabban Yohanan ben Zakkai; see also *Siphre Deut.* 305 (Finkelstein, *Sifre on Deuteronomy,* 324).

42. See Goldin, *Rabbi Nathan,* 194 n.5. For parallels, see B30,65; *Siphre Deut.* 305 (Finkelstein, *Sifre on Deuteronomy,* 324–25); and Ginzberg, *Legends,* vol. 3, 396–400 on the "Appointment of Joshua." In Moses's statement—"This people that I pass on [*moser*] to you"—the use of "pass on" echoes the chain of transmission that opens *The Fathers* and some witnesses of *Rabbi Nathan* (*Fathers* 1:1; B1,2; contrast A1,2; see also Num. 27:15–23). For other interpretations of Songs 1:8 see A17,65; *Exod. Rab.* 2:4; *Songs Rab.* 1:8; *Num. Rab.* 21:15.

43. This observation was made by Valentina Izmirlieva during a discussion of this material at the Institute for the Advanced Study of Religion, University of Chicago, 1999. For comparisons of humans to animals and angels in general, see A37,109; also *Gen. Rab.* 8 to 1:27 (Theodor and Albeck, *Bereshit Rabba,* 64–65 and notes). According to teaching discussed earlier in this chapter, though, animals do not have the bad *yetzer.*

44. The metaphor "Torah is fire" has exegetical origins that can be found in

early rabbinic texts. The opening of Moses's final blessing, Deut. 33:2, is interpreted to describe the giving of the Torah at Sinai: "[F]rom His right hand [there emerged] a fire of law for them" (*Siphre Deut.* 343; Finkelstein, *Sifre on Deuteronomy,* 399 and his references; Fraade, *From Tradition,* 46–48; and Fishbane, *Exegetical,* 9 and notes). This passage has numerous parallels, and in *Rabbi Nathan B* the metaphor appears with Deut. 33:2 as a prooftext in a list of "Four that are called fire" (B43,121; along with Torah, the other three are God, Israel, and the world to come). For an extensive study of the trope of Torah being fire, see Hoshen, "The Fire Symbol," especially 38–53. The metaphor that the bad *yetzer* is metal appears also in a *baraita* of the school of Rabbi Ishmael. The agent of transformation is the study house, and if the student brings his bad *yetzer* there, it will split apart *(mitpotzetz).* One of the prooftexts is Job 14:19, which in the story of Rabbi Akiba in *Rabbi Nathan A* is the source for the image of the water wearing away rock. See *b. Qidd.* 30b and *b. Sukk.* 52b, and compare A6,28–29, analyzed in the introduction. The image of iron being placed in fire appears in a practice prescribed in the Mishnah. If a person buys a metal spit or grill from "worshippers of stars," the object must "be cleansed in fire" *(lelabben be'or)* (see *m. 'Abod. Zar.* 5:12 and *b. 'Abod. Zar.* 75b). Prov. 25:21–22 is also the source for a different midrashic interpretation concerning *yetzer,* focusing on "enemy" but not the coals/fire (*b. Sukk.* 52a; also *Siphre Deut.* 45, Finkelstein, *Sifre on Deuteronomy,* 103–4). The metaphor of fire appears in other passages of *Rabbi Nathan* that are related to, but do not directly address, the topic of ethical transformation. In one epigram, the presence of the sages is compared to coal—they may "warm" the student but also can be dangerous and burn him (A15,62; B29,92; *Fathers* 2:10; Hoshen, "The Fire Symbol," 45–46).

45. Prov. 25:21–22 employs terminology that could easily yield an interpretation in terms of divine reward and punishment *(yeshallem),* but this midrash firmly situates the verse in terms of self-transformation: "Do not read 'will repay you [*yeshallem lakh*]' but 'will put him [the bad *yetzer*] at peace with you [*yashlimennu lakh*].'" See also midrash Proverbs to that verse. On "do not read" *('al tiqrey),* see Michael Fishbane, *The Garments of Torah: Essays in Biblical Hermeneutics,* 19–32.

46. I have learned much from Jeff Estrin's and Sarah Rosenblum's comments on this passage. An image of physical labor appears in another teaching about Torah, among the narratives of Rabbi Akiba's career. The intellectual work of learning Torah is portrayed as cutting away stone. This trope upholds a scholastic virtue of persistence (A6,29; B12,29).

47. Schechter suggests correcting "from here" in the printed edition to "from where" (A16,64 n.28).

48. See Kister, *Studies,* 215. He writes that this is a common teaching from the period after Bar Kokhba. A very different agricultural image, of "growing" the Torah within oneself, appears in *Sed. El. Rab.* 2 (Friedmann, *Seder Eliahu,* 8). For other agricultural metaphors in rabbinic sources, see Fraade, *From Tradition,* 108–9 and notes. Many parables of agricultural labor appear in the New Testament. See

especially Matt. 20:1–16 and also Matt. 5:18–32; Luke 13:18–19; Williams, *Paul's Metaphors*, 36–40. On parables in rabbinic literature generally, see Stern, *Parables in Midrash.*

49. This focus on compassion is also present in Ps. 103 as a whole, which Fishbane writes is "a sustained appeal for divine compassion" (*Biblical Interpretation,* 348). The verse prior to the prooftext (Ps. 103:13) states that God has compassion for those who fear Him, as a father has compassion for his children. The goal of Rabbi Simeon ben Yohai's petition, then, is an attempt to transform God's response from judgment to compassion. On the theme of God's responsibility for the existence of the bad *yetzer,* and the need for divine compassion, see Schechter, *Aspects of Rabbinic Theology,* 280–84. A parable that makes a similar point, but using the trope of a potter who makes an imperfect pot, appears in *Exod. Rab.* 46:4 (note Williams, *Paul's Metaphors,* 168–69). Ps. 103:14 is the source of other midrashic interpretations concerning *yetzer.* One passage begins with Gen. 8:21 and develops the metaphors that God is a baker (who "forms" the dough), and human impulses are leaven. See *Gen. Rab.* 34:4 to Gen. 8:21 (Theodor and Albeck, *Bereshit Rabba,* 320); leaven also appears as a metaphor on *b. Ber.* 17a. Fishbane argues, moreover, that Ps. 103:14—"For He knows our formation [*yitzrenu*]. He is mindful that we are dust"—is itself an interpretation of other biblical verses that underlie the rabbinic notion of *yetzer.* Remember that Gen. 2:7 and 8:21 are central to the exegetical construction of *yetzer.* Fishbane writes that "in so far as the stem appears to relate to mankind's creaturehood, as 'formed' from the earth, it may be suggested that v. 14 is also an aggadic adaptation of Gen. 2:7 'And YHWH Elohim formed [*y.tz.r.*] the man from the dust ['*.p.r.*] of the earth.'" Fishbane also suggests that the notion of "formation" echoes Gen. 8:21. He summarizes, "Taken together, one may venture to propose that Ps. 103:14 is an exegetical reuse of Gen. 2:7 while simultaneously punning on 8:21, so as to deepen the exegetical thrust" (*Biblical Interpretation,* 348–49).

50. Fishbane, *Kiss of God,* 12 and generally 3–13. On this theme among Jews and Christians in the first two centuries CE, see Peter Brown, *Body and Society,* 33–44.

51. Henry Fischel argues that Ben Zoma employs the Stoic rhetorical form of *paradoxa,* which "belong to the most popular rhetorical formulas of antiquity, especially in the period from 100 B.C. to 200 A.D. They state in an extreme and abrupt form some of the major ethical premises of the Stoic concept of the sage." He adds that the "*paradoxon* is not paradoxical in the contemporary sense. It is, rather . . . *para—doxon,* generally held by the public, i.e., startling, contrary, nonconventional but not a-logical, contrary to reason." See Fischel, *Rabbinic Literature,* 70–73 and notes. On tropes of warfare in the New Testament, see Williams, *Paul's Metaphors,* 213–16. This maxim appears in the section of *Rabbi Nathan* concerning the four sages who "entered the garden"; see my discussion in chapter 1b on the arrangement of maxims.

52. In *Midr. Prov.* to Prov. 15:18, a parallel to this statement appears as an anonymous *baraita.*

53. Recall Rabbi Nehurai's statement comparing the learning of Torah to the "breaking" of a heifer. His word for "breaking"—*kibbeshuha*—means literally "they conquered her," and it is the same word that Ben Zoma uses for conquering the *yetzer*. Rabbi Nehurai's teaching appears in the chapter that begins with Ben Zoma's maxim (A23,75–76).

54. Ben Zoma's maxim, then, could be interpreted as a potentially universalist strand of rabbinic instruction, while the commentary shows a strong concern with the particular tradition of Torah as central to transformation. See my discussions in the introduction and chapter 1a regarding universal and particular/locative ways of framing ethics. Goldin cites this passage in building his argument that *Rabbi Nathan A* shows greater concern with Torah than *Rabbi Nathan B*, which gives relative weight to good deeds (*Studies in Midrash*, 90–91).

55. The final words of Prov. 21:22 and of Ps. 103:20 are not quoted in the printed edition but do appear in some manuscripts. See Schechter's comments in A23,75 nn.4, 5.

56. In *Lev. Rab.* 31:5, we find several different interpretations of Prov. 21:22. In some of them, the "stronghold" (*'oz*) is glossed as Torah, so the verse is understood to describe not a man confronting his impulses but a student facing the challenges of learning Torah.

57. Marcus Aurelius employs a somewhat similar metaphor to characterize the intellect when separated from passions—he writes that it is a citadel in which humans can take refuge (Hadot, *Inner Citadel*, 122). For the rabbinic commentators to Ben Zoma's maxim, it is not the intellect separate from tradition but rather Torah that brings one to a point of refuge.

58. This citation concludes a passage that I analyzed earlier in this chapter. It begins, "They said, the bad *yetzer* is thirteen years older than the good *yetzer*. From the belly of a person's mother it grows and comes with him." Both of these passages are in the commentary to the maxim of Rabbi Yehoshua, "The malicious eye, the bad *yetzer*, and hatred of creatures cast a man out from the world" (A16,62).

59. Following the printed edition and MS O, I read *mit'annin*, which could also imply making him suffer. See the discussion of the variants in Kister, *Studies*, 50–51. Schechter amends *mit'atztzelin* (A16 n.7).

60. See for example B16,36; *Eccles. Rab.* to Eccles. 4:13–14; and *Midr. Psalms* to Ps. 9:2. Note that "wisdom" in rabbinic interpretation is often understood as Torah. So when the "wise child" is the good *yetzer*, this may imply another link between the good *yetzer* and Torah. See also the comparison of Jewish and Christian receptions of these verses in Marc Hirshman, *A Rivalry of Genius: Jewish and Christian Biblical Interpretation in Late Antiquity*, 100–102.

61. From the word for "prison house" (*hasurim*), a midrashically minded reader will find also the "prohibitions" (*'asurim*) from which those governed by the bad *yetzer* will "turn" (*surim*). Implicit in this passage is the rabbinic correspondence

between the 248 body parts and the 248 positive commandments (*b. Mak.* 23b; *m. 'Ohol.* 1:8; Fishbane, *Kiss of God,* 131 n.7; Urbach, *Sages,* 360–65 and notes).

62. My analysis here follows, with some modifications, that of Fishbane in *Kiss of God,* 8–10. Elizabeth Shanks Alexander has given me helpful comments. A similar account appears in *Seder Eliyahu Zuṭa.* The limbs and sensory organs, which are sources of sin, appear as ten rulers of the body. Wisdom and Torah are stronger than they are, though, and ultimately come to rule (*Sed. El. Zuṭa* 1; Friedmann, *Seder Eliahu,* supplement 1–4). On the broader issue of interrelations and contrasts between rabbinic and Hellenistic conceptions of the body, see Boyarin, *Carnal Israel* and *A Radical Jew.*

63. This addition is suggested by Schechter based on MS H (B13,30 n.1).

64. There is a parallel in *Midr. Prov.* to Prov. 24, though the explanation *(nimshal)* is placed before the parable *(mashal).* Also, there the passage is not connected with the maxim "and drink with thirst their words."

65. Note also a passage in *Midr. Psalms* stating that the bad *yetzer* has no power over those with Torah in their hearts (*Midr. Psalms* 119:7, commenting on Ps. 119:11). Regarding the trope of the king occupying an empty room, Saldarini comments, "This parable may be modeled on the travels of the Roman emperors in the East who commanded nightly resting places" (*Fathers According to Rabbi Nathan B,* 98 n.2). If so, then this parable would be another example of rabbis drawing upon their experience of subjection to imperial power in figuring their elected subordination to tradition and God.

66. Rabbi Tzadok controls his gaze and avoids looking at the woman in a way that is also somewhat similar to Job in the account of his "fence" (A2,13), which I discussed in chapter 2a.

67. See especially *b. Sukk.* 51a–52b; also Porter, "*Yeçer,*" 123, 127, 129.

68. Following Fishbane, *Kiss of God,* 7. Another translation is "pierced."

69. See the analysis in Fishbane, *Kiss of God,* 7–8. On the significance of the plural "judges" of Ps. 109:31 in the exegesis, see Goldin, *Rabbi Nathan,* 130, 205 n.14. In *Genesis Rabbah,* an interpretation of Gen. 8:21 expresses similar concepts employing the term "heart." The wicked are controlled by their hearts, but for the righteous, their hearts are under their control. *Gen. Rab.* 34 to Gen. 8:21 (Theodor and Albeck, *Bereshit Rabba,* 320).

70. The broader literary context is a series of lists organized by the number ten, which include the creation of the world, the genealogy from Adam to Abraham, the trials of Abraham, and miracles in the Temple (A31–35,90–106; B36–39,90–108; *Fathers* 5:1–6; Finkelstein, *Introduction,* 81–114). The list "Ten generations from Adam to Noah" is interpreted homiletically, beginning with the question, "For what need do inhabitants of the world have of this? It is to teach you that . . ." (A32,92). The first set of interpretations concerns the flood and the interrelation of human righteousness and divine punishment. Then the compilers of *Rabbi Nathan A* introduce a more general discussion of divine justice centered on

Genesis 6:3. On the homiletical interpretation of these numerical lists, see my discussion in chapter 1b; also A31,90; A32,93; *Fathers* 5:1–2; Kister, *Studies*, 42; Towner, *Enumeration*, 246.

71. This passage has textual difficulties, as is noted by Schechter (A32,93 n.8). In *Genesis Rabbah* we find a different midrash of Rabbi Yose ha-Gelili based on Gen. 6:3, but the verse is interpreted not in relation to *yetzer* but to the attributes of God: "Rabbi Yose ha-Gelili said, I will no longer judge the measure of justice opposite [*keneged*] the measure of compassion" (*Gen. Rab.* 26 to Gen. 6:3; Theodor and Albeck, *Bereshit Rabba*, 252).

72. I follow Fishbane's analysis of *b. Ber.* 61b in *Kiss of God*, 7. Another translation is "pierced." Goldin chooses "wounded" (*Rabbi Nathan*, 130). Both Fishbane and Goldin cite Rashi's commentary to *b. Ber.* 61b (Fishbane, *Kiss of God*, 130 n.14; Goldin, *Rabbi Nathan*, 205 n.10).

73. In *b. Sukk.* 52b, an amoraic tradition in the name of Rabbi Samuel bar Nahmani tells of the bad *yetzer* testifying against a person in the world to come.

74. The first part of the biblical verse, though not glossed by the commentators, implies that all hope is not lost: "He will stand on the right of the needy." The statement of harsh judgment is softened by hope for those who repent in their need of divine support.

75. My analysis here focuses on the psychological dimensions of the rabbis and their Torah. Jacob Neusner highlights the public dimension of the sage as a figure of Torah. He describes the Babylonian rabbis as religious figures who embody the Torah and represent it to the broader Jewish public. See for example his *The Wonder-Working Lawyers of Talmudic Babylonia*, especially 39–138.

76. On rabbinic accounts of women as temptresses, see Satlow, *Tasting the Dish*, 158–67.

77. This story is one example of many legends that circulated in Roman late antiquity concerning Joseph's encounter with Potiphar's wife. On this material, with a focus on the exegetical features of the teachings, see Kugel, *Potiphar's House.*

78. Kugel writes that the name "Joseph the Righteous" is based on his behavior during the incident with Potiphar's wife (*Potiphar's House*, 25). This epithet for Joseph appears a number of times in rabbinic literature, including *t. Ber.* 4:16; *Gen. Rab.* 84 to Gen. 37:25 (Theodor and Albeck, *Bereshit Rabba*, 1021); *Gen. Rab.* 91 to Gen. 42:1 (Theodor and Albeck, *Bereshit Rabba*, 1118); *b. Ketub.* 111a. See also Rudolph Mach, *Der Zaddik in Talmud und Midrasch*, 242–45. In *Rabbi Nathan*, Moses is also called "the Righteous" in A2,9; see my discussion in chapter 2a concerning Moses's fence.

79. I use "exile" following Goldin's interpretation of "Aramean." Goldin writes that "Aramean" often appears in rabbinic literature to mean "pagan." Here, though, he suggests it may mean "stranger"—"i.e., she threatened Joseph that she would exile him to a far off land . . . and reduce him to the status of strangers, who generally have no rights and are helpless; hence Joseph's answer." He also raises the possibility that the word may refer to proselytes (Goldin, *Rabbi Nathan*, 193 n.7).

Kister notes the oddness of this passage (*Studies,* 221); compare *Gen. Rab.* 87 to
Gen. 39:21–22 (Theodor and Albeck, *Bereshit Rabba,* 1075–1076).

80. As Michael Lyons has pointed out to me, a portrayal of internalized traditional discourse appears in Matthew 4:1–11: Jesus is presented as quoting from
Deuteronomy when facing temptation.

81. *Gen. Rab.* 87 to Gen. 39:21–22 (Theodor and Albeck, *Bereshit Rabba,* 1075–
76); Kugel, *Potiphar's House,* 52–53. Kugel writes that the story in *Rabbi Nathan* is
"early" and may be right, but he does not justify his dating. On the uses of this
psalm, compare the morning blessings in the prayer book and the second blessing
of the Amidah in Philip Birnbaum, *Daily Prayerbook,* 15–18, 83–84. Jonathan Malamy has pointed out to me that in the edition of *Rabbi Nathan* by the Gaon Rabbi
Elijah of Vilna, the story only includes verses that appear in the morning blessings.

82. On this expression as indicating distinction, see Hezser, *Social Structure of
the Rabbinic Movement,* 301–6.

83. Schechter suggests this addition based on manuscripts (it also appears in
MS N, which Schechter did not have).

84. The phrase for "slander" *('okhilu qurtza')* echoes Daniel 3:8, where elite
Jews working in the king's administration are accused of not engaging in proper
worship. On the vocalization, note Marcus Jastrow, *A Dictionary of the Targumim,
the Talmud Babli and Yerushalmi, and the Midrashic Literature,* 1425.

85. Or, "sit and recite the Mishnah" *(yosheb veshoneh).*

86. I have specified the subjects of certain verbs. The word I translate as "general" is difficult. Schechter's text, MS O, and MS N have *hegemon,* a word that
changed meaning over time but indicates a powerful military leader—often a
"general" but also sometimes "emperor." Note that the Wilna-Romm edition has
shilton—"ruler, governor." David Stern translates "general" in his recent analysis
of the story (see "The Captive Woman," 91–127). Moshe David Herr, who argues
that this story is evidence for a historical event, translates "prefect." See his "Dialogues Between Sages and Roman Dignitaries," 123–50. Joshua Holo has helped
me research these terms. On the general issue of rabbis traveling, including travel
in order to meet representatives of the government, see Hezser, *Social Structure of
the Rabbinic Movement,* 165–71; Schwartz, *Imperialism and Jewish Society,* 114.

87. Stern, "The Captive Woman," 98–99, 116. Stern argues that such narratives in rabbinic literature represent a "deep Hellenization," in which Greco-
Roman culture is central to "the most profound, fundamental constructs of Rabbinic Judaism, including the very way the Rabbis conceived the world and
themselves within it" (115–16).

88. Herr explains this answer in terms of Rabbi Tzadok's subordinate position.
He "was a captive, a slave. Hence his mistress wanted to mate him a slave-woman
with whom to beget slave children. Rabbi Tzadok could hardly have disclosed the
true reason for his conduct—a slave, after all, is subservient to the will of his master. He therefore accounted for his refusal to consort with the slave-woman by his
ancient and noble descent" ("Dialogues," 137). Whether or not one follows Herr's

analysis, Rabbi Tzadok's answer is likely a strategic reply. The issue of bastardy appears in *Rabbi Nathan* in A12,53.

89. Herr writes of the "view of universal human brotherhood which had become strong in Rome after 96 CE. Such Roman views clashed with the Jewish tendency to separate themselves from gentiles in food and marriage" ("Dialogues," 136–37). See also Goldin, *Rabbi Nathan,* 193 n.11. Peter Schäfer presents a sophisticated treatment of Greco-Roman hostility to Jews and addresses numerous cases in which Jews are accused of xenophobia, starting at least as early as the Egyptian priest Manetho at Heliopolis in the third century BCE; see *Judeophobia,* 15–33, 66–67, 167–69, 170–79, 183–86, 208–10. The statements by the Roman in the narrative appear to emerge from Greco-Roman anti-Jewish polemic more than Christian, given the appeal to universalism, but criticisms of dietary observance and particularism were taken up by Christians as well. See Samuel Krauss, *The Jewish-Christian Controversy,* vol. 1, 20–21 and generally 13–26. Joshua Holo has helped me research these issues.

90. Both David Stern and Marc Hirshman have argued that the figure of Rabbi Akiba is often associated with rabbinic ideals of particularism and suspicion of Roman society. See Stern, "The Captive Woman," and Hirshman, "Rabbinic Universalism," 115. This is the second case we have seen in which a non-rabbi appeals to creation in challenging a rabbi—compare the story of Rabbi Simeon ben Eleazar discussed in chapter 1c. There seems to be a rabbinic concern that their own theology of creation undermines their claims to distinctiveness.

91. *Nebelot* are animals not slaughtered according to ritual requirements; *terephot* are animals with a fatal organic disease; and *sheratzim* are unclean reptiles. The combination of *nebelot* and *terephot,* along with other terms, is quite common in rabbinic literature, though this particular triad is not. For other examples of women being compared with food, see *b. Ned.* 20b; *b. Shabb.* 13a; and Michael Satlow, "'Texts of Terror': Rabbinic Texts, Speech Acts, and the Control of Mores," 282–83.

92. Note that no laws are mentioned or cited. In particular, if we can read this story in relation to others about Rabbi Akiba, he would have been married long before he attained any authoritative status as a rabbi, so adultery would have been an issue. See the brief reference in A6,30 and generally the references in note 8 of my introduction.

93. We have reason, then, not to discount Rabbi Akiba's last line as deceptive speech in relation to a powerful Roman man. On rabbinic "trickster" speech in such contexts, see Boyarin, *Dying for God,* 42–66.

94. On the distinction between self-controlled and fully virtuous, see Rosalind Hursthouse, *On Virtue Ethics,* 91–107. I thank Philip Ivanhoe for this observation. On the contrast between continence and temperance, see for example, Aristotle, *Nicomachean Ethics,* 196, and more generally, Foucault, *Use of Pleasure,* 63–91. As Herr has observed, the closest parallel to these two stories appears in the Babylonian Talmud *Qiddushin* 39b–40a. Comparing the talmudic stories with those in

Rabbi Nathan, several distinctive features of the *Rabbi Nathan* versions correlate with the broader interests of the text. The Babylonian stories do not present explicit threats in the way that the ones in *Rabbi Nathan* do, and these threats are central to the commentary upon "from the prison house he comes to rule," with its complex ideals that combine self-governance and resistance to Roman power. Also, the accounts in the Talmud do not have the same concern as we find in *Rabbi Nathan* with the sage's desire (Rabbi Tzadok's struggle and Rabbi Akiba's disgust) and with the role of traditional learning in controlling that desire (in the story of Rabbi Tzadok). Herr has examined these stories as part of a narrative type: "dialogues between rabbinic sages and Roman dignitaries." His focus is on historical questions—whether or not the events could have happened in the first centuries CE—rather than the redactional and literary problems that I address here. See Herr, "Dialogues," 100–22, 136–37, 149–50.

95. Kister states that the story in the Palestinian Talmud is the source of the one in *Rabbi Nathan* (*Studies*, 210 n.452).

96. On laws concerning female minors, see Judith Romney Wegner, *Chattel or Person? The Status of Women in the Mishnah*, 21–39.

97. Following the printed edition. The Leiden manuscript has "wife." Ilan suggests that the original text may have had the name of Rabbi Eliezer's wife, Imma Shalom (see *Mine and Yours*, 112–13 n.46).

98. Scholars of demographics debate the median age of marriage for both males and females in the eastern Roman Empire, with some holding that marriage soon after puberty was quite common, and others disputing this claim. Literary evidence appears to indicate at least that it was an aristocratic ideal. See Brent Shaw, "The Age of Roman Girls at Marriage: Some Reconsiderations"; M. K. Hopkins, "The Age of Roman Girls at Marriage"; also Brown, *Body and Society*, 6. Rabbi Eliezer is known among sages for his legal consistency concerning the status of a girl who is a minor. See the sources and discussion in Itzchak Gilath, *R. Eliezer ben Hyrcanus: A Scholar Outcast*, 128–29. Neusner comments on this passage, "Abbahu's story illustrates Eliezer's view that marriage of a minor counts for nothing. . . . This is the sort of story that would follow the formulation of an apodictic law. Whether Abbahu had heard or made it up for himself we do not know, but since he comes late in the formulation of the traditions about Eliezer, it stands to reason that the story depends upon the antecedent law, already known in the Mishnah-Tosefta, and combines that law with the theme of the sages' respect for their mothers and fathers" (*Eliezer ben Hyrcanus: The Tradition and the Man,* part 1, 170–71).

99. In rabbinic law, a "handmaid" (*'amah*) is a minor, while a "maidservant" (*shiphḥah*) is not (see for example *m. Qidd.* 1:2). The underlying midrash may be a concretization of *hinneh 'amatekha leshiphḥah,* such that the phrase is not simply "your handmaid is a maidservant," but "your child-servant is now an adult-servant." Also, Abigail appears as a paradigm of virtue in some rabbinic teachings (*m. Sanh.* 2:4; *b. Sanh.* 21a; see 1 Sam. 25:3). Willis Johnson has helped me research these points.

100. On this epithet see Hezser, *Social Structure of the Rabbinic Movement*, 301–6.

101. Schechter follows MS O, which reads, "he got her permission, betrothed her, and had intercourse with her." MS N does not have the clause about permission, stating, "he betrothed her and had intercourse with her." Note that according to the Mishnah, intercourse is itself a method of betrothal (*m. Qidd.* 1:1).

102. In comparing the two versions of the story, note also the shift in the niece's statement from saying that she will wash "the feet of the servants of my lord" (in 1 Sam. 25:41 and the Palestinian Talmud) to "the feet of your students." The scholastic setting is more prominent in *Rabbi Nathan*. The image of a woman tending the sages is reminiscent of New Testament accounts, such as Luke 10: 38–42; John 11:1–2; also Matt. 26:6–13. In *Rabbi Nathan* Rabbi Eliezer is often lauded for his great knowledge. See A6,30–31; A16,63; A19,70; A25,80; B13,30–33.

103. See especially *b. Nidd.* 44b–45a, in which the age of three years and one day is a key point of legal significance. Note the criticisms of marrying young girls in *Rabbi Nathan B* on B8,24; B48,131; also Saldarini, *Fathers According to Rabbi Nathan B*, 80–81 n.31, 298 n.11 (the latter note gives citations concerning the early marriage of girls in rabbinic literature).

104. These last three paragraphs are inspired by the discussion that ensued after I presented my paper, "Structure and Editing of Rabbinic Traditions Concerning *Yetzer* (Inclination)," at the Annual Meeting of the Association for Jewish Studies in December of 2000. I thank David Kraemer for his thoughtful comments. He has suggested to me that the very act of Rabbi Eliezer sleeping in bed with his niece may be problematic by standards articulated in the Babylonian Talmud. He highlights the legal material in *m. Qidd.* 4:12 regarding a man sleeping in bed with his daughter as well as the commentary in *b. Qidd.* 81b, which raises concerns regarding a maturing girl's own *yetzer*. Kraemer points out that, while the Mishnah permits a man to sleep with his daughter until she has reached puberty, in the talmudic commentary there is a recognition "that there is something amiss about the Mishnah's permission; girls have sexual feelings long before they develop, and the absence of the actual father-daughter taboo (Rabbi Eliezer was only his niece's social father) would render this that more complicated" (personal correspondence).

105. Deborah Green has helped me in formulating this summary.

2c. Rabbinic Tradition: Conclusion

1. Other sources portray a more optimistic view of Torah growing within the self. Also, the Torah can be water, bread, milk, or wine that nourishes or quenches thirst (see for example *Sed. El. Rab.* 2 and 13; Friedmann, *Seder Eliahu*, 8 and 195).

2. See, for example, Foucault, *Use of Pleasure*, 63–72, and *Care of the Self*, 81–95; Hadot, *Inner Citadel*, 122; Brown, *Body and Society*, 34.

3. Daniel Boyarin has discussed in a number of works the differences and

interrelations between Hellenistic and rabbinic accounts of the body (see *Carnal Israel, A Radical Jew,* and *Dying for God*).

4. Compare to my account of the rabbinic sages: Ivanhoe, *Confucian Moral Self-Cultivation,* especially 1–42 (note also page 85 for images of conquest); Schofer, "Virtues in Xunzi's Thought." Philip J. Ivanhoe has pointed out to me that metaphors of fences and animal training are absent in early Confucian ethics. Regarding the latter, for Confucians, one takes on the tradition in order to become *unlike* an animal. Along with the great difference at the metaphysical level, there are unexpected similarities. For example, the accumulation of virtue *(de)* in very early Chinese sources implies an accumulation of power that inspires a sense of debt in others (Ivanhoe, *Confucian Moral Self-Cultivation,* ix–xvii). This could be juxtaposed in interesting ways with rabbinic notions of divine pay and debt discussed in part 3. On a completely different line of comparison, note also that the trope of a "yoke" appears in South Asian traditions, as in the word "yoga."

5. MacIntyre, *After Virtue,* 220–23. He formulates the category in *After Virtue,* but he has much more detailed accounts of tradition in *Whose Justice? Which Rationality?* and *Three Rival Versions,* 127–215. Also, Ivanhoe employs and develops the category in his *Confucian Moral Self-Cultivation.*

6. On revelation and tradition, see Gershom Scholem, "Revelation and Tradition"; on canon and exegesis, Jonathan Z. Smith, *Imagining Religion,* 36–52, and Fishbane, *Exegetical;* on intertextuality, Boyarin, *Intertextuality.* For another example of conceptual formulation that has an overly strong focus upon reasoning that is specifically philosophical, see Thomas Kasulis's definition of "metapraxis" ("Philosophy as Metapraxis," 174) and note 29 of my introduction.

7. See my introduction as well as MacIntyre, *Three Rival Versions,* 61–68, 82–104; Ricoeur, *Oneself as Another,* 156–57; Asad, *Genealogies of Religion,* 83–167, especially 130, 136; Mahmood, *Women's Piety and Embodied Discipline,* and "Feminist Theory, Embodiment, and the Docile Agent"; and Butler, *Psychic Life.*

Part 3. Rabbinic Theology

1. Newman emphasizes theology in his study of Jewish ethics, but not the pervasive pictures of divine involvement in the world that I address here (see *Past Imperatives,* 83–115). MacIntyre, despite his strong interest in medieval Christianity, writes little about God's role in his Augustinian or Thomist formulations of virtue and tradition (note, though, the discussion in *After Virtue,* 278). Particularly in *Three Rival Versions,* where Thomas Aquinas is a key figure, God is curiously absent or at least concealed. Hadot has criticized Foucault's lack of attention to the role of an "Other"—whether nature or universal reason—in Greco-Roman ethics ("Reflections on the Idea of the 'Cultivation of the Self,'" in *Philosophy as a Way of Life,* 206–13). Yearley argues explicitly for the value of focusing upon "practical" rather than "secondary" theory in the comparative study of virtues (*Mencius and*

Aquinas, 175–82). My analysis of human action shows that, at least for the case of late ancient rabbis, such a separation is difficult to maintain. Charles Taylor gestures at the significance of theology for Western ethics in *Sources of the Self*, but his lack of explicitness on the issue is ultimately problematic. For a recent review and discussion of this point, with references, see William Greenway, "Charles Taylor on Affirmation, Mutilation, and Theism: A Retrospective Reading of *Sources of the Self*."

2. In *Rabbi Nathan*, we find images of God as warrior fighting Egypt at the Sea of Reeds (A27,83–84; A33,95–96; B11,28) and of God as bestowing a kiss upon the righteous at death (A12,49–50; B25,51; B12,28). On such anthropomorphic imagery in rabbinic literature, see Fishbane, *Kiss of God* and *Exegetical*, 22–104; *Rabbinic Mythmaking*, 95–249, 325–401; Stern, *Midrash and Theory*, 73–93. Note also the passages concerning the multiple images of God in *Mek. R. Ishmael* to Exod. 15:3 (Horovitz and Rabin, *Mechilta d'Rabbi Ishmael*, 129–30) and *Pesiq. Rab. Kah.* 4 (Mandelbaum, *Pesikta de Rav Kahana*, 222–24).

3. As was discussed in chapter 1c, the image of "reward and punishment" itself implies metaphors of monetary exchange and of law. *Sakhar* (reward or pay) is a rabbinic term drawn from the realm of human monetary exchange, while *'onesh* (punishment) is drawn from legal discourse. While both terms are common in rabbinic literature, the phrase *sakhar va'onesh* as such does not appear until very late midrashic collections and medieval literature. A search in the Bar-Ilan Responsa Project CD-ROM shows only one case in rabbinic literature, in *'Otzar ha-Midrashim*, 66: *sekhar va'onesh ha-tzaddiqim umishpat* (reward and punishment of the righteous and judgment). These terms are exegetically derived from Ps. 89:15 *(tzedeq umishpat mekhon kis'ekha)*, where *tzedeq* is interpreted as *sekhar va'onesh ha-tzaddiqim*.

4. I use the term "order" in the same sense, and with the same reservations, as does Lennart Boström in his study of the Book of Proverbs. He argues that Proverbs portrays "a world which is characterized by regularity, order, and harmony." However, he adds that, "The problem with using the term 'order' to designate the world-view of the sages lies in the connotations: it designates a particular world view . . . in which 'order' is regarded as an impersonal principle governing all things in the world. Thus this view countenances a kind of deism in which justice and order are inherent in the structure of the world, rendering God's continued involvement redundant." He concludes that the concept of "order" is appropriate for interpreting the Book of Proverbs, with the reservation that "the Lord is above or independent of this order" (*The God of the Sages*, 136–37; see nn.205–9 for references to previous scholarship and debates concerning the term "order").

5. See Gannath Obeyesekere, *Imagining Karma: Ethical Transformation in Amerindian, Buddhist, and Greek Rebirth;* Wendy Doniger O'Flaherty, ed., *Karma and Rebirth in Classical Indian Traditions;* Charles F. Keyes and E. Valentine Daniel, eds., *Karma: An Anthropological Inquiry;* Eliot S. Deutsch, "Karma as a 'Convenient Fiction' in the *Advaita Vedānta*."

6. The intellectual currents that are now named as "modern" were very much counter to this sensibility. The great critique of divine justice is Friedrich Nietzsche's *On the Genealogy of Morals*. An important treatment of rewards and punishments in modernity is Foucault's *Discipline and Punish* (especially on theological issues and religious institutions see 34, 45–47, 90–91, 122–26, 146–47, 149–51, 161–62, 226, 238).

7. This treatment of divine reward and punishment aims to develop further the scholarly literature concerning the ethical dimensions of rabbinic theology. Of these studies, I draw most upon Ephraim Urbach's *The Sages,* particularly his extensive discussion of "Man's Accounting and the World's Accounting" (420–523). My analysis attends to the tropes and genres of rabbinic thought and strives for greater precision both in the conceptual framing and in the treatment of specific passages. Earlier major studies of this topic include Schechter, *Aspects of Rabbinic Theology,* especially 21–115, and "The Doctrine of Divine Retribution," in *Studies in Judaism,* first series, 213–32; Büchler, *Studies in Sin and Atonement;* Moore, *Judaism in the First Centuries;* Kadushin, *The Theology of Seder Eliahu,* especially 163–211; David Kraemer, *Responses to Suffering in Classical Rabbinic Literature.* A short but very insightful piece is Gershom Scholem's "On Sin and Punishment: Some Remarks Concerning Biblical and Rabbinical Ethics," 163–77. There is also a massive scholarly literature on related topics in the Hebrew Bible, which I draw upon and cite as relevant.

8. Judah Goldin, in his analysis of the differences between *Rabbi Nathan A* and *Rabbi Nathan B,* states the now well-known thesis that *Rabbi Nathan A* gives relative weight to Torah, while *Rabbi Nathan B* emphasizes good deeds *(maʿaśim ṭobim).* My analysis supports this point, though in somewhat different terms— *Rabbi Nathan A* is a richer source of material concerning Torah and related concepts, and *Rabbi Nathan B* often has more developed accounts of divine reward and punishment. Judah Goldin, "The Two Versions of *Abot de-Rabbi Nathan,*" in *Studies in Midrash,* 83–100; also Saldarini, *Scholastic Rabbinism,* 122–24.

3a. Divine Reward and Punishment

1. Hebrew: *metzudah perusah.* The image of the "net" may derive from Eccles. 9:12, which employs a simile of "fish caught in an evil net" *(bimtzodah raʿah).* In the Vatican manuscript of *Rabbi Nathan A,* the base passage is only, "All is given on pledge, and a net is spread." A teaching in the name of Rabbi Ishmael interprets the "net" as "a net of death" (See Schechter, *Rabbi Nathan,* 162). In a *baraita* cited in *b. Pesaḥ* 3b, the phrase *metzudah perusah* appears in a narrative and connotes political influence.

2. In the printed edition of *Rabbi Nathan A,* the maxim does not appear in full. It states, "All is given on pledge. A net is cast over all that live, etc." I follow Schechter, who draws upon MS E (see A39,117 n.3). A version with commentary appears in MS V, printed in Schechter, *Rabbi Nathan,* 162. In *Rabbi Nathan B,* the

epigram is attributed to Rabbi Eliezer the son of Rabbi Yose ha-Gelili (B44,123), and in *The Fathers* it appears in a list of epigrams of Rabbi Akiba (*Fathers* 3:12–16; note Urbach, *Sages,* 437; Kraemer, *Responses to Suffering,* 62–63). There are some differences between the parallels in *Rabbi Nathan A* and in *Rabbi Nathan B.* In *Rabbi Nathan A,* the divine/human relation highlights human indebtedness to God, with all being "given on pledge," whereas *Rabbi Nathan B* emphasizes God's foreknowledge, the centrality of human deeds *(ma'aseh),* and the truth of divine judgment. Also, the scene on high differs somewhat in each case. In *Rabbi Nathan A* God sits as judge, while *Rabbi Nathan B* emphasizes the arranged table (perhaps for an eschatological banquet) and God's handwriting. Finally, in describing the collector, *Rabbi Nathan A* uses the plural, implying some band of angels, while *Rabbi Nathan B* uses the singular—either God himself or the angel of death (for the angel of death appearing in a narrative, see A12,50; B25,51–52). In both *Rabbi Nathan A* and *Rabbi Nathan B,* this theological epigram is followed by other passages discussing divine payment and credit (A39,116–19; B44,123).

3. Royal and judicial tropes also appear together in the maxim of Akabya ben Mahalalel (A19,69; B32,69; *Fathers* 3:1), which I quote and analyze in chapter 3b. In *Rabbi Nathan B,* a list of names praising God includes both "king" and "judge" (B38,100–101). In chapter 1c I discuss the metaphor "God is a king" when introducing the concept of "tension," and several of the passages presented in my analysis of *yetzer* (chapter 2b) make reference to God's kingship and judgment. On biblical materials, see E. Theodore Mullen, *The Divine Council in Canaanite and Early Hebrew Literature;* Brettler, *God Is King* (on God's role as a judge, see 109–16, 122–24, and for qualifications regarding the link between metaphors of kingship and those of judgment, see 113). A classic study of the metaphor in the Bible is Martin Buber, *Kingship of God.* On judicial tropes in Paul's writings, see Williams, *Paul's Metaphors,* 141–64. The comparison between divine rulers and human rulers also appears in classical Greek sources, such as Book Ten of Plato's *Laws.*

4. On deathbed scenes, see my discussion in chapter 1b as well as Saldarini, "Deathbed," and Fishbane, *Kiss of God,* 51–86. This passage appears in a chapter of *Rabbi Nathan A* that opens with maxims by Ben Azzai, one of the "four who entered the garden." Several of these sayings concern the bodily position of a person who has died, stating whether or not a given position is a good "sign" or a bad one (A25,79; following the interpretation of Goldin in *Rabbi Nathan,* 105). The implicit issue at stake appears to be one's status at the moment of divine judgment, and Ben Azzai claims to be able to divine that status from the dead body. The editors of *Rabbi Nathan A* begin their commentary upon this series with this narrative of Rabban Yohanan ben Zakkai, developing the theme of one's status before God at death. On the compilation of this unit, see Kister, *Studies,* 171–72.

5. In printed versions and manuscripts, there is inconsistency whether the key verb here is "sentence/imprison" *('.s.r.)* or "chastise" *(y.s.r.).* See Schechter's comments in A25,79 nn.8, 9, and Finkelstein's discussion in *Introduction,* 158–59. The use of "chastise" may result from an attempt to soften an earlier, stronger image.

6. For "kneel" in Ps. 22:30, Goldin translates "be sentenced" (*Rabbi Nathan*, 106), probably interpreting the midrash as based on the sense of *k.r.ʻ.* in the *hiphʻil* as "to outweigh" or "to decide." A parallel to this passage appears in *b. Ber.* 28b. Fränkel presents a subtle analysis of the talmudic account in *Studies in the Spiritual World*, 52–56. For an analysis and synoptic presentation of the versions, see Neusner, *Legend*, 221–24, and *Judaism and Story*, 130–31; also Büchler, *Studies in Sin and Atonement*, 45–56.

7. See also A16,64; A19,69; B32,69; B38,100–101; *Fathers* 3:1.

8. The term for "bribe" *(sh.ḥ.d.)* appears often in the Bible as an attempt to pervert justice. See for example Exod. 23:8 and Deut. 16:19.

9. In *The Fathers*, the epigram is attributed to Rabbi Eliezer ha-Kappar (*Fathers* 4:21–22).

10. At the end of the maxim in *Rabbi Nathan B*, we find the monetary image of an "account" *(ḥeshbon)*, as well as the epithet that God is the King of the kings of kings (B34,77). In *Fathers* 4:21, we read right after the parallel to the quoted passage that "All is according to the account" *(ha-kol lephi ha-ḥeshbon)*.

11. For a discussion of these terms and citations of examples, see Daniel Sperber, *A Dictionary of Greek and Latin Legal Terms in Rabbinic Literature*, 123–26 (on *sanhedrin*), 126–30 (on *senigur* and related terms), and 178–80 (on *qaṭeygur* and related terms). On the opposition of *senigur* and *qaṭeygur*, see Saldarini, *Fathers According to Rabbi Nathan B*, 206–7 n.10. Lee Levine challenges the view that there was a "Sanhedrin" in Palestine during the talmudic period (*Rabbinic Class*, 76–83; also Hezser, *Social Structure of the Rabbinic Movement*, 186–95).

12. The literary context of this passage is a numerical list of generations from Adam to Noah. The mention of Noah gives rise to a discussion of the flood and the nature of divine justice, part of which centers on Gen. 6:3. This passage concludes the series of teachings, and the first one is that of Rabbi Yose ha-Gelili concerning *yetzer*, analyzed in chapter 2b.

13. For another use of "court" in relation to the ministering angels, see A20,72.

14. Saldarini translates *ketarim* as "shields," not the more literal "crowns" (*Fathers According to Rabbi Nathan B*, 207).

15. The specific features of this advocacy and prosecution are not specified. We do not know whether each act generates an attorney for an immediate judgment, or if one accumulates many defenders and prosecutors over the course of a lifetime, all to meet at a final hearing after death.

16. This passage appears in the commentary upon Moses's "fence" for his words (see my discussion in chapter 2a). An account of Moses's decision to break the tablets of the covenant opens by describing his ascent on high to receive them from God. For other examples of angels opposing either Moses receiving the tablets or the creation of Adam, see *b. Sanh.* 38b; *b. Shabb.* 88b; *Psiq. R.* 20 (Friedmann, *Pesiqta Rabbati*, 96b–98b); *Midr. Ps.* 8 (Buber, 78–79); *Gen. Rab.* 8 to Gen. 1:26 (Theodor and Albeck, *Bereshit Rabba*, 61).

17. Urbach highlights the significant innovation in terminology by the rabbis in *Sages,* 4.

18. Following Goldin and Saldarini, who understand *'orekhey ha-dayyanin* as the equivalent of *'rky-qrytys* (Greek: *archikritēs*) in *Gen. Rab.* 50 to Gen. 19:1 (Theodor and Albeck, *Bereshit Rabba,* 519 and notes). See Goldin, *Rabbi Nathan,* 58, 187 n.2; Saldarini, *Fathers According to Rabbi Nathan B,* 129 n.7.

19. In *Rabbi Nathan B,* the maxim is attributed to Simeon ben Shetah.

20. In addition to the passages I have quoted, in a discussion of the events in Eden the commentators employ the term *d.y.n.* to describe God's sentencing of the snake: "The Holy One, blessed be He, said, "If I do not judge [*dan*] the snake . . ." (A1,7). Another example is an epigram attributed in *Rabbi Nathan B* to Rabbi Eliezer the son of Rabbi Eleazar ha-Kappar. He plays on the metaphoric tension between human and divine judgment, advising, "do not be a judge alone, for none is a judge alone but One" (B34,76; in *Fathers* 4:8, the saying is attributed to Rabbi Ishmael son of Rabbi Yose). Both God and a human judge enact judgment, but a human judge must be situated in a community and a tradition. God, and God alone, can enact judgment alone. For examples of the root *d.y.n.* in *Rabbi Nathan,* see A1,5; A1,7; A3,17; A8,35; A8,37; A10,42; A10,43; A12,49; A13,57; A16,64; A20,72; A21,74; A32,93; A36,106–8; A39,117; A41,33; B1,8; B2,8–10; B8,23–24; B20,43; B25,50; B26,52; B32,69; B34,76; B42,116; B42,117; B43,119.

21. On A33,94 another passage employs these terms to depict human legal processes in the context of a narrative concerning Aaron.

22. Urbach also discusses the link between *tz.d.q.* and notions of purity and cleanliness (*Sages,* 483–85). For examples of this root being used in *Rabbi Nathan,* see A1,5; A2,9; A2,11; A3,14–15; A9,38–39; A12,54; A13,57; A16,63; A25,79; A28,85– 86; A32,92; A34,103; A36,106–8; A39,118; A40,128; A41,133; B3,12; B10,25–26; B16,35; B22,46–47; B25,51; B27,54; B33,73; B42,116; B43,120; B43,121; B45,125.

23. For examples of the root *z.k.h.* in *Rabbi Nathan,* see A1,1; A6,29; A8,35; A8,37; A9,42; A10,42–43; A12,54; A19,70; A35,104–5; A36,107; A40,120; A41,131; A41,134; B11,27; B12,29–30; B13,32–33; B14,34; B19,40; B20,43; B22,46–47; B24,49–50; B25,50; B26,54; B27,54; B29,62; B35,80–81; B45,124–26; B48,131.

24. In translating the verse from Ecclesiastes, I follow Choon-Leong Seow, who writes that the *lamed* preceding *kheleb* is emphatic, and that the verse should not be translated, "It is better than for a living dog" (*Ecclesiastes: A New Translation with Introduction and Commentary,* 301). Here I quote the passage simply to exemplify its use of terms, and I discuss it further later in this chapter.

25. For examples of *h.v.b.,* see A2,10; A2,11; A3,15; A3,16; A6,29; A10,43; A11,44; A11,47–48; A12,48; A12,55; A12,56; A17,65–66; A20,72; A25,80; A33,94; A38,114; B2,10; B3,14; B9,25; B14,33; B18,39; B21,44–45; B22,47; B25,50; B26,52; B27,55–57; B42,117; B46,129. For examples of *g.z.r.,* see A1,6–7; A3,17; A8,36; A39,117; B25,51; B42,116–17. For examples of *'.n.sh.,* see A9,39–40; B32,70; note also terms such as *z.q.q.* (*hiph'il*— "to bind, obligate") on A2,11; and *p.t.r.* (to acquit or exempt) on A3,15.

26. On the difference between systematic metaphors and isolated, unsystematic, "dead" metaphors, see Lakoff and Johnson, *Metaphors We Live By,* 52–55 and my discussion in chapter 1c.

27. I quote from Schechter's addition in A27,84 based on the Epstein manuscript. The passage is not in the printed edition of *Rabbi Nathan A,* but it appears in both the Epstein and Oxford manuscripts. The parallels in B35,84 and *Fathers* 2:14 do not mention the future to come.

28. For examples of *sakhar,* see A1,3; A5,25–26; A8,36–37; A11,44; A16,64; A18,67; A25,81; A27,84; A30,89; A32,93; A33,94–95; A35,104; A35,105; B10,25–26; B15,34–35; B18,40; B21,44–45; B27,55–56; B32,70; B33,72–73; B35,85–86; B36,92–93; B36,94; B44,123; B45,126. Note that *s̆.k.r.* is absent in A17,66 but present in a parallel version in *Fathers* 2:14. The theological sense is most common, though on A35,104, *sekhar miṭṭot* denotes payment for a night on a bed. On this term generally, see Morton Smith, *Tannaitic Parallels to the Gospels,* 46–77, 161–84. Biblical examples of theological uses of *sakhar* include Gen. 15:1; Ps. 127:3; and Eccles. 9:5; Michael Fox, *A Time to Tear Down and a Time to Build Up: A Rereading of Ecclesiastes,* 293. On the general concepts of pay, reward, or recompense in Greek literature, the Hebrew Bible, and the New Testament, see the problematic but informative treatment of *misthos* in Gerhard Kittel, ed., *Theological Dictionary of the New Testament,* vol. 4, 695–728. This passage and its parallels have some resemblance to parables in the New Testament in which a person is an agricultural laborer before God, such as Matt. 9:37, Luke 10:2, and John 4:35–38. For other exchange metaphors in the New Testament, see Williams, *Paul's Metaphors,* 170–71, 179–92.

29. Fränkel has suggested that the maxim juxtaposes suffering and reward in a manner that reveals the implicit "employer" to be unique, for generally a worker is paid according to the product or the hours of labor, not based in the degree of suffering (*Ways,* 402). Divine pay is thus based on a different assessment of work than human pay. In *Rabbi Nathan A,* the maxim is attributed to Hillel (A12,55). In *Rabbi Nathan B* and *The Fathers* it is attributed to Ben He He (B27,55; *Fathers* 5:23). Saul Lieberman claims that it "was a popular adage current in Palestine, and various sages were credited with it" (*Greek in Jewish Palestine,* 160 n.113). Fränkel discusses the maxim as an example of Hillel's influence upon later sages (*Ways,* 402). Note another use of the root *tz.ʿ.r.* (suffering), implying the same principle, in a narrative describing Rabbi Akiba's wife's suffering and her ensuing reward (A6,28–30). On Hillel's maxims and their commentary, see generally A12,48–56; B24–27,48–57; *Fathers* 1:12–14; Fränkel, *Ways,* 396–402; and my discussion in chapter 1b.

30. A *seʾah* is a measure of volume, and a *dinar* is a unit of currency.

31. This epigram appears as part of a commentary to the numerical catalogue, "Five do not have forgiveness" (A39,116). Several examples that I analyze here are drawn from chapters 39 and 40 of *Rabbi Nathan A,* which present and comment upon numerical catalogues based on the numbers five and four. These chapters do not have strict thematic consistency, but the tropes of reward and punishment are

prominent. Note that the passage with which I opened this chapter is from A39,116–17. Kister points out that A39,116–18 parallels B44,123–24 (*Studies,* 160). On numerical catalogues, see my discussion in chapter 1b as well as Towner, *Rabbinic Enumeration.*

32. Schechter emends the text, "The wicked are paid as people who observed the Torah with good intention and nothing wrong is ever found with them. The righteous are given credit as people who observed the Torah with bad intention and nothing good is ever found in them" (A39,118 n.5). His emendation is probably correct, as the extant text is probably the result of a euphemistic change that softens the argument. The issues of intentionality are complex here—what does it mean to observe the Torah with bad intention?

33. The last line of the passage is difficult. See Schechter's comments in A39,118 n.5. Kister cites this passage as one of several cases in *Rabbi Nathan* for which he identifies an original text that is not found among any of the manuscript witnesses (*Studies,* 42). Parallels include *Siphre Deut.* 307 (Finkelstein, *Sifre on Deuteronomy,* 345); *Gen. Rab.* 33:1 (Theodor and Albeck, *Bereshit Rabba,* 298–303); *Lev. Rab.* 27:1.

34. In B44,123, the terms are used differently. The text states that the wicked receive credit now, in this world, but receiving "credit" means that the rewards are loaned in this world, such that all merit is used up before one reaches the world to come. See also A35,105; B27,54.

35. Earlier in the same chapter, a short epigram states, "The ease of the wicked—its end is bad" (A39,117), and a passage later in the chapter, in the name of Eliezer bar Tzadok, expresses the same point using purity motifs (A39,119). Also see A25,79; B33,73; *Fathers* 4:15. On the topic of theodicy in rabbinic literature, see Urbach, *Sages,* 511–23, and Schofer, "Protest or Pedagogy?" On the formulation, "the ease of the wicked," note Jer. 12:1–2.

36. A parallel appears in the Mishnah at the opening of laws concerning the corners of agricultural fields to be left for the poor. Here, the play between agricultural produce and the "produce" of one's actions is prominent (*m. Pe'a* 1:1). Moore comments concerning this passage, "It will be noted that all the items of this 'capital in heaven' are things that cannot be defined or measured by law—things that by nature are 'committed to the heart' of the individual" (*Judaism in the First Centuries,* vol. 2, 92). See also Urbach, *Sages,* 441–42; Diamond, *Holy Men,* 59–64. A more developed discussion of this topic appears in *t. Pe'a* 1:1–4. In *b. Shabb.* 127a–b, an amoraic tradition expands from this tannaitic material to list six actions with "fruits" in this world and "capital" remaining in the next. This passage appears in the Morning Blessings of the prayer book (Birnbaum, *Daily Prayerbook,* 15–16). An extended talmudic exposition citing and developing this material appears in *b. Qidd.* 39b–40a. The section addresses many of the same topics as A40,119–20 and includes a parallel to a teaching in A40,120 that states, "Merit [*zekhut*] has capital and fruits." It also contains much material on *yetzer,* including a story concerning Rabbi Tzadok that parallels one in A16,62 discussed in chapter 2b; also see *Sed. El.*

Rab. 11/12 (Friedmann, *Seder Eliahu,* 59). For another example of *qeren* being employed as a trope, see *m. B. Qam.* 9:7.

37. The figurative use of "fruit" as the results of one's deed or actions appear in Is. 3:10 and Jer. 17:10; note that Is. 3:10 is cited as a prooftext for the epigram "Merit has capital and fruits" (A40,120).

38. For examples of *n.ḥ.l.,* see A40,120; B10,25–26; B26,54; B29,62; B45,126. For *p.d.ḥ.,* B27,54. For *maʿaleh,* A4,18; A8,36; A12,53; A13,57; A23,75; A23,78; A26,82; A28,85; A30,89; A31,90; B18,40; B23,48; B26,53–54; B30,66; B32,70; B36,90.

39. See B30,66; Saldarini, *Fathers According to Rabbi Nathan B,* 179 n.19. See also B17,38 and Schechter's comments in n.12; Saldarini, *Fathers According to Rabbi Nathan B,* 118 n.14; and *b. B. Metz.* 69b.

40. On this exegetical opening, see my discussion in chapter 1b as well as Kister, *Studies,* 45. It appears in A31,90; A32,92; A33,93; B36,90; B36,94; and *Fathers* 5:1–2.

41. For a person receiving credit for causing another to do something, see A23,78. For examples of negative cases, see A26,83; A30,89. The phrase "as if" *(keʾilu)* often marks simulation or substitution. See Fishbane, *Kiss of God,* 87–124, and *Exegetical,* 123–35. For a case of "Scripture accounts it to him as if . . ." specifically indicating a substitution for sacrificial acts, see A4,18. Yadin examines the rabbinic idea that Scripture has agency in *Scripture as Logos,* 22–33, 122–141.

42. On *purʿanut,* see Diamond, *Holy Men,* 67–74. For the understanding of metaphor that underlies this claim, see my discussion in chapter 1c and Lakoff and Johnson, *Metaphors We Live By,* 89–96.

43. This does not mean that every account of action depicts these three features. However, this is the basic model or structure implied by the diverse teachings of *Rabbi Nathan.* See Lakoff's discussion of "idealized cognitive models" in *Women, Fire, and Dangerous Things,* 68–90. For another treatment of these issues, see Morton Smith's study of divine "pay" *(misthos/śakhar)* in early rabbinic literature and the New Testament (*Tannaitic Parallels,* especially 46–77 and 161–84). I do not give a full treatment of the possibilities for intervention: ways that rabbis aim to influence God's judgment and appeal to divine compassion. In short, they appear in three forms—repentance, ritual atonement, and forceful petition. Numerous passages in *Rabbi Nathan* stress the importance of repentance, which can be a regular activity or can occur at specific times, particularly the crucial day of one's death (A15,62; B29,62; *Fathers* 2:10; Urbach, *Sages,* 467). Passages that stress the importance of repentance include A12,54; A28,88; A32,92; B22,47; B33,73; B35,81; *Fathers* 4:11; see also the general discussion of Urbach, *Sages,* 110, 462–71, 728 n.33). Several teachings stress that for some sins, repentance alone is not sufficient, and ritual atonement is necessary (A29,88; B32,71; *Fathers* 5:18). Atonement has origins in the sacrificial cult, and in the rabbinic context this sacrifice is sublimated into various ritual activities, particularly the annual Day of Atonement or

Yom Kippur (A4,21; B8,22; Fishbane, *Exegetical,* 128–29). A teaching attributed to Rabbi Ishmael interprets four biblical verses to distinguish four kinds of ritual atonement for four kinds of sin (A29,88; note *m. Yoma* 8:8). For both repentance and atonement, we find a great concern in *Rabbi Nathan* with the individual's intention—such practices must be sincere, not just ways to find a loophole in procedures of divine justice (A39,116; A40,120; *m. Yoma* 8:9). As for the third form in intervention, petition, *Rabbi Nathan* has examples of forceful "law court" prayers—strong attempts in the form of a legal argument that petitions God to change divine judgment. One such prayer appears in a narrative of Benjamin the Righteous, and it is placed in the mouth of the angels (A3,17; *b. B. Bat.* 11a; Schechter, *Rabbi Nathan,* 155; compare the angels' petition with A31,90–91; see also Goldin, *Studies in Midrash,* 116, and generally in this chapter, 101–17; Finkelstein, *Introduction,* 147; Kister, *Studies,* 209). On the "law court" prayer in rabbinic literature, see Joseph Heinemann, *Prayer in the Talmud,* 194–204. Note the challenges to Heinemann posed by William Scott Green in "Palestinian Holy Men," 629 n.52, 638 n.75. Another example of a law court prayer in *Rabbi Nathan* is that of Nakdimon ben Gurion for rain (A6,32).

44. This issue has received much attention in biblical studies due to the work of Klaus Koch. Koch argues against the view that the texts of the Hebrew Bible present a "doctrine of retribution" *(Vergeltungsdogma).* Rather, he holds that there is a connection or nexus between act and consequence, such that good actions bring blessings and bad actions bring disaster. See "Gibt es ein Vergeltungsdogma im Alten Testament?," 130–80. An abridged English translation is Koch, "Is There a Doctrine of Retribution in the Old Testament?" Koch's arguments have also been criticized by Boström as well as Patrick Miller and Michael Fox. See Boström, *The God of the Sages,* 90–113 (Boström also discusses the comparison between Israelite understanding of consequences and Egyptian conceptions of *ma'at* on 94–96); Patrick D. Miller, *Sin and Judgment in the Prophets: A Stylistic and Theological Analysis,* 121–39; Fox, *A Time To Tear Down,* 53–55 and generally 51–70. I also offer a more extended discussion of this issue in *Rabbi Nathan* in my dissertation, *The Making of a Sage,* 263–69.

45. On the paradigmatic rabbinic violations of idolatry, incest, and murder, see my discussions in part 2 as well as A38,113–15; B41,113–16; *Fathers* 5:9. See also *b. Shabb.* 32b–33a; Finkelstein, *Introduction,* 94–97; and Saldarini, *Fathers According to Rabbi Nathan B,* 243 n.1. On ritual activity, see A26,82; B35,87; *Fathers* 3:11; Schechter, *Aspects,* 220–221; Goldin, *Studies in Midrash,* 112 and 200 nn.14–17; Finkelstein, *Introduction,* 160–61. On the *Shema,* the *Amidah,* and phylacteries, see B3,14; B27,55; B38,101. On women's ritual activities, particularly those specified in the Mishnah (menstrual purity, lighting of Sabbath candles, and the *ḥallah*), see A2,8; B9,25; B42,117; also *m. Shabb.* 2:6; *b. Shabb.* 32b and generally 31b–34a; Urbach, *Sages,* 437; Fonrobert, *Menstrual Purity,* especially 29–37.

46. The epigram is not found in *The Fathers.* See *t. Sukk.* 4:3; *b. Sukk.* 53a; also Saldarini, *Fathers According to Rabbi Nathan B,* 160 n.11.

47. The midrash is a subtle case of "sublimation of sacrifice" in rabbinic thought and practice. On Exod. 20:21 in its biblical context, see Fishbane, *Biblical Interpretation*, 251–52. A this-worldly result of diligence in study appears in narratives of Rabbi Akiba and Rabbi Eliezer ben Hyrcanus. Both characters suffer hardship, but in the end they not only become great sages but also attain great wealth. While neither story states explicitly that God rewards them for their actions, they imply that a consequence of becoming learned is to become wealthy. I have quoted from and referred to these stories at several points above (A6,27–31; B13,27–33; *Fathers* 1:4).

48. Other passages threaten punishment for not consulting the sages (A12,56; B27,56–57) and for teaching improperly (A11,47–48; B22,47; *Fathers* 1:11). For other examples of study and teaching as actions that result in divine reward and punishment, see B5,18; B15,34–35; B18,40; B22,46; B48,131.

49. The three major sins of idolatry, incest, and murder are often the basis of hyperbolic expressions that uphold some nonlegal ideal. Several teachings link the cardinal sins with the men of Sodom through an atomistic exegesis of Gen. 13:13—"The men of Sodom are bad [*ra'im*] and sin [*hata'im*] against the Lord a great deal" (Gen 13:13) (A36,106). This midrash, and the three paradigmatic transgressions, appear in commentaries to Hillel's instruction to "love all people" (A12,52) and to Rabbi Yehoshua's epigram concerning the danger of "hatred of people" (B30,64). On malicious speech, see also A9,39–42; B16,36. On God's punishment "in this world and in the world to come" (A40,120), contrast the passage that describes virtuous actions for which one enjoys the "fruits" in this world and the "capital" in the next (A40,119; also A40,120). For other teachings concerning interpersonal relations, see Elisha ben Abuyah's assertion that one can gain divine credit by influencing others to observe the commandments (A23,78). For a negative corollary, where others may get credit for stopping a person from transgressing, see a teaching of Ben Azzai on A25,81. Also, Rabbi Akiba states that those who accompany people committing transgression or observing the commandments, even if they themselves do nothing, receive the punishment or reward (A30,89). For an example of reward and punishment applying to relations with those outside the community, see the instructions concerning giving to the poor in B14,34.

50. Note the use here of the technical expression, "Scripture accounts it to him as if" *(ma'aleh 'alav ha-katub ke'ilu)*, which marks a divine response that appears disproportionate to the act. Rabbinic views concerning gift giving appear to continue ancient Near Eastern values, according to which intention and volition are central to the validity of the exchange. See Yochanan Muffs, *Love and Joy: Law, Language, and Religion in Ancient Israel*, 166, 186. Many other passages in *Rabbi Nathan* describe internal states that bring divine reward and punishment. A story of the martyrdom of Rabbi Simeon and Rabbi Ishmael focuses on arrogance (A38,114–15; B41,114–15; Finkelstein, *Introduction*, 100–101; Goldin, *Studies in Midrash*, 94–96; Kister, "Metamorphoses," 213–20; Schofer, "Protest or Pedagogy?"); other passages address the significance or lack thereof of intentionality

(A1,5; A30,89); on the topic of intentionality more generally, see Eilberg-Schwartz, *The Human Will in Judaism*. Also, in *Rabbi Nathan B,* one teaching states that thinking about doing a commandment counts as doing so (B18,40).

51. Correct action can bring a number of unspecified rewards: one may receive a "good reward" (*śakhar ṭob;* A16,64 and A35,105); Scripture may "account" a reward or punishment (as discussed earlier in this chapter); or one's reward may be "received on high" (*śekharo mitqabbel ba-marom;* A8,36–37, three times). This latter phrase implies an interesting question—are there cases in which one may have reward (*śakhar*) that is not received by God?—but this topic is not developed in the text. Punishment, as well as reward, may be unspecified. For example, Rabbi Simeon ben Eleazar midrashically interprets "Love your neighbor as yourself" (Lev. 19:18) by attributing to God the words, "If you love him, I am faithful to pay you a good reward *śakhar ṭob*], and if not, I am the judge to punish [*dayyan liph-roaʿ*]" (A16,64). In some cases, the consequence of an action may be an extended life span or an early death. One story tells of God granting additional years to the life of a pietist *(ḥasid)* because of an act of charity (A3,17). Often threats of death are hyperbolic. Epigrams of Hillel preserved in Aramaic counsel, "One who does not learn is guilty of death [*qaṭlaʾ ḥayyab*]," and "One who does not serve the sages is guilty of death [*qaṭlaʾ ḥayyab*]" (A12,48 and 56; B27,56; *Fathers* 1:13). Other teachings state that a person is guilty of "death" or "for his life" *(benaphsho)* (A2,10–11; A25,80; B3,14). A few sayings begin with the question, "Why do students of the sages die when they are young?" (or "before their time"). The answer is that they are punished for particular omissions or transgressions (A26,82; A29,88; B35,81). Punishments just short of death, such as disease and exile, are threatened for malicious speech or false teaching (A11,47–48; B22,47; A9,38–39). Note that this concrete sense of life as a reward contrasts with the fuller notion of "life" as happiness and well-being found in Deuteronomy (Weinfeld, *Deuteronomy and the Deuteronomic School,* 307–13), which would be closer to the spiritual rewards described later in this chapter. In *Rabbi Nathan B* we find a teaching stating that the human status of facing divine judgment itself comes from transgression. The tenth of a list of ten decrees passed by God against Adam is "that he in the future will stand in judgment" (B42,117; based on a midrashic reading of the end of Eccles. 11:9). In contrast, a list of paradigmatic sinners in *Rabbi Nathan A*—the men of Sodom, Korah and his followers, and so on—are described as those who "do not live and are not judged" (A36,106–8). According to this series, not being subject to divine judgment is the greatest punishment: such people are beyond the range of human interaction with God.

52. For a similar categorization, see Morton Smith, *Tannaitic Parallels,* 62–65.

53. This epigram opens the chapter in which it appears. I discuss the contrast between study and neglect of Torah in chapter 2a. On the term "end" *(soph),* see my dissertation, *The Making of a Sage,* 263–69.

54. On Rabbi Eliezer ben Hyrcanus, see A6,30–31; B13,31. I have discussed both of these stories at various points above. Other passages describe physical rewards

and punishments for action. One promises wealth for giving money to the poor and threatens poverty for not doing so (B14,34). Another describes a wealthy man whose fellows interpret this wealth as a sign of God's favor (A11,46). The numerical catalogue of "Seven kinds of punishment come to the world because of seven types of transgression" includes punishments such as "the sword" and exile (A38,113–15; B41,113–15; *Fathers* 5:8; Urbach, *Sages,* 438). Also, passages that describe substitutes for sacrifice present cosmic and social well-being as dependent upon such action (A4,18–21; B5,18–19). Schechter discusses the significance of physical/material punishments in his essay, "The Doctrine of Divine Retribution"; Schechter, *Studies in Judaism,* first series, 216–17.

55. See, for example, A7,35; A15,62; A16,64; A12,52. On "Gehenna," see Urbach, *Sages,* 4, 262, 282, 395, 407, 510, 613, 674, 692; also the many sources listed in Ginzberg, *Legends,* vol. 7, 177.

56. On mysticism in rabbinic literature generally, see, for example, Fishbane, *Kiss of God* and *Exegetical,* 56–72; note Fishbane's treatment of a passage from *Rabbi Nathan* describing a mysticism that does not draw upon the theology of reward and punishment but rather centers upon the internalization of virtues that are hypostasized as serving before the divine throne (A37,110 in *Exegetical,* 67–70); Moshe Idel, "Ancient Jewish Theurgy," in *Kabbalah: New Perspectives,* 156–72. Not all spiritual rewards described in *Rabbi Nathan* are mystical. *Rabbi Nathan B* lists several spiritual rewards such as strength, wisdom, and "calm of spirit" *(naḥat ruaḥ)* that describe a general sense of well-being and calm rather than an intense experience of divine presence. See B43,120; Saldarini, *Fathers According to Rabbi Nathan B,* 260 n.33 for a list of the sources; and Finkelstein, *Introduction,* 101–2, for an analysis of this section of *Rabbi Nathan B.* The phrase *naḥat ruaḥ* also appears in *Rabbi Nathan A,* not as a divine reward but as a worldly consequence of a humble household (A7,34). Other rewards of spiritual well-being include "pleasure of spirit" *(qorat ruaḥ)* in the world to come (B33,73); see also Kadushin, *Organic Thinking,* 88–89, 101. In an encyclopedia article on "Reward and Punishment," L. I. Rabinowitz cites a maxim of Ben Azzai, "The reward *[śakhar]* of a commandment (observed) is a commandment (observed). The reward of a transgression is a transgression" (A25,81; B33,72; *Fathers* 4:2) *(Encyclopedia Judaica,* vol. 14, 134–39). This epigram employs the terminology of reward and punishment *(śakhar)* to highlight the benefits and dangers of habituation: observance leads to more observance, and transgression to more transgression. Urbach also gives much attention to Ben Azzai's maxim in *Sages,* 249, 268–72, 349, 514.

57. For a discussion of this passage and its manuscript variants, see Finkelstein, *Introduction,* 41, 137. In B11,28, we find the expression "they were fit that the Holy Spirit would rest upon them."

58. Kadushin characterizes rabbinic spirituality generally as a "normal" mysticism that is experienced in daily events and activities (*Rabbinic Mind,* 194–272), and he analyzes the term Shekhinah as a significant concept for such mysticism (222–62).

59. On the parallel in *Fathers* 3:2, see Urbach, *Sages,* 42. A similar passage appears in B34,74; compare A8,36–37, which frames the reward not in terms of divine presence but through the language of accounting. According to another passage in *Rabbi Nathan A,* on the Sabbath the righteous may dine in the splendor of the Shekhinah (A1,5). On the expression, "splendor of the Shekhinah" *(ziv ha-shekhinah),* see Urbach, *Sages,* 44–46. Urbach devotes a full chapter to the Shekhinah. He summarizes, "The designation Shekhina connotes the personification and hypostasis of God's presence in the world, that is, of God's immanence" *(Sages,* 40; also 43, 47).

60. The passage appears as part of the commentary to an epigram of Hillel, "Be one of the students of Aaron. Love peace and pursue peace. Love all humans and bring them close to the Torah" (note my discussions in the introduction and chapter 2a concerning proximity or being "close" to the Torah). The editors of both *Rabbi Nathan A* and *Rabbi Nathan B* combine the first two elements of this maxim through stories of Aaron bringing peace among the Israelites. These stories culminate in accounts of how much the Israelites love him and ultimately weep at his funeral. A following series focuses on his honor at death, including being lamented by angels (A12,48–50; B24–25,48–51). The commentary then turns to Moses, stating that he wishes for such a death, and we read a number of accounts concerning him (A12,50–51; B25,50–52).

61. This follows the printed edition. Schechter omits the first occurrence of 1 Sam. 29, arguing that it is a scribal error (A50 n.23).

62. In B12,28, the kiss of God is promised as a reward for toil in the Torah; see also *b. B. Bat.* 17a; Fishbane, *Kiss of God,* especially 17–18. Concerning 1 Sam. 25:29, often the "bundle of the life" *(tzeror ha–ḥayyim)* is interpreted as a "treasure-house" *('otzar)* in which souls are stored. See for example, *Siphre Deut.* 344 (Finkelstein, *Sifre on Deuteronomy,* 401); *Eccles. Rab.* 3:21; Urbach, *Sages,* 238–42, and "Treasures Above," 117–24. On the "soul" in rabbinic literature, see Rubin, "The Sages' Conception of the Body and Soul." On the Throne of Glory, for the motif of seven measures or hypostases of God's virtues serving before it, see A37,110; Fishbane, *Exegetical,* 67–70 and generally 56–72. On the primordial nature of the throne, see *Gen. Rab.* 1:1 (Theodor and Albeck, *Bereshit Rabba,* 6–8; see notes for parallels); Urbach, *Sages,* 684. The Throne of Glory also appears in A26,82. For other sources, see *b. Shabb.* 152b; *b. Ḥag.* 12b–13a; *Sed. El. Rab.* 4 (Freidmann, *Seder Eliahu Rabba,* 18); Saldarini, *Fathers According to Rabbi Nathan B,* 150 n.18; Ginzberg, *Legends,* vol. 1, 10; vol. 5, 10–11 n.22. *Rabbi Nathan B* has a number of other mystical images. One passage speaks of the "light of the righteous" *('or ha-tzaddiqim)* (B37,95) and another asserts that the righteous may see God—some will see "the King" but not "the Face," and others will see both (B43,120).

63. The concepts of "this world" and/or "the world to come" appear on A1,7; A2,9; A5,25–26; A9,42; A12,50–56; A14,58; A15,62; A19,70; A25,79; A25,80; A26,82; A27,84; A28,85–86; A29,87; A36,108; A39,118; A40,119; A40,120; A41,133; B10,25–26; B12,29–30; B15,34–35; B18,40; B22,46–47; B25,51; B26,54; B27,54;

B27,56; B29,62; B31,66; B32,70–71; B33,72–73; B34,73; B34,76; B35,79–80; B35,87; B36,94; B37,98; B43,121; B45,125; B45,126; note also *'olam 'aḥer* on A5,25–26. One teaching emphasizes the significance of reward in the world to come through the motifs of a palace and an eschatological banquet for the righteous. Rabbi Yaakob states that this world is merely a foyer before the world to come, which is a banquet hall (B33,73; *Fathers* 4:16). In some cases, rabbis interpret a biblical verse by way of the binary opposition (A1,14; A12,53; A21,74; A25,79; B18,40; B39,66; B35,79–80; *Fathers* 6:9; see also the epigram and parable attributed to Rabbi Yehudah the Patriarch on A28,85–86). The commentary in *Rabbi Nathan* may also add "the world to come" to a maxim in *The Fathers* (compare A14,58 and *Fathers* 2:1,9; Goldin, *Studies in Midrash*, 68; also A27,84 with *Fathers* 2:9; Kister, *Studies*, 65). I analyze in detail one case of such an addition in chapter 3b (A5,25–26; B10,25–26). Urbach discusses the concepts in *Sages*, 4, 131, 249, 262, 268–72, 349, 445, 510, 514, 543, 649, 652–53, 672. Morton Smith points out with respect to tannaitic literature that rewards and punishments in the world to come are usually not specified (*Tannaitic Parallels*, 65). One passage in *Rabbi Nathan A* describes something like purgatory for people who are neither completely righteous nor completely wicked: those who are in between go to a place where they are "refined," or more literally, "smelted" *(metzarephin 'otam)* (see A41,133).

64. See my discussion earlier in this chapter of A39,118; also A39,119; B22,46–47; B42,116. Arthur Marmorstein claims that Rabbi Akiba was the first rabbi to emphasize this teaching in response to theodicy (*The Doctrine of Merits in Old Rabbinic Literature*, 186). Urbach discusses providence and theodicy in *Sages*, 268–72, 445.

65. The question of whether God responds to humans as individuals or as a group was present in ancient Israel, as can be seen in the difference between wisdom and Deuteronomic materials. The former focus on individual action and divine response, while the Deuteronomists emphasize the level of the nation (Weinfeld, *Deuteronomy and the Deuteronomic School*, 307). See also, for example, Ezek. 14:12–23. On Sodom, A12,52; A36,106; B30,64. On Israel, for God's response to cultic activities, see A4,18–25; A38,113–15; B5,18–25; B41,113–15. Regarding more general observance of God's will and commandments, see A34,100; A17,65–66. On rabbinic interpretations of Adam and Eve, see my discussions in chapters 1a and 2a concerning women as excluded from the scholastic community and concerning Adam's fence. *Rabbi Nathan* follows the biblical account in taking Adam's curses to bring human mortality and labor and Eve's curses to bring women's subordination to men and pain during childbearing. In *Rabbi Nathan A,* midrashic readings add women's menstruation, as well as rabbinic prescriptions for modest dress and isolation at home, to God's curses upon Eve. We see more attention in *Rabbi Nathan B* than in *Rabbi Nathan A* to the body as well as to differentiation of and hierarchy between the sexes. According to *Rabbi Nathan B*, Adam's curse not only concerns sweat in labor but also human defecation as well as bodily decay after death. Eve's curses account for specific ritual requirements expected of

women and even positions appropriate for sexual intercourse (see A1,4–7; B1,6–8; B8–9,22–25; B42,116–17; also *m. Shabb.* 2:6; *b. Shabb.* 32b and generally 31b–34a; Urbach, *Sages,* 437; Boyarin, *Carnal Israel,* 77–106; Fonrobert, *Menstrual Purity,* 29–37; Lapin, "Hegemony and Its Discontents"). The significance of the transgression in Eden appears elsewhere as well. In the story of Moses's death in *Rabbi Nathan B,* God tells Moses that he must die due to "the decree of [*gezerat-*]" Adam (B25,51). One etiological story concerning the human lifespan reverses the usual temporal direction of reward and punishment. Adam is rewarded by God for the righteous men that will, in the future, descend from him (B42,116). In some cases, particularly in material concerning the destruction of Jerusalem and the Second Temple in 70 CE, the suffering of Jews is strikingly *not* interpreted in terms of God's punishment for past sins (A4,22–25; A17,65–66; B6–7,19–22); on this point, see Schofer, "Protest or Pedagogy?"

66. Regarding the relation between individual and community, Rabbi Akiba states, "Anyone who clings to transgressors [*'oberey 'aberah*], even if he does not act according to their deeds, receives punishment [*pur'anut*] along with them. Anyone who clings to those who observe commandments [*'osey mitzvah*], even if he does not act according to their deeds, receives reward [*sakhar*] along with them" (A30,89). Rabbi Akiba thus emphasizes the influence of the group upon the individual. A more complex image of the individual being punished with or because of the group appears in a series of stories portraying Jerusalem after the Roman destruction of the temple. Here, the storytellers focus upon the suffering of one woman as illustrating or exemplifying the suffering of many Jews under Roman rule. In two of these narratives, a character interprets the suffering in terms of God's punishment for Israel, or the Jews (A17,65–66; one of these concerns the daughter of Nakdimon ben Gurion, and for this figure see also A6,30–32; B13,30–32). On the sage bringing merit to those surrounding him, an anonymous teaching speaks of one who "brings merit to [*mazkeh*] the multitudes" in contrast with one who "makes the multitudes sin [*mahati*]" (A40,120; B45,125; *Fathers* 5:18). Also, the commentary in *Rabbi Nathan B* to the instruction, "May your house be a meeting house for the sages," states that when the sages and their students enter a house, the entire household "is blessed because of their merit" (B11,27). More generally on the individual and the collective, see Urbach, *Sages,* 436.

67. The classic study of *sakhar* and *zekhut* is Arthur Marmorstein's, *Doctrine of Merits.* He argues that the term *sakhar* is linked with the school of Rabbi Ishmael (6–8, 11); this connection is not apparent in *Rabbi Nathan.* Both Urbach and Marmorstein attend to themes concerning merit in rabbinic literature that are not prominent in *Rabbi Nathan,* including the role of ancestral merit (particularly the merit of the patriarchs), the view that the living endow the dead with merit, and the view that merits can bring miracles (Marmorstein, *Doctrine of Merits;* Urbach, *Sages,* 113, 258, 265, 498–510).

68. This issue was also debated in ancient Israel. One example is the inner-biblical exegesis of the divine attributes, centered upon Exod. 34:6–7, as found in the Books of Jeremiah and Ezekiel. See Jer. 32:28–29; Ezek. 18:1–32; 33:12–20. Other relevant passages are Num. 14:17–18; Deut. 5:9–10, 7:9–10, 24:16; Fishbane, *Biblical Interpretation,* 337–45; Moshe Greenberg, *Ezekiel 1–20: A New Translation with Introduction and Commentary,* 334–47; also Ezek. 14:12–23. Interestingly, the prophetic motif of teeth being "set on edge" appears in *Rabbi Nathan B,* describing Adam's response to eating from the Tree of Knowledge of Good and Evil (B1,6).

69. Fishbane discusses interpretations of this maxim in early Hasidism. See "Action and Non-Action in Jewish Spirituality."

70. Schechter suggests omitting "in my lifetime" (A12,54 n.57), but Goldin retains it in his translation (Goldin, *Rabbi Nathan,* 69 and 190 n.34). Note also that the commentary employs a different prepositional phrase than the maxim: the maxim has *li,* the commentary *bi.*

71. This gloss may reflect a "midrashic" repointing of Hillel's statement, reading *keshe-'ani* ("when I am" for myself) as *keshe-'eyni* ("when I am not" for myself). See Goldin, *Rabbi Nathan,* 190 n.34.

72. For other variants of this passage, see Schechter's comments in *Rabbi Nathan,* 141, 143. The last part—the "another opinion"—was quoted and discussed earlier in this chapter as an example of technical terms drawn from legal language.

73. In his commentary to Ecclesiastes, Choon-Leong Seow writes, "The use of the dog as a metaphor for the living is ironic. Dogs were among the most despised creatures in the ancient Near East. . . . In contrast, the lion is the most admired of creatures. The irony is especially bitter, since dogs may have been associated with death and the underworld" (*Ecclesiastes,* 301).

74. This focus on merit implies a midrash to the following verse, Eccles. 9:5, which states that the dead have no more "recompense" (*sakhar*) because their memory has been forgotten. To rabbinic interpreters, this line may have suggested that the dead have no ability to gain "merit" (*sakhar/zekhut*).

75. See a similar view expressed in A12,53. Fränkel claims that this interpretation in terms of merit is implicit in the maxim itself (*Ways,* 396–97, 660 n.19). In *Rabbi Nathan B,* the teachings concerning merit transfer are more complex. On one hand, the parallel interpretation of Hillel's maxim, "If I am not for me . . ." is longer and more developed, and makes similar claims (B27,54). On the other hand, earlier in the text we find a teaching in the name of Rabbi Yose that responds to the challange of theodicy with an elaborate set of explanations in terms of transgenerational reward and punishment. He begins with a statement that captures the problem in the starkest possible terms: "A righteous one, and it goes well for him. A righteous one, and it goes badly for him. A wicked one, and it goes well for him. A wicked one, and it goes badly for him" (B22,46; see also B42,116; *Sed. El. Zuṭ.* 6; Friedmann, *Seder Eliahu,* 183; *b. Ber.* 7a; Schechter, *Studies in Judaism,* first series, 218–19; the Hebrew is far more elegant, capturing the issue in

merely twelve words). Rabbi Yose explains the situation through transfer of merit and demerit. For example, to take the problem of bad things happening to good people, "A righteous one, and it goes badly for him. This is a righteous one who is a son of a wicked one. His actions [*ma'aśav*] are good, but the actions [*ma'aśeh*] of his fathers are not good. His fathers did not merit [*zakhu*] him to eat in this world, and he merited [*zakhah*] himself to eat in the life of the world to come" (B22,46). Rabbi Yose employs a similar logic for the other three cases. Sons are punished for their fathers' transgressions in this world. However, if the sons earn merit, they can gain life and reward in the world to come. In contrast with passages in both *Rabbi Nathan A* and *Rabbi Nathan B* that deny merit transfer, here the wicked benefit from the merits of their fathers, and the righteous suffer for the bad deeds of past generations. Note also that Marmorstein collects a large number of rabbinic teachings that elaborate beliefs in transgenerational reward *(Doctrine of Merits).*

76. On "measure for measure," see Ishay Rosen-Zvi, "The Sin of Concealment of the Suspected Adultress" (Hebrew). See also *m. Soṭa* 1:7–9; Urbach, *Sages,* 438–40 and notes, especially 881 n.68; Kadushin, *The Theology of Seder Eliahu,* 177–78. I have learned a tremendous amount concerning these issues from Robert Yelle, who employs the categories "similarity" and "contiguity" in a comparison of legal punishment and sympathetic magic ("Rhetorics of Law and Ritual: A Semiotic Comparison of the Law of Talion and Sympathetic Magic"). I also draw upon Patrick D. Miller, *Sin and Judgment in the Prophets,* especially pages 1 on content and style, 105–10 on exact or "talionic" correspondence, and generally 111–19. On the biblical law of talion, a classic study is Bernard Jackson, "The Problem of Exodus 21:22–5 *(Ius Talionis),*" 75–107. Also see the discussions and references in Fishbane, *Biblical Interpretation,* 92–93 and notes; Urbach, *Sages,* 881 n.68.

77. Following Goldin, I translate the last word in accord with the Oxford manuscript (A55,69; Goldin, *Rabbi Nathan,* 190 n.45). Kister discusses all the variants in *Studies,* 125–26. B27,56 and *Fathers* 2:6 have "will be drowned" in place of "others will drown." In *Rabbi Nathan B* the character is Rabbi Yehoshua.

78. The anecdote (in colloquial Aramaic) makes no mention of God. It simply makes an observation about causality in the world, and the theology must be inferred. See Fränkel, *Ways,* 402–3, for a valuable analysis. The story has received much attention by both modern scholars and traditional commentators. See Goldin, *Studies in Midrash,* 4–6; Lieberman, *Hellenism in Jewish Palestine,* 137 n.87.

79. See also my survey of sage narratives in chapter 1b. A similar story appears on A8,36; B19,41–42; also note the parallel to the maxim and story on *b. Shabb.* 127b.

80. An example of punishment that has exact correspondence of both content and style is attributed to Elisha ben Abuyah in *Rabbi Nathan B.* He quotes God as saying, "My children, if you keep [*meshammerim*] the Torah, you keep [*meshammerim*] your lives. If you lose [*me'abbedim*] the Torah, you lose [*me'abbedim*] your life" (B35,77). The syntactic terms "just as . . . so . . ." *(keshem she- . . . kakh . . .)*

can convey correspondence in cases where divine reckoning is not explicit. For example, in the account of Rabbi Eliezer ben Hyrcanus's early career, the version of *Rabbi Nathan B* tells that at one point he fasted until the smell from his mouth offended his fellows. Later, when his teacher Rabban Yohanan ben Zakkai hears of his fasting, he says, "Just as [*kashem she-*] the smell of your mouth rose before me, so [*kakh*] the Mishnah of your mouth will go out from one end of the world to the other" (B13,31). The statement does not say whether Rabbi Eliezer's future success will be based on divine reckoning or worldly causes. However, Rabban Yohanan describes a correspondence that has elements of contiguity (the mouth is both the site of the odor and the source of the teaching) and similarity (the smell going up, the teaching going out).

81. This exegetical unit has been analyzed at length by Goldin, who writes, "For the editor of *R. Nathan A,* therefore, 'Akiba is not only an articulate advocate of the proposition that one should raise many disciples, . . . 'Akiba is in addition himself a splendid example of the consequences of Hillelite policy in practice" (Hillelite policy being that one should teach every man, not only those who are talented, meek, and wealthy) (Goldin, *Studies in Midrash,* 112 and generally 101–17).

82. There may be a correspondence of similarity if one presumes that the person digs the pit in order that something fall in or that he breaks the fence in order to injure someone else. Choon-Leong Seow, however, argues against interpreting the images as implying such intentions (*Ecclesiastes,* 316, 326; also see Fox, *A Time to Tear Down,* 304–5).

83. Note, though, that here the correspondence in content is not conveyed through similarity in language—the intention is that someone would "die," while the result is that "they will bury him during their lives." Another example of correspondence between intention and consequence can be seen in an account of God's punishment for the snake after the events in Eden (A1,5). On the topic of intention in rabbinic law, see Eilberg-Schwartz, *The Human Will in Judaism.*

84. On distraction from study, see A26,82; A29,81; B35,81. On arrogance, see A38,114–15; B41,114–15. I also have quoted in this chapter a passage in which malicious speech is held to be a greater sin than idolatry, incest, and murder. In another story, a man's early death is attributed to an apparently minor transgression of norms concerning his wife's menstrual impurity (A2,8–9; Schofer, "Protest or Pedagogy"). In yet another, Job's extreme suffering is said to come because, while he exemplifies great hospitality, he is nonetheless not as hospitable as Abraham (A7,33–34). See also the list of "Three who spoke the truth yet perished from life in this world and life of the world to come" (B45,125–26).

85. Wendy Doniger suggested to me this sense of a sage's fragility.

86. See *m. Pe'ah* 8:9; also *b. Kethub.* 68a.

87. Michael Fishbane pointed out to me this stylistic correspondence.

88. On *rahamim* and *din,* see A3,17; B38,100–101; also the similar distinction between "measure of goodness" *(middat ha-tob)* and "measure of retribution" *(middat pur'anut)* (A30, 89–90); God's compassion is implied in the teaching of

Rabbi Simeon ben Yohai in A16,64, discussed in chapter 2b. One statement asserting the inability of humans to understand God's working in the world, given the
"ease of the wicked," is on B33,73; *Fathers* 4:15. The claim that humans cannot
understand God's action, however, appears in dramatic and extensive form in
other Jewish texts. For example, *Seder Eliyahu Zuṭa* depicts Moses at Sinai, posing
the challenge of theodicy as, "A righteous one and things go well for him . . ."
While in *Rabbi Nathan* the problem is explained in terms of transgenerational
merit transfer (see B22,46), in *Seder Eliyahu Zuṭa* God's answer is "you cannot
stand upon My measures" *(la'amod 'al middotay). Sed. El. Zuṭ.* 6 (Friedmann,
Seder Eliahu, 183); also *b. Ber.* 7a.

3b. Motivation and Emotion

1. This unpredictability is most explicit in the deathbed scene of Rabban Yohanan ben Zakkai when he expresses his intense anxiety at the prospect of divine
judgment. He says, after emphasizing the momentous nature of God's judgment,
that, "He has two paths, one to the Garden of Eden, and one to Gehenna. I *do not
know* if He will sentence me to Gehenna or if He will have me enter the Garden of
Eden" (A25,79; emphasis added). A great founder of rabbinic Judaism, upon his
deathbed, does not know what his sentence will be, and in this uncertainty he
cries. The ordinary student should be all the more anxious. Fränkel emphasizes
this point in *Studies in the Spiritual World,* 52–56. For an explicit statement that
humans lack knowledge concerning divine judgment, see B32,70.

2. For a similar interpretation, see Moore's overview of motivation in relation
to divine reward and punishment. He also quotes and cites parallel themes in the
Gospels and in Jewish apocalyptic literature (*Judaism in the First Centuries,* vol. 2,
89–92). On the general topic of motivation before God, see also Büchler, *Sin and
Atonement,* 119–211.

3. The most common sense of *histakkel* is seeing or observation, but it can
have an intellectual and perhaps contemplative dimension. Marcus Jastrow translates the term as "to look at, observe, to reflect, to keep in mind." In the passages I
focus upon here, it has been rendered as "consider," "mark well," and "meditate
upon." I translate the imperative as "attend to." See Jastrow, *Dictionary,* 990;
Goldin, *Rabbi Nathan,* 236; Saldarini, *Fathers According to Rabbi Nathan B,* 189;
William G. Braude and Israel J. Kapstein, *Tanna Debe Eliyahu: The Lore of the
School of Elijah,* 375. Rubenstein translates *mistakkel* of *m. Ḥag.* 2:1 as "contem-
plate" and "look into" in *Talmudic Stories,* 100. A strange appearance of "meditate"
as a translation of *mistakkel* appears in Israel Abraham's translation of Urbach's discussion of *m. Ḥag. 2:1* in *Sages,* 193, 772 n.37. Urbach's Hebrew text does not convey this sense. He glosses *histakkelut* in terms of *hitbonnenut* (observation, consideration, reflection) and *yedi'ah* (knowledge), and then he cites the use of *histakkel*
in *Fathers* 3:1. See Ephraim Urbach, *The Sages* (Hebrew), 169 and 169 nn.36–37.
We have thus come full circle, where the scholarship cites for clarification the texts

we are trying to understand herein. On biblical meanings, see Michael Fox, *Proverbs 1–9*, 147. In *The Fathers* and *Rabbi Nathan,* we find teachings that advocate certain things or images that one should "attend to" *(mistakkel).* By contrast, Mishnah *Ḥagigah* lists certain forms of theological or metaphysical speculation that should *not* be the objects of *mistakkel* (*m. Ḥag.* 2:1). S. E. Loewenstamm has analyzed this passage and its variants. He suggests that in this passage, because of the use of the verb *d.r.sh.* at the opening, *mistakkel* refers not just to reflection or attention, but also to reading or expositing out loud. "On an Alleged Gnostic Element in Mishna *Ḥagiga* ii, 1" (Hebrew), 114 n.3 and generally 112–22. Urbach rejects this position (*Sages,* 772 n.37).

4. The phrasing varies, but the key elements are the verb "give" *(n.t.n.)* and the noun "heart" *(leb):* including, "give . . . to one's heart" *(noten 'el libbo),* "place . . . upon one's heart" *(noten 'al libbo),* and "give one's heart to . . ." *(noten libbo le-).* The heart, as discussed in part 2, is a seat of emotions and impulses, but it also has intellectual dimensions and can be rendered as "heart/mind."

5. For discussions of all these variants, and speculations concerning their influences upon each other and from historical context, see Finkelstein, *Introduction,* 64–70; Steinmetz, "Distancing and Bringing Near," 78–81 and throughout.

6. Goldin translates, "He who takes to heart four things will sin no more" (*Rabbi Nathan,* 93).

7. Saldarini translates, "Mark well four things and you will not fall into the clutches of sin" (*Fathers According to Rabbi Nathan B,* 189; he lists parallels in 189 n.15).

8. Herbert Danby translates, "Consider three things and thou wilt not fall into the hands of transgression" (*The Mishnah,* 449; also quoted in Goldin, *Rabbi Nathan,* 236).

9. This passage has received much scholarly attention. The claim that people go "to a place of darkness and gloom" does not appear in *The Fathers;* on this point and generally on the textual variations, see Finkelstein, *Introduction,* 53–55 and 64–67; in English, Saldarini, *Fathers According to Rabbi Nathan B,* 189 n.15. In addition to the appearances in *Rabbi Nathan A, Rabbi Nathan B,* and *The Fathers,* the teaching is quoted in *Lev. Rab.* 18:1 and *Eccles. Rab.* 12:1. A parallel to the material in A19,69–70 is in *Der. Er. Rab.* 3, though the maxim is in the name of Ben Azzai. In *Kalla Rab.* 6, the material of *Der. Er. Rab.* 3 appears as a "mishnah" to which there is a commentary.

10. On "worm and maggot," see Job 25:6 and Is. 14:11. Akabya ben Mahalalel's saying likely predates much of the other material in *Rabbi Nathan.* However, in the intertextual contexts of both *Rabbi Nathan* and *The Fathers,* the trope of "worms and maggots" carries extremely strong resonances of mortality, contingency, and the limits of corporeal existence. For example, the image is used as a reason for humility: "Rabbi Levitas of Jamnia says: Be very very humble of spirit, for the end of man is a worm and of humans a maggot" (B34,74; also *Fathers* 4:4). "Worm and maggot" also has more negative connotations. In one case, "worm

and maggot rule over him" describes one of the curses for Adam's transgression (B42,116–17). In another, a narrative about the destruction of Jerusalem, God speaks to Titus after Titus desecrates the Temple sanctuary. God insults Titus calling him, "Evil one. Stinking secretion. Dust, worm, and maggot" (B7,21). The trope is also used to contrast humans and God in B40,111. The image of worm and maggot is often coupled with a focus on semen, excrement, and sweat. See, in addition to the insult to Titus, A19,70; B42,116. On sweat and excrement as distinctive of human embodiment, see B34,74. While *Rabbi Nathan* contains teachings advocating care and honor of the body (such as in B30,66), the image of "worm and maggot" consistently invokes the body with negative evaluation, challenging people to move out of a concern with embodied existence toward a focus on the greatness of God; see Schofer, "The Beastly Body." On similar images in mystical sources, see Swartz, *Scholastic Magic,* 69, 166–70.

11. Urbach, *Sages,* 224–25. For a full study of anthropomorphic and other dualisms in rabbinic thought, see Rubin, "The Sages' Conception of the Body and Soul."

12. The commentary in *Rabbi Nathan A* focuses upon Akabya ben Mahalalel's characterization of human finitude, and we find various answers to the questions of where one comes from, where one goes, and what one will become. Finkelstein argues that the version of Akabya ben Mahalalel's maxim in *Rabbi Nathan A* is the earliest form. He holds that the other versions of the maxim (in B32,69 and *Fathers* 3:1), as well as the commentaries concerning the "four things," are attempts to insure that the saying does not conflict with rabbinic views concerning the afterlife (*Introduction,* 64–67). Saul Lieberman argues that one of these interpretations of the "four things"—that of Rabbi Simeon ben Eleazar—is a response to Gnostic views articulated in the Gospel of Thomas, 55 (see *Tosefta Ki-fshutah,* 1292–1293 to *t. Ḥag.* 2:5, 7; in English, Saul Lieberman, "How Much Greek in Jewish Palestine?," 136–37). Kister disagrees with Lieberman on this point (*Studies,* 107). In *Rabbi Nathan A,* after the material concerning the "four things," the commentators develop the theme of finitude through accounts of Rabbi Eliezer ben Hyrcanus upon his deathbed. This scene also teaches that one should attend to God's presence. Rabbi Eliezer's instruction to his students concludes, "At the time when you pray, know before whom you stand to pray, for through this thing you will merit life in the world to come" (A19,70; in the parallel of *Der. Er. Rab.* 3, the deathbed scene names Rabbi Eleazar ben Azariah not Rabbi Eliezer ben Hyrcanus). See also the passage in *Seder Eliyahu Zuṭa* that opens, "Upon three things a person must attend [*mistakkel/yistakkel*] every day." Here the focus of attention is everyday life—actions such as going to the bathroom, drawing blood, and standing over the dead (*Sed. El. Zuṭ.* 3; Friedmann, *Seder Eliahu,* 176). Braude and Kapstein translate, "There are three occasions that a man ought to meditate upon every day" (*Tanna Debe Eliyahu,* 375).

13. Saldarini translates *Rabbi Nathan B,* "Mark well three things and you will not fall into the clutches of sin" (*Fathers According to Rabbi Nathan B,* 191–92).

Danby translates *The Fathers* 2:1, "Consider three things" (Danby, *Mishnah,* 447; Goldin, *Rabbi Nathan,* 233). Finkelstein argues that this epigram is a shortened form of the one attributed to Akabya ben Mahalalel (*Introduction,* 66–67); Albeck makes a similar comment; Chanoch Albeck, *The Six Orders of the Mishnah,* vol. 4, 495. See also the discussion in Steinmetz, "Distancing and Bringing Near," 80–81.

14. See also *Gen. Rab.* 1:10 to Gen. 1:1 (Theodor and Albeck, *Bereshit Rabba,* 8– 9 and notes). Urbach points out that in some cases, *ma'alah* takes the place of the divine epithet *'elyon* (Most High) (*Sages,* 79).

15. These motifs appear in a number of places in the Bible. On God's eye and ear, see Pss. 34:7 and 94:9; Job 34:21; on the book, Mal. 3:16 and Dan. 7:10; also Albeck, *Mishnah,* vol. 4, 357; Saldarini, *Fathers According to Rabbi Nathan B,* 191 n.24. Recall also the "ledger" in the passage quoted at the opening of this chapter (A39,116–17); parallels to that epigram also contain the motif of a hand writing (B44,123; *Fathers* 3:16).

16. Later in the collection of teachings that follow the maxim of Akabya ben Mahalalel, the editors of *Rabbi Nathan B* place two other epigrams of Rabbi Yehudah the Patriarch. Neither of these specifies a distinct theological image—king, judge, or employer. Rather, they set out a correspondence between God and humans as willing beings. Both maxims prescribe intense focus on the divine will (*ratzon*) such that all of one's actions are in accord with God. The first maxim counsels orientation toward God's will, "Rabbi Yehudah the Patriarch says: Do His will as your will, so that He will do your will as His will. Cancel your will before His will so that He will cancel the will of others before your will" (B32,70; *Fathers* 2:4. The text is difficult; I follow the suggestions of Schechter in B32,71 and Saldarini, *Fathers According to Rabbi Nathan B,* 193. See also Tirosh-Samuelson, *Happiness in Premodern Judaism,* 121–23). Such orientation, though, is not the most radical form of service to God, for it maintains self-centeredness. The sage aligns his will with God's will, but he still can act according to his own will. A more stringent demand calls for orientation toward, yet separation from, the divine will. When one does God's will, recognizing that one does so *only* because it is God's will and not one's own, then one attains a truly God-centered consciousness. Such a position appears in the next teaching of Rabbi Yehudah the Patriarch, which begins, "If you have done His will as your will, you have not done His will as His will. If you have done His will not as your will, you have done His will as His will" (B32,71, again following Schechter's text; see B32,70 n.26 and Saldarini, *Fathers According to Rabbi Nathan B,* 193). This statement is the strongest prescription in *Rabbi Nathan* for a God-centered consciousness—the ideal that action should be centered upon God, not upon the desires, emotions, and motivations of the self-centered subject (see also Fishbane, "Action and Non-Action," 321). I examine another example of such "attempts to purify sanctioned actions from self-centeredness" later in this chapter in the maxim of Antigonus of Sokho (A5,25–26; B10,25–26; *Fathers* 1:3). For other passages prescribing that one do God's will, see A30,89; A41,133; B48,133. For a contemporary discussion of

whether it is a greater virtue to act well easily (as in "Do His will as your will") or through struggle (as in, "If you have done His will not as your will, . . ."), see Hursthouse, *On Virtue Ethics,* 91–107.

17. See the discussion of the names and sources in Finkelstein, *Introduction,* 53, 67–70, 73, 122–24, and Saldarini, *Fathers According to Rabbi Nathan B,* 186 n.39, 187 n.1. See also *Fathers* 3:5 and *Sed. El. Zuṭ.* 16 (Friedmann, *Seder Eliahu,* appendix, 2). Schechter quotes other parallel sources in *Rabbi Nathan,* 145.

18. Saldarini translates, "He who gives his heart to words of Torah" (*Fathers According to Rabbi Nathan B,* 187).

19. Perhaps implicit in this instruction is the metaphor discussed in chapter 2b that the heart is a container, which can be filled either with Torah or with other words, though this point would be strengthened if one were to place the words upon the heart (as in Rabbi Hananiah's maxim that follows) rather than give one's heart to Torah.

20. This follows the printed edition and most manuscripts. See A20,70 n.1; Finkelstein, *Introduction,* 122–24. Schechter follows MS E, which reads "many sinful desires" *(hirhurim harbeh)* (A20,70 n.1). Goldin does the same (*Rabbi Nathan,* 94). The phrase *hirhurey ḥereb* appears in a parallel source in *Sed. El. Zuṭ.* 16 (Friedmann, *Seder Eliahu,* supplement, 2–3; Friedmann discusses variants in n.10). Braude and Kapstein translate it as "anxiety about a war's threat to his life" (*Tanna Debe Eliyahu,* 429). Kadushin translates, "thoughts (i.e., fears) of the sword (i.e., government)" (*Organic Thinking,* 71).

21. Or, as Finkelstein suggests, "the wife of one's neighbor" *('eshet rea').* The pairing of *yetzer* and a wife also appears in A14,58; see also B29,59 and compare *Fathers* 2:9. For a talmudic example of this connection, see the prayer of Mar son of Ravina in *b. Ber.* 17a.

22. MSS N and R attribute this to Rabbi Nehuniah ben ha-Kanah. A parallel appears in *Seder Eliyahu Zuṭa.* It opens, "Rabbi Simeon ben Yohai said: Anyone who gives/places the words of Torah upon his heart [*kol ha-noten dibrey torah 'al libbo*] eliminates desires of transgression" (*Sed. El. Zuṭ.* 16; Friedmann, *Seder Eliahu,* supplement, 2). Braude and Kapstein translate, "He who takes words of Torah to heart is relieved of anxiety about his transgression" (*Tanna Debe Eliyahu,* 429).

23. Goldin translates "preoccupations" (*Rabbi Nathan,* 94–95). Jastrow suggests, generally, "thought, meditation, heated imagination, impure fancies" (*Dictionary,* 366). Philip J. Ivanhoe has helped me on this issue.

24. His phrasing collapses the common binary opposition between the words of Torah and meaningless words *(debarim beṭelim),* since the words of Torah are what "cancel" *(mebaṭṭelim)* wayward desire; on the opposition, see the opening section of my discussion in part 2 concerning Torah.

25. Such an experience is portrayed in the narrative of Rabban Yohanan ben Zakkai crying upon his deathbed. Adolf Büchler points out that in both the deathbed scene of Rabban Yohanan ben Zakkai and the maxim of Akabya ben

Mahahalel, the focus is upon God's power more than upon "the method of His judgment or punishment" (*Studies in Sin and Atonement,* 46). In the passage to which we now turn, this "method" is of central concern.

26. This maxim appears in the name of Nittai the ha-Arbeli in A9,38 and *Fathers* 1:6, and in the name of Yehoshua ben Perahiah in B16,35 (in B, both have the title of Rabbi). Regarding "distance yourself" *(harḥeq),* I discuss the motif of "distancing" *(r.ḥ.q.)* and its contrast with proximity as part of analyzing Torah and transgression in chapter 2a. On "befriend" *(titḥabber),* note that the root of this verb—*ḥ.b.r.*—is used as a technical term for fellowship among the students of the sages; see my discussion in chapter 1a on the scholastic community. The line may mean, "Do not make a *ḥaber* of the wicked." Modern scholars have translated the third element in a variety of ways. Examples include "And do not lose hope of the final reckoning" (Goldin, *Rabbi Nathan,* 58) and "And do not shrug off all thought of calamity" (Saldarini, *Fathers According to Rabbi Nathan B,* 116). Saldarini collects others (*Fathers According to Rabbi Nathan B,* 116 n.1). I follow Jastrow, *Dictionary,* 560.

27. For other examples of "Woe is me," see A12,48–49; A30,89; A32,93; B24,49–50.

28. The Hebrew term is *ha-maqom.* On this epithet for God, see Urbach, *Sages,* 66–79. He writes that the term, which literally means "place," is "used metonymically and refers to the God who reveals Himself in whatever place He wishes; this epithet thus expresses God's nearness" (72).

29. The righteous person would always assume that he has accumulated no merit, even if in fact he might have. He then maintains something analogous to a "fence" around his actions, insuring that "capital" remains for the world to come. See my discussion in chapter 2a on the image of the fence and A1–2,3–14; B1–3,3–14; *Fathers* 1:1.

30. On Antigonus's name and date, see Elias Bickerman, "Maxim of Antigonus."

31. Scholars have also debated whether *'al menat le-* should be rendered "for the sake of" or "on the condition of." See Bickerman, "Maxim of Antigonus," 270–89; Urbach, *Sages,* 402–4, 861 nn.21–23; also Goldin, *Rabbi Nathan,* 39; Saldarini, *Fathers According to Rabbi Nathan B,* 85; Büchler, *Studies in Sin and Atonement,* 156–57.

32. The metaphoric tension in the maxim is noted by Bickerman, who writes, "[W]e must remember that *ebed* means not only slave, but also subject, worshipper" ("Maxim of Antigonus," 279). J. Albert Harrill has examined conceptions of slavery in Greek philosophy and in Roman law, arguing that Roman law recognized a slave as having inner subjectivity and moral agency, and that an ideal slave could anticipate the master's wishes and take initiative to fulfill them. This picture may underlie the image of slave in the maxim. Harrill presents this account in "The Apostle Paul on the Slave Self." Also see Harrill, *The Manumission of Slaves*

in Early Christianity; Williams, *Paul's Metaphors,* 111–40; and volume 83/84 of the journal *Semeia* edited by Callahan, Horsley, and Smith, which is devoted entirely to the topic of slavery.

33. Fishbane sees this maxim as countering self-centeredness ("Action and Non-Action," 318–29). Bickerman interprets the passage in terms of theodicy: "you have to serve the Lord, even if he, like a heartless owner, refuses your *peras,* your daily bread." He also writes that "fear of Heaven," historically understood, means simply "piety" (and only later was interpreted in terms of contrasts between fear and love of God) ("Maxim of Antigonus," 280–82). I find Bickerman's historical reconstruction persuasive, but, as I am arguing herein, I do not believe that the passage is best interpreted in terms of theodicy. For other cases of "fear of Heaven," see A27,84–85; B34,76; Urbach, *Sages,* 66–79. An even stronger denial of self-interest is present in a variant of the maxim preserved in quotations, a *genizah* fragment, and B5,25. Antigonus is said to advise: "[B]e like slaves who serve the master *for the sake of not* ['*al menat she-lo*] receiving a reward" (Kister, *Studies,* 127 n.59, 156 n.195; Bickerman, "Maxim of Antigonus," 270 n.2). In this case, the person acts before God not only without expectation of divine response but also with active rejection of reward for right action. Action is purely and intentionally intrinsic. Bickerman claims that this reading could not be the original text ("Maxim of Antigonus," 289 n.76), but Kister disagrees concerning *Rabbi Nathan* based on manuscript evidence (*Studies,* 156 n.195). While the dominant trend in rabbinic exegesis is to soften the maxim, a number of later sources preserve this radical ethical ideal. Both Rabbenu Yonah and *Midrash Shemuel* on *Fathers* 1:3 quote and weigh the significance of both versions. The strongest statement upholding the rejection of self-interest in *Rabbi Nathan* is a maxim of Rabbi Yehudah the Patriarch, preserved in *Rabbi Nathan B* (B32,71), which I discussed in note 16 of this chapter.

34. *Rabbi Nathan B* has a more expansive addition, which has significant textual difficulties (B10,25–26; see Schechter's comments in B10,26 n.2; Saldarini, *Fathers According to Rabbi Nathan B,* 85; Kister, *Studies,* 128). As I discussed in note 63 of chapter 3a, these passages are not the only cases in which *Rabbi Nathan* adds "the world to come" to an epigram found in *Fathers.*

35. Bickerman states, "Antigonus speaks not of reward given to a free man but of food allocation to a slave." Then he adds in a footnote, "Note that in the paraphrase given in *Abot Rabbi Nathan* free workers are substituted for slaves of Antigonus' maxim and that . . . the term *sokar* (wages) is substituted for *peras*" ("Maxim of Antigonus," 279 especially n.38).

36. An additional shift may be imbedded in the difference between action "for the sake of" a response from God (as in the short form of the maxim), and action that occurs "so that" a divine response will occur. In the first case, a person would be motivated directly by the payment or food allowance, while in the second, the relation between result and motivation is more ambiguous (this point was suggested by a number of faculty members at Stanford University and at the University of Nebraska at Omaha, January and February 2000).

37. While the rabbis are not, by any means, proto-Kantians, the distinction between theoretical and practical standpoints is helpful here. From the standpoint of a person describing the world, the concept of "the world to come" implies theoretical claims about the nature of temporality and human life. But from the standpoint of a choosing agent, "the world to come" is a practical concept that shapes desire and motivation. On the language of "standpoints," see Christine M. Korsgaard, "Morality as Freedom," 23–48.

38. The commentary also includes a narrative concerning the Sadducees and the Boethusians that appears, with variations, in both *Rabbi Nathan A* and *Rabbi Nathan B*. This passage has received much scholarly attention. See Bickerman "Maxim of Antigonus," 289; Finkelstein, *Introduction*, 35–38; Kister, *Studies*, 32–34, 155–57, 269–70. The commentary in *Rabbi Nathan A* ends with this narrative. In *Rabbi Nathan B*, the commentary continues with the passages that I discuss here.

39. Shmuel Safrai links language and images in *Seder Eliyahu* with the ḥasidim ri'shonim (see *Temple and Mishnah*, vol. 2, 518–539, and my discussion and notes concerning the ḥasidim ri'shonim in chapter 1a). I follow Safrai's observations concerning thematic similarities but not his view that *Seder Eliyahu* was composed early in the classical rabbinic period.

40. *Sed. El. Rab.* 3–5/6 (Friedmann, *Seder Eliahu*, 14–31). See also the commentary in *Eccles. Rab.* to Eccles. 3:15, "What is, already was," which expresses a similar view and uses the terms "*mi-qetzat . . .* in this world."

41. Saldarini translates "the righteous receive only a partial reward" (*Fathers According to Rabbi Nathan B*, 87); see also Schechter's discussion in B10,26 n.6. I realize that I am skirting the complex issues concerning the relative dating of *Rabbi Nathan* and *Seder Eliyahu*. This passage in *Rabbi Nathan B* can very well be late in the development of the text, as it is not paralleled in *Rabbi Nathan A*. Moreover, *Sed. El. Rab.* may have a later final redaction but still preserve the terminology and belief to which *Rabbi Nathan B* refers. Braude presents a survey of the opinions concerning the dating of *Sed. El. Rab.* and *Sed. El. Zut.* (*Tanna Debe Eliyahu*, xv–xxiv; also Strack and Stemberger, *Introduction to the Talmud and Midrash*, 340–42).

42. On this phrase, see also *Siphre Deut.* 330 (Finkelstein, *Sifre on Deuteronomy*, 380) and Neh. 10:1.

43. The last line is also difficult, and I interpret it as a reversal or rejection of the view presented at the opening. One might expect that some of the reward for the righteous is present in this world. However, because of the greedy eyes of those who lack faith, God defers that very portion of reward (the part that would be present in this world), along with the rest, to the world to come. See also Schechter's comments in B10,26 n.6.

44. The general observations have been made and elaborated upon by a number of scholars, including Schechter, *Aspects*, 72; Büchler, *Studies in Sin and Atonement*, 119–211; and Urbach, *Sages*, 400–419. Note also Bickerman, "Maxim of Antigonus," 281–82. In *Rabbi Nathan*, love and fear are paralleled in A37,109;

A41,133; and B45,124. See also my discussions in chapter 1a and the opening of part 2 concerning "awe, fear, trembling, and shaking" as ideal modes of comportment; also A1,1; A6,27–28; B10,26; B11,28; Kister, *Studies,* 140–42; Finkelstein, *Introduction,* 29–35.

45. On the term "will" *(ratzon)* used for the will of God, see the teachings of Rabbi Yehudah the Patriarch in B32,71 and my discussion in note 16 of this chapter. See also A30,89; A41,133; B48,133.

46. This text is a seventeenth-century commentary to *Rabbi Nathan A* by Yom Tov ben Moses Tzahalon, who cites from *Rabbi Nathan B* (MS Halberstam: Oxford Bodleian, Neubauer 2635). Schechter quotes the passage in A5,26 n.10; see also Finkelstein, *Introduction,* 32–35; Saldarini, *Fathers According to Rabbi Nathan B,* 87–88 n.13.

47. The quotation in *Rabbi Nathan B* differs from the Masoretic text, which reads, "I fear the Lord, God of the Heavens" (Jonah 1:9).

48. Schechter comments that the passage is "strange" (B10,16–17 n.11) as does Büchler (*Studies in Sin and Atonement,* 159 n.2). Finkelstein attributes the emphasis on fear and awe to early Shammaitic editing of the text (*Introduction,* 32–35). Urbach calls the passage a "Baraita" and writes, "its strangeness is not sufficient ground for assigning to it a late date" (*Sages,* 403, also 861–62 n.24).

49. See Urbach, *Sages,* 400–419.

50. Also see *Mekh. of Rabbi Simeon ben Yohai* 20:6; *Num. Rab.* 22. Contrast the commentary in *Siphre Deut.* to Deut. 6:5, "You shall love the Lord your God . . ." (*Siphre Deut.* 32; Finkelstein, *Sifre on Deuteronomy,* 54). The midrash upon "you shall love" upholds love over fear.

51. For Finkelstein's argument, see *Introduction,* especially 18–39; also Saldarini, *Fathers According to Rabbi Nathan B,* 87–88 and nn.12–14. On the *ḥasidim ri'shonim,* see my discussion in chapter 1a and the studies cited there. On *y.r.'.* in the expression "fear of sin," see Hirshman, "Towards a Clarification of the Term 'Fear of Sin.'"

52. See Fishbane, *Kiss of God.*

3c. Rabbinic Theology: Conclusion

1. Michael Fox in particular has challenged and encouraged my thinking on this point.

2. Except for the figure of a king, there is little overlap between tropes of God's justice and those that appear in relation to Torah. Note, though, Hillel's comparison of himself to a donkey, discussed in chapter 3a, and the tropes of animal training discussed in chapter 2b.

3. Hadot's studies of spiritual exercises run through his works, including *Plotinus, or, The Simplicity of Vision; Philosophy as a Way of Life; Inner Citadel.* Key methodological statements appear in "Spiritual Exercises" and "Ancient Spiritual Exercises and Christian Philosophy," in *Philosophy as a Way of Life,* 81–144. An

important predecessor is Paul Rabbow, *Seelenführung: Methodik der Exerzitien in der Antike.*

4. Hadot, *Philosophy as a Way of Life,* 82–83, 107.

5. Ibid., 102.

6. Ibid., 83, 99, 183, 211.

7. For a different and very important approach to the intersection of rabbinic study and *askēsis,* see Satlow, "*Talmud Torah* and Rabbinic Asceticism."

8. While there are no parallels made between physical exercise and engagement with Torah or the commandments, a narrative of Hillel in *Rabbi Nathan B* asserts that going to the Roman baths fulfills a commandment (B30,66; citing Gen. 9:6, which states that God made humans in the divine image). I discuss this passage as well as other teachings in *Rabbi Nathan* concerning the body in "The Beastly Body." Regarding instructions for specific practices to be done at specific times, other texts such as *Derekh Eretz Zuṭa* and *Derekh Eretz Rabbah* set out guidelines for daily activities such as dining and using the toilet. These latter two texts, both in form and content, can be described as "manuals" for conduct in ways that *Rabbi Nathan* is not. On this characterization, see Sperber, "Manuals of Rabbinic Conduct."

9. Hadot, *Philosophy as a Way of Life,* 84, and generally 84–86.

10. Ibid., 87–88 (on physics), 89–93 (on Socratic dialogue), and 93–101 (on training for death).

11. In addition, while *Rabbi Nathan* does not contain dialogues similar to those of Plato, the exegesis of the epigrams often replicates a dialogue or classroom discussion in its own way. This is particularly clear in passages that comment upon a given epigram with the exegetical opening, "How so? This teaches that . . ." *(keytzad? melammed she-).* Such a format echoes a discussion in which a teaching is cited, then someone asks, "How so?" and then an answer is given. See also Goldin, "A Philosophical Session," in *Studies in Midrash,* 57–76, and my discussion of commentary in chapter 1b.

12. Marcus Aurelius, *Meditations,* 7:54; following the translation in Hadot, *Philosophy as a Way of Life,* 84, 132.

13. Hadot, *Philosophy as a Way of Life,* 132.

14. Saul Lieberman makes a similar point in comparing the maxim of Akabya ben Mahalalel with one of Seneca ("How Much Greek," 136 n.13). Urbach comments, in discussing the same maxim, "Concepts derived from foreign sources, and for which there is no Biblical authority, were bounded by the belief in reward and punishment and the postulate of free will" (*Sages,* 224).

15. Hadot, *Philosophy as a Way of Life,* 93–101.

16. On Rabban Yohanan ben Zakkai's emotions on his deathbed, see my discussion in chapter 3a as well as note 1 of chapter 3b; also Fränkel, *Studies in the Spiritual World,* 52–56. Another point of potentially fruitful comparison is that Hadot quotes exercises aiming for "the transformation of the will so that it becomes identified with the divine will" (*Philosophy as a Way of Life,* 136). Teachings

of Rabbi Yehudah the Patriarch, discussed above in note 16 to chapter 3b, call for such identification but are not centered on tropes of reward and punishment: "Do His will as your will, so that He will do your will as His will. Cancel your will before His will so that He will cancel the will of others before your will" (B32,70; *Fathers* 2:4).

17. Sara McClintock has helped me in refining this set of points. The specific image of shared discursive space comes from Schäfer, "Introduction," in Schäfer and Hezser, *The Talmud Yerushalmi and Graeco-Roman Culture,* vol. 1, 14–16 and generally 1–23; see also my discussion in chapter 1a concerning the contextualization of *Rabbi Nathan.* It may be worth exploring further the observation that most of the instructions for attention that I have examined generated a complex reception by the editorial stream of *Rabbi Nathan:* the maxim of Antigonus of Sokho for its strong rejection of self-interest; the maxim of Akabya ben Mahalalel for its conception of finitude; and perhaps also the sayings of Rabbi Nehuniah ben ha-Kanah and Rabbi Hananiah. Saul Lieberman and Elias Bickerman in particular have examined some of that material as evidence for Hellenistic influence upon the rabbis. I am not sure what to make of these observations, but they appear to link these "exercises" with doctrines that came to be on the margins of rabbinic thought and culture. See my discussion and notes in chapter 3b, and especially Bickerman, "Maxim of Antigonus"; Lieberman, *Tosefta Ki-fshutah,* 1292–93 to *t. Ḥag.* 2:5, 7; in English, "How Much Greek," 136–37; and Kister, *Studies,* 107.

Conclusion

1. This variety contrasts with modern scholarship, where these dynamics are often discussed through a narrow range of motifs, particularly those of bondsman/ servant/slave and lord/master. Such imagery appears only once in the instruction of *Rabbi Nathan*—in the maxim of Antigonus of Sokho—and the commentators explicitly soften it to portray a free servant before an employer. Note also that, while I have selected the sage, Torah, and God as the three most prominent clusters of concepts in *Rabbi Nathan* for analysis of its ethics, there are many others, including the body, purity, and the will. I examine the body in "The Beastly Body in Rabbinic Self-Formation." On purity, key works to consider in relation to rabbinic ethics are Klawans, *Impurity and Sin in Ancient Judaism,* and Fonrobert, *Menstrual Purity.* The category of "will" *(ratzon)* appears only a few times in *Rabbi Nathan.* See the teachings of Rabbi Yehudah the Partriarch in B32,70–71 and *Fathers* 2:4 and my discussion in note 16 to chapter 3b; also A30,89; A41,133; B48,133. Another important passage is attributed to Rabbi Akiba in *Fathers* 3:15 (note also that in one case, Goldin translates *da'ato shel adam* as "man's will"; see A39,116 and Goldin, *Rabbi Nathan,* 161). More generally, I realize at the end of this project that the broad issues of temporality and spatiality need to be addressed more directly for understanding both rabbinic ethics and ethics in general.

2. A next step in research can be comparative study centering upon the varieties of character formation through chosen subjection. Comparisons of ethical instruction in Roman late antiquity may help us characterize more fully the nature of rabbinic participation in Hellenistic culture and areas of possible contact between elites of the Eastern Empire. My analysis has drawn attention to points of similarity, including tropes of conquest and governance as well as spiritual exercises of attention. At the same time, rabbinic ethics differs greatly from that of philosophical schools, focusing on a particular tradition and deity and showing little explicit concern with reason, the will, and medical and therapeutic practices and metaphors. More generally, I have noted that processes of chosen subjection appear in religious traditions that are, in some respects at least, contiguous with Judaism—including Christianity, Islam, and Manichaeism. I believe that the notion of chosen subjection may also illuminate ethical outlooks in cultures far beyond this range (see Schofer, "Self, Subject, and Chosen Subjection").

3. Hirshman raises this issue in his discussion of rabbinic universalism, asking, "Is a person's ability to achieve divine status innate, encoded in creation? Or is it an acquired trait that needs to be renewed continuously through the study of Torah?" ("Rabbinic Universalism," 106).

4. One response is to say that early socialization is crucial for the creation of the good *yetzer*. This puts weight on dimensions of life that *Rabbi Nathan* does not discuss—childrearing and education. A second is to see the good *yetzer* as nascent and growing within the self from the beginning, though this is never stated in the text. A third is simply to say that the text offers no answer to this problem, but the rabbis are not unique in this way: for example, a similar problem appears for the Confucian thinker Xunzi. See Philip J. Ivanhoe, "Human Nature and Moral Understanding in the *Xunzi*," in Kline and Ivanhoe, *Virtue, Nature, and Moral Agency,* 243–46.

5. A person would already have to accept a rabbinic account of divine justice; if not, then the discourse would be ineffective.

6. Another problem concerning the unity of *Rabbi Nathan* is the relation between the concept of the "fence" and narratives of sages being "tested." Fences are ways of distancing oneself from transgression, while tests show highly cultivated figures surrounded by temptation. One could say that these two forms of instruction are complementary—the fence being a day-to-day strategy for bounding in desire and the tests as modeling correct behavior in exceptional situations. Such a connection, though, is never made in *Rabbi Nathan* itself.

7. One particular problem in considering different accounts of subject formation is characterizing the subtleties of the movement from outside to inside, and specifically identifying when the process ends or resolves. If the goal of chosen subjection is an expansion of the self through incorporation of that which is other, then we should attend to the specific point at which the other (an external rule or authority) becomes part of the self. When and how, if at all, does the subject

emerge fully as a choosing and independent agent? This shift can be framed in a number of ways, each with its own nuances: from self-control to full virtue, from continence to temperance, from superego to ego, from needing preservative virtues (such as will power and endurance) to being free of them. *Rabbi Nathan* does not offer a clear answer to this question, though the concern seems to be implied in the hierarchy of sage stories, in which a crucial difference is between the character of Rabbi Tzadok (struggling through the night to fill his heart with Torah and stave off temptation) and the tempered desires of Rabbi Akiba and Rabbi Eliezer. This problem is a central concern for Butler; see *Psychic Life*, 12–18 and throughout. Philip J. Ivanhoe has discussed the problem with me in conversation, not specifically in relation to rabbinic sources. See also my discussion of Xunzi's account of the sage's virtue in "Virtues in Xunzi's Thought," in Kline and Ivanhoe, *Virtue, Nature, and Moral Agency*, 81–82.

8. Also, the role of the self in its transformation likely involves a greater sense of agency than the tropes in *Rabbi Nathan* indicate. As I emphasized in the introduction and throughout, the interpretative procedures of rabbinic commentary reveal that rabbis received and developed both biblical and later traditions with a tremendous amount of innovation. While the text frames a student's formation through Torah in terms of strong imagery of subordination and internalization, it also conveys that participation in the tradition includes a significant dimension of creativity.

Bibliography

Manuscripts of *The Fathers According to Rabbi Nathan*

For a full description of all the textual witnesses to *Rabbi Nathan,* see Menahem Kister, *Studies in Avot de-Rabbi Nathan: Text, Redaction, and Interpretation* (Hebrew) (Jerusalem: The Hebrew University Department of Talmud, 1998), 225–37.

Rabbi Nathan A

MS O (Oxford): Oxford Bodleian, Neubauer 408.
MS N (New York): The Jewish Theological Seminary of America, Catalog Brommer, Rab. 25.
MS V (Vatican): Vatican 44; Schechter published this manuscript as "Appendix B to Version A" of his edition.
MS E (Epstein): This manuscript was lost in the Holocaust. Schechter made use of it in his edition and quotes from it in his notes.

Rabbi Nathan B

MS R (Romi): Vatican Assemani 303, folios 195–221; the basis of Schechter's edition.
MS P (Parma): Biblioteca Palatina in Parma; de Rossi 327.
MS H (Halberstam): Oxford Bodleian, Neubauer 2635; this seventeenth-century commentary on *Rabbi Nathan A* by Yom Tov ben Moses Tzahalon cites extensively from Version B.
MS N (Neve Shalom): Solomon Taussig, *Neweh Shalom I* (Munich: 1872).

Books and Articles

Aaron, David. *Biblical Ambiguities.* Leiden: Brill, 2001.
Abrahams, Israel. *Hebrew Ethical Wills.* New York: Jewish Publication Society, 1976.

Abrams, Judith Z. *The Women of the Talmud.* Northvale, NJ: J. Aronson, 1995.

Abramson, Shraga. "Four Topics in Midrash *Halakhah.*" *Sinai* 74 (1973): 1–7.

———. "From the Language of the Sages." *Leshonenu* 19 (1953–54): 61–71.

Adler, Cyrus, et al., ed. *The Jewish Encyclopedia.* New York: Funk and Wagnalls.

Agnon, S. Y. *Present at Sinai.* Philadelphia: Jewish Publication Society, 1995.

Albeck, Chanoch. *The Six Orders of the Mishnah.* 6 volumes. Jerusalem: Musad Bialek, 1988.

Alexander, Elizabeth Shanks. "Art, Argument and Ambiguity in the Talmud: Conflicting Conceptions of the Evil Impulse in *b. Sukkah* 51b–52a." *Hebrew Union College Annual* 73 (2003): 97–132.

———. "Casuistic Elements in Mishnaic Law: Examples from Mishnah *Shevu'ot.*" *Jewish Studies Quarterly* 10, no. 3 (2003): 189–243.

Althusser, Louis. "Ideology and Ideological State Apparatuses (Notes Towards an Investigation)." In *Lenin and Philosophy and Other Essays.* Translated by Ben Brewster. New York: Monthly Review Press, 1971.

Aristotle. *Nicomachean Ethics.* Translated by Terence Irwin. Indianapolis: Hackett Publishing Company, 1985.

Asad, Talal. *Genealogies of Religion: Discipline and Reasons of Power in Christianity and Islam.* Baltimore, MD: Johns Hopkins University Press, 1993.

Baskin, Judith. *Midrashic Women: Formations of the Feminine in Rabbinic Literature.* Hanover, NH: Brandeis University Press, 2002.

BeDuhn, Jason David. *The Manichaean Body in Discipline and Ritual.* Baltimore, MD: Johns Hopkins University Press, 2000.

Benveniste, Emile. *Problems in General Linguistics.* Translated by Mary Elizabeth Meek. Coral Gables, FL: University of Miami Press, 1971.

Bettelheim, Bruno. *Freud and Man's Soul.* New York: Random House, 1982.

Bickerman, Elias. "La Chaîne de la Tradition Pharisienne." *Revue Biblique* 60 (1952). Reprinted in *Studies in Jewish and Christian History.* Vol. 2. Leiden: E. J. Brill, 1980.

———. "The Maxim of Antigonus of Socho." *Harvard Theological Review* 44 (1951): 153–65.

———. *Studies in Jewish Christian History.* Vol. 2. Leiden: E. J. Brill, 1980.

Birnbaum, Philip. *Daily Prayerbook.* New York: Hebrew Publishing Company, 1995.

Black, Max. *Models and Metaphors.* Ithaca, NY: Cornell University Press, 1962.

Borges, Jorge Luis. *Ficciones.* New York: Alfred A. Knopf, 1993.

Borowitz, Eugene B., and Frances W. Schwartz. *The Jewish Moral Virtues.* Philadelphia: Jewish Publication Society, 1999.

Boström, Lennart. *The God of the Sages.* Stockholm: Almqvist and Wiksell International, 1990.

Bourdieu, Pierre. *The Logic of Practice.* Translated by Richard Nice. Stanford, CA: Stanford University Press, 1990.

Bowersock, G. W., et al., eds. *Late Antiquity: A Guide to the Postclassical World.* Cambridge, MA: Harvard University Press, 1999.

Boyarin, Daniel. *Carnal Israel.* Berkeley: University of California Press, 1993.

———. *Dying for God: Martyrdom and the Making of Christianity and Judaism.* Stanford, CA: Stanford University Press, 1999.

———. *Intertextuality and the Reading of Midrash.* Bloomington: Indiana University Press, 1990.

———. "Masada or Yavneh? Gender and the Arts of Jewish Resistance." In *Jews and Other Differences: The New Jewish Cultural Studies.* Edited by J. Boyarin and D. Boyarin. Minneapolis: University of Minnesota Press, 1997.

———. "On the Status of the Tannaitic Midrashim." *Journal of the American Oriental Society* 112, no. 3 (1992): 455–65.

———. *A Radical Jew: Paul and the Politics of Identity.* Berkeley: University of California Press, 1994.

———. *Unheroic Conduct: The Rise of Heterosexuality and the Invention of the Jewish Man.* Berkeley: University of California Press, 1997.

Brakke, David. *Athanasius and Asceticism.* Baltimore, MD: Johns Hopkins University Press, 1998.

Brakke, David, Michael Satlow, and Steven Weitzmann. *Self-Revelations: Religion and the Self in Antiquity.* Bloomington, IN: Indiana University Press, forthcoming.

Braude, William G., and Israel J. Kapstein. *Tanna Debe Eliyahu: The Lore of the School of Elijah.* Philadelphia: Jewish Publication Society, 1981.

Braudel, Fernand. *On History.* Translated by Sarah Matthews. Chicago: University of Chicago Press, 1980.

Bregman, Mark. "An Early Fragment of *Avot de Rabbi Natan* from a Scroll." *Tarbiz* 52 (1982–83): 201–22.

———. "Introduction." In *The Four Who Entered Paradise.* Edited by H. Schwartz. London: Jason Aronson Inc., 1995.

———. "Pseudepigraphy in Rabbinic Literature." In *Pseudepigraphic Perspectives: The Apocrypha and Pseudepigrapha in Light of the Dead Sea Scrolls.* Edited by E. Chazon and M. Stone. Leiden: Brill, 1999.

Brettler, Marc. *God Is King: Understanding an Israelite Metaphor.* Sheffield: Sheffield Academic Press, 1989.

Brody, Robert. *The Geonim of Babylonia and the Shaping of Medieval Jewish Culture.* New Haven, CT: Yale University Press, 1998.

Brooten, Bernadette J. *Women Leaders of the Ancient Synagogue: Inscriptional Evidence and Background Issues.* Chico, CA: Scholars Press, 1982.

Brown, Francis, et al. *The Brown-Driver-Briggs Hebrew and English Lexicon.* Peabody, MA: Hendrickson Publishers, 2000.

Brown, Peter. "Bodies and Minds: Sexuality and Renunciation in Early Christianity." In *Before Sexuality: The Construction of Erotic Experience in the Ancient*

World. Edited by D. M. Halperin, J. J. Winkler, and F. I. Zeitlin. Princeton, NJ: Princeton University Press, 1990.

———. *The Body and Society: Men, Women, and Sexual Renunciation in Early Christianity*. New York: Columbia University Press, 1988.

Buber, Martin. *I and Thou*. Translated by Walter Kaufman. New York: Charles Scribner's Sons, 1970.

———. *Kingship of God*. Translated by Richard Scheimann. New York: Harper and Row, 1967.

Buber, Solomon. *Midrash Psalms*. Jerusalem, 1977.

Büchler, Adolph. *Studies in Sin and Atonement in the Rabbinic Literature of the First Century*. New York: Ktav Publishing House, 1967.

Burrus, Virginia. *"Begotten, Not Made": Conceiving Manhood in Late Antiquity*. Stanford, CA: Stanford University Press, 2000.

Butler, Judith P. *The Psychic Life of Power: Theories in Subjection*. Stanford, CA: Stanford University Press, 1997.

Cabezón, José Ignacio. *Buddhism and Language: A Study of Indo-Tibetan Scholasticism*. Edited by F. Reynolds and D. Tracy. Albany: State University of New York Press, 1994.

———, ed. *Scholasticism: Cross-Cultural and Comparative Perspectives*. Albany: State University of New York Press, 1998.

Callahan, Allen Dwight, Richard A. Horsley, and Abraham Smith, eds. "Slavery in Text and Interpretation." *Semeia* 83–84 (1998).

Carrithers, Michael, Steven Collins, and Steven Lukes, eds. *The Category of the Person: Anthropology, Philosophy, History*. Cambridge: Cambridge University Press, 1985.

Cassuto, Umberto. *A Commentary on the Book of Exodus*. Jerusalem: Magnes Press, 1983.

Coakley, Sarah. *Power and Submissions: Spirituality, Philosophy, and Gender*. Oxford: Blackwell Publishers, 2002.

Cohen, Aryeh. *Rereading Talmud: Gender, Law, and the Poetics of Sugyot*. Atlanta: Scholars Press, 1998.

Cohen, Jeremy. *"Be Fertile and Increase, Fill the Earth and Master It."* Ithaca, NY: Cornell University Press, 1989.

Cohen, Norman. "Leviticus Rabbah, Parashah 3: An Example of a Classic Rabbinic Homily." *Jewish Quarterly Review* 72 (1981): 18–31.

———. "Structure and Editing in the Homiletic Midrashim." *Association for Jewish Studies Review* 6 (1981): 1–20.

Cohen, Shaye. "Patriarchs and Scholars." *Proceedings of the American Academy for Jewish Research* 48 (1981): 57–85.

———, ed. *The Synoptic Problem in Rabbinic Literature*. Providence, RI: Brown Judaic Studies, 2000.

Cohen, Stuart. *The Three Crowns*. New York: Cambridge University Press, 1990.

Cohen-Stuart, G. H. *The Struggle in Man Between Good and Evil.* Kampen: Uitge-versmaatschappij J. H. Kok, 1984.

Collins, Steven. *Selfless Persons.* Cambridge: Cambridge University Press, 1982.

———. "What Are Buddhists *Doing* When They Deny the Self?" In *Religion and Practical Reason.* Edited by Frank Reynolds and David Tracy. Albany: State University of New York Press, 1994.

Cook, Johann. "Towards the Dating of the Tradition 'The Torah as a Surrounding Fence.'" *Journal of Northwest Semitic Studies* 24, no. 2 (1998): 25–34.

Coshdan, Eli. *'Aboth d'Rabbi Nathan.* In *The Minor Tractates.* Edited by Abraham Cohen. London: Soncino Press, 1984.

Crisp, Roger, and Michael Slote, eds. *Virtue Ethics.* New York: Oxford University Press, 1998.

Dan, Joseph. *Hebrew Ethical and Homiletical Literature.* Jerusalem: Keter Publishing House, 1975.

Danby, Herbert. *The Mishnah.* London: Oxford University Press, 1974.

Daube, David. "Rabbinic Methods of Interpretation and Hellenistic Rhetoric." *Hebrew Union College Annual* 22 (1949): 239–64.

Davidson, Arnold. "Archaeology, Genealogy, Ethics." In *Foucault: A Critical Reader.* Edited by D. C. Hoy. New York: Basil Blackwell, 1986.

———. "Ethics as Ascetics: Foucault, the History of Ethics, and Ancient Thought." In *Foucault and the Writing of History.* Edited by J. Goldstein. Cambridge, MA: Basil Blackwell, 1994.

Deleuze, Gilles. *Foucault.* Translated by Seán Hand. Minneapolis: University of Minnesota Press, 1988.

Deutsch, Eliot S. "Karma as a 'Convenient Fiction' in the *Advaita Vedānta.*" *Philosophy East and West* 15, no. 1 (1965): 3–12.

Diamond, Eliezer. *Holy Men and Hunger Artists.* New York: Oxford University Press, 2004.

Dorff, Elliot N., and Louis E. Newman, eds. *Contemporary Jewish Ethics and Morality: A Reader.* New York: Oxford University Press, 1995.

Eco, Umberto. *The Name of the Rose.* Translated by William Weaver. New York: Random House, 1983.

Eilberg-Schwartz, Howard. *The Human Will in Judaism: The Mishnah's Philosophy of Intention.* Atlanta: Scholars Press, 1986.

———. *The Savage in Judaism: An Anthropology of Israelite Religion and Ancient Judaism.* Indianapolis: Indiana University Press, 1990.

Fernandez, James W., ed. *Beyond Metaphor: The Theory of Tropes in Anthropology.* Stanford, CA: Stanford University Press, 1991.

———, ed. *Persuasions and Performances: The Play of Tropes in Culture.* Bloomington: Indiana University Press, 1986.

Fine, Steven. *This Holy Place: On the Sanctity of the Synagogue during the Greco-Roman Period.* Notre Dame, IN: University of Notre Dame Press, 1997.

Finkelstein, Louis. *Akiba: Scholar, Saint, and Martyr.* New York: Atheneum, 1975.

———. *Introduction to the Treatises Abot and Abot of Rabbi Nathan.* New York: Jewish Theological Seminary, 1950.

———. "Introductory Study to *Pirke Abot.*" *Journal of Biblical Literature* 57 (1938): 13–50.

———. "The Maxim of the *Anshe Keneset Ha-Gedolah,*" *Journal of Biblical Literature* 59 (1940): 455–69.

———, ed. *Sifre on Deuteronomy.* New York: Jewish Theological Seminary, 1993.

Fisch, Menachem. *Rational Rabbis: Science and Talmudic Culture.* Indianapolis: Indiana University Press, 1997.

Fischel, Henry. *Rabbinic Literature and Greco-Roman Philosophy.* Leiden: E. J. Brill, 1973.

———. "Story and History." In *Essays in Greco-Roman and Related Talmudic Literature.* Edited by H. Fischel. New York: Ktav Publishing House, 1977.

Fishbane, Michael. "Action and Non-Action in Jewish Spirituality." *Judaism* 33, no. 3 (1984): 318–29.

———. *Biblical Interpretation in Ancient Israel.* New York: Clarendon Press, 1985.

———. *Biblical Myth and Rabbinic Mythmaking.* Oxford: Oxford University Press, 2003.

———. *The Exegetical Imagination: On Jewish Thought and Theology.* Cambridge, MA: Harvard University Press, 1998.

——— *The Garments of Torah: Essays in Biblical Hermeneutics.* Bloomington: Indiana University Press, 1989.

———. *The Kiss of God: Spiritual and Mystical Death in Judaism.* Seattle: University of Washington Press, 1994.

———. "Torah." In *Encyclopedia Miqra'it.* Jerusalem: Bialik Institute, 1982.

———. "The Well of Living Water: A Biblical Motif and Its Ancient Transformations." In *Sha'arei Talmon.* Edited by M. Fishbane and E. Tov. Winona Lake, IN: Eisenbrauns, 1992.

Flusser, David. *Judaism and the Origins of Christianity.* Jerusalem: Magnes Press, 1988.

———. "Which Is the Right Way that a Man Should Choose for Himself?" *Tarbiz* 60, no. 2 (1991): 163–78.

Flusser, David, and Shmuel Safrai. "The Essene Doctrine of Hypostasis and Rabbi Meir." In *Judaism and the Origins of Christianity.* Edited by D. Flusser. Jerusalem: Magnes Press, 1988.

Fonrobert, Charlotte. *Menstrual Purity: Rabbinic and Christian Reconstructions of Biblical Gender.* Stanford, CA: Stanford University Press, 2000.

Foucault, Michel. *The Archaeology of Knowledge and The Discourse on Language.* Translated by A. M. Sheridan Smith. New York: Pantheon Books, 1972.

———. *The Care of the Self.* Translated by Robert Hurley. New York: Random House, 1986.

———. *Discipline and Punish: The Birth of the Prison.* Translated by Alan Sheridan. New York: Random House, 1977.

———. *Dits et Écrits: 1954–1988.* Paris: Editions Gallimard, 1994.

———. *The History of Sexuality: Part 1, An Introduction.* Translated by Robert Hurley. New York: Random House, 1978.

———. *The Order of Things: An Archaeology of the Human Sciences.* New York: Random House, 1970.

———. *The Use of Pleasure.* Translated by Robert Hurley. New York: Random House, 1985.

———. "What Is an Author?" Translated by Josué Harari. In *The Foucault Reader.* Edited by P. Rabinow. New York: Pantheon Books, 1984.

Fox, Marvin, ed. *Modern Jewish Ethics: Theory and Practice.* Columbus: Ohio State University Press, 1975.

Fox, Michael. *Proverbs 1–9: A New Translation with Introduction and Commentary.* New York: Doubleday, 2000.

———. *A Time to Tear Down and a Time to Build Up: A Rereading of Ecclesiastes.* Grand Rapids, MI: William B. Eerdmans Publishing Company, 1999.

Fraade, Steven D. *From Tradition to Commentary: Torah and Its Interpretation in the Midrash Sifre to Deuteronomy.* Albany: State University of New York Press, 1991.

———. "Rabbinic Views on the Practice of Targum and Multilingualism in the Jewish Galilee of the Third-Sixth Centuries." In *The Galilee in Late Antiquity.* Edited by Lee I. Levine. New York and Jerusalem: Jewish Theological Seminary, 1992.

Fränkel, Yonah. *Studies in the Spiritual World of the Sages.* Tel Aviv: Hakibbutz Hameuchad Publishing House, 1981.

———. *The Ways of the Aggadah and Midrash.* Israel: Hotz'et Yad Le-Talmud, 1991.

Freud, Sigmund. "Dissection of the Psychical Personality." In *New Introductory Lectures in Psychoanalysis.* Translated by James Strachey. New York: W. W. Norton and Co., 1964.

Friedmann, Meir. *Pesiqta Rabbati.* Vienna, 1880.

———. *Seder Eliahu Rabba, Seder Eliahu Zuṭa, and Pseudo-Seder Eliahu Zuṭa.* Jerusalem: Wahrmann Books, 1969.

Gadamer, Hans-Georg. *Truth and Method.* Second edition. Translated by Joel Weinsheimer and Donald Marshall. New York: Crossroads, 1989.

Gerhardsson, Birger. *Memory and Manuscript: Oral Tradition and Written Transmission in Rabbinic Judaism and Early Christianity.* Translated by Eric Sharpe. Lund: Almqvist and Wiksells, 1961.

Gilath, Itzchak. *R. Eliezer ben Hyrcanus: A Scholar Outcast.* Jerusalem: Menahem Press, 1984.

———. *Studies in the Development of the Halakhah.* Jerusalem: Bar-Ilan University Press, 1992.

Ginzberg, Louis. *The Legends of the Jews.* 7 volumes. Translated by Henrietta Szold and Paul Radin. Philadelphia: Jewish Publication Society, 1909–38.

Gleason, Maude. *Making Men: Sophists and Self-Presentation in Ancient Rome.* Princeton, NJ: Princeton University Press, 1995.

Goldberg, Abraham. "Form-Analysis of Midrashic Literature as a Method of Description." *Journal of Jewish Studies* 36 (1988): 159–74.

Goldin, Judah. *The Fathers According to Rabbi Nathan.* New Haven, CT: Yale University Press, 1983.

———. "The First Chapter of *Abot de Rabbi Nathan.*" In *The Mordecai Kaplan Jubilee Volume.* New York: Jewish Theological Seminary, 1953.

———. "The Freedom and Restraint of Haggadah." In *Midrash and Literature.* Edited by G. Hartman and S. Budick. New Haven, CT: Yale University Press, 1986.

———. "Not by Means of an Angel and Not by Means of a Messenger." In *Religions in Antiquity: Essays in Memory of Erwin Randall Goodenough.* Edited by J. Neusner. Leiden: E. J. Brill, 1968.

———. "On Honi the Circle-Maker: A Demanding Prayer." *Harvard Theological Review* 56, no. 3 (1963): 233–37.

———. "Something Concerning the Study House of Rabban Yohanan ben Zakkai." In *The Harry Wolfson Jubilee Volume.* Jerusalem: Central Press, 1965.

———. *Studies in Midrash and Related Literature.* Edited by Barry L. Eichler, and Jeffrey H. Tigay. Philadelphia: Jewish Publication Society, 1988.

Goodblatt, David. "The Beruriah Traditions." *Journal of Jewish Studies* 26, no. 1 (1975): 68–85.

———. *Rabbinic Instruction in Sasanian Babylonia.* Leiden: E. J. Brill, 1975.

Goodman, Martin. *State and Society in Roman Galilee, AD 132–212.* Totowa, NJ: Rowman and Allanheld, 1983.

Goshen-Gottstein, Alon. *The Sinner and the Amnesiac: The Rabbinic Invention of Elisha ben Abuya and Eleazar ben Arach.* Stanford, CA: Stanford University Press, 2000.

Graham, Angus C. *Two Chinese Philosophers.* LaSalle, IL: Open Court Press, 1992.

Green, Arthur. *Keter: The Crown of God in Early Jewish Mysticism.* Princeton, NJ: Princeton University Press, 1997.

Green, William Scott. "Palestinian Holy Men: Charismatic Leadership and Rabbinic Tradition." In *Aufstieg und Niedergang der römischen Welt,* II:19:2. Edited by H. Temporini and W. Haase. New York: Walter de Gruyter, 1979.

———. "What's in a Name? The Problematic of Rabbinic Biography." In *Approaches to Ancient Judaism: Theory and Practice.* Edited by William Scott Green. Missoula, MT: Scholars Press, 1978.

Greenberg, Moshe. *Ezekiel 1–20: A New Translation with Introduction and Commentary.* New York: Doubleday, 1983.

Greenway, William. "Charles Taylor on Affirmation, Mutilation, and Theism: A Retrospective Reading of *Sources of the Self.*" *Journal of Religion* 80, no. 1 (2000): 23–40.

Hadot, Pierre. *The Inner Citadel: The Meditations of Marcus Aurelius.* Translated by Michael Chase. Cambridge, MA: Harvard University Press, 1998.

———. *Philosophy as a Way of Life: Spiritual Exercises from Socrates to Foucault.* Translated by Michael Chase. New York: Blackwell, 1995.

———. *Plotinus, or, The Simplicity of Vision.* Translated by Michael Chase. Chicago: University of Chicago Press, 1993.

Halbertal, Moshe, and Avishai Margalit. *Idolatry.* Translated by Naomi Goldblum. Cambridge, MA: Harvard University Press, 1992.

Halivni, David Weiss. *Midrash, Mishnah, and Gemara: The Jewish Predilection for Justified Law.* Cambridge, MA: Harvard University Press, 1986.

Harrill, J. Albert. "The Apostle Paul on the Slave Self." In *Self-Revelations: Religion and the Self in Antiquity.* Edited by D. Brakke, M. Satlow, and S. Weitzman. Bloomington: Indiana University Press, forthcoming.

———. *The Manumission of Slaves in Early Christianity.* Tübingen: J. C. B. Mohr, 1995.

Harvey, David. *Justice, Nature, and the Geography of Difference.* Oxford: Blackwell, 1996.

———. *Spaces of Hope.* Berkeley: Univerisity of California Press, 2000.

Harvey, Van. *Feuerbach and the Interpretation of Religion.* Cambridge: Cambridge University Press, 1995.

Hasan-Rokem, Galit. *The Web of Life: Folklore and Midrash in Rabbinic Literature.* Translated by Batya Stein. Stanford, CA: Stanford University Press, 2000.

Hayes, Christine. *Between the Babylonian and Palestinian Talmuds: Accounting for Halakhic Difference in Selected Sugyot from Tractate Avodah Zarah.* New York: Oxford University Press, 1997.

———. "Displaced Self-Perception: The Deployment of *Minim* and Romans in B. Sanhedrin 90b–91a." In *Religious and Ethnic Communities in Later Roman Palestine.* Edited by Hayim Lapin. Bethesda: University Press of Maryland, 1998.

Hegel, G. W. F. *Phenomenology of Spirit.* Translated by A. V. Miller. New York: Oxford University Press, 1977.

Heinemann, Joseph. *Prayer in the Talmud.* New York: Walter de Gruyter, 1977.

———. "The Proem in the Aggadic Midrashim." In *Scripta Hierosolymitana.* Vol. 22. *Studies in Aggadah and Folk Literature.* Edited by J. Heinemann and D. Noy. Jerusalem: Magnes Press, 1971.

Herr, Moshe David. "Dialogues Between Sages and Roman Dignitaries." In *Scripta Hierosolymitana.* Vol. 22. *Studies in Aggadah and Folk Literature.* Edited by J. Heinemann and D. Noy. Jerusalem: Magnes Press, 1971.

Hezser, Catherine. "Rabbis and Other Friends." In *The Talmud Yerushalmi and Graeco-Roman Culture,* vol. 2. Edited by Peter Schäfer and Catherine Hezser. Tübingen: Mohr Siebeck, 2000.

———. *The Social Structure of the Rabbinic Movement in Roman Palestine.* Tübingen: Mohr Siebeck, 1997.

Hirshman, Marc. "Rabbinic Universalism in the Second and Third Centuries." *Harvard Theological Review* 93, no. 2 (2000): 101–15.

——. *A Rivalry of Genius: Jewish and Christian Biblical Interpretation in Late Antiquity.* Translated by Batya Stein. Albany: State University of New York Press, 1996.

Hirshman, Menahem. "Towards a Clarification of the Term 'Fear of Sin.'" In *A Tribute to Sara: Studies in Jewish Philosophy and Kabbalah Presented to Professor Sara O. Heller Wilensky.* Edited by M. Idel, D. Dimant, and S. Rosenberg. Jerusalem: Magnes Press, 1994.

Hobsbawm, Eric J., and Terence O. Ranger, eds. *The Invention of Tradition.* New York: Cambridge University Press, 1992.

Hock, Ronald F., and Edward O'Neil. *The Chreia in Ancient Rhetoric, Volume I: The Progymnasmata.* Atlanta: Scholars Press, 1986.

Holtz, Avraham. *Rabbinic Thought: An Introduction to the Works of M. Kadushin.* Tel Aviv: Sifriath Poalim, 1978.

Hopkins, M. K. "The Age of Roman Girls at Marriage." *Population Studies* 18, no. 3 (1965): 309–27.

Horovitz, H. S., and I. A. Rabin. *Mechilta d'Rabbi Ishmael.* Jerusalem: Shalem Books, 1997.

Hoshen, Dalia. "The Fire Symbol in Talmudic-Aggadic Exegesis." Ph.D. thesis, Bar-Ilan University, 1989.

Hursthouse, Rosalind. *On Virtue Ethics.* New York: Oxford University Press, 1999.

Idel, Moshe. *Kabbalah: New Perspectives.* New Haven, CT: Yale University Press, 1988.

——. "Secrecy, Binah, and Derishah." In *Secrecy and Concealment: Studies in the History of Mediterranean and Near Eastern Religions.* Edited by H. Kippenberg and G. Stroumsa. New York: E. J. Brill, 1995.

Ilan, Tal. *Mine and Yours Are Hers: Retrieving Women's History from Rabbinic Literature.* Leiden: E. J. Brill, 1997.

Ivanhoe, Philip J. *Confucian Moral Self-Cultivation.* Revised second edition. Indianapolis: Hackett Publishing Co., 2000.

——. *Ethics in the Confucian Tradition: The Thought of Mencius and Wang Yang-ming.* Revised second edition. Indianapolis: Hackett Publishing Co., 2002.

Izmirlieva, Valentina. *The Christian Art of Listing: Naming God in Slavia Orthodoxa.* Ann Arbor: University of Michigan Dissertation Services, 1999.

Jackson, Bernard. "The Problem of Exodus 21:22–5 *(Ius Talionis)*." In *Essays in Jewish and Comparative Legal History.* Edited by B. Jackson. Leiden: Brill, 1975.

Jaffee, Martin. "The Oral-Cultural Context of the Talmud Yerushalmi: Greco-Roman Paideia, Discipleship, and the Concept of Oral Torah." In *Transmitting Jewish Traditions: Orality, Textuality, and Cultural Diffusion.* Edited by Y. Elman and I. Gershoni. New Haven, CT: Yale University Press, 2000.

——. "A Rabbinic Ontology of the Written and Spoken Word: On Discipleship, Transformative Knowledge, and the Living Texts of the Oral Torah." *Journal of the American Academy of Religion* 65, no. 3 (1997): 525–49.

———. *Torah in the Mouth: Writing and Oral Tradition in Palestinian Judaism 200 BCE–400 CE.* New York: Oxford University Press, 2001.

Jastrow, Marcus. *A Dictionary of the Targumim, The Talmud Babli and Yerushalmi, and the Midrashic Literature.* New York: The Judaica Press, 1992.

Kadushin, Max. "Introduction to Rabbinic Ethics." In *Yehezkel Kaufmann Jubilee Volume.* Edited by M. Haran. Jerusalem: Magnes Press, 1960.

———. *Organic Thinking: A Study in Rabbinic Thought.* New York: Jewish Theological Seminary, 1938.

———. *The Rabbinic Mind.* Second edition. New York: Blaisdell Publishing Company, 1965.

———. *The Theology of Seder Eliahu: A Study in Organic Thinking.* New York: Bloch Publishing Company, 1932.

Kagen, Zipporah. "Divergent Tendencies and Their Literary Moulding in the Aggadah." In *Scripta Hierosolymitana.* Vol. 22. *Studies in Aggadah and Folk Literature.* Edited by J. Heinemann and D. Noy. Jerusalem: Magnes Press, 1971.

Kalmin, Richard. *The Sage in Jewish Society of Late Antiquity.* New York: Routledge, 1999.

Kasulis, Thomas. "Philosophy as Metapraxis." In *Discourse and Practice.* Edited by F. Reynolds and D. Tracy. Albany: State University of New York Press, 1992.

Kemp, Anthony. *The Estrangement of the Past: A Study in the Origins of Modern Historical Consciousness.* New York: Oxford University Press, 1991.

Keyes, Charles F., and E. Valentine Daniel, eds. *Karma: An Anthropological Inquiry.* Berkeley: University of California Press, 1983.

Kimelman, Reuven. "*Birkat Ha-Minim* and the Lack of Evidence for an Anti-Christian Jewish Prayer in Late Antiquity." In *Jewish and Christian Self-Definition.* Vol. 2. Edited by E. P. Sanders, et al. London: SCM Press, 1981.

Kippenberg, Hans, et al., eds. *Concepts of Person in Religion and Thought.* New York: Mouton de Gruyter, 1990.

Kister, Menahem. "Introduction." In *Avoth de-Rabbi Nathan: Solomon Schechter Edition.* New York: Jewish Theological Seminary, 1997.

———. "Metamorphoses of Aggadic Traditions." *Tarbiz* 60, no. 2 (1991): 179–224.

———. *Studies in Avot de-Rabbi Nathan: Text, Redaction, and Interpretation.* Jerusalem: The Hebrew University Department of Talmud, 1998.

Kittel, Gerhard, ed. *Theological Dictionary of the New Testament.* Vol. 4. Translated by Geoffrey W. Bromiley. Grand Rapids, MI: William B. Eerdmans Publishing Company, 1967.

Klawans, Jonathan. *Impurity and Sin in Ancient Judaism.* New York: Oxford University Press, 2000.

Kline, Moshe. "The Art of Writing the Oral Tradition: Leo Strauss, the Maharal of Prague, and Rabbi Judah the Prince." *Torah, Mishnah, Kabbalah.* N.d. http://www.chaver.com/Articles/TheArt-H.HTM.

Kline, T. C., and Philip J. Ivanhoe, eds. *Virtue, Nature, and Moral Agency in the Xunzi.* Indianapolis: Hackett Publishing Company, 2000.

Koch, Klaus. "Gibt es ein Vergeltungsdogma im Alten Testament?" In *Um das Prinzip der Vergeltung in Religion und Recht des Alten Testaments.* Edited by K. Koch. Darmstadt: Wissenschaftliche Buchgesellschaft, 1972.

———. "Is There a Doctrine of Retribution in the Old Testament?" In *Theodicy in the Old Testament.* Edited by James Crenshaw. Translated by Thomas H. Trapp. Philadelphia: Fortress Press, 1983.

Kojève, Alexandre. *Introduction to the Reading of Hegel.* Translated by James Nichols. Ithaca, NY: Cornell University Press, 1969.

Koltun-Fromm, Naomi. "Zippora's Complaint: Moses Is Not Conscientious in the Deed! Exegetical Traditions of Moses' Celibacy." In *The Ways That Never Parted: Jews and Christians in Late Antiquity and the Early Middle Ages.* Edited by Adam H. Becker and Annette Yoshiko Reed. Tübingen: Mohr Siebeck, 2003.

Korsgaard, Christine M. "Morality as Freedom." In *Kant's Practical Philosophy Reconsidered.* Edited by Yirmiyahu Yovel. Boston: Kluwar Academic Publishers, 1989.

Kraemer, David. *Responses to Suffering in Classical Rabbinic Literature.* New York: Oxford University Press, 1995.

Krauss, Samuel. *The Jewish-Christian Controversy.* Vol. 1. Edited and revised by W. Horbury. Tübingen: Mohr Siebeck, 1995.

Kugel, James. *In Potiphar's House: The Interpretative Life of Biblical Texts.* Cambridge, MA: Harvard University Press, 1990.

LaCapra, Dominick. *Rethinking Intellectual History: Texts, Contexts, Language.* Ithaca, NY: Cornell University Press, 1983.

Lakoff, George. *Women, Fire, and Dangerous Things: What Categories Reveal about the Mind.* Chicago: University of Chicago Press, 1987.

Lakoff, George, and Mark Johnson. *Metaphors We Live By.* Chicago: University of Chicago Press, 1980.

Lapin, Hayim. "Hegemony and Its Discontents: Rabbis as a Late Antique Provincial Population." In *Jewish Culture and Civilization under the Christian Roman Empire.* Edited by R. Kalmin and S. Schwartz. Leuven: Peeters, 2002.

———. "Rabbis and Cities: Some Aspects of the Rabbinic Movement in its Graeco-Roman Environment." In *The Talmud Yerushalmi and Graeco-Roman Culture,* vol. 2. Edited by Peter Schäfer and Catherine Hezser. Tübingen: Mohr Siebeck, 2000.

Lau, D. C. *Mencius.* New York: Penguin Books, 1970.

Leiman, Shnayer Z. *The Canon and the Masorah of the Hebrew Bible.* New York: Ktav Publishing House, 1974.

———. *The Canonization of Hebrew Scripture: The Talmudic and Midrashic Evidence.* Hamden, CT: Archon Books, 1976.

Lerner, M. B. "The Tractate *Avot.*" In *The Literature of the Sages.* Edited by S. Safrai. Philadelphia: Fortress Press, 1987.

Levine, George, ed. *Constructions of the Self.* New Brunswick, NJ: Rutgers University Press, 1992.

Levine, Lee. "The Jewish Patriarch (Nasi) in Third Century Palestine." In *Aufstieg und Niedergang der römischen Welt,* II:19:2. Edited by H. Temporini and W. Haase. New York: Walter de Gruyter, 1979.

———. *The Rabbinic Class of Roman Palestine in Late Antiquity.* New York: Jewish Theological Seminary, 1989.

Lieberman, Saul. "The Discipline of the So-Called Dead Sea Manual of Discipline." *Journal of Biblical Literature* 71 (1952): 199–206.

———. *Greek in Jewish Palestine.* New York: Jewish Theological Seminary, 1994.

———. *Hellenism in Jewish Palestine.* New York: Jewish Theological Seminary, 1994.

———. "How Much Greek in Jewish Palestine?" In *Biblical and Other Studies.* Edited by Alexander Altman. Cambridge, MA: Harvard University Press, 1963.

———. "The Martyrs of Caesarea." *Annuaire de l'institute de philologie et d'histoire orientales et slaves* 7 (1939–44): 395–446.

———. "Notes on the First Chapter of Qoheleth Rabbah." In *Studies in Mysticism and Religion.* Edited by E. E. Urbach, R. J. Zwi Werblowski, and Ch. Wirszubski. Jerusalem: Magnus Press, 1967.

———. "Roman Legal Institutions in Early Rabbinics and in the Acta Martyrum." *Jewish Quarterly Review* 35 (1944): 1–57.

———. *Tosefta Ki-fshutah: A Comprehensive Commentary on the Tosefta.* New York: Jewish Theological Seminary, 1992.

Loewe, Raphael. "The 'Plain' Meaning of Scripture in Early Jewish Exegesis." *Annual of the Institute of Jewish Studies* 1 (1964): 140–85.

Loewenstamm, S. E. "On an Alleged Gnostic Element in Mishna Hagiga ii, 1." In *Yehezkel Kaufmann Jubilee Volume.* Edited by Menahem Haran. Jerusalem: Magnes Press, 1960.

Maass, Fritz. *Formgeschichte der Mischna: mit besonderer Berücksichtigung des Traktats Abot.* Berlin: Junker und Dünnhaupt Verlag, 1937.

Mach, Rudolph. *Der Zaddik in Talmud und Midrasch.* Leiden: E. J. Brill, 1957.

MacIntyre, Alasdair C. *After Virtue: A Study in Moral Theory.* Second edition. Notre Dame, IN: University of Notre Dame Press, 1984.

———. *Three Rival Versions of Moral Inquiry: Encyclopedia, Genealogy, and History.* Notre Dame, IN: University of Notre Dame Press, 1990.

———. *Whose Justice? Which Rationality?* Notre Dame, IN: University of Notre Dame Press, 1988.

Mahmood, Saba. "Feminist Theory, Embodiment, and the Docile Agent: Some Reflections on the Egyptian Islamic Revival." *Cultural Anthropology* 16, no. 2 (2001): 202–36.

———. *Women's Piety and Embodied Discipline: The Islamic Resurgence in Contemporary Egypt.* Ann Arbor: University of Michigan Dissertation Services, 1998.

Mandelbaum, Bernard. *Pesikta de Rav Kahana.* Second edition. New York: Jewish Theological Seminary, 1987.

Marcus, Ivan G. *Rituals of Childhood: Jewish Acculturation in Medieval Europe.* New Haven, CT: Yale University Press, 1996.

Margulies, Mordecai. *Midrash Wayyikra Rabbah.* New York: Jewish Theological Seminary, 1993.

Markus, R. A. *The End of Ancient Christianity.* New York: Cambridge University Press, 1990.

Marmorstein, Arthur. *The Doctrine of Merits in Old Rabbinic Literature.* London: Jews College Publications, 1920.

Marrou, H. I. *A History of Education in Antiquity.* Translated by George Lamb. New York: Sheed and Ward, 1956.

Martin, Luther H., Huck Gutman, and Patrick H. Hutton, eds. *Technologies of the Self: A Seminar with Michel Foucault.* Amherst: University of Massachusetts Press, 1988.

Mauss, Marcel. "A Category of the Human Mind: The Notion of Person; the Notion of Self," in *A Category of the Person: Anthropology, Philosophy, History.* Edited by Michael Carrithers, Steven Collins, and Steven Lukes. Cambridge: Cambridge University Press, 1985.

———. *Sociology and Anthropology.* Translated by Ben Brewster. Boston: Routledge, 1979.

McGinn, Bernard, ed. *Meister Eckhart and the Beguine Mystics.* New York: Continuum Publishing Company, 1994.

Miller, Patrick D. *Sin and Judgment in the Prophets: A Stylistic and Theological Analysis.* Chico, CA: Scholars Press, 1982.

Moore, George Foot. *Judaism in the First Centuries of the Christian Era.* 3 volumes. Peabody, MA: Hendrickson Publishers, 1997.

Muffs, Yochanan. *Love and Joy: Law, Language, and Religion in Ancient Israel.* New York: Jewish Theological Seminary, 1992.

Mullen, E. Theodore. *The Divine Council in Canaanite and Early Hebrew Literature.* Chico, CA: Scholars Press, 1980.

Nash, June. *Mayan Visions: The Quest for Autonomy in an Age of Globalization.* New York: Routledge, 2001.

Neusner, Jacob. *Development of a Legend: Studies of the Legends Concerning Yohanan ben Zakkai.* Leiden: E. J. Brill, 1970.

———. *Eliezer ben Hyrcanus: The Tradition and the Man.* Leiden: E. J. Brill, 1973.

———. *The Fathers According to Rabbi Nathan: An Analytical Translation and Explanation.* Atlanta: Scholars Press, 1986.

———. *Form-Analytical Comparison in Rabbinic Judaism: Structure and Form in The Fathers and The Fathers According to Rabbi Nathan.* Atlanta: Scholars Press, 1992.

———. *Judaism and Story.* Chicago: University of Chicago Press, 1992.

———. *A Life of Yohanan ben Zakkai.* Leiden: E. J. Brill, 1970

———. *The Wonder-Working Lawyers of Talmudic Babylonia.* New York: University Press of America, 1987.

Newman, Louis. *Past Imperatives: Studies in the History and Theory of Jewish Ethics.* Albany: State University of New York Press, 1998.

Nietzsche, Friedrich. *On the Genealogy of Morals and Ecce Homo.* Translated by Walter Kaufmann. New York: Random House, 1967.

Novak, David. *Natural Law in Judaism.* New York: Cambridge University Press, 1998.

Nussbaum, Martha. *The Therapy of Desire: Theory and Practice in Hellenistic Ethics.* Princeton, NJ: Princeton University Press, 1994.

Obeyesekere, Gannath. *Imagining Karma: Ethical Transformation in Amerindian, Buddhist, and Greek Rebirth.* Berkeley: University of California Press, 2002.

O'Flaherty, Wendy Doniger, ed. *Karma and Rebirth in Classical Indian Traditions.* Berkeley: University of California Press, 1980.

Pagels, Elaine. *Adam, Eve, and the Serpent.* New York: Random House, 1988.

Patai, Raphael. *Man and Temple in Ancient Jewish Myth and Ritual.* Second edition. New York: Ktav Publishing, 1967.

Pease, Donald. "Author." In *Critical Terms for Literary Study.* Second edition. Edited by Frank Lentricchia and Thomas McLaughlin. Chicago: University of Chicago Press, 1995.

Perkins, David. *Is Literary History Possible?* Baltimore, MD: Johns Hopkins University Press, 1992.

Plaskow, Judith. "Standing Again at Sinai: Jewish Memory from a Feminist Perspective." *Tikkun* 1, no. 2 (1986): 28–34.

———. *Standing Again at Sinai: Judaism from a Feminist Perspective.* San Francisco: Harper and Row, 1990.

Porter, F. C. "The *Yeçer Hara:* A Study in the Jewish Doctrine of Sin." In *Biblical and Semitic Studies: Yale Historical and Critical Contributions to Biblical Science.* Yale Bicentennial Publications. New York: Charles Scribner's Sons, 1901.

Preuss, Julius. *Biblical and Talmudic Medicine.* Translated by Fred Rosner. Northvale, NJ: Jason Aronsen, 1978.

Rabbow, Paul. *Seelenführung: Methodik der Exerzitien in der Antike.* Munich: Kösel-Verlag, 1954.

Rabinow, Paul, ed. *The Foucault Reader.* New York: Pantheon Books, 1984.

Rabinowitz, L. I. "Reward and Punishment." In *Encyclopedia Judaica.* Vol. 14. Jerusalem: Keter Publishing House, 1972.

Reames, Kent. "Metaphysics, History, and Rational Justification." *Journal of Religious Ethics* 27, no. 2 (1999): 257–81.

Reynolds, Frank, and David Tracy, eds. *Religion and Practical Reason: New Essays in the Comparative Philosophy of Religions.* Albany: State University of New York Press, 1994.

Ricoeur, Paul. *Hermeneutics and the Human Sciences.* Translated by John B. Thompson. Cambridge: Cambridge University Press, 1981.

———. *Interpretation Theory: Discourse and the Surplus of Meaning.* Fort Worth: Texas Christian University Press, 1976.

———. *Oneself as Another*. Translated by Kathleen Blamey. Chicago: University of Chicago Press, 1992.

———. *The Rule of Metaphor: Multi-Disciplinary Studies of the Creation of Meaning in Language*. Translated by Robert Czerny. Toronto: University of Toronto Press, 1977.

———. *Time and Narrative*. 3 volumes. Translated by Kathleen McLaughlin and David Pellauer. Chicago: University of Chicago Press, 1984, 1985, 1988.

Rosen-Zvi, Ishay. "Evil Desire and Sexuality: A Chapter in Talmudic Anthropology." *Theory and Criticism* 14 (1999): 55–84.

———. "The Sin of Concealment of the Suspected Adulteress." *Tarbiz* 70 (2001): 367–401.

Rubenstein, Jeffrey L. *The History of Sukkot in the Second Temple and Rabbinic Periods*. Atlanta: Scholars Press, 1995.

———. *Talmudic Stories: Narrative Art, Composition, and Culture*. Baltimore, MD: Johns Hopkins University Press, 1999.

Rubin, Nissan. "The Sages' Conception of the Body and Soul." In *Essays in the Social Scientific Study of Judaism and Jewish Society*. Edited by S. Fishbane and J. N. Lightstone. Montréal, Québec: Concordia University, 1990.

Safrai, Shmuel. *In Times of the Temple and Mishnah: Studies in Jewish History*. 2 volumes. Jerusalem: Magnes Press, 1996.

———. "Jesus and the Hasidim." *Jerusalem Perspective* 42–44 (1994): 1–22.

———. "Tales of the Sages in the Palestinian Tradition and the Babylonian Talmud." In *Scripta Hierosolymitana*. Vol. 22. *Studies in Aggadah and Folk Literature*. Edited by J. Heinemann and D. Noy. Jerusalem: Magnes Press, 1971.

———. "Teaching of Pietists in Mishnaic Literature." *Journal of Jewish Studies* 16 (1965): 15–33.

———. "The Term *Derekh Erez*." *Tarbiz* 60, no. 2 (1991): 147–62.

Saldarini, Anthony. "The End of the Rabbinic Chain of Tradition." *Journal of Biblical Literature* 93 (1974): 97–106.

———. *The Fathers According to Rabbi Nathan (Abot de Rabbi Nathan) Version B*. Leiden: E. J. Brill, 1975.

———. "Johanan ben Zakkai's Escape from Jerusalem: Origin and Development of a Rabbinic Story." *Journal for the Study of Judaism* 6 (1975): 189–204.

———. "Last Words and Deathbed Scenes in Rabbinic Literature." *Jewish Quarterly Review* 68 (1977): 28–45.

———. *Scholastic Rabbinism: A Literary Study of the Fathers According to Rabbi Nathan*. Chico, CA: Scholars Press, 1982.

Sarason, Richard. "Kadushin's Study of Midrash: Value Concepts and Their Literary Embodiment." In *Understanding the Rabbinic Mind: Essays on the Hermeneutic of Max Kadushin*. Edited by P. Ochs. Atlanta: Scholars Press, 1990.

Satlow, Michael. "'And on the Earth You Shall Sleep': *Talmud Torah* and Rabbinic Asceticism." *Journal of Religion* 83, no. 2 (2003): 204–24.

———. *Jewish Marriage in Antiquity.* Princeton, NJ: Princeton University Press, 2001.

———. *Tasting the Dish: Rabbinic Rhetorics of Sexuality.* Atlanta: Scholars Press, 1995.

———. "'Texts of Terror': Rabbinic Texts, Speech Acts, and the Control of Mores." *Association for Jewish Studies Review* 21, no. 2 (1996): 273–97.

Schäfer, Peter. "Die Flucht Johanan ben Zakkais aus Jerusalem und die Grüdung des 'Lehrhauses' in Jabne." In *Aufstieg und Niedergang der römischen Welt,* II: 19:2. Edited by H. Temporini and W. Hasse. New York: Walter de Gruyter, 1979.

———. *Judeophobia: Attitudes Towards Jews in the Ancient World.* Cambridge, MA: Harvard University Press, 1997.

Schäfer, Peter, and Catherine Hezser, eds. *The Talmud Yerushalmi and Graeco-Roman Culture.* 2 volumes. Tübingen: Mohr Siebeck, 2000.

Schechter, Solomon. *Aspects of Rabbinic Theology: Major Concepts of the Talmud.* New York: Schocken Books, 1961.

———. *Studies in Judaism.* First series. Philadelphia: Jewish Publication Society, 1938.

———. *Studies in Judaism.* Second series. Philadelphia: Jewish Publication Society, 1908.

Schechter, Solomon, and Menahem Kister. *Avoth de-Rabbi Nathan: Solomon Schechter Edition.* New York: Jewish Theological Seminary, 1997.

Schofer, Jonathan. "The Beastly Body in Rabbinic Self-Formation." In *Self-Revelations: Religion and the Self in Antiquity.* Edited by D. Brakke, M. Satlow, and S. Weitzman. Bloomington: Indiana University Press, forthcoming.

———. *The Making of a Sage: The Rabbinic Ethics of Abot de Rabbi Natan.* Ann Arbor: University of Michigan Dissertation Services, 2000.

———. "Protest or Pedagogy? Trivial Sin and Divine Justice in Rabbinic Narrative." *The Hebrew Union College Annual* 74 (2003).

———. "The Redaction of Desire: Structure and Editing of Rabbinic Teachings Concerning Yeṣer (Inclination)." *Journal of Jewish Thought and Philosophy* 12, no. 1 (2003): 19–53.

———. "Self, Subject, and Chosen Subjection: Rabbinic Ethics and Comparative Possibilities." *The Journal of Religious Ethics* 33 (2005).

———. "Spiritual Exercises in Rabbinic Culture." *Association for Jewish Studies Review* 27, no. 2 (2003): 203–26.

———. "Virtues in Xunzi's Thought." *Journal of Religious Ethics* 21, no. 1 (1993): 117–36.

Scholem, Gershom. "On Sin and Punishment: Some Remarks Concerning Biblical and Rabbinical Ethics." In *Myths and Symbols: Studies in Honor of Mircia Eliade.* Edited by J. M. Kitagawa and C. H. Long. Chicago: University of Chicago Press, 1969.

———. "Revelation and Tradition as Religious Categories in Judaism." In *The Messianic Idea in Judaism and Other Essays on Jewish Spirituality.* New York: Schocken Books, 1971.

Schwartz, Howard, ed. *The Four Who Entered Paradise.* London: Jason Aronson, 1995.

Schwartz, Seth. "Gamaliel in Aphrodite's Bath: Palestinian Judaism and Urban Culture in the Third and Fourth Centuries." In *The Talmud Yerushalmi and Graeco-Roman Culture,* vol. 1. Edited by Peter Schäfer and Catherine Hezser. Tübingen: Mohr Siebeck, 2000.

———. *Imperialism and Jewish Society, 200 BCE to 640 CE.* Princeton, NJ: Princeton University Press, 2001.

———. "The Patriarchs and the Diaspora." *Journal of Jewish Studies* 50, no. 2 (Autumn 1999): 208–22.

Scott, R. B. Y. *Proverbs. Ecclesiastes.* New York: Doubleday, 1965.

Segal, Alan. *Rebecca's Children: Judaism and Christianity in the Roman World.* Cambridge, MA: Harvard University Press, 1986.

———. *Two Powers in Heaven.* Leiden: E. J. Brill, 1977.

Seow, Choon-Leong. *Ecclesiastes: A New Translation with Introduction and Commentary.* New York: Doubleday, 1997.

Shaw, Brent. "The Age of Roman Girls at Marriage: Some Reconsiderations." *Journal of Roman Studies* 77 (1987): 30–46.

Shils, Edward. *Tradition.* Chicago: University of Chicago Press, 1981.

Smith, Jonathan Z. *Imagining Religion: From Babylon to Jonestown.* Chicago: University of Chicago Press, 1982.

———. *Map Is Not Territory: Studies in the History of Religions.* Chicago: University of Chicago Press, 1978.

———. "No Need to Travel to the Indies: Judaism and the Study of Religion." In *Take Judaism, For Example.* Edited by J. Neusner. Chicago: University of Chicago Press, 1983.

Smith, Morton. *Tannaitic Parallels to the Gospels.* Philadelphia: Society of Biblical Literature, 1951.

Sommer, Benjamin. "Revelation at Sinai in the Hebrew Bible and in Jewish Theology." *Journal of Religion* 79, no. 3 (1999): 422–51.

Soskice, Janite. *Metaphor and Religious Language.* Oxford: Clarendon Press, 1985.

Sperber, Daniel. *Commentary on Derech Erez Zuṭa, Chapters Five to Eight.* Ramat Gan: Bar-Ilan University Press, 1990.

———. *A Dictionary of Greek and Latin Legal Terms in Rabbinic Literature.* Jerusalem: Bar-Ilan University Press, 1984.

———. "Manuals of Rabbinic Conduct." In *Scholars and Scholarship.* Edited by L. Landman. New York: Yeshiva University Press, 1990.

Steigman, Emero. "Rabbinic Anthropology." In *Aufstieg und Niedergang der römischen Welt,* II:19:2. Edited by H. Temporini and W. Haase. New York: Walter de Gruyter, 1979.

Stein, Siegfried. "The Concept of the 'Fence': Observations on Its Origin and Development." In *Studies in Jewish Religious and Intellectual History: Presented to Alexander Altmann on the Occasion of His Seventieth Birthday.* Edited by S. Stein and R. Loewe. University: University of Alabama Press, 1979.

Steinmetz, Devora. "Distancing and Bringing Near: A New Look at Mishnah Tractates *'Eduyyot* and *'Abot.*" *Hebrew Union College Annual* 73 (2003): 49–96.

Stern, David. "The Captive Woman: Hellenization, Greco-Roman Erotic Narrative, and Rabbinic Literature." *Poetics Today* 19, no. 1 (1998): 91–127.

———. "Midrash and Indeterminacy." *Critical Inquiry* 15 (1988): 132–61.

———. *Midrash and Theory: Ancient Jewish Exegesis and Contemporary Literary Studies.* Evanston, IL: Northwestern University Press, 1996.

———. *Parables in Midrash.* Cambridge, MA: Harvard University Press, 1991.

Strack, H. L., and Gunter Stemberger. *Introduction to the Talmud and Midrash.* Translated by Marcus Bockmuehl. Second edition. Minneapolis: Fortress Press, 1996.

Swartz, Michael. *Scholastic Magic: Ritual and Revelation in Early Jewish Mysticism.* Princeton, NJ: Princeton University Press, 1996.

———. "Scholasticism as a Comparative Category and the Study of Judaism." In *Scholasticism: Cross-Cultural and Comparative Perspectives.* Edited by J. I. Cabezón. Albany: State University of New York Press, 1998.

Taussig, Solomon. *Neweh Shalom I.* Munich, 1872.

Taylor, Charles. *Sources of the Self: The Making of the Modern Identity.* Cambridge, MA: Harvard University Press, 1989.

Taylor, Mark C. *Critical Terms for Religious Studies.* Chicago: University of Chicago Press, 1998.

Theodor, J., and Ch. Albeck. *Midrash Bereshit Rabba.* Second printing. Jerusalem: Shalem Books, 1996.

Tirosh-Samuelson, Hava. *Happiness in Premodern Judaism: Virtue, Knowledge, and Well-Being.* Cincinnati: Hebrew Union College Press, 2003.

Toer, Pramoedya Ananta. *The Mute's Soliloquy.* Translated by Willem Samuels. New York: Penguin Books, 1999.

Towner, Wayne Sibley. *The Rabbinic "Enumeration of Scriptural Examples."* Leiden: E. J. Brill, 1973.

Twersky, R. Yitzhak. "Make a Fence for the Torah." *Torah U-Madda Journal* 8 (1998–99): 25–42.

Urbach, Ephraim. *The Sages: Their Concepts and Beliefs* (Hebrew). Jerusalem: Magnes Press, 1971.

———. *The Sages: Their Concepts and Beliefs.* Translated by Israel Abrahams. Cambridge, MA: Harvard University Press, 1979.

———. "Treasures Above." In *Hommage à Georges Vajda.* Edited by G. Nahon and Charles Touati. Louvain: Éditions Peeters, 1980.

Van Loopik, Marcus. *The Ways of the Sages and the Ways of the World.* Tübingen: J. C. B. Mohr, 1991.

Veyne, Paul. *The Roman Empire.* Translated by Arthur Goldhammer. Cambridge, MA: Harvard University Press, 1997.

Visotzky, Burton. *Midrash Mishle.* New York: Jewish Theological Seminary, 1990.

Viviano, Benedict T. *Study as Worship: Aboth and the New Testament.* Leiden: E. J. Brill, 1978.

Wacholder, Ben Zion. "The Date of the Mekilta De-Rabbi Ishmael." *Hebrew Union College Annual* 39 (1968): 117–44.

Watts, Edward. "The Student Self in Late Antiquity." In *Self-Revelations: Religion and the Self in Antiquity.* Edited by D. Brakke, M. Satlow, and S. Weitzman. Bloomington: Indiana University Press, forthcoming.

Wegner, Judith Romney. *Chattel or Person? The Status of Women in the Mishnah.* New York: Oxford University Press, 1988.

Weinfeld, Moshe. *Deuteronomy and the Deuteronomic School.* Winona Lake, IN: Eisenbrauns, 1992.

Williams, David J. *Paul's Metaphors: Their Context and Character.* Peabody, MA: Hendrickson Publishers, Inc., 1999.

Winquest, Charles. "Person." In *Critical Terms for Religious Studies.* Edited by Mark C. Taylor. Chicago: University of Chicago Press, 1998.

Yadin, Azzan. "Hammer on the Rock: Mekhilta Deuteronomy and the Question of Rabbinic Polysemy." *Jewish Studies Quarterly* 9 (2002): 1–27.

———. *Scripture as Logos: Rabbi Ishmael and the Origins of Midrash.* Philadelphia: University of Pennsylvania Press, 2004.

———. "*Shnei Ketuvim* and Rabbinic Intermediation." *Journal for the Study of Judaism* 33 (2002): 386–410.

Yearley, Lee. *Mencius and Aquinas: Theories of Virtue and Conceptions of Courage.* Albany: State University of New York Press, 1990.

———. "Recent Work on Virtue." *Religious Studies Review* 16, no. 1 (1990): 1–9.

———. "Teachers and Saviors." *Journal of Religion* 65, no. 2 (1985): 225–43.

Yelle, Robert. "Rhetorics of Law and Ritual: A Semiotic Comparison of the Law of Talion and Sympathetic Magic." *Journal of the American Academy of Religion* 69 (2001): 627–47.

Zeitlin, Solomon. "An Historical Study of the Canonization of the Hebrew Scriptures." In *The Canon and the Masorah of the Hebrew Bible.* Edited by S. Z. Leiman. New York: Ktav Publishing House, 1974.

Zlotnick, Dov. *The Tractate "Mourning" (Regulations Relating to Death, Burial, and Mourning).* New Haven, CT: Yale University Press, 1966.

Index of Sources

Ancient sources cited in the main text are indexed below. The endnotes contain numerous discussions and citations of parallel passages and related materials that can be located by referring to the relevant analysis in the main text.[*]

Rabbinic Sources

'Abot de Rabbi Natan (cited by version and chapter)

A1: 4, 32, 42, 47, 68, 71, 73, 74, 76
A1–13: 45
A2: 75, 77, 78, 79, 80, 81, 128
A3: 4, 44, 83, 144, 145
A4: 35–36, 43
A5: 155, 157, 265n.16
A6: 4, 6, 32, 39, 49, 65–66, 102, 138
A7: 47
A8: 33, 50, 66, 143–44
A9: 152, 153
A10: 128
A12: 43, 48, 129, 130, 136, 139–40, 141, 142, 143
A13: 137
A14: 139
A14–18: 45
A15: 50, 51, 52
A16: 4, 86, 87, 88, 89, 96, 97, 100–101, 103, 107, 108–9, 112
A17: 94
A18: 93
A19: 52, 148, 149
A19–20: 151
A19–22: 45

A20: 150
A22: 44
A23: 93, 99
A23–26: 45
A25: 126
A26: 136
A27: 129–30
A29: 103, 136
A30: 138, 265n.16
A31: 134
A31–35: 46
A31–41: 45
A32: 60, 104–5
A33: 127
A35: 60
A39: 125, 132, 152
A40: 133, 137, 153
A41: 38, 62–63, 265n.16
A90–106: 46
B1: 4, 42, 68, 71, 73, 74
B1–3: 47
B1–27: 45
B2: 79, 80
B3: 75, 77, 81
B4: 144
B5: 43
B10: 155, 156, 157, 158, 265n.16
B11: 4, 32, 65–66, 102

[*] Indexes prepared by Michael Lyons.

Index of Names,
Ancient and Modern

Ancient Names

Akabya ben Mahalalel
    sayings about "giving one's heart"/
        "attending to," 148–49, 264n.12
Akiba, 176n.8, 177n.9, 208n.25
    as exemplar, 49
    control of sexual desire tested by Ro-
        mans, 106, 108–11, 114–15, 116
    model for shaping heart with Torah,
        5–6
    narratives about, 48
    poverty and wealth of, 138
    teaching about act and consequence,
        144–45
    teaching about early death of stu-
        dents, 136
    teaching about individual and com-
        munity, 258n.66
Antigonus of Sokho
    "Be like slaves who serve the master,"
        154–55, 157, 159, 161–62, 268n.33

Ben Zoma
    metaphor of warrior conquering a
        city, 98–100, 116

Eleazar ben Azariah
    teaching on words of Torah as a goad,
        92–93
Eliezer ben Hyrcanus, 208n.25
    control of sexual desire tested, 106,
        111–15

    instruction at deathbed scene of, 52
    narratives about, 48

Hananiah
    saying about words of Torah cancel-
        ing desires, 150–51
Hillel
    epigram about merit, "If I am not for
        me, who is for me?," 141–42
    epigram about study, "If you come to
        my house . . . ," 136
    Hillel and the donkey driver, 130–32
    Hillel and the floating skull (epigram
        about punishment), 143
    narratives about, 48, 208n.25
    patience of, 50–52
    stance on accepting students, 4–5
    teaching value of Oral Torah, 51–52

Joseph, and Potiphar's wife, 106–8, 116,
    238n.78

Nehuniah ben ha-Kanah
    epigram on yoke of Torah, 92
    giving one's heart to words of
        Torah vs. words of foolishness,
        150
Nehurai
    teaching on Torah student as trained
        calf, 93–94
Nittai ha-Arbeli, 267n.26
    "Do not give up [the idea of] retribu-
        tion," 151–52, 162

25, 226nn.38, 41, 228n.5, 230n.21,
232n.34, 233n.40, 237n.70, 246n.5,
252nn.43, 45, 253n.50, 255nn.56,
57, 263nn.5, 9, 264n.12, 265n.13,
266nn.17, 20, 21, 269n.38, 270nn.44,
46, 48, 51
Fisch, Menachem, 232nn.35, 36
Fischel, Henry, 195n.23, 205n.7, 207n.18,
210n.33, 235n.51
Fishbane, Michael, 177n.11, 178n.12,
208n.29, 209n.31, 211n.45, 212n.3,
213n.8, 214n.12, 215nn.3, 4, 19, 217n.11,
218n.18, 219n.2, 220n.8, 228nn.9, 10,
233n.38, 234nn.44, 45, 235nn.49, 50,
237nn.61, 62, 68, 69, 238n.72, 243n.6,
244n.2, 246n.4, 251n.41, 252n.43,
253n.47, 255n.56, 256n.62, 259nn.68,
69, 260n.76, 261n.87, 265n.16,
268n.33, 270n.52
Flusser, David, 205n.7, 217–18n.16,
228n.10, 233nn.37, 39
Flusser, David, and Shmuel Safrai, 177n.11,
178n.12, 217n.11
Fonrobert, Charlotte, 180n.19, 195n.21,
200nn.45, 48, 201n.51, 214n.11,
223n.23, 252n.45, 258n.65, 272n.1
Foucault, Michel, 8, 11, 17, 18, 19, 178n.13,
180–81n.21, 181n.24, 182nn.27, 29,
183n.30, 186n.47, 186–87n.48, 187n.50,
187–88n.53, 188nn.54, 55, 188–89n.56,
192n.7, 231nn.28, 29, 240n.94, 242n.2,
243n.1, 245n.6
Fox, Michael, 216n.8, 226n.36, 249n.28,
252n.44, 261n.82, 263n.3, 270n.1
Fraade, Steven D., 177n.11, 179n.17,
180n.18, 191n.2, 192n.6, 194n.20,
195n.23, 206n.14, 209n.29, 213n.11,
217nn.11, 15, 226n.43, 233n.36,
234nn.44, 48
Fränkel, Yonah, 42, 43, 194n.20, 204nn.2,
5, 6, 247n.6, 249n.29, 259n.75,
260n.78, 262n.1, 271n.16
Freud, Sigmund, 184n.42, 186n.45, 188n.55,
229n.17

Gadamer, Hans-Georg, 178n.13, 215n.1
Gilath, Itzchak, 229n.16, 241n.98

Ginzberg, Louis, 215–16n.4, 216n.8,
224n.32, 225n.33, 233n.42, 255n.55,
256n.62
Gleason, Maude, 181n.21, 192n.6, 195n.21
Goldin, Judah, 74, 176nn.3, 5, 179n.16,
193n.12, 194n.15, 195n.23, 196n.26,
197n.28, 198n.37, 199n.40, 202n.56,
203nn.58, 62, 204n.3, 205n.7,
207nn.21, 22, 208nn.25, 26, 210n.39,
211n.47, 216nn.6, 7, 8, 217nn.11, 14, 15,
218nn.16, 17, 18, 219nn.18, 3, 220nn.10,
11, 221nn.13, 14, 16, 17, 223nn.22, 25,
226nn.38, 39, 233n.42, 236n.54,
237n.69, 238nn.72, 79, 240n.89,
245n.8, 246n.4, 247n.6, 248n.18,
252nn.43, 45, 253n.50, 257n.63,
259nn.70, 71, 260nn.77, 78, 261n.81,
262n.3, 263nn.6, 8, 265n.13, 266nn.20,
23, 267nn.26, 31, 271n.11, 272n.1
Goshen-Gottstein, Alon, 177n.11, 206n.12,
207n.18
Graham, Angus C., 231n.30
Green, William Scott, 194n.20, 203n.58,
252n.43

Hadot, Pierre, 8, 163, 164, 165, 178n.13,
180n.21, 194n.20, 196n.26, 236n.57,
242n.2, 243n.1, 270n.3, 271nn.4, 9,
12, 13, 15, 16
Halbertal, Moshe, and Avishai Margalit,
219n.2, 226n.41
Halivni, David Weiss, 187n.50
Harvey, David, 12, 13, 14, 18, 20, 21,
183nn.33, 34, 184n.35, 189n.60
Harvey, Van, 190n.65
Hayes, Christine, 193nn.10, 11, 202n.57
Hegel, G. W. F., 18, 187n.49, 188n.55,
189n.57
Herr, Moshe David, 239nn.86, 88,
240nn.89, 94, 241n.94
Hezser, Catherine, 175n.1, 193n.9, 195n.22,
196n.25, 197nn.27, 28, 29, 32, 33,
198nn.33, 36, 202n.56, 203n.62,
206n.14, 215n.19, 239nn.82, 86,
242n.100, 247n.11, 272n.17
Hirshman, Marc, 175n.2, 202n.58, 203n.63,
236n.60, 240n.90, 270n.51, 273n.3

Index of Subjects

fence *(seyyag)*, 4, 42, 47, 48, 74–83, 195n.23,
 221nn.14, 15, 221–22n.18,
 222n.19, 224n.30
field, as trope, 92, 97–98
fire, as trope, 57, 59, 69, 82, 84, 95, 96, 116,
 117, 170
formation, of character or self, 8–11, 17–22,
 44, 119, 181n.24, 182n.29
 See also cultivation, of self;
 transformation
"Four Who Entered the Garden," 45, 46,
 207n.18, 246n.4
"From the prison house he comes to rule,"
 98, 100–101, 106, 108, 110, 111,
 113, 116, 236n.61
fruits (interest) and capital, 132–34, 153,
 162, 250n.36, 251n.37, 253n.49,
 267n.29

ḥaber ("fellow"), 33, 38, 50, 139
hailing the subject, 21, 44, 65, 190–91n.63
heart *(leb)*
 as center of emotion, 86
 as seat of transgressive tendencies, 86,
 88, 168
 as term for psyche, 84, 228n.10
 "give to one's heart," 148–50, 161,
 263n.4, 266n.22
 metaphors for, 5–7, 64, 266n.19
 transforming impact of Torah on,
 5–7, 106–15, 117, 151
 tropes for transformation of, 90–105
histakkel. See "attend to"

impulses, viii, 4, 11, 57, 71, 84–105, 168–69,
 227n.1
 self-destructive, 88–90, 231n.27
 See also yetzer
inclination. *See yetzer*
individual, and community, 258n.66
interest. *See* fruits (interest) and capital
internalization, 7, 20–21, 88, 101, 106, 107,
 111, 116–17, 151, 161–62, 167,
 273n.7
 internalized figurative language about
 God, 147–56, 161

internalized speech, 151–53
internalized traditional discourse,
 7, 17, 88, 106, 107, 111, 116–17,
 119, 161
iron, as trope, 6, 64, 92, 95–96, 116, 117, 170

judge
 as trope for God, 50, 57, 60, 104, 122,
 125–27, 129, 137, 145, 147–49,
 161–62, 246n.3, 248n.20
 as trope for the *yetzer* ("inclination"),
 104–5
"Judge every man with the scales weighted
 in his favor," 49–50, 66, 143–44
judgment, divine, 125–29, 142–48, 248n.20
justice
 occurrences of *tz.d.q.* ("to be righteous, just") in *'Abot de Rabbi
 Nathan*, 248n.22
 of God, 36, 55–57, 58–60, 122, 127–28,
 130, 135, 140, 141, 147, 167–69,
 212nn.6, 8, 245n.6, 270n.2

king
 as trope for God, 36, 57–58, 125–
 26, 147, 149, 161–62, 165, 170,
 214n.12, 246n.3, 270n.2
 as trope for the *yetzer* ("inclination"),
 100–101, 116–17
 as trope for Torah, 102–3, 117
kiss of God, as reward, 11, 139–41, 256n.62

lashon ha-ra'. See speech, malicious speech
leb. See heart
love, 86, 148, 165
love and fear, as different responses or motivations, viii, 11, 157–60, 162,
 168, 268n.33, 269n.44, 270n.50
 See also motivation; self-interested
 desire and fear

maxims, 4, 14, 42–48
merit *(zekhut)*, 60, 128–33, 141–42, 151,
 153, 162, 248n.23, 258nn.66, 67,
 259n.75
metaphor. *See* tropes